BLACK WOMEN AND PUBLIC HEALTH

SUNY Series in Black Women's Wellness

Stephanie Y. Evans, editor

BLACK WOMEN AND PUBLIC HEALTH

STRATEGIES TO NAME, LOCATE, AND CHANGE SYSTEMS OF POWER

Edited by

Stephanie Y. Evans, Sarita K. Davis,
Leslie R. Hinkson, and Deanna J. Wathington

Afterword by

Jasmine Ward

Cover art entitled "Loving Comfort (Byllye Avery)"; used by permission.

Published by State University of New York Press, Albany

For information, contact State University of New York Press, Albany, NY
www.sunypress.edu

Library of Congress Cataloging-in-Publication Data

Names: Evans, Stephanie Y., editor. | Davis, Sarita K., editor. | Hinkson, Leslie R.,
    editor. | Wathington, Deanna J., editor.
Title: Black women and public health : strategies to name, locate, and change
    systems of power / Stephanie Y. Evans, Sarita K. Davis, Leslie R. Hinkson,
    and Deanna J. Wathington, editors.
Description: Albany : State University of New York Press, [2022] | Series:
    SUNY series in Black Women's Wellness | Includes bibliographical references and
    index.
Identifiers: ISBN 9781438487311 (hardcover : alk. paper) | ISBN 9781438487335
    (ebook) | ISBN 9781438487328 (pbk. : alk. paper)
Further information is available at the Library of Congress.

10 9 8 7 6 5 4 3 2 1

Contents

Part II. Locate Disparity

Part III. Act for Change

Acknowledgments

Stephanie Y. Evans: I extend thanks to coeditors Sarita Davis, Leslie Hinkson, and Deanna Wathington; the chapter authors; and Jasmine Ward. Your willingness to help shape this important discussion will certainly have an impact on many generations to come as we work to improve the quality of life for ourselves and others. A special thanks is extended to Camara Jones, a leader in thought and practice. As always, thanks to Dr. Rebecca Colesworthy and the SUNY Press team for supporting this research agenda. Of course, I remain grateful for the love and support of my husband, Dr. Curtis Byrd.

Sarita K. Davis: I want to thank Dr. Stephanie Evans for including me in this book project. Her visionary leadership in documenting the health and mental health of Black women is inspirational and encourages me to dream bigger. I also want to thank Drs. Gail E. Wyatt, Gina Wingood, Faye Belgrave, and Cynthia Prather for embodying the spirit of warrior women fighting to reclaim the health of Black women and girls. Together we can.

Leslie R. Hinkson: I extend my gratitude to Stephanie Y. Evans for inviting me to be a part of this project. Equal parts Black girl magic and Black girl wisdom and knowledge, I hope this volume will play a significant role in a new era of Black girl healing and wellness.

Deanna J. Wathington: I would like to thank coeditors Stephanie Y. Evans, Sarita Davis, and Leslie Hinkson as well as contributor Jasmine Ward. It has been a pleasure to work with these powerful and brilliant women. I would also like to thank my sister, Melissa L. Wathington, who was a true profile in courage, an incredible author, and a role model for living a faith-filled life.

Introduction

Race, Gender, and Public Health: Social Justice and Wellness Work

STEPHANIE Y. EVANS, SARITA K. DAVIS, LESLIE R. HINKSON, AND DEANNA J. WATHINGTON

> The three tasks of becoming actively antiracist are to name racism, ask "How is racism operating here?" and organize and strategize to act.
>
> —Camara Jones (2016, p. 3)

Dr. Camara Phyllis Jones, former president of the American Public Health Association (APHA), constructed her national platform as a call for action to fight racism in order to achieve health equity. Dr. Jones (who holds MD, MPH, and PhD degrees) spent the duration of her 2016 tenure as a national leader fighting for social justice; her APHA platform offers a fundamental framework for how this book approaches the topic of race, gender, and public health.

Jones (2014) wrote in the journal *Medical Care* that "equity is assurance of the conditions for optimal health for all people. Achieving health equity requires valuing all individuals and populations equally, recognizing and rectifying historical injustices, and providing resources according to need. Health disparities will be eliminated when health equity is achieved" (p. S74). This book is comprised of essays that directly address the challenge Jones issued in her leadership, scholarship, and service to the field of public health. Authors share research and strategies to name, locate, and change inequitable systems. As a research collective, we present a scholar-activist discussion of social justice wellness work.

Black Women and Public Health: Strategies to Name, Locate, and Change Systems of Power seeks to create an interdisciplinary dialogue that bridges gaps between researchers, practitioners, educators, and advocates. Black women's work in public health is a regenerative practice with a rich history. Just as Anna Julia Cooper wrote in her 1892 essay "Womanhood: A Vital Element in the Regeneration and Progress of a Race," we look backward, inward, and forward as we work to improve the quality of life for ourselves and others. Dr. Cooper, a historian and educator, argued that those who wish to advance society must look back for wisdom, look inward for strength, and look forward for hope. In her articulation of "social regeneration," the concept of conscious progress, she centered Black women as both recipients of social service and agents of change (Cooper, 1998).

Regeneration is a helpful theoretical framework by which to best understand Black women's history, practice, and planning in public health. Black women's life stories, scholarship, and community engagement represent a continuum of insight—what Cooper (1998) called "retrospection, introspection, and prospection" (p. 61). As Cooper argued in *A Voice From the South: By a Black Woman of the South* (1892), social justice is the desired goal of education, and we all have a responsibility to work in our individual capacities toward the common good. This collection of researchers represents an ongoing dialogue to improve education, training, and practice in public health by centering race and gender in order to advance health equity.

This project, as a deliberate submission to the SUNY book series *Black Women's Wellness*, also answers a call from mental health policy researchers Daniel Dawes and Keisha Brathwaite Holden of the Morehouse School of Medicine, who recently published a book chapter titled "Transformative Mental Health Policy" in *Black Women's Mental Health: Balancing Strength and Vulnerability*. Dawes and Holden call for culturally appropriate wellness tool kits that center Black women's voices. As the lead editor of that volume, as with this present collection, Stephanie Evans was mindful of the need to include policy experts to shape recommendations for next steps. Dawes and Holden (2017) call for culturally relevant measures to improve access to and quality of health-care service: "Researchers, clinicians, public health professionals, and policymakers have a responsibility to implement action-oriented steps that may be a catalyst for changes in diverse communities. In particular, we must: Design and establish innovative models and wellness tool-kits for prevention of mental illness and the promotion of stigma reduction in ethnically and culturally diverse communities" (p. 278). By centering Black women's history, theory, identity, academic disciplinary expertise, and various locations, *Black Women and Public Health* advances extant literature in public health, mental health, and related fields. The design for a wellness toolkit is grounded in Black women's intellectual history, including Camara Jones's articulation of the relationship between personal behaviors, social determinants of health, and social determinants of equity. For every public health question—from wellness practices to family planning and from vaccines to housing and policing—centering Black women's experience and articulation of both the problem and solutions is essential.

Community-centered public health involves asking, What does your research *do*, how does your work center perspectives of those who are being researched, and who is the research meant to impact? Though leaps and bounds have been made in the discipline over the past four decades, unfortunately, public health research, policy, and programming is too often offered from a perspective that does not center or benefit Black women. This is often the case even when Black women are the imagined audience.

> Frequently, we take the "public" out of public health and allow the practice to become extremely narrow, limited to experts telling the public what's best for them. But in reality, there are not enough public health educators to treat and teach the public. This means that people—the public—must participate in a much more active way. . . . Who, then, does the work of public health? We all do. (Avery, 2002, p. 571)

There is no lack of access to Black women intellectuals and experts, but rather a lack of commitment to representation at all levels of inquiry, research, analysis, practice, application, and assessment in higher education institutions. Ideas matter, and Black women's reflective writing is at once abstract and applicable, specific and universal. Thus, a holistic approach to public health must include an expressed appreciation of Black women's robust historical contributions to the intellectual inquiry, applied history, and creative practice of public health.

Health-disparity research by bodies like APHA clearly shows how interpersonal and institutional inequities impact Black women disproportionately. In fields like legal studies that are adjacent to public health, Kimberlé Crenshaw's intersectionality research advances understanding about how oppressive and inequitable systems are formed. Professor Crenshaw explains how the law fails to adequately address how race, class, and gender compound to place Black women in violent situations and exacerbate disempowerment through legal dispossession. In addition to understanding community involvement and the goal of promoting health in communities, during her tenure as the president of APHA, Dr. Camara Jones advanced understanding about the social determinants of health and how health systems constitute another area of disproportionate power. *Black Women and Public Health* builds on these foundations of inquiry and activism.

Accordingly, this book is a research collective of scholars who investigate how to "prevent disease, prolong life, and promote health" in ways that specifically impact Black women (Winslow, 1920). According to the American Public Health Association (APHA, n.d.), "Public health works to track disease outbreaks, prevent injuries and shed light on why some of us are more likely to suffer from poor health than others. The many facets of public health include speaking out for laws that promote smoke-free indoor air and seatbelts, spreading the word about ways to stay healthy and giving science-based solutions to problems." Dr. Jones has made significant advancements in the discussion of racism and public health. Her detailed approach and program coordination literally put racism on the map as a subject of interest for public health professionals: Her tenure as leader of APHA focused squarely on providing resources to institutionalize discussions in the profession. In multiple talks around the nation, Dr. Jones has demonstrated how racism fosters internalized, personally mediated, and institutionalized oppression. After clearly delineating the personal, social, and structural impact of racism, she has shown how various positionalities, such as gender, economic class, sexuality, and disability, also follow the same patterns.

Dr. Jones's definition of racism as a public health issue is in line with the Centers for Disease Control and Prevention's initial assessment of their National Intimate Partner and Sexual Violence Survey (NISVS) of 2010 (Black et al., 2011). Both racism and sexual violence are duly recognized as preventable social diseases. Jones proposes three steps of "health equity" as a way to address the disease of violence: (1) value all individuals and populations equally, (2) recognize and rectify historical injustices, and (3) provide resources according to need. In line with Jones's vision of health equity and the 2010 CDC NISVS report, *Black Women and Public Health* offers a tool kit to center Black women's voices, unearth and counteract roots of violence against Black women (restorative), and provide resources useful for culturally sensitive counseling of survivors of violence (curative) as well as resources to construct alternate futures that reduce this violence (preventative).

African American women have a deep history in public health, dating back to nineteenth-century professionals. Though we highlight the intellectual leadership of Dr. Camara Jones, multitudes of Black women have historically contributed to the work of public health, including Mary Eliza Mahoney, Dr. Rebecca Lee Crumpler, Dr. Rebecca Cole, Dr. Susan Smith McKinney Steward, and Dr. Eliza Grier in the nineteenth century. Twentieth-century innovators include Dr. Bessie Delany, Dr. May Chin, Dr. Helen Dickens, Dr. Dorothy Boulding Ferebee and Alpha Kappa Alpha Sorority's Mississippi Health Project, Byllye Avery, the Center for Black Women's Wellness, Black Women's Health Imperative, Dr. Edith Irby Jones, Dr. Rosalyn Epps, Dr. Patricia Harris, Dr. Jocelyn Elders, Dr. Jewel Plummer Cobb, Dr. Mae Jemison, and Dr. Gayle Helene. These women are part of an international community of global wellness workers such as Mary Seacole, Dr. Wangari Maathai, Dr. Princess Nothemba Simelela, and Maria de Jesus Bringelo (Dona Dijé). Whether trained medical professionals, community activists, university professors, or a combination of these identities, Black women have been at the center of the push for healthy individuals, families, communities, and nations.

As Sarita K. Davis clearly outlines in her review of the origins of public health in her editor reflections later in this chapter, race clearly matters in how the field is developed, practiced, and advanced. Black women's voices are too often left out of the discussion of curative, restorative, and preventative solutions to the public health issue of violence. In addition to scholarship produced by and about Black women within the field of public health, disciplines such as history, African American studies, and women's studies have advanced discussions about the meaning and implications of practice and policy. Prime examples of cross-fertilization between science, social science, and humanities include Susan Smith's *Sick and Tired of Being Sick and Tired: Black Women's Health Activism in America, 1890–1950*, Marie Jenkins Schwartz's *Birthing a Slave: Motherhood and Medicine in the Antebellum South*, Rebecca Wanzo's *The Suffering*

Will Not Be Televised: African American Women and Sentimental Political Storytelling, and Deirdre Cooper Owens's *Medical Bondage: Race, Gender, and the Origins of American Gynecology.*

Comprehensive research projects, particularly the Boston University Black Women's Health Study presented in section 2, provide abundant data on areas from epidemiology to environmental justice. Several resources exist via the Black Women's Health Imperative, the CDC, and the American Psychological Association. Black women on the APHA Executive Board have included Ayanna Buckner, U. Tara Hayden, Ella Greene-Moton, Linda Rae Murray, and Deanna Wathington. The history and experience of Black women in public health can most readily be seen in the work of Byllye Avery and in a grassroots movement of Black women organizing for healing, health, and wellness.

Black Women's Public Health Project:
The Living Legacy of Byllye Avery

Susan Smith wrote a groundbreaking history of African American public health initiatives titled *Sick and Tired of Being Sick and Tired: Black Women's Health Activism in America, 1890–1950.* This outstanding book chronicles the advocacy and organizing efforts of women groups like Alpha Kappa Alpha Sorority's Mississippi Health Project and collective efforts to raise health awareness and expand care options in rural areas, especially in the South. Byllye Avery's work with the Gainesville Women's Health Center in 1974, the Black Women's Health Project in the 1980s, and the development of the Black Women's Health Imperative (BWHI) and Center for Black Women's Wellness (CBWW) built on a long history of collective action by Black women to improve their own health and the quality of life in their own communities highlighted in Smith's work.

Avery, a public health scholar-activist, created a model of Black women's health that centered narratives and storytelling. In an article titled "Who Does the Work of Public Health?" published in the *American Journal of Public Health*, she reminisced about the 1983 national meeting she held for Black women's health at Spelman College in Atlanta, Georgia, "We were moved by what happened, but even more, it dawned on me that that conference defined the true meaning and spirit of public health. When women make their stories public, without the shame and embarrassment that keep us silent about our health, we become active participants in our health, and those who listen to them and support them benefit as well" (Avery, 2002, p. 573).

One of the most widely known Black women's health activists, Byl-lye Avery was raised in DeLand, Florida, and graduated from Talladega College and the University of Florida. She became an activist in the 1970s and remains active as a cornerstone of continuing movements, including the CBWW in Atlanta and BWHI in Washington, DC. Self-care is a fundamental part of her mantra about health activism; she acknowledges that there is no "rest" in seeking justice and resources for proper health care, but there are two ways that activists can ensure sustainability: first, pay attention to your own needs, and second, pass the baton to a new generation of activists (Our Bodies Ourselves, 2011).

Avery is the personification of a quest for wellness on all levels of social location. Her experiences in her Florida community led to her advocacy for those around her and blossomed into lifelong activism for women's health and reproductive rights.

CBWW in Atlanta was established in 1988, and empowerment is a central theme in its mission. The clinic offers programs to broaden awareness, positively impact maternal and infant health, help youth and adolescents develop healthy habits, and promote Black women's economic self-sufficiency. The gynecological services (including Pap tests, pelvic exams, HIV testing, and mammograms) are supplemented with prevention programs, so the facility fills in health care gaps for the most vulnerable family and community populations (CBWW, n.d.).

Several publications emerged from the Black Women's Health Project that were spearheaded by BWHI: *The Black Women's Health Book* (1990), *Health First! The Black Woman's Wellness Guide* (2012), and *IndexUS: What Healthy Black Women Can Teach Us About Health* (2016). *The Black Women's Health Book* captures the agenda of many women intimately involved in the 1980s activism and community organizing. *Health First!* built on the first collection by providing in-depth data-driven research about the top ten health risks Black women face at every stage of their lives (Hoytt & Beard, 2012). *IndexUS* is a forward-thinking report: it is "the first health index focused exclusively on healthy Black women. It's based on 20 years of data from the Boston University Black Women's Health Study (BWHS), specifically, information from 38,706 BWHS participants who reported their health as excellent or very good" (Black Women's Health Imperative,

2016, p. 3). In 2013, when participants responded to questions about their health, the average age of women in this study was in the mid-fifties. As stated in the introduction to the report, "IndexUS is the first time Black women's health story is being told from a position of strength. Instead of studying what makes us sick, IndexUS takes more than two decades of research in the Black Women's Health Study and explores what keeps us healthy" (Blount, 2016, p. 4).

BWHI's *IndexUS* report is a contemporary example of the efforts of twentieth-century women's groups to impact their communities. Advancements including the election of the first Black woman president of APHA, Dr. Jessica Henderson Daniel, in 2017, come as a direct result of work done over a century ago. The ongoing research in Black women's public health is making important strides to better understand underlying aspects of health, health disparities, and optimal health.

The lead editor for this project, Stephanie Evans, came to the work of public health through her interest in Black women's intellectual history and mental health in memoirs. While investigating race, gender, and wellness through the threshold concept of what she calls historical wellness, she was heavily influenced by Byllye Avery, who clearly articulated the relationship between mental health and public health in works such as *Health First! The Black Woman's Wellness Guide*. The coeditors and author of the afterword who were invited to help shape this current book project—Sarita K. Davis, Leslie R. Hinkson, Deanna J. Wathington, and Jasmine Ward—have all committed their careers to public health through social justice scholarship, advocacy, and community organizing for the greater good. Below, the members of the editorial team share their reflections about how this new volume contributes to public health work.

Editor Reflections: Collectively Defining the History, Practice, and Planning of Public Health

Race, class, and gender violence impact health outcomes. This disciplinary evidence in public health supports findings in other areas, including women's studies and higher education. As a prime example, we can consider the widely reviewed, critically acclaimed, and provocatively titled *Presumed Incompetent: The Intersections of Race and Class for Women in Academia* (2012). The editors of *Presumed Incompetent* argue that intervention is imperative to counteract negative results women of color face when simply striving to operate in a constantly hostile environment: "Mounting public health evidence suggests that chronic stress—like the pressure of being continually misperceived or belittled or having to fight off micro-aggressions—can result in higher levels of hypertension, cardiovascular disease, and coronary heart disease" (Harris & González, 2012, p. 7). In the foreword to the book, Bettina Aptheker (2012) notes, "We are in the university. We are in the labs. We are in the law schools and courtrooms, medical schools and operating theaters. We prevail, but sometimes it is at enormous costs to ourselves, to our sense of well-being, balance, and confidence" (p. xi). As academic women, the editors of *Black Women and Public Health* band together to contribute to the ongoing discussion of scholar-activists dedicated to impacting wellness inside and beyond the academy. If carefully studied, historical, educational, and several other disciplinary models have much to offer public health research and practice.

As the editors demonstrate, these topics include mental health and wellness as a social justice issue (Evans), unpacking social constructs (Wathington), and the right to quality medical and health care (Hinkson). In her chapter contribution as well as her summary reflection, Davis summarizes the meaning of this collection by showing how self-definition is an essential part of self-determination in challenging and changing oppressive systems that maintain health inequality.

Sarita K. Davis: Framing Black Women and Public Health

In March of 2020, a dual public health crisis ravaged Black and brown communities in the United States. A highly contagious and deadly virus had developed through animal-to-human transmission. Called the *novel coronavirus*, the resulting condition was known first as COVID-19 and later as SARS-CoV-2. The second public health crisis that emerged during this same period was the antipolice protests. Protestors took to the streets across the United States and the globe to make their discontent known about the unwarranted police brutality that took the lives of unarmed Black citizens like Tony McDade, Breonna Taylor, George Floyd, and countless other Black people who have been killed at the hands of law enforcement officers. In a CNN podcast episode with Dr. Sanjay Gupta on June 5, 2020, on the two viruses—the pandemic and police violence—Dr. Camara Jones, epidemiologist and former president of the APHA, said that Black people in the United States are at disproportionate risk of sickness and death from both COVID-19 and systemic racism in policing. Jones said, "We have to protest . . . because we are not okay" (Gupta, 2020). At the heart of both of these public health crises is the long-standing disregard for Black life.

The failure of the federal government under the Trump administration is in large part responsible for the devastation visited upon our communities during this pandemic, from both anemic responses to states' needs for coronavirus testing, contact tracing, and personal protective equipment and capitalist-driven desires to "reopen" states while the rates of COVID-19 continued to rise—along with the administration's militarized response to peaceful protestors against police brutality. The result is the indisputable fact that racism must be recognized as a systemic public health issue that requires brutally honest conversations about public health history, policy changes, and practices on a national level.

Historical research like Deirdre Cooper Owens's work *Medical Bondage: Race, Gender, and the Origins of American Gynecology* documents foundational negative encounters with public health officials. In popular discourse, some associate this history with higher levels of medical mistrust—a particularly devastating consequence in the middle of a pandemic that necessitates prompt medical care and testing. In addition to the complicated history with the medical field, the complicated history of police and community patrols exacerbates public health challenges. The deaths of unarmed Black citizens like Ahmaud Arbery, Floyd, McDade, and Taylor brought many Americans and global citizens onto the streets in protest against systemic racism and police brutality. Amidst great concern and personal risk, protesters took to the streets en masse and showed that masked demonstrations could be very effective in bringing about local and national change in short order.

Still, many health experts are debating the risk of transmission against the need for public protests in light of irrefutable social injustices. If we are totally honest with ourselves, we must acknowledge that people are willing to risk their lives to protest their fears about systemic racism in public health and police brutality. The people have issued a decree stating that they are no longer willing to endure disproportionate mortality and morbidity from police brutality or flawed public health practices that devalue Black lives.

This book, *Black Women and Public Health*, is poised to explore the long and fraught history of systemic inequality and biased treatment of Black girls and women as it pertains to public health in the United States. The historical narrative about racial inferiority has exacerbated discriminatory health care practices, in turn negatively affecting the quality and types of health care provided to Black women. The book contains essays, research, and analyses that serve as a pointed critique on the state of Black women's health in America by Black women scholars, researchers, medical professionals, social workers, and public health advocates who acknowledge America's continuing gendered and racial disparities and advocate for interdisciplinary reforms.

The Public Health Crisis Among Black Women and Girls

The politically charged times in which we currently live demand unprecedented leadership from Black women laboring in and around the field of public health. At a time when Black women are disproportionately experiencing health crises in heart disease, maternal and infant mortality, breast cancer, and HIV, scholar-activism is not an option—it is a mandate (Abdou & Fingerhut, 2014; Earnshaw et al., 2013; Jones, 2000; Wyatt, 1997). The research clearly shows that Black women in the US are in a health crisis. For example, Black women are disproportionately subject to various factors—from poor-quality environments in impoverished neighborhoods to food deserts to a lack of access to health care—that make them more likely to contract life-threatening diseases, from HIV to cancer. Nationally, Black women account for 66 percent of new cases of HIV among all women. HIV/AIDS-related illness is the leading cause of death among Black women ages 25–34 (Centers for Disease Control and Prevention [CDC], 2017). There are also drastic gaps in access to high-quality, culturally competent health care for Black women, meaning the diseases they contract are more likely to be life threatening. While Black women have a lower rate of breast cancer diagnosis than White women, they have a substantially higher rate of mortality as a result of the disease. The breast-cancer death rate for Black women ages 45–64 is 60 percent higher than for White women (CDC, 2016).

Many people assume that the educational gains and the professional statuses of Black women mitigate these health concerns. They are wrong. Advanced degrees and professional success have not translated into good health for Black women. The stress of anti-Black racism and sexism, coupled with the stress of serving as the primary caretakers of their communities, may have taken a toll on Black women's health even if they have the economic privilege to send their children to good schools, have more professional career options, and live in a wealthy neighborhood. In fact, well-educated Black women have worse birth outcomes than White women who haven't finished high school. Some researchers, like Cooper Owens (2017) and Dorothy Roberts (1997), have concluded that the primary issues plaguing the health of Black women today are linked to the deeply embedded sexist, racist, and discriminatory systems built into the very fabric of this country, including the origins and evolutions of the public health system. These facts place Black women public health scholars and researchers in the crosshairs of the conversation. We are simultaneously researcher and victim, thus making our point of view uniquely qualified to initiate this conversation. In moving forward in framing this discussion, we must address a few fundamental questions. First, what was the foundational goal of public health? Second, how has racism influenced the public health agenda? And third, how is the historical treatment of Black women's bodies linked to contemporary public health issues?

The Origins of Public Health

In the late 1700s, public health emerged as a field of practice and study out of concern for how communities treated and managed contagions threatening the population. The primary goal of public health was to reduce exposure to disease and death among the broad community (Tulchinsky & Varavikova, 2014). The history of public health tells a story about the search for ways of securing health and preventing disease in the population. Epidemic and endemic infectious disease stimulated thought and innovation about how to prevent disease on a practical level, oftentimes before the cause was scientifically identified. The prevention of disease in populations revolves around defining diseases, measuring their occurrence, and seeking effective interventions.

The evolution of public health is based on trial and error and has often involved controversial testing methods rooted in natural disaster, war, and racism. The need for organized public health is anchored in urbanization and social reform. Public health is arguably fueled by religious and societal beliefs, which have influenced approaches to explaining and attempting to control communicable disease by sanitation, civil planning, and provision of medical care (van Brakel et al., 2017). Religions and social systems have also viewed scientific investigation and the spread of knowledge as threatening, resulting in the inhibition of developments in public health, including the modern examples of opposition to sexual and reproductive rights, immunization, and food security.

Scientific controversies, such as the contagionist and anticontagionist disputations during the nineteenth century and opposition to social reform movements, were ferocious and resulted in long delays in adoption of the available scientific knowledge. Such debates still continue into the twenty-first century despite a melding of methodologies proven to be interactive, incorporating the social sciences, health promotion, and translational sciences, bringing the best available evidence of science and practice together for greater effectiveness in policy development for individual and population health practices.

The evolution of public health is a continuing process; pathogens change, as do the environment and the host. In order to face the challenges ahead, it is important to have an understanding of the past. Although there is much in this age that is new, many of the current debates and arguments in public health are echoes of the past. Experience from the past is a vital tool in the formulation of health policy, especially regarding marginalized populations such as Black women. An understanding of the evolution and context of those challenges as they pertain to Black women can help us to navigate the public health issues past, present, and future.

Racism and the Public Health Agenda

According to scholars, marginalized communities including Indigenous communities, enslaved Africans, women, prisoners, disabled people, LGBTQIA communities, and youth have rarely been included in the broad public health agenda (Washington, 2008). In her book *Medical Apartheid*, Harriet Washington points to pathologic public health responses to two issues affecting the Black community: tuberculosis (TB) in the early 1900s and HIV in the 1980s. In both instances, when poor, gay, and Black people were identified as vectors of the disease, they were treated as a threat of infection to Whites and often as criminals, locked up and isolated in prisons. Regarding the response to TB, Washington says, Whites and Blacks demonstrated different approaches:

> In the 1930s and 1940s, African American public-health advocates following in the footsteps of Booker T. Washington promoted such initiatives as Negro Health Week to provide

tuberculosis prevention and care to blacks who rarely gained entrée to quality medical care. But white support of such initiatives was predicated on concerns that the black domestics who cared for their children, cleaned their homes, drove their cars, and prepared their meals might import tuberculosis into white households. (p. 326)

Washington goes on to point out a similar public health response to HIV. While the legal restraints initially applied to gay white men in the early 1980s have been relaxed, they were forcefully applied to Black men in the 1990s. Testing laws are now rigorously applied to pregnant women and prisoners. According to Washington, twenty-nine states punish or incarcerate those who pass the virus on to others. A statement by Dr. Walter Shervington, a New Orleans psychiatrist and former president of the National Medical Association, said of the practice, "It has bothered me that when more punitive laws have come up, it is black people who are affected" (qtd. in Washington, 2008, p. 337).

The pathologizing response to public health issues in the Black community favors criminalization over treatment, further relegating infected and affected people to the margins of inequitable health care. Historically, public health has failed to recognize the social, historical, and cultural determinants of health, thus rendering it silent on issues related to access to medical care and treatment, inequitable economic and human-rights issues, and biases in medical practices.

In 1984, Margaret Heckler, then secretary of the US Department of Health and Human Services, dissatisfied with the way health disparities were being reported to Congress, provided the first comprehensive review of health disparities endured by Black and minority groups compared with Whites; the report laid the foundations for action to eliminate these disparities through health education and promotion and access to health care. One of the most significant outcomes of the 1985 *Report of the Secretary's Task Force on Black and Minority Health,* also known as the Heckler Report, was the creation of the Office of Minority Health (OMH) in 1986. The mission of OMH was to improve the health of racial and ethnic minority populations through the development of health policies and programs to eliminate health disparities. The Heckler Report called health disparities among minority groups an affront to public health ideals and American medicine (Heckler, 1985; OMH, n.d.).

Thirty-six years after the Heckler Report was released, Blacks still endure unacceptable health disparities and lack the power over policy and actions that could enable the changes to eliminate such disparities. We must be willing to challenge the inequalities and racial bias woven into the fabric of public health theory, practice, and policy. Otherwise, the lofty goals of community well-being and equal access for all will never be met. The sheer number of Black women who live below the level of poverty, live in food deserts, have limited access to health clinics, suffer maternal and infant mortality across socioeconomic lines, and have the highest risk of HIV among all women should force us to reconsider and reimagine the public health paradigm.

The Link Between History and Black Women's Contemporary Health Issues

Many researchers exploring the health and well-being of Black women and girls have suggested that there is a link between historical health-related experiences and our contemporary health issues. The race-based mistreatment of Black women is well documented over the four hundred years spanning enslavement, Jim/Jane Crow, the civil rights movement, through contemporary times. The inability of enslaved and freed Black women to exercise agency over their bodies resulted in violence, sexual exploitation, rape, childbearing for profit, medical experimentation, and forced sterilization. Often, the poor treatment Black women experienced was codified into law and public health practices, further disenfranchising Black women from the "common good" mission on which public health was founded.

A CDC report authored by Prather et al. (2018) links the historical antecedents of racism experienced by Black women to current health outcomes. The authors link the historical time periods from enslavement to now, including the personal experiences of Black women that contribute to disparities in sexual and reproductive health, with the parallel health care experiences of Black women over time. The authors concluded that the field of public health must examine the root causes of health inequities from multidisciplinary angles that include historical and cultural lenses in order to address the health inequities affecting Black women.

Black women are frequently referred to as the "conscience" of this country because we know that when the rest of America gets a cold, Black folks get pneumonia. This book, *Black Women and Public Health*, brings together the knowledgeable but often muted voices of Black women scholars and researchers who have been actively working in the trenches serving the health and medical needs of Black girls and women across the United States. Our goal is to amplify the voices of Black women who through their research and scholarship in health and wellness are seeking equity, dignity, and humanity for Black women and girls nationwide and across the globe.

After hundreds of years of social segregation and discrimination, existing health data confirm that Black women are the least healthy ethnic and gendered group in this country. Although the resources and policies to eliminate disparities exist in the United States, there has been inadequate long-term commitment to successful strategies and to the funding necessary to achieve health equity. Black women have not been in the fiscal nor political positions to assure the successful implementation of long-term efforts; the health of Black women has not been a priority for decision makers. For these reasons, Black women working at the intersection of health and gender need to assume positions of education, mentorship, advocacy, and leadership to lend our voices, experiences, and scholarship to the cause of social justice.

Deanna J. Wathington: Social Constructs, Lived Experience, and Science

Overall, I believe this work provides the opportunity to observe the effects of various social constructs (race, gender, class, etc.) on the health, beliefs, and behaviors of Black women. Even more telling is the opportunity to examine the effects of these constructs as a "prescription" for society and the health system as a whole in their interactions with Black women. In other words, the constructs weave a tale that allows others to feel comfortable in offering health promotion, preventive services, pharmaceuticals, and health care to Black women based for the most part on minimal amounts of correct knowledge and on stereotypes. These constructs have created a story wherein Black women can be seen as "other" and therefore not of the same value. As a physician and public health practitioner, I have often experienced and seen this in real time.

This book provides a space and a place to hear from Black women who are practitioners, researchers, academics, and scientists about how Black women are living within all the aforementioned social constructs and how their health is suffering from all of those constructs. We engage in discourse about our health experiences and health outcomes and the acknowledgment that we are not a uniform or monolithic group.

The breadth of our voices and our experiences are presented here along with the opportunity to learn through our research, data, and practice. We acknowledge our painful history in this space, meet the myths and fallacies about who we are in this space, and urge the reader to see and understand the reality of who we actually are and can become. We acknowledge and affirm the World Health Organization's (2014) definition of *health* as "a state of complete physical, mental and social well-being and not merely the absence of disease or infirmity" while understanding there is much we and our society must do to achieve that goal for Black women (p. 1).

This book is significant to me because the scope of the contributions within touch and intersect with the practice and research I have engaged for much of my career. Reproductive health, maternal and child health, and LGBTQ health are cornerstones upon which my journey into public health began (these encompassed interpersonal violence and emerging STIs). Over the years, these have been shaped and built upon by the larger connecting pieces of disparities in health status; inequities in care; diversity in the health professions; policy advocacy; interprofessional education; and the social, structural, and environmental determinants of health—all while I have still actively practiced medicine and public health.

My present and future work still sits squarely within the health-equity framework, with a bigger focus on active policy advocacy and development. And I will continue to work tirelessly to increase the presence of our faces and experiences in the health professions through the creation of relevant academic programming and successful graduation and placement of my students. After over thirty years of engaging in such work, I am blessed to have mentored and taught Black women who are now graduates working in various health fields and am comforted by the knowledge that that they are fully engaged in providing the best care to current and future generations.

Leslie R. Hinkson: Ain't I a Woman?

As a Black woman from a low-income immigrant family, I can attest to the glaring differences between the life and opportunities I had as a child growing up in a very segregated Brooklyn and those my three daughters enjoy in a mostly White suburb of Washington, DC. As my life prospects have improved, so has my environment and the resources I have available to me. This includes my access to quality health and medical care.

I had my first daughter right before starting graduate school. My obstetrician was one of the best in New York. His practice was in the most upscale neighborhood in Brooklyn at the time. However, he was affiliated with a nearby hospital in Brooklyn as well as a very posh one in Manhattan. I chose to give birth in the Brooklyn hospital. I knew it served a largely Black and Latino population, but, given its location in a wealthy neighborhood, I never questioned the quality of care I would receive there. I was wrong. While my doctor was excellent, the nurses who were charged with my care pre- and post-labor were not. While I had never given birth before, I didn't expect I'd be told to be quiet after yelling through my first push. If I were White, would I have been left in the delivery room for over twenty minutes surrounded by what looked like the detritus of battle until a kind custodian found me in there when she came to clean up and informed the nurse that I should be cleaned up and moved to my room? Would that same shushing nurse have brought my dinner to the delivery room where, surrounded by blood and tissue, she insisted that I eat? And when I made it clear that I would not eat in that environment, would she have informed me that I was not being a good mother? I don't know.

I do know that I had my second daughter in Princeton, New Jersey. My second obstetrician was just as great as my first. What differed was where I gave birth. In a hospital that served a predominantly White, affluent clientele, there was no nurse to tell me I couldn't scream as loud as I wanted to considering I was the one giving birth. I was not forgotten as soon as I pushed the baby out and was stitched up. I had a private room. And a volunteer came around every afternoon with a sundae cart! The total cost of both births was nearly identical. The quality of care could not have been more different.

I share this story because while the literature in my field of study helps inform my empirical research, so does my lived experience. As a social scientist, I strive to attain as much objectivity as possible in how I approach my work. As a critical sociologist, however, I also understand that everything down to the way I frame my research question, to the ways in which I conceptualize and operationalize key concepts, and to the way I interpret my findings are all informed by the way I see and experience the world.

One of my primary research interests involves medical knowledge, particularly as it relates to race. Since its institutionalization as a profession in the late nineteenth century, medicine in the US, as a discipline and a practice, has been significantly informed by both the dominant scientific and popular discourses surrounding race of a given time. Even as those discourses change, remnants of scientific racism still haunt medicine. The fact that Black adults and *children* are less likely to have their pain taken seriously and treated adequately in emergency departments nationwide than their White counterparts, the fact that Blacks are still thought to have lower lung capacity than Whites due to some inherent difference—these are two examples of how medical practices and insights, developed by plantation doctors blind to the lived realities of slavery as anything other than beneficial to slaves, are still alive in medical practice today. To what extent have African Americans been under- or overtreated for certain diseases and conditions simply because of their race? To what extent are health disparities the result of structural constraints that determine not just access to and quality of care but kind of care?

As a sociologist, while committed to the use of empirical evidence in uncovering fact, I also understand that the interpretation of fact is reliant on one's lived experience and one's location within our stratified society. These differences in interpretation lead to the creation of different truths. Often, one's position within the social hierarchy determines whether their truth will be believed and embraced. That is why I am so excited to be a part of this volume. Black women in America are often unseen and unheard. This volume promises to add fuel to a small but growing movement in public health that recognizes the value of Black women and their health and wellness but also the value of Black women in leading the charge to improve Black women's health. This volume embraces the truth about Black women's health as written by Black women.

I remember, as a child, seeing the old news footage from the civil rights movement as I watched the documentary series *Eyes on the Prize*. I distinctly remember thinking to myself as so many men carried posters that read "I AM A MAN!" that none of the Black women had posters that read "I AM A WOMAN!" Each chapter in this volume declares in some way, "I AM A BLACK WOMAN!" By imagining a public health that puts the concerns of Black women front and center, by focusing on Black women not as defective Black men or White women but as the standard, the contributors to this volume help us to dream a world in which Black women are afforded the care and consideration that will allow them to continue being the bedrock of their communities without sacrificing their mental and physical health to do so.

Stephanie Evans: Wellness as a Social Justice Issue

In the CDC's *Public Health 101* lecture series, the instructor, Susie McCarthy (2014), emphasizes that public health focuses on groups rather than individuals, and she argues that "at the core of public health, there is this principle of social justice, that people have the right to be healthy and to live in conditions that support their health." She cites C.-E. A. Winslow's portrayal of public health work as communities organizing to "prevent disease, prolong life, and promote health." I come to public health as a scholar of intellectual history seeking to insert Black women's visions of social justice into how communities are organized. In particular, my research centers Black women's memoir and autobiography as a source of information, evaluation, and planning. While individual responses are not sufficient evidence to create policy, a collection of narrative voices over time offer crucial insight into patterns and changes that can inform research questions and interpretations.

Social justice education is at the core of Black women's educational history and is the heart of Black women's studies. As Gloria Hull and Barbara Smith wrote, the goal of Black women's studies is "to save Black women's lives" (Hull et al., 1982, p. xxxi). It should be evident then, that Black women and public health are intertwined areas of critical race and gender research. Yet, as a survivor of sexual violence, I also have a deeply personal interest in deepening the commitment to social justice work in public health in ways that specifically save the lives of Black women and girls. Numerous memoirs (by authors like Maya Angelou, Tina Turner, Gabrielle Union, and Tarana Burke) demonstrate how personal reflections, when viewed collectively, can and should inform interpretation of public health problems and solutions.

The authors in this collected volume address multiple topics through variant research methods, yet all chapters center Black women's voices, and much of this work is grounded in personal experience. Life narratives as a source of health education that reinforce centering community perspectives in public health efforts and incorporating narrative analysis can certainly increase the efficacy of community interest, awareness, and collaboration. The power of collaborative work can be seen, for example, in the partnering of ideas with activism, as demonstrated in the case of the #MuteRKelly campaign against continued support of sexual abusers. In response to protests waged by Kenyette Barnes and Oronike Odeleye, I coined the hashtag #MuteRKelly, which became the galvanizing rallying cry of a movement decades in the making. The relationship of public health scholarship to activism is as deep as the relationship of activism to public health scholarship.

While most people recognize Kenyette Barnes as an activist, few realize her training in public health. In reflecting on the meaning of her work, Barnes exemplified the connection of public health to social justice that Susie McCarthy articulated in the CDC *Public Health 101* lecture. When I asked her to share reflections about her work for this book project, Barnes articulated,

> The intersection of public health and social justice, as it relates to the lived experiences of Black and other Women of Color, is a subject required within the public health discourse. Having had a background in both—I'm an alumna of Temple University's Department of Public Health—I have, throughout my career walked the delicate tightrope that connects social trauma, injustice and inequality directly to health disparities. For instance, when we explore health disparities of maternal health, abysmal childbirth outcomes, violence, and sexual trauma, we have, in real time, evidence that public health and social justice are interconnected and proximal to each other. HIV infection, sexual violence, cardiovascular disease, mental illness (including post traumatic stress disorder), are just a handful of public health issues that often have made themselves present in social justice spaces, as evidenced by contemporary movements such as #DoingIt, #GoRed, #MeToo, #MuteRKelly, #YouOKSis, and several others.
>
> As an example, sexual violence as a public health issue focuses solely on the individual and social determinants of risk. This view posits that in addressing ecological and interpersonal variables, we would in turn eradicate the issue. Yet, according to the Bureau of Justice Statistics, more than 2/3rd of Black ciswomen will experience sexual trauma (to include, forcible rape, incest and molestation, pornography, and sex trafficking). To assert that the sole responsibility to address this

adversity rests solely within the public health arena is short-sighted. Without a doubt, social justice is a valued partner in the combined labor in addressing public health disparity. (K. Barnes, personal communication, January 26, 2019)

Much like Barnes envisions in her scholar-activist work, the authors who contributed to *Black Women and Public Health* create much-needed dialogue about a rich past, critical current issues, and imperative recommendations for interventions that will impact the future of Black women in the United States and in the African diaspora. This collection is an opportunity for specialists and generalists to foster mutual understanding for the benefit of all.

Because of my personal and professional experiences, I am committed to healing practices as a form of social justice—sharing lessons from life narratives is part of a critical pedagogy to do so. My work in mental health led me from studying memoirs and portraits of women like Anna Julia Cooper as case studies of scholarly achievement to studying Cooper as a case study in wellness—as a centenarian who lived to be 105. Women like Cooper who exemplified mindfulness and holistic health and Black women elders who practiced yoga (including Harriet Jacobs, Sadie and Bessie Delany, Eartha Kitt, Rosa Parks, Jan Willis, and Tina Turner, in addition to the profile of Alice Coltrane presented in this book) show that public health issues like stress must be studied from an intersectional lens. Still other traditions, like those of musicians, singers, and dancers, reveal the very real healing properties embedded in joy and culture, as medical doctor and music therapist Deforia Lane wrote about in her memoir, *Music as Medicine* (1994).

The stress and self-care chapters in this book by Portia Jackson Preston and Dakota King-White are examples of how this collection on public health is intimately connected to what can be seen as a companion text, *Black Women's Mental Health: Balancing Strength and Vulnerability* (2017), which offers a framework to positively impact Black women's wellness. This collection, along with the edited volume on mental health, serves the *Black Women's Wellness* series's goal to "draw on and further expand BWST's engagement with various theoretical frameworks, questions of identity, different disciplines, activism and social justice work, and location-based analysis" (SUNY Press, n.d.).

Ultimately, I argue that wellness is a social justice issue, and I have introduced the concept of #HistoricalWellness to enhance visibility of Black women's lived experience and meaning making in public health and mental health. Historical wellness, as a concept, expands the understanding of self-care as it operates in Black women's lives by revealing a long history of healing traditions. Narratives of #HistoricalWellness provide longitudinal insight into interesting public health topics. For example, my current research is beginning to uncover how alcohol consumption (specifically narratives of wine in Black women's memoirs) has simultaneously served as a site of pleasure, pain, and power. Listening to women's voices, like those expressed in memoir, introduce intellectual history to health studies so Black women can be recognized as theorists and knowledge producers about issues that impact our well-being.

Life narratives carry lessons for public health scholars that are closely related to other foundational ideas in Black women's studies and history, such as Gloria Hull, Patricia Bell-Scott, and Barbara Smith's creative survival; Evelyn Brooks Higginbotham's politics of respectability; Kimberlé Crenshaw's intersectionality; Darlene Clark Hine's culture of dissemblance; and Farah Jasmine Griffin's textual healing. Like these scholars of race, gender, and history, Black women public health scholars should be at the center of grants, training practices, and education of the next generation who will engage in public health policies, especially those that will directly impact Black women.

Conclusion: A Regenerative Framework for Building Community

The theoretical framework for this book is derived from Cooper's notion of regeneration, and the methodological frame for organizing this work answers the call by Jones to name, locate, and act to change oppressive systems of power. The chapters are organized to reflect the history, practice, and planning of public health in ways that expand the vast and growing body of critical race and gender research. We explicitly contribute to antiracist work as outlined by Dr. Jones (2014) in her concept where she seeks to "braid the strands" between public health workers and disability-rights communities:

> There can be convergent strength between the antiracism community and the disability rights community in terms of expanding advocacy agendas, integrating research agendas, and sharing successful policy strategies. The 3 tasks that I

have historically identified with regard to addressing racism as a threat to the health and well-being of the nation have their parallels when addressing able-ism as a threat to the health and well-being of the nation. They are: (1) put racism/able-ism on the agenda. Name racism/able-ism as forces determining the other social determinants of health. Routinely monitor for differential exposures and opportunities (as well as outcomes) by "race"/disability status. (2) Ask "How is racism/able-ism operating here?" Identify mechanisms in structures, policies, practices, norms, and values. Attend to both what exists and what is lacking. (3) Organize and strategize to act. Join in grassroots organizing around the conditions of people's lives. Identify the structural factors creating and perpetuating those conditions. Link with similar efforts across the country and around the world. (p. S74)

Here her work is quoted at length to demonstrate how Black women's work in this volume seeks to name, locate, and act in ways that foster health and wellness. This book is part of the broader public health project that contributes to developing "convergent strength" in the antiracist public health community. For each third of the book, our coeditors provide section summaries that situate each chapter in relation to the larger project. These brief introductions show how each chapter contributes a piece of the puzzle in the overall picture of how to improve the quality of life through research.

Black women's research in public health is growing, and organizations like Black Ladies in Public Health, founded by Jasmine Ward in 2016 and hosting 13,100 online members, indicate more breakthroughs to come. Fittingly, Ward provides the afterword for this volume, as these scholars are joined by an interdisciplinary group of researchers that have defined aspects of Black women's public health, healing, and wellness.

The World Health Organization (2006) offered a definition of *wellness* that is at once helpful and problematic: "Wellness is the optimal state of health of individual and groups. There are two focal concerns: the realisation of the fullest potential of an individual physically, psychologically, socially, spiritually, and economically, and the fulfillment of one's role expectations in the family, community, place of worship, workplace and other settings." The idea of optimal health is important, but fulfilment of role expectations for women is often part of the problem that prevents one from realizing her full potential. For example, if the expectation is to stay in abusive relationships, families, communities, or nations, Black women's wellness would not be achievable. However, many Black women have been able to record their paths to wellness in ways that offer alternatives to violence and operate as a preventative measure for the next generation of would-be abusers and victims.

This collection of researchers, activists, practitioners, and teachers embodies a collective will to move public health toward wellness and to offer a diversity of pathways to move in that direction. In Dr. Anna Julia Cooper's words, this book is an exercise in "retrospection, introspection, and prospection," a look backward, inward, and forward toward ever-better individual, social, and global systems of health, healing, and wellness.

References

Abdou, C. M., & Fingerhut, A. W. (2014). Stereotype threat among black and white women in health care settings. *Cultural Diversity and Ethnic Minority Psychology, 20*(3), 316–323.

American Public Health Association. (n.d.). *What is public health?* Retrieved July 17, 2018, from https://www.apha.org/what-is-public-health

Aptheker, B. (2012). Foreword. In G. Gutiérrez y Muhs, Y. F. Niemann, C. G. González, & A. P. Harris (Eds.), *Presumed incompetent: The intersections of race and class for women in academia* (pp. xi–xiv). University Press of Colorado.

Avery, B. (2002). Who does the work of public health? *American Journal of Public Health, 92*(4), 570–575.

Black, M. C., Basile, K. C., Breiding, M. J., Smith, S. G., Walters, M. L., Merrick, M. T., Chen, J., & Stevens, M. R. (2011). *The National Intimate Partner and Sexual Violence Survey (NISVS): 2010 summary report.* National Center for Injury Prevention and Control, Centers for Disease Control and Prevention.

Black Women's Health Imperative. (2016). *IndexUS: What healthy Black women can teach us about health.*

Blount, L. G. (2016). What's right with us [Letter from the publisher]. In *IndexUS: What healthy Black women can teach us about health* (pp. 4–5). Black Women's Health Imperative.

Center for Black Women's Wellness. (n.d.). *Wellness program.* https://www.cbww.org/cbwwprograms

Centers for Disease Control and Prevention. (2016). *Breast cancer rates among black women and white women.* https://www.cdc.gov/cancer/dcpc/research/articles/breast_cancer_rates_women.htm

Centers for Disease Control and Prevention. (2017). *HIV and women.* https://www.cdc.gov/hiv/group/gender/women/index.html

Cooper, A. J. (1998). *The voice of Anna Julia Cooper: Including* A voice from the South *and other important essays, papers, and letters* (C. Lemert & E. Bhan, Eds.). Rowman & Littlefield.

Cooper Owens, D. (2017). *Medical bondage: Race, gender, and the origins of American gynecology.* University of Georgia Press.

Dawes, D. E., & Holden, K. B. (2017). Transformative mental health for African American women: Health policy considerations. In S. Y. Evans, K. Bell, & N. K. Burton (Eds.), *Black women's mental health: Balancing strength and vulnerability* (pp. 265–285). State University of New York Press.

Earnshaw, V. A., Rosenthal, L., and Lewis, J. B., Stasko, E. C., Tobin, J. N., Lewis, T. T., Reid, A. E., & Ickovics, J. R. (2013). Maternal experiences with everyday discrimination and infant birthweight: A test of mediators and moderators among young, urban women of color. *Annals of Behavior Medicine, 45*(1),13–23.

González, C. G., & Harris, A. P. (2012) Introduction. In G. Gutiérrez y Muhs, Y. F. Niemann, C. G. González, & A. P. Harris (Eds.), *Presumed incompetent: The intersections of race and class for women in academia* (pp. 1–16). University Press of Colorado.

Gupta, S. (Host). (2020, June 5). Two viruses: Dr. Sanjay Gupta's coronavirus podcast for June 5 [Podcast episode transcript]. *Coronavirus: Fact vs. fiction with Dr. Sanjay Gupta.* CNN. https://www.cnn.com/2020/06/05/health/gupta-coronavirus-podcast-wellness-june-5/index.html

Heckler, M. M. (1985). *Report of the secretary's task force on Black and minority health* (vol. I: Executive summary). U.S. Department of Health and Human Services. http://www.minorityhealth.hhs.gov/assets/pdf/checked/1/ANDERSON.pdf

Hoytt, E. H. & Beard, H. (2012). *Health first! The Black woman's wellness guide.* Black Women's Health Imperative.

Hull, G. T., Bell Scott, P., & Smith, B. (Eds.). (1982) *All the women are White, all the Blacks are men, but some of us are brave: Black women's studies.* Feminist Press.

Jones, C. P. (2000). Levels of racism: A theoretic framework and a gardener's tale. *American Journal of Public Health, 90*(8),1212–1215.

Jones, C. P. (2014). Systems of power, axes of inequity: Parallels, intersections, braiding the strands. *Medical Care,* 52(10, Suppl. 3), S71–S75. https://doi.org/10.1097/MLR.0000000000000216

Jones, C. P. (2016). How understanding of racism can move public health to action: Allegory highlights dual reality of privilege. *The Nation's Health,* 46(1), 3.

McCarthy, Susie. (2014). Introduction to public health. In *Public health 101* [Lecture series]. U.S. Department of Health and Human Services, Centers for Disease Control and Prevention. https://www.cdc.gov/publichealth101/public-health.html

Office of Minority Health. (n.d.). *OMH Home*. United States Department of Health and Human Services. Retrieved January 19, 2020, from http://minorityhealth.hhs.gov/omh/browse.aspx?lvl=2&lvlid=1

Our Bodies Ourselves. (2011, November 1). *Byllye Avery on the impact of Our bodies ourselves* [Video]. YouTube. https://www.youtube.com/watch?v=6vFcuV4aCAg

Prather, C., Fuller, T. R., Jeffries, W. L., Marshall, K. J., Howell, A. V., Belyue-Umole, A., & King, W. (2018). Racism, African American women, and their sexual and reproductive health: A review of historical and contemporary evidence and implications for health equity. *Health Equity*, *2*(1), 249–259.

Roberts, D. (1997). *Killing the Black body: Race, reproduction, and the meaning of liberty*. Vintage Books.

SUNY Press. (n.d.). *Series*. https://www.sunypress.edu/l-49-series.aspx

Tulchinsky, T. H., & Varavikova, E. A. (2014). *The new public health* (3rd ed.). Academic Press.

van Brakel, W. H., Post, E., Saunderson, P. R., & Gopal, P. K. (2017). Leprosy. In S. R. Quah (Ed.), *International encyclopedia of public health* (2nd ed., pp. 391–401). Academic Press.

Washington, H. A. (2008). *Medical apartheid: The dark history of medical experimentation on Black Americans from colonial times to the present*. Harlem Moon.

Winslow, C.-E. A. (1920). The untilled fields of public health. *Science*, *51*(1306), 23–33.

World Health Organization. (2006). *Health promotion glossary update*. http://www.who.int/healthpromotion/about/HPR%20Glossary_New%20Terms.pdf

World Health Organization. (2014). Constitution of the World Health Organization. In *Basic Documents* (48th ed., pp. 1–19). (Originally published in 1946)

Wyatt, G. E. (1997). *Stolen women: Reclaiming our sexuality, taking back our lives*. Wiley.

PART I

NAME INEQUITY

SECTION OUTLINE: LESLIE R. HINKSON

Until the lion learns how to write, every story will glorify the hunter.

—African proverb

Since its institutionalization as a profession in the late nineteenth century, medicine in the United States as a discipline and a practice has been significantly informed by the dominant scientific and popular discourses surrounding race. In the early twentieth century, the rise of the medical profession and the biomedical model of disease exerted formative influences on the development of public health as a field in the US. What this meant in practice was a public health discipline that largely framed discussions of Black health and illness in terms that downplayed the effects of environmental and societal factors and highlighted notions of alleged biological racial inferiority to explain the health profile of a people newly freed from slavery and having to navigate a society that not only seemed to begrudge them their freedom but their very lives as well.

W. E. B. Du Bois's seminal works *The Philadelphia Negro* (1899) and "The Health and Physique of the Negro American" (1906) are perhaps the earliest published public health studies in the US. Challenging the predominant notion that Black and White differences in both mortality and morbidity were driven by innate biological difference, Du Bois illustrated

29

the significant role that environmental conditions (e.g., poor sanitation, high rates of population density) and socioeconomic status played in explaining these disparities. Yet even as Du Bois's methodological innovations would in many ways revolutionize the study of disease in the US, it would take decades before his contribution would be widely recognized. Just as importantly, his theoretical framing of "Negro health" as primarily informed by environment and resources would go largely ignored by the mainstream of both American medicine and public health. Yet, a growing number of Black lions—and lionesses—would join Du Bois in not only questioning the predominant narrative of Black biological inferiority in explaining health disparities but centering that narrative around the lived experiences of African Americans through the twentieth century and the significant role that racism, discrimination, and racial oppression played in explaining them.

The first four chapters of this volume focus on the history of Black women in public health—both as active agents in improving the health of Black women and communities and as the victims of a history of dehumanization that would inform both clinical practices and social policies that worked to undermine their health and well-being for over a century. In all four chapters, the authors illustrate the importance of naming and framing public health through the history and experiences of Black women in order to understand the present-day challenges they face in attaining wellness and health justice.

In "Reversing the Dehumanization of Black Women," Tiffany D. Thomas and Mandy Hill examine the history of reproductive health in the US in order to shed light on the historical abuse and present-day neglect of Black women and their health. The chapter reveals how the broader societal dehumanization of Black women throughout the history of the US was translated into clinical practice. Just as disturbing, the authors highlight how the historical dehumanization of Black women became internalized within Black communities, leading to behaviors that have contributed to poor reproductive and sexual health outcomes.

Next, Rebekah Israel Cross, Brittney Butler, and Mya L. Roberson highlight the contributions of Black women activists from the late nineteenth century to the present in their chapter, "An Overview of the Past, Present, and Future of Black Women in Health Policy." While almost none of the women included in the chapter contributed directly to the crafting of health policy or to the fields of medicine or health more broadly, their activism focused on improving areas of life that research on the social determinants of health has subsequently identified as crucial to supporting the health and well-being of the populace writ large and Black women in particular. Given that at least since the nineteenth century Black women have been advocating for improvements in housing, education, sanitation, nutrition and food access, health care, and a host of issues directly linked to better health outcomes, why haven't we incorporated their activism into the history of public health and its development as a field? Why was much of their work largely ignored in the crafting of public health policy in their day? And how might deliberately incorporating the voices of Black women activists into public health research and policy significantly improve the health of Black women and communities today and into the future?

Jovonni R. Spinner, Sheila Carrette, and Joylene John-Sowah describe the disproportionately high rates of maternal mortality among Black women in the United States. The authors of "The Maternal Mortality Crisis in the Black Community" detail the biological, medical, and environmental causes of maternal mortality rates. Issues related to racism and implicit bias are also explored as contributing factors. The authors conclude with some innovative practice, community, and policy recommendations for reducing the disparities in maternal mortality rates among Black women.

In their chapter "Promoting Self-Care and Awareness of Stress, the Strong Black Woman Schema, and Mental Health Among African American Women," Dakota King-White, Kelly Yu-Hsin Liao, and Elice E. Rogers examine stress-related factors and their role as obstacles (impediments) to prime physical and mental health for Black women. The chapter provides a salient discussion of types of stress, intersectionality, and the impact of tropes and stereotypes followed by strategies to help effectively manage these detrimental factors.

These chapters open the door to discussions of how to unpack characteristics of disparity, presented in the next section.

Chapter 1

Reversing the Dehumanization of Black Women

TIFFANY D. THOMAS AND MANDY HILL

Modern America perpetuates the false idea that Black women are not fully human and do not feel pain. Cultural and social norms here in the United States of America embrace ideals that render Black women unseen or unheard (McLellan-Lemal et al., 2013). Failure to recognize and acknowledge Black women as human beings with feelings and voices undermines the full human capacity of the Black woman. This is modern-day dehumanization. One aspect of the dehumanization of Black women is the process of racial devaluation. As it relates to Black women and health, racial devaluation in the medical encounter is a phenomenon whereby a Black woman's race increases the likelihood that she will be "denied more advanced and riskier medical technologies" as part of her care and treatment regimen, in part because her position within the racial hierarchy deems her less worthy of these goods and services (Hinkson, 2015). The dehumanization of Black women, however, goes beyond processes of racial devaluation, calling into question not simply the worth of Black women because of their race but their humanity itself. Evidence of this motif permeates society and manifests as a wide array of health disparities, particularly in the areas of reproductive and sexual health. Black women have been dehumanized and continue to disproportionately experience negative outcomes stemming from the intersection between racism, sexism, and classism relative to other racial and gender groups (Centers for Disease Control and Prevention [CDC], 1999; Prather et al., 2018; Sheats et al., 2005; Wallace et al., 2013). This chapter explores the experience of Black women in totality, retells the history, evaluates societal implications on the human experience of Black women, and culminates with a plan to leverage clinical care as the change agent for the lived experience of Black women. In examining reproductive health specifically, the chapter sheds light on the historical abuse and present neglect of Black women and their health.

The Historical Timeline of Black Women as Less-Human Patients in Health Care

The current health-care system perpetuates the false idea that Black women do not feel pain. Failure to acknowledge pain creates a barrier to adequate health care for Black women whereby they are not heard and subsequently not treated. We cannot challenge the quality of health care Black women receive without examining the complex national race story.

Since slavery, and through the evolution of the US health-care system, Black women were excluded from full social citizenship, the ability to access and participate in political, civil, and social rights, and womanhood (Plous & Williams, 1995). This fact is evident in the countless examples of medical mistrust demonstrated through medical journals, institutional practices, and physicians' writings, often supported by the law, particularly when it came to sexual reproduction. Half of the original articles in the 1836 *Southern Medical and Surgical Journal* issue deal with experiments performed on enslaved Blacks (Savitt, 1981).

Slave owners were motivated to provide a source of health care to their slaves based on economic return rather than humane compassion. Therefore, owners consented to medical treatment on their behalf without the consent of those being treated and regardless of the pain and level of recovery. Slaves did not have the agency to refuse, and, when they did, the slaveholders often ignored and disregarded their complaints.

James Marion Sims, who is lauded as the "father of gynecology," is known for believing Black women did not feel pain (Hoffman et al., 2016). He promoted the idea by refusing to provide anesthesia to the Black women and girl slaves he used and abused to perfect his vesicovaginal fistula technique. Sims expressed that administering medication to reduce pain was not worth the trouble or risk and that his procedures were not painful enough for medication. One could argue his defense of refusal, especially since the use of anesthesia was in its infancy at the time. However, Sims always administered anesthesia to his White female patients in need of repairs to their vagina in 1840 (Harris, 1950).

For Black women, forced experimentation was the standard practice of care. Dr. François Marie Prevost, a physician from Donaldson, Louisiana, enslaved Black women for the sole purpose of practicing cesarean sections to perfect the procedure; between 1822 and 1831 he performed thirty-seven experiments on women, and thirty of them were oppressed Black women (Fisher, 1968; Slack, 1835; Louisiana State Medical Society, 1880). These incredibly painful surgeries were deemed too dangerous to perform on White women.

The medical community has benefited from the "greater good" of the medical trauma placed upon Black women while absorbing none of the pain or risks. A Black woman named Henrietta Lacks paid the ultimate price, without consent, for the advancement of medicine. Physicians voluntarily abandoned their ethical responsibilities when they stole cultured cells from a malignant tumor in her cervix and named them HeLa cells while she underwent treatment for cervical cancer. HeLa cells continue to revolutionize medical research at the expense of a Black woman. Today, HeLa cells have contributed to medical breakthroughs in science involving the polio vaccine, the AIDS virus, and cancer worldwide.

"The best way to hate a nigger is to hate him before he is born."

—Louisiana Judge Leander Perez

Medical control of Black women's reproductive roles evolved from forcing them to produce children to supply a workforce to removing their ability to reproduce, both without their consent. Fannie Lou Hamer is known for her bold and unapologetic stances regarding the political activities of Blacks. However, many are unaware it was her "Mississippi appendectomy" that motivated and shaped her political involvement (Hamer, 1967). In a Mississippi appendectomy, a doctor would tell a Black woman they needed their appendix removed and would ultimately give them a hysterectomy. Hamer was a granddaughter of slaves, daughter of sharecroppers, and one of the youngest out of her eighteen siblings caught in the cycle of poverty and uneducated. In 1961, during a routine uterine fibroid tumor removal surgery, Hamer's uterus was removed from her body—without consent and more importantly without her knowledge. She was a victim of eugenics, a social movement to improve the genetic quality of a human population by discouraging reproduction by people with "undesirable" qualities, i.e., Black race (Black, 2003).

This is yet another example of how the US health care system medically misled Black women by refusing to extend to them full social citizenship. This practice was common, as procedures were often extended to women deemed feeble-minded, promiscuous, poor, or unfit to have children (Roberts, 1997). In reality, the targets of the eugenics practices like the Mississippi appendectomy were overwhelmingly women of color of all classes and poor women of all ethnicities. In this way, it served as a policy informed primarily by dominant intersecting systems of oppression—namely, racism, classism, and sexism.

Between the 1960s and 1970s, federally funded welfare programs promoted the forced sterilizations of thousands of poor Black women after giving birth in rural hospitals in the US South (Roberts, 1997). If Black women refused the service, their medical treatment or welfare benefits would be in jeopardy. Therefore, they "consented" to sterilization procedures through pressure. Continued discrimination through federal programming continued when social workers would perform "night raids" on the homes of Black women receiving welfare (Neubeck & Cazenave, 2001). If a man was identified in the house, their benefits were either threatened or they were offered sterilization as an option to guarantee no new children would be birthed for the state to support, promoting a single-parent family structure for poor Black families. The perpetual implications continue to persist today.

Failed social policies have continued to impact the health outcomes of Black women, as they have generally been drafted, passed, and enforced by legislation in states led by White, wealthy men. The Virginia Sterilization Act of 1924, which called for involuntary sterilization of individuals, heavily influenced the popularity of local states' adoption of eugenic programming and legislation of their own. The Sterilization Act of 1924 was upheld by the United States Supreme Court in the case *Buck v. Bell*, 274 U.S. 200 (1927; Antonios, 2011). Between 1924 and 1979, Virginia sterilized seven thousand people, and this was never called unconstitutional. By 1956, twenty-four states had adopted legislation supporting involuntary eugenics, resulting in 59,000 victims over fifty years (Kaelber, 2012). However, the

Virginia General Assembly (2001) issued a joint resolution acknowledging the misuse of the Act and how it embodied racist views.

The residual effects of the Sterilization Act of 1924 were evident as of November 2018, as fourteen states refused the Affordable Care Act's Medicaid expansion, and the overwhelming majority of those states were in the South. The South is often looked at as backward when considering social policies, but teaching hospitals in New York City also participated in medically misleading Black women. Unnecessary hysterectomies were performed on poor Black and Puerto Rican women that included further abuses, such as pressuring patients to consent and incomplete medical records of these procedures (Roberts, 1997).

Patient-doctor relationships are critical to quality care (Cuevas, 2013; Meredith et al., 2001). Medical mistrust continued in the relationship between obstetricians and Black women when they were sterilized after giving birth. Forged consent forms and falsified medical records reflecting incorrect procedures such as "appendectomy" or "gallbladder removal" due to inaccurate accounts served as catalysts to erase evidence accounting for complete and accurate numbers of Black women sterilized without their knowledge.

In 1973, the Southern Poverty Law Center filed a class-action suit against Casper Weinberger, Secretary of the U.S. Department of Health, Education, and Welfare representing Mary Alice Relf (age twelve) and her sister Minnie (age fourteen), who were sterilized by the Montgomery Community Agency, a federally funded program (Relf v. Weiberger, 1974). Their parents were illiterate and signed over consent with an X. Neither parent was aware their daughters were sterilized. Findings in the lawsuit led to the discovery that 100,000–150,000 women had been sterilized using federal funding (Relf v. Weiberger, 1974). Half of those women were Black.

Margaret Sanger, most notably recognized as the founder of Planned Parenthood and a powerful defender of women's rights, was also an ardent eugenics advocate—particularly for Black women. She routinely recruited Black leaders and luminaries such as Mary McLeod Bethune, W. E. B. Dubois (Du Bois, 1939), Charles Spurgeon Johnson, and Adam Clayton Powell Jr. to write articles for her Birth Control Review as an avenue to support sterilization. By creating relationships through respected voices in the Black community, the pervasiveness of racism was often modeled and encouraged within systems. Yet again, this violated sacred spaces for Black people and their families such as places of worship and educational institutions.

Societal Implications of Widespread Perceptions that Black Women Are Less Human

The societal implications of pervasive and consistent historical references to the Black woman are far-reaching, invading public and intimate social spheres and interrupting the human need to foster connection. Evidence of this is made clear in the prevalence of sexual violence and sexual exploitation and the disproportionate burden of health disparities for Black women, globally and nationally (CDC, 2015; Blythe et al., 2006; Bowleg et al., 2004; Broaddus et al., 2016).

Black women have been hypersexualized in the US through imagery (Benard, 2016). This history has provided a theoretical framework that interventionists and program developers utilize to better understand the negative mental, physical, and sexual health consequences of degrading images that shape societal perceptions of Black women in the US and abroad. The sexual script theory (Boutin-Foster et al., 2010; Jones & Hostler, 2002; Kim et al., 2007; Parsons et al., 2004; Reed & Weinberg, 1984; Stokes, 2007; Tolman et al., 2007) and the theory of gender and power (Albarracin et al., 2001; DePadilla et al., 2011; Hennessy et al., 2010; Hill et al., 2017; Tolman et al., 2007; Wingood & DiClemente, 1992, 1998, 2000) are two established theories that collectively describe sexual scripts with significant cultural relevance to Black women. Stephens' and Phillips' (2005) focus of sexual script development research on Black women explores ways culture shapes perception, expression of appropriate and socially acceptable sexual behavior, individual-level expectations, and experiences of behaviors that occur in series (Jones, 2006) within a population at high risk for HIV and communicable diseases that include hepatitis C and a myriad of sexually transmitted infections (STIs) (Boutin-Foster et al., 2010; Bowleg et al., 2004; Erickson et al., 2013; Holman & Sillars, 2012; Hussen et al., 2012; Jones & Oliver, 2007; McLellan-Lemal et al., 2013; Robinson et al., 2002; Ross & Coleman, 2011; Roye et al., 2013; Vannier & O'Sullivan, 2011; Wiederman, 2005).

Gender-based power imbalances strongly influence the sexual behaviors that place Black women at high risk for HIV and STIs and constrain a woman's ability to assert their sexuality and desire and grant enthusiastic consent (Pulerwitz et al., 2002). Influence and constraint are compounded by feelings of powerlessness and meekness (DePadilla et al., 2011). Gina Wingood led the focusing of Connell's theory of gender and power on the powerlessness of Black women in sexual decision-making (Wingood & DiClemente, 1992, 1998, 2000).

Within sexual scripts of Black women, there is a double standard wherein the power in the sexual relationship favors the man, and inconsistent condom use is attributed to low sexual-relationship power (Amaro, 1995; Amaro et al., 2001; Bowleg, 2004; Bowleg et al., 2004; Crepaz et al., 2009; Fullilove et al., 1990; Jones, 2006; Jones & Oliver, 2007; McLellan-Lemal et al., 2013; Pulerwitz et al., 2002; Roye et al., 2013; Wingood et al., 2003), supporting a dynamic where the woman is vulnerable to decisions made by her partner (Martyn & Hutchinson, 2001; McLellan-Lemal et al., 2013). This power dynamic is reminiscent of that between the White slave master and the Black woman centuries ago, wherein the Black woman had no power to negotiate. For Black women, survival sex with the slave master was a worthy sacrifice for the survival of not only themselves but their families (Bridges, 2011; Collins, 2006). *Survival sex* today is a term used to describe women who engage in sex to meet a fundamental need (i.e., food, water, shelter; Mallory & Stern, 2000; Wojcicki, 2002). Sexual script theory and the theory of gender and power demonstrate the influence of societal factors and gender roles on sexual behaviors among Black women (Jones, 2006; Jones & Hostler, 2002; Kim et al., 2007; Wingood & DiClemente, 1998, 2000).

Subsequent to the powerless condition of sexual scripts imposed upon Black women are disparities in the incidence of disease as a sexual health consequence. Young adult Black women have the highest human papillomavirus (HPV) rates in the US (Dunne et al., 2007) and are two times more likely to develop HPV-related cervical cancer than their White counterparts (American Cancer Society, 2019; Horner, 2009; Pickle et al., 2007; National Cancer Institute, 2021). Black women are also twice as likely to die from cervical cancer as White women (American Cancer Society, 2019; Horner, 2009; Pickle et al., 2007; National Cancer Institute, 2021). Worsened health outcomes of HPV are an important example of how health disparities for Black women manifest in disease incidence, morbidity, and mortality.

Beyond disease, the racial homogeneity among Black people in social networks means that they are generally comprised of members who are also at high risk for health disparities due to behaviors that are embraced as culturally normative. High-risk sex behaviors (e.g., inconsistent condom use) among Black women are driven by societal pressures to tolerate unhealthy behaviors such as partner infidelity (Jones, 2004, 2006; Sikkema et al., 1995; Wagstaff et al., 1995) in order to maintain relationships (Bowleg et al., 2004), use of sex as currency (Jones & Oliver, 2007; Ross & Coleman, 2011), and greater value of intimacy, romance, and trust in the relationship (Jones & Oliver, 2007; McLellan-Lemal et al., 2013).

The human right to procreate has been violated for Black women, as they experience a vastly disproportionate burden of maternal mortality. In Texas, Black women are at higher risk of dying from pregnancy complications than any other group, suffering 27.8 deaths per 100,000 live births, which is twice the rate for White and Hispanic women (13.6 per 100,000 and 11.5 per 100,000 respectively; Baeva et al., 2018). Furthermore, the risk for maternal death among Black mothers remains high across the socioeconomic spectrum (Maternal Mortality and Morbidity Task Force [MMMTF], 2018).

Recently, in 2016, a healthy Black woman named Kira Dixon Johnson died twelve hours after giving birth because her health concerns were ignored and dismissed. This example offers one piece of historical evidence of the dehumanization of Black women that has occurred in medicine throughout American history. Failure to completely extend womanhood to Black women has resulted in systemic mistrust of the medical system among this group (H. L. Gamble et al., 2009; V. N. Gamble, 1997). The current maternal mortality rates among Black women underscore historical unethical medical treatment (Baeva et al., 2018; CDC, 1995, 1999; MMMTF, 2018), whereby the dehumanization of Black women is an accepted norm among medical providers. This disparity persists even when controlling for significant factors like socioeconomic status and education, illustrating that race is the principal determinant of health for Black women who need reproductive care.

On November 28, 2018, Judge Glenda Hatchett shared the devastating story of the maternal health care for her daughter-in-law, Kira Hatchett, during her final twenty-four-hour period as a living Black woman. Kira's obstetrician performed a second cesarean-section (c-section) delivery procedure in a record time of two minutes (the standard period for a second c-section is twelve to fifteen minutes; 4Kira4Moms, 2018). Judge Hatchett said of the physician's performance, "He butchered her." The most striking part, after Kira was allowed to bleed for several hours, is that the physician did not provide the family with the professional courtesy of delivering the news of Kira's death under his care. Instead, the physician exited out of the back door to avoid the family. The utter disrespect and apparent subpar value placed on the human life of a Black woman in this story illustrate a broader societal problem. According to the CDC (2018), Black women are three to four times more likely to die during childbirth than women of every other race, even after controlling for traditional confounders like socioeconomic status, education, and access to care. This health outcome is because Black women are still not being seen or heard when describing their pain and pregnancy symptoms. As a consequence, their health care is compromised, and the threat of their death remains imminent.

"The voice of a Black woman should always be HERSELF"

—Malebo Sephodi

The integration and application of culturally responsible community-development models is desperately needed to reinstate full social citizenship to Black women in this nation. To this end, practitioners have activated the asset-based community development (ABCD) model as a tool to create a culture of involvement and collaboration around community issues, typically around housing and economic development (Kretzmann & McKnight, 1993). ABCD has eight guiding principles that inform facilitators how to engage with communities for a more inclusive approach complete with results; these principles can fully influence health outcomes and perceptions of Black women as human when power is diffracted to reverse powerlessness from the patient and neutralize power from the physician (Mathie et al., 2017). The "listen" principle encourages the premise that decisions should come from conversations where people feel heard. We have the opportunity to use the "listen" concept to institute strategies aimed at holding researchers and practitioners accountable through training and recruitment of culturally responsive faculty members (Kington et al., 2001).

White physicians spend more time creating connection with and treatment plans for as well as educating their White patients than they do for their Black patients due to levels of comfort between both parties (Norman et al., 2001). As such, physicians are less likely to spend time discussing treatment plans with Black female patients or their caregivers due to the inaccurate and pervasive imagery of Black women and perceptions of the type of care and respect we deserve. Physicians operate in positions of visible, hidden, and invisible power (McGee, 2017). Visible power includes formal rules and procedures, such as decision-making. Hidden power is when powerful people marginalize the concerns of people and their voices. Invisible power operates within the framework of belief systems that are created about others, such as negative stereotypes. By removing these power elements from the physician-patient experience, we can implement a three-tiered transition of the relationship from power *over* the patient to power *to* the patient to power *with* the patient in order to create a more balanced approach and mutual respect between physicians and patients (Mathie et al., 2017). Without this transition, the unconscious trifecta of a physician's power wills their use of race and gender to influence their bias while interacting with patients at any moment (Hinkson, 2015).

The untoward consequence to this misuse of power manifests in the way Black women experience the nation's health-care system. Black women consistently report miscommunication as a barrier to their care (Scheppers et al., 2006). Implementing the "listen" principle within the US health-care system allows Black women to re-create a culturally sensitive relationship wherein they are heard. Consistent utility of the "listen" principle presents an opportunity for the standard narrative and practice to shift regarding health care outcomes for Black women. By listening to Black women and hearing them, practitioners will involve them, as equal stakeholders, in decisions regarding their health outcomes with consent (Mathie et al., 2017; Rim et al., 2011).

Conclusion: Leveraging Clinical Care as a Change Agent to Societal Perceptions of the Black Woman

By systematically building cultural competency and cultural sensitivity for Black women within the health-care system, we can create an environment that serves as a catalyst to transform societal perceptions of Black women that are void of value and humanity. Black women have led the nation for decades in health disparities among women for many health conditions, consistently bearing a disproportionate burden of disease, injury, death, and disability (CDC, 2005). Data demonstrating this disparity suffered by this race and gender group continue to be produced; however, clinicians and policy makers who can effect change either lack the power to evoke change or do not value Black women as a priority group deserving of investment and quality-of-life preservation. Epidemiologic studies generally do not explore how our nation's history of racism negatively influences the present-day health outcomes of Black women (Prather et al., 2018). Thus, future aims to promote equity among all Americans in this nation must consider this history and move forward with framing culturally appropriate strategies that acknowledge this history. According to the CDC (2005), "eliminating these disparities will require culturally appropriate public health initiatives, community support, and equitable access to quality health care" (p. 1).

In the absence of cultural considerations, public health sequelae manifest as underutilization of physical and mental health services by Black women. For instance, a group of researchers, social workers, policy makers, public health practitioners, and community activists recently organized themselves as the Black Mamas Community Collective in Texas to require state legislators to address the disproportionate mortality rates from pregnancy complications of Black women (Puente, 2019). This group is bringing attention to the dire need for a dual approach with capabilities to offer culturally relevant, cutting-edge research opportunities and newly tested interventions for Black women. Texas Representative Shawn Thierry filed House Bill 607, a bill purposed to address health disparities through education, requiring cultural competency and bias training as part of state licensing for physicians who provide care to the general population, including primary care, pediatrics, and obstetrics and gynecology (Puente, 2019). This is an important step toward changing societal perceptions of Black women.

Legislative action requires reinforcement by health-care providers to produce systemic change. Unconscious bias, often referred to as implicit bias, is explained by the Association of American Medical Colleges as "attitudes outside of our awareness" that can extend beyond race and ethnicity and may relate to demographic variables like sexual orientation, gender, weight, age, social class, or height (Glicksman, 2016). Educating health-care providers on unconscious bias at every level of the health care spectrum, from medical-student training to continuing education for licensed providers, should be standardized. Exposure to unconscious-bias training exposes students, faculty members, and clinicians to people who are different from themselves and helps to reprogram thoughts and expectations of the public. Through reprogramming, students can think about bias before they become physicians, and practicing physicians can shed stereotypes that serve as barriers to achieving health equity. Dr. LaTanya Love at the University of Texas Health Science Center at Houston is leading this charge through development of workshops on unconscious-bias training for both medical students and faculty members (Glicksman, 2016). By requiring unconscious-bias training throughout the US medical system, we position providers to interrupt current treatment-plan models that are negatively influenced by race and gender. This type of systemic change could result in equity in disease incidence and health outcomes across races among women and equity in clinical responses to patients' self-reporting of pain across gender and race. The result is a general improvement in health equity to the lay public with positive implications for Black women as a part of the whole.

Translating theoretical equity to practical equity for Black women requires increased awareness of the subconscious bias among clinicians that is driven by societal perceptions of Black women. Clinicians must show fidelity to their Hippocratic Oath principles in treating Black women in a systematic way. Health-care providers have the opportunity to shift the narrative of Black women, in whose experience asking to be heard and not being listened to abounds, regardless of income, education, or marital status. By esteeming the fundamental medical ethic to "first, do no harm," clinical care teams can deliver better, more equitable, and compassionate care to all cross-sections of humanity, including Black women.

References

Albarracin, D., Johnson, B. T., Fishbein, M., & Muellerleile, P. A. (2001). Theories of reasoned action and planned behavior as models of condom use: A meta-analysis. *Psychological Bulletin, 127*(1), 142–161.

Amaro, H. (1995). Love, sex, and power: Considering women's realities in HIV prevention. *American Psychologist, 50*(6), 437–447.

Amaro, H., Raj, A., & Reed, E. (2001). Women's sexual health: The need for feminist analyses in public health in the decade of behavior. *Psychology of Women Quarterly, 25*, 324–334.

American Cancer Society. (2019). Cancer Facts and Figures for African Americans 2019–2021. https://www.cancer.org/content/dam/cancer-org/research/cancer-facts-and-statistics/cancer-facts-and-figures-for-african-americans/cancer-facts-and-figures-for-african-americans-2019-2021.pdf

Antonios, N. (2011). Sterilization Act of 1924. *The Embryo Project encyclopedia.* http://embryo.asu.edu/handle/10776/2090

Baeva, S., Saxton, D. L., Ruggiero, K., Kormondy, M. L., Hollier, L. M., Hellerstedt, J., Hall, M., & Archer, N. P. (2018). Identifying maternal deaths in Texas using an enhanced method, 2012. *Obstetrics and Gynecology, 131*(5), 762–769.

Benard, A. A. F. (2016). Colonizing Black female bodies within patriarchal capitalism: Feminist and human rights perspectives. *Sexualization, Media, & Society, 2*(4), 1–11.

Black, E. (2003). *War against the weak: Eugenics and America's campaign to create a master race*. Dialog Press.

Blythe, M. J., Fortenberry, J. D., Temkit, M., Tu, W., & Orr, D. P. (2006). Incidence and correlates of unwanted sex in relationships of middle and late adolescent women. *Archives of Pediatrics and Adolescent Medicine, 160*(6), 591–595.

Boutin-Foster, C., McLaughlin, N., Gray, A., Ogedegbe, A., Hageman, I., Knowlton, C., Rodriguez, A., & Beeder, A. (2010). Reducing HIV and AIDS through Prevention (RHAP): A theoretically based approach for teaching HIV prevention to adolescents through an exploration of popular music. *Journal of Urban Health, 87*(3), 440–451.

Bowleg, L. (2004). Love, sex, and masculinity in sociocultural context. *Men and Masculinities, 7*(2), 166.

Bowleg, L., Lucas, K. J., & Tschann, J. M. (2004). "The ball was always in his court": An exploratory analysis of relationship scripts, sexual scripts, and condom use among African American women. *Psychology of Women Quarterly, 28*(1), 70–82.

Bridges, K. M. (2011). *Reproducing race: An ethnography of pregnancy as a site of racialization*. University of California Press.

Broaddus, M., Owczarzak, J., Pacella, M., Pinkerton, S., & Wright, C. (2016). Partnership-level analysis of African American women's risky sexual behavior in main and non-main partnerships. *AIDS and Behavior, 20*(12), 2893–2903.

Centers for Disease Control and Prevention. (1995). Differences in maternal mortality among black and white women—United States, 1990. *MMWR: Morbidity and Mortality Weekly Report, 44*(1), 6–7, 13–14.

Centers for Disease Control and Prevention. (1999). State-specific maternal mortality among black and white women—United States, 1987–1996. *MMWR: Morbidity and Mortality Weekly Report, 48*(23), 492–496.

Centers for Disease Control and Prevention. (2005). Health disparities experienced by black or African Americans—United States. *MMWR: Morbidity and Mortality Weekly Report, 54*(1), 1–3.

Centers for Disease Control and Prevention. (2010). *National health and nutrition examination survey*. www.cdc.gov/nchs/nhanes.htm

Centers for Disease Control and Prevention. (2015). HIV and African American women. *Gateway to health communication and social marketing practice*. https://www.cdc.gov/healthcommunication/toolstemplates/entertainmented/tips/hivwomen.html

Centers for Disease Control and Prevention. (2018). *Pregnancy mortality surveillance system*. https://www.cdc.gov/reproductivehealth/maternalinfanthealth/pregnancy-mortality-surveillance-system.htm

Collins, P. (2006). New commodities, new consumers. *Journal of Sex and Black Women*, 6(3), 297–317.

Crepaz, N., Marshall, K. J., Aupont, L. W., Jacobs, E. D., Mizuno, Y., Kay, L. S., Jones, P., McCree, D. H., & O'Leary, A. (2009). The efficacy of HIV/STI behavioral interventions for African American females in the United States: A meta-analysis. *American Journal of Public Health*, 99(11), 2069–2078.

Cuevas, A. G. (2013). *Exploring four barriers experienced by African Americans in healthcare: Perceived discrimination, medical mistrust, race discordance, and poor communication* [Master's thesis, Portland State University].

DePadilla, L., Windle, M., Wingood, G., Cooper, H., & DiClemente, R. (2011). Condom use among young women: Modeling the theory of gender and power. *Health Psychology*, 30(3), 310–319.

Du Bois, W. E. B. (1939). *Negroes and birth control*. Smith Libraries Exhibits.

Dunne, E. F., Unger, E. R., Sternberg, M., McQuillan, G., Swan, D. C., Patel, S. S., & Markowitz, L. E. (2007). Prevalence of HPV infection among females in the United States. *JAMA*, 297(8), 813–819.

Erickson, P. I., Badiane, L., & Singer, M. (2013). The social context and meaning of virginity loss among African American and Puerto Rican young adults in Hartford. *Medical Anthropology Quarterly*, 27(3), 313–329.

Fisher, W. (1968). Physicians and slavery in the antebellum *Southern Medical Journal*. *Journal of the History of Medicine and Allied Sciences*, 23(1), 36–49.

4Kira4Moms. (2018). *4Kira4Moms*. https://4kira4moms.com/

Fullilove, R. E., Fullilove, M. T., Bowser, B. P., & Gross, S. A. (1990). Risk of sexually transmitted disease among Black adolescent crack users in Oakland and San Francisco, Calif. *JAMA*, 263(6), 851–855.

Gamble, H. L., Klosky, J. L., Parra, G. R., & Randolph, M. E. (2009). Factors influencing familial decision-making regarding human papillomavirus vaccination. *Journal of Pediatric Psychology*, 35(7), 704–715.

Gamble, V. N. (1997). Under the shadow of Tuskegee: African Americans and health care. *American Journal of Public Health*, 87(11), 1773–1778.

Glicksman, E. (2016, September 27). Unconscious bias in academic medicine: Overcoming the prejudices we don't know we have. *AAMCNews*. https://news.aamc.org/diversity/article/unconscious-bias/

Hamer, F. L. (1967). *To praise our bridges: An autobiography*. KIPCO.

Harris, M. D. (1950). *Women's surgeon: The life story of J. Marion Sims*. Macmillan.

Hennessy, M., Bleakley, A., Fishbein, M., Brown, L., Diclemente, R., Romer, D., Valois, R., Vanable, P. A., Carey, M. P., & Salazar, L. (2010). Differentiating between precursor and control variables when analyzing reasoned action theories. *AIDS and Behavior*, 14(1), 225–236.

Hill, M., Granado, M., & Stotts, A. (2017). Theoretical implications of gender, power, and sexual scripts for HIV prevention programs aimed at young, substance-using African-American women. *Journal of Racial and Ethnic Health Disparities*, 4(6), 1175–1180.

Hinkson, L. (2015). The right profile? An examination of race-based pharmaco-logical treatment of hypertension. *Sociology of Race and Ethnicity, 1*(2), 255–269.

Hoffman, K., Trawalter, S., Axt, J., & Oliver, M. N. (2016). Racial bias in pain assessment and treatment recommendations, and false beliefs about bio-logical differences between blacks and whites. *PNAS, 113*(16), 4296–4301.

Holman, A., & Sillars, A. (2012). Talk about "hooking up": The influence of college student social networks on nonrelationship sex. *Health Communication, 27*(2), 205–216.

Horner, M. J., Ries, L. A., Krapcho, M., Neyman, N., Aminou, R., Howlader, N., Altekruse, S. F., Feuer, E. J., Huang, L., Mariotto, A., Miller, B. A., Lewis, D. R., Eisner, M. P., Stinchcomb, D. G., & Edwards, B. K. (Eds.). (2009). *SEER Cancer Statistics Review, 1975–2006.* http://seer.cancer.gov/csr/1975_2006/

Hussen, S. A., Bowleg, L., Sangaramoorthy, T., & Malebranche, D. J. (2012). Par-ents, peers and pornography: The influence of formative sexual scripts on adult HIV sexual risk behaviour among Black men in the USA. *Culture, Health & Sexuality, 14*(8), 863–877.

Jones, R. (2004). Relationships of sexual imposition, dyadic trust, and sensation seeking with sexual risk behavior in young urban women. *Research in Nursing and Health, 27*(3), 185–197.

Jones, R. (2006). Sex scripts and power: A framework to explain urban women's HIV sexual risk with male partners. *Nursing Clinics of North America, 41*(3), 425–436, vii.

Jones, R., & Oliver, M. (2007). Young urban women's patterns of unprotected sex with men engaging in HIV risk behaviors. *AIDS and Behavior, 11*(6), 812–821.

Jones, S. L., & Hostler, H. R. (2002). Sexual script theory: An integrative exploration of the possibilities and limits of sexual self-definition. *Journal of Psychology and Theology, 30*(2), 120–130.

Kaelber, L. (2012). *Eugenics: Compulsory sterilization in 50 American states.* Retrieved from https://www.uvm.edu/~lkaelber/eugenics/

Kim, J. L., Sorsoli, C. L., Collins, K., Zylbergold, B. A., Schooler, D., & Tolman, D. L. (2007). From sex to sexuality: Exposing the heterosexual script on primetime network television. *Journal of Sex Research, 44*(2), 145–157.

Kington, R., Tisnado, D., & Carlisle, D. M. (2001). Increasing racial and ethnic diversity among physicians: An intervention to address health disparities? In *The right thing to do, the smart thing to do: Enhancing diversity in the health professions—Summary of the symposium on diversity in health professions in honor of Herbert W. Nickens, M.D.* National Academies Press.

Kretzmann, J., & McKnight, J. (1993). *Building communities from the inside out: A path toward finding and mobilizing a community's assets.* ACTA Publications.

Louisiana State Medical Society. (1880). *The New Orleans medical and surgical journal.* J. A. Gresham.

Mallory, C., & Stern, P. N. (2000). Awakening as a change process among women at risk for HIV who engage in survival sex. *Qualitative Health Research*, *10*(5), 581–594.

Martyn, K. K., & Hutchinson, S. A. (2001). Low-income African American adolescents who avoid pregnancy: Tough girls who rewrite negative scripts. *Qualitative Health Research*, *11*(2), 238–256.

Maternal Mortality and Morbidity Task Force. (2018, September). *Maternal Mortality and Morbidity Task Force and Department of State Health Services joint biennial report*. Texas Health and Human Services. https://www.dshs.texas.gov/mch/pdf/MMMTFJointReport2018.pdf

Mathie, A., Cameron, J., & Gibson, K. (2017). Asset-based and citizen-led development: Using a diffracted power lens to analyze the possibilities and challenges. *Progress in Development Studies*, *17*(1), 54–66.

McGee, R. (2017). Invisible power and visible everyday resistance in the violent Colombian Pacific. *Peacebuilding*, *5*(2), 170–185.

McLellan-Lemal, E., Toledo, L., O'Daniels, C., Villar-Loubet, O., Simpson, C., Adimora, A. A., & Marks, G. (2013). "A man's gonna do what a man wants to do": African American and Hispanic women's perceptions about heterosexual relationships: A qualitative study. *BMC Women's Health*, *13*, Article 27.

Meredith, L. S., Orlando, M., Humphrey, N., Camp, P., & Sherbourne, C. D. (2001). Are better ratings of the patient-provider relationship associated with higher quality care for depression? *Medical Care*, *39*(4), 349–360.

National Cancer Institute. 2021. Seer Cancer Statistics Review, 1975–2018. Table 1.25 and SEER*Explorer [Accessed 7/22/2021]. https://seer.cancer.gov/csr/1975_2018/; https://seer.cancer.gov/explorer/

Neubeck, K., and Cazenave, N. (2001). *Welfare racism: Playing the race card against America's poor*. Routledge.

Norman, O. M., Goodwin, M. A., Gotler, R. S., Gregory, P. M., & Stange, K. C. (2001). Time use in clinical encounters: Are African-American patients treated differently? *Journal of the National Medical Association*, *10*, 380–385.

Parsons, J. T., Vicioso, K. J., Punzalan, J. C., Halkitis, P. N., Kutnick, A., & Velasquez, M. M. (2004). The impact of alcohol use on the sexual scripts of HIV-positive men who have sex with men. *Journal of Sex Research*, *41*(2), 160–172.

Pickle, L. W., Hao, Y., Jemal, A., Zou, Z., Tiwari, R. C., Ward, E., Hachey, M., Howe, H. L., & Feuer, E. J. (2007). A new method of estimating United States and state-level cancer incidence counts for the current calendar year. *CA: A Cancer Journal for Clinicians*, *57*(1), 30–42.

Plous, S., & Williams, T. (1995). Racial stereotypes from the days of American slavery: A continuing legacy. *Journal of Applied Social Psychology*, *25*, 795.

Prather, C., Fuller, T. R., Jeffries, W. L., IV, Marshall, K. J., Howell, A. V., Belyue-Umole, A., & King, W. (2018). Racism, African American women, and their sexual and reproductive health: A review of historical and contemporary evidence and implications for health equity. *Health Equity, 2*(1), 249–259.

Puente, A. (2019, February 26). Group calls for legislative action to address Texas' high maternal mortality rate for black women. *The Austin Chronicle.* https://www.austinchronicle.com/daily/news/2019-02-26/group-calls-for-legislative-action-to-address-texas-high-maternal-mortality-rate-for-black-women/

Pulerwitz, J., Amaro, H., De Jong, W., Gortmaker, S. L., & Rudd, R. (2002). Relationship power, condom use and HIV risk among women in the USA. *AIDS Care, 14*(6), 789–800.

Reed, D., & Weinberg, M. S. (1984). Premarital coitus: Developing and established sexual scripts. *Social Psychology Quarterly, 47*(2), 129–138.

Relf v. Weinberger, 372 F. Supp. 1196 (D.D.C. 1974). Civil action nos. 73–1557.

Rim, S. H., Hall, I. J., Fairweather, M. E., Fedorenko, C. R., Ekwueme, D. U., Smith, J. L., Thompson, I. M., Keane, T. E., Penson, D. F., Moinpour, C. M., Zeliadt, S. B, & Ramsey, S. D. (2011). Considering racial and ethnic preferences in communication and interactions among the patient, family member, and physician following diagnosis of localized prostate cancer: Study of a US population. *International Journal of General Medicine, 4,* 481–486.

Roberts, D. (1997). *Killing the black body: Race, reproduction, and the meaning of liberty.* Pantheon Books.

Robinson, B. B., Bockting, W. O., Rosser, B. R., Miner, M., & Coleman, E. (2002). The sexual health model: Application of a sexological approach to HIV prevention. *Health Education Research, 17*(1), 43–57.

Ross, J. N., & Coleman, N. M. (2011). Gold digger or video girl: The salience of an emerging hip-hop sexual script. *Culture, Health & Sexuality, 13*(2), 157–171.

Roye, C. F., Tolman, D. L., & Snowden, F. (2013). Heterosexual anal intercourse among Black and Latino adolescents and young adults: A poorly understood high-risk behavior. *Journal of Sex Research, 50*(7), 715–722.

Savitt, T. (1981). *Medicine and slavery: The diseases and health care of blacks in antebellum Virginia.* University of Illinois Press.

Scheppers, E., van Dongen, E., Dekker, J., Geertzen, J., & Dekker, J. (2006). Potential barriers to the use of health services among ethnic minorities: A review. *Family Practice, 23*(3), 325–348.

Sheats, N., Lin, Y., Zhao, W., Cheek, D. E., Lackland, D. T., & Egan, B. M. (2005). Prevalence, treatment, and control of hypertension among African Americans and Caucasians at primary care sites for medically under-served patients. *Ethnicity and Disease, 15*(1), 25–32.

Sikkema, K. J., Koob, J. J., Cargill, V. C., Kelly, J. A., Desiderato, L. L., Roffman, R. A., Norman, A. D., Shabazz, M., Copeland, C., Winett, R. A., Steiner, S. & Lemke, A. L. (1995). Levels and predictors of HIV risk behavior among women in low-income public housing developments. *Public Health Reports, 110*(6), 707–713.

Slack, C. (1835). *The American journal of the medical sciences.* Smithsonian Libraries.

Stephens, D. P., & Phillips, L. (2005) Integrating Black Feminist Thought into Conceptual Frameworks of African American Adolescent Women's Sexual Scripting Processes. Sexualities, Evolution and Gender, 7, 37–55. http://dx.doi.org/10.1080/14616660500112725

Stokes, C. (2007). Representin' in cyberspace: Sexual scripts, self-definition, and hip hop culture in Black American adolescent girls' home pages. Culture, Health, & Sexuality, 9(2), 169–184.

Tolman, D. L., Kim, J. L., Schooler, D., & Sorsoli, C. L. (2007). Rethinking the associations between television viewing and adolescent sexuality development: Bringing gender into focus. Journal of Adolescent Health, 40(1), 84.e9–16.

Vannier, S. A., & O'Sullivan, L. F. (2011). Communicating interest in sex: Verbal and nonverbal initiation of sexual activity in young adults' romantic dating relationships. Archives of Sexual Behavior, 40(5), 961–969.

Virginia General Assembly. (2001). House joint resolution no. 67 (2001 Session).

Wagstaff, D. A., Kelly, J. A., Perry, M. J., Sikkema, K. J., Solomon, L. J., Heckman, T. G., & Anderson, E. S. (1995). Multiple partners, risky partners and HIV risk among low-income urban women. Family Planning Perspectives, 27(6), 241–245.

Wallace, K., Hill, E. G., Lewin, D. N., Williamson, G., Oppenheimer, S., Ford, M. E., Wargovich, M. J., Berger, F. G., Bolick, S. W., Thomas, M. B., & Alberg, A. J. (2013). Racial disparities in advanced-stage colorectal cancer survival. Cancer Causes and Control, 24(3), 463–471.

Wiederman, M. W. (2005). The gendered nature of sexual scripts. The Family Journal, 13(4), 496–502.

Wingood, G. M., & DiClemente, R. J. (1992). Cultural, gender, and psychosocial influences on HIV-related behavior of African-American female adolescents: Implications for the development of tailored prevention programs. Ethnicity and Disease, 2(4), 381–388.

Wingood, G. M., & DiClemente, R. J. (1998). Partner influences and gender-related factors associated with noncondom use among young adult African American women. American Journal of Community Psychology, 26(1), 29–51.

Wingood, G. M., & DiClemente, R. J. (2000). Application of the theory of gender and power to examine HIV-related exposures, risk factors, and effective interventions for women. Health Education and Behavior, 27(5), 539–565.

Wingood, G. M., DiClemente, R. J., Bernhardt, J. M., Harrington, K., Davies, S. L., Robillard, A., & Hook, E. W., III. (2003). A prospective study of exposure to rap music videos and African American female adolescents' health. American Journal of Public Health, 93(3), 437–439.

Wojcicki, J. M. (2002). "She drank his money": Survival sex and the problem of violence in taverns in Gauteng province, South Africa. Medical Anthropology Quarterly, 16(3), 267–293.

Chapter 2

An Overview of the Past, Present, and Future of Black Women in Health Policy

REBEKAH ISRAEL CROSS, BRITTNEY BUTLER,
AND MYA L. ROBERSON

Social determinants of health are factors outside of the health-care system, such as socioeconomic status, education, neighborhood physical environment, employment, and social support networks, that are known to influence health outcomes (Artiga & Hinton, 2018). Recently, there has been formal acknowledgment of the importance of policies relating to these factors in affecting health outcomes with the Health in All Policies framework created by the Public Health Institute, American Public Health Association, and California Department of Health. The mission of this framework is that policy makers are aware and knowledgeable of the health consequences of various policy options (Rudolph et al., 2013). Using this social determinants of health framework, we are operating under the assumption that policies addressing these determinants fall under the purview of health policy. Thus, environmental policy, housing policy, social-welfare policy, and so on all fall under the umbrella of health policy. The purpose of this chapter is to describe Black women's influence on policies affecting health, historically and currently, and to name health-policy issues that will be important to Black women in the future.

Selection Criteria

This chapter is organized in three sections: the past, the present, and the future. This chapter does not seek to present an exhaustive list of Black women's contributions to health policy throughout history. Instead, the examples selected for inclusion in each section were chosen because they exemplify Black women's contributions to pertinent health-related policy issues during that time frame. The examples outlined in the first section focus on Black women's activism in housing, social welfare, and communicable disease. These health issues were selected based on a literature search on the history of public health. Specific examples were selected based on their influence on health-related policy. Examples discussed in the "Past" section were found through the keyword searches "Black women AND housing activism," "Black women AND social services," and "Black women AND infectious disease" in history and social science databases and limited to US history up until the civil rights era. Examples discussed in the "Present" section were selected to highlight the breadth of Black women's roles in various sectors and health outcomes.

It is important to note that there were substantial challenges in searching for and finding examples outlining specific contributions of Black women to health policies. Rather than this being a reflection of a lack of examples, we posit that Black women's contributions in this area have been largely overlooked except by other Black women. This chapter seeks to highlight Black women's underacknowledged narratives and contributions to health policy.

Black Women in Health Policy: The Past

Much like in the present, the presumed behavioral and moral shortcomings of Black people were blamed for racial disparities in mortality in the late nineteenth and early twentieth centuries. State and local governments largely ignored the health needs of Black residents during this time. Black women filled this gap by community organizing, building institutions to provide social services, and implementing community health programs. Many of their interventions have had significant implications for health-related policy (Neverdon-Morton, 1989).

Across the United States, but particularly in the South, Black women were invested in providing social-welfare support for Black youth—especially orphans. The relationship between social welfare and health is well documented (Gregory & Deb, 2015). In the late nineteenth century, the need for social-welfare assistance was dire for Black people. After the Civil War, newly emancipated Black citizens were largely excluded from mainstream social services including hospitals, mental health facilities, and orphanages (Rabinowitz, 1974). The precariousness experienced by Black youth and elders with little to no institutional support fueled public health concerns regarding disease and premature death (Rabinowitz, 1974). In Atlanta, in 1890, a formerly enslaved woman, Carrie Steele, started a home for orphans to fill a critical gap in the social-welfare system for Black youth. An orphan herself, she was passionate about providing a space for young, Black, impoverished children to thrive. To raise money for the orphanage, she solicited private donations, sold her home, and worked as a railroad laborer (Neverdon-Morton, 1989). The Carrie Steele-Pitts Home started with five children but expanded to over two hundred before her death. Today, the home still fills an important gap in the social and health services for Black youth and the surrounding Atlanta community, including programs that promote mental and physical well-being. The Carrie Steele-Pitts Home is joined by numerous other orphanages and youth homes in the city of Atlanta and recently received funding from the City to expand its services to young adults up to age twenty-four (Carrie Steele-Pitts Home, n.d.). Carrie Steele's success in building a sustainable institution for orphaned and neglected Black youth is significant for health-related policy because it exemplifies how Black women are equipped to address the social and health needs of their communities. This is especially true when their work is backed by institutional resources.

Black women health activists understood early on that social environment impacted health. These women organized around improving the social realities that are inextricably linked to health. Affordable, decent housing is considered an important social determinant of health (Artiga & Hinton, 2018). Quality affordable housing provides people with security and refuge and potentially a foundation to pursue health in other arenas. In the twentieth century, public housing was a vital component of the housing stock for impoverished Americans. Black women, in particular, relied on public housing for reliable, affordable, decent housing (Williams, 2004). Toward the end of the 1950s, however, conservative lawmakers began to shift the public image of federally subsidised housing by restricting use to the very poor and limiting the amount of funding developments received (Goetz, 2013). Black women organized to respond to the growing deterioration of housing projects, and one woman, Joyce Thorpe, unintentionally turned her advocacy into federal policy. An organizer living in public housing in Durham, North Carolina, Joyce Thorpe was evicted in 1965 from McDougald Terrace in Durham, a federally subsidized housing development, after being elected as the building's Parents' Club president. Thorpe sued the Housing Authority to overturn her eviction, but it was upheld by both the appeals court and the North Carolina Supreme Court in 1967 (*Thorpe v. Housing Authority of the City of Durham* [1969]). Thorpe's case eventually moved up to the US Supreme Court, and while it was pending the US Department of Housing and Urban Development instituted a new policy that public housing residents cannot be evicted without just cause and notification. The US Supreme Court unanimously ruled in Thorpe's favor and concluded that the Durham Housing Authority must adhere to the new policy (Williams, 2009). Thorpe's activism has protected thousands of public housing residents from being evicted without just cause. Her court case still has implications for housing policy today. Just-cause eviction laws are considered effective tools for reducing the likelihood of landlord abuse often used to displace impoverished residents and maximize property profits.

Finally, Black women's history of organizing for health led to improved health outcomes and health-related policies. In the late nineteenth and early twentieth centuries, maternal and child mortality rates were disproportionately high among Black women in the South (Smith, 1995). Additionally, rates of infectious diseases were high due to poor sanitation and minimal access to health care. During this time, Black women in the Black Midwifery Movement organized to directly improve outcomes in maternal and child health and infectious diseases in Mississippi (Smith, 1995). In the early to mid twentieth century, the Mississippi government—at the behest of the federal government—attempted to intervene in the practice of Black midwifery in the state through strict regulations. The government claimed that Black midwives, in particular, performed "unsanitary and unscientific" work (Smith, 1995). Rather than resist the regulations, Black midwives in the state used them as an opportunity to improve their services for Black, poor, rural Mississippians. Black midwives coordinated with white public health nurses to barter services—midwives provided them support, and nurses provided midwives additional training to adhere to the new regulations. Black midwives' main role included improving the maternal and child health outcomes of their mostly poor, rural clients. They were a necessary part of the health-professional community because mainstream doctors were simply unavailable to poor Black women. Records indicated that Black midwives' services were as safe as those of physicians (Logan, 2013).

In addition to maternal and child health outcomes, Black midwives were also responsible for public health promotion and venereal disease control. Black midwives helped control the transmission of disease by encouraging expecting mothers, their partners, and other community members to get screened (United States Public Health Service, 1925). Some midwives even promoted the services offered at the venereal-disease clinics at local churches and schools and directly in people's homes (Mississippi State Board of Health, 1944). They were also instrumental in increasing the rate of vaccinations among Black community members for typhoid fever, smallpox, and diphtheria (Smith, 1995). Despite the earlier tension between the Black midwives and the government, their work eventually became incorporated into the Mississippi public health system to the extent that the state relied on them for the collection of vital statistics such as live births, stillbirths, venereal disease, and tuberculosis.

Black women have contributed significantly to the betterment of Black communities through organizing, institution building, and public health programs. They have, sometimes unintentionally, altered health-related policies to provide vital social services, reduce institutional discrimination, and improve access to and quality of care. Recovering this history can help inform current health-policy debates and public health research, particularly as they relate to Black women and communities.

Black Women in Health Policy: The Present

Black women continue to be more likely to live in poverty (Park, 2017) and to have higher rates of housing insecurity (Desmond, 2014), higher rates of exposure to environmental toxins (Williams and Mohammed, 2009), and increased barriers to accessing necessary health-care services (Kaiser Family Foundation, 2018), all of which have been linked to growing disparities in many disease outcomes. Before health was formalized into the policy lexicon, Black women understood that antiracist and social policies were at the core of changing health outcomes and closing the large disparity gaps that we see today.

America's pressing social challenges, including but not limited to affordable housing, segregation, police brutality, educational disparities, and incarceration disparities, are linked to the nation's continued legacy of inequality and racial discrimination against Black Americans (Gillborn, 2008; Alexander, 2012; Tonry, 2011; Rothstein, 2017) and have consistently been shown to have direct impacts on health in the Black community (Acevedo-Garcia & Lochner, 2003; Schnitticker et al., 2011). Black women are especially equipped to understand the nuanced experiences that contribute to poor health in the community and how policies can directly impact the communities without explicitly naming health as an outcome.

The Black Panther Party (BPP) held health activism as a key value and developed key programs to fight the social and health inequities of its time. While many of the BPP's efforts to address health equity were led by the men of the organization, most were conceptualized and organized by Black women (Nelson, 2011). BPP members like Cleo Silvers and Marie Branch were critical in developing and implementing community programs to address growing health concerns. Silvers developed community health surveys to better understand and address health concerns of Black communities in Harlem and also helped develop the door-to-door sickle-cell monitoring program (Nelson, 2011, 2016). Branch was vital in the party's development of the Free People Medical Clinics (Nelson, 2011). Not only were Black women critical in the development of these programs, their day-to-day involvement was critical to the programs' success, and their ranks included public health figures notable today such as Dr. Mary Bassett (Bassett, 2016), who has worked tirelessly to gain equity in health outcomes by addressing social policy both in the US and internationally. Dr. Bassett previously served as the commissioner for the New York City Department of Health and Mental Hygiene and currently serves as the director of the FXB Center for Health and Human Rights at Harvard University, where she continues to explore how policies impact health outcomes among vulnerable populations.

While the Black Panther Party eventually disbanded in 1982, it popularized a set of beliefs that identified health as a social justice issue for Black families and that influences public health to this day (Bassett, 2016) and laid the framework for many current national and institutional policies such the USDA school breakfast program, patient navigators and coordinated care models, the Nixon administration's funding for sickle cell anemia, and universal newborn screening for genetic diseases (Morabia, 2016).

Black women have continued to make strides in improving and maintaining optimal health through policy efforts through their roles in academic institutions, national appointments, congressional appointments, grassroots organizations, and large research foundations and nonprofit organizations addressing various issues such as access to care, environmental justice, maternal mortality, drug usage, and educational disparities. While this is not an exhaustive list, we highlight notable Black women in a few of these sectors:

A notable example of a Black woman presently in health policy is Dr. Marsha Lillie-Blanton, who has dedicated her career to fighting for equity in health-care access for individuals in the racial and ethnic minority. Dr. Lillie-Blanton is currently an associate research professor at George Washington University in Washington, DC. Prior to this position, she served in numerous senior-level positions in both federal agencies such as the Centers for Medicare and Medicaid Services and large foundations including the Henry J. Kaiser Family Foundation. Her research focuses on the role of insurance in decreasing health disparities. Research is an integral aspect of developing and advocating for health policy, though often unseen and without recognition. Dr. Lillie-Blanton has used her research to develop policy briefs and testimonies that have been given in numerous congressional hearings. Dr. Lillie-Blanton has also served as director of three programs designed to train scholars of color in health-policy leadership. She was elected to the National Academy of Social Insurance in 1996 and has continues to serve as an expert to improve policies related to health-care access.

Similar to historical efforts, Black women have continued to create grassroots organizations and nonprofits to fight for the health of Black women. Byllye Avery cofounded the Gainesville Women's Health Center, fighting for abortion rights and providing an alternative birthing center. In 1983, she founded the National Black Women's Health Project. Avery understood that the special health problems of Black women were integrally tied to the variety of challenges faced by Black families such as poverty, unemployment, family fragmentation, and inadequate education (Avery, 1987).

Now named the Black Women's Health Imperative (BWHI), this organization has remained the only national organization dedicated solely to improving the health and wellness of Black women and girls. BWHI's mission is to solve the most pressing health issues that affect Black women and girls in the US. Through investments in evidence-based strategies, they deliver bold new programs and advocate health-promoting policies. The group has been instrumental in moving forward policies on the local, state, and federal levels through their commitment to ensuring that all Black women have access to health care. Some of their notable achievements have been policies to ensure that insurers in New York and Texas cover 3D mammograms with no out-of-pocket expenses as a way to more accurately diagnose breast cancer for Black women. Another policy success has been ensuring that New York insurers cover all medically necessary abortions as outlined in the Patient Protection and Affordable Care Act and provide at least twelve months of contraceptives with no copayment following the procedure. Additionally, for the 2018 primaries, the organization developed a voting report card to engage voters and increase political power by outlining criteria that candidates could be scored on based on their commitment to policies that directly impact Black women's health issues (Blount et al., 2018).

Black women nationwide are boldly leading a growing effort to heighten public awareness of how environmental issues like pollution and climate change affect Black communities. In 1988, Peggy Shepard cofounded a New York City-based environmental justice organization named WE ACT for Environmental Justice. The organization aids low-income and minority communities to fight against environmental policies in five main areas: climate justice, clean air, good jobs, healthy homes, and sustainable and equitable land use. Currently, WE ACT for Environmental Justice has campaigns centered around asthma disparities, healthy and sustainable public housing, clean air, and how Environmental Protection Agency budget cuts can have grave effects on this vulnerable community. They use their community campaigns to advocate for policy changes in these communities. In 2015, approximately 46 percent of all public housing in New York City was occupied by Black families, and 48 percent of those were female-led households (New York City Housing Authority, 2015). WE ACT for environmental justice understood that social, environmental, and economic factors have more to do with health than access to a doctor or hospital. Health and well-being start in homes, schools, workplaces, neighborhoods, and communities. With that in mind, they developed a partnership with the Dyckman Houses to create a political advocacy plan to address the environmental hazards in their community.

Black women continue to lead grassroots efforts around environmental justice to address ongoing social injustices in Black communities. Black Millennials for Flint, founded by LaTricea Adams, is a grassroots environmental justice and civil rights organization with the purpose of bringing like-minded organizations together to collectively act and advocate against the crisis of lead exposure specifically in Black and Latino communities throughout the nation. In Flint, Michigan, Black women make up approximately 30 percent of the population, and a large portion of them are of reproductive age. Maternal lead poisoning has been linked to preterm birth and low birth weight and developmental delays in infants (Dietrich et al., 1987; Koval, 2018). Racial disparities in reproductive health outcomes exist nationwide for Black women, and lead exposure only exacerbates this risk. In addition to their advocacy work, Black Millennials for Flint developed a health-education campaign to educate Black women about their pregnancy risks from lead poisoning.

The ultimate act of moving policies related to health forward is having elected congresspeople introduce, support, and vote for these policies. Many Black women have held positions in the United States Congress and have consistently fought for direct health issues, cosponsored key pieces of legislation for equity, and fought for inclusion in existing bills to increase equity for health outcomes. Shirley Chisholm, the first Black woman to be elected to Congress, was a pioneer for using policy to address social determinants of health. During her tenure, Chisholm pushed for the expansion of the food-stamps program and was critical in the development of supplemental nutrition for women, infants, and children. She also pushed for minimum-wage policies, introduced legislation for universal day care to ease the burden of single working mothers of color, and introduced legislation to improve Medicaid services for low-income children and pregnant women.

Another congresswoman who has consistently fought for the health of Black women is Congresswoman Maxine Waters. Her top priorities have always incorporated the inclusion of women of color and their health outcomes, with a special focus on HIV/AIDS. The congresswoman developed the Minority AIDS Initiative in 1998. The Minority AIDS Initiative provides grants for HIV/AIDS treatment and prevention programs that serve minority communities and enables health-care providers and community-based organizations to expand their capacity to serve these communities. Congresswoman Waters introduced the Stop AIDS in Prison Act in 2009, which was ultimately signed into law. This law requires the Bureau of Prisons to test all federal-prison inmates for HIV when they enter prison and again prior to their release from prison, to provide HIV/AIDS-prevention education for all inmates, and to give comprehensive treatment to inmates who test positive. In 2012, she also introduced the Routine HIV/AIDS Screening Coverage Act, a bill to require health-insurance plans to cover routine HIV/AIDS tests under the same terms and conditions as other routine health screening. Most recently, Congresswoman Waters proposed amendments to two house bills aimed at expanding Medicaid to cover opioid treatment to cover all substance-abuse disorders so that all communities have the same opportunities and access to treatment and care and to address the disparities in punitive treatment associated with some substances and communities.

Byllye Avery, Shirley Chisholm, and Maxine Waters also collaborated, along with thirteen other Black women, in 1990 to develop an organization, African American Women for Reproductive Freedom, to provide Black women with a platform to support *Roe v. Wade*. The organization sought to convey that abortion was a conscious choice for Black women, who they argued faced additional stigma and judgement for seeking out a legal abortion. Avery, Chisholm, and Waters's arguments included the historical narrative of rape, torture, and other forms of abuse experienced by Black women and made the case that Black women would continue to exist on the margins of society if they continued to be treated as if they could not make independent decisions (Gillespie, 1989).

In the 2018 midterm elections, the United States saw an unprecedented movement with the notable election of several Black women to Congress. This was the first year in which there were more than twenty Black women serving. One newly elected representative, Congresswoman Lauren Underwood, is a nurse from Illinois whose campaign platforms included priorities for reproductive and environmental justice. The inclusion of Black medical professionals in Congress will bring additional Black female voices to help educate and advocate for awareness that most policies have impacts on health.

Black Women in Health Policy: The Future

Essential to the future of Black women in health policy is diversifying the pool of health services and health-policy researchers. In 1978, 95 percent of health services and health-policy researchers identified as non-Hispanic White (Pittman & Holve, 2009). Slow incremental progress had been made by the mid-2000s, when researchers found that 84 percent of the health-services research and health-policy workforce identified as non-Hispanic White; however, just 3.1 percent of this population identified as African American or Black (McGinnis & Moore, 2009). In order to advance the health of Black women, Black women must be substantively involved in the research and decision-making processes.

AcademyHealth, the largest health-services research and health-policy professional society in the country, issued a report in 2015 entitled *The Future of Diversity and Inclusion in Health Services and Policy Research: A Report on the AcademyHealth Workforce Diversity 2025 Roundtable.* This report named several recommendations for increasing diversity in the society: making a public commitment to diversity and inclusion, collecting better data on member demographics and reporting it publicly, and improving the pipeline of people from underrepresented backgrounds involved in health-services research and health policy (Edmunds et al., 2015).

Central to the mission of including more Black women in the health-services and health-policy workforce is the development and continuation of educational and training pipeline programs. Previous training programs have included the Kaiser Family Foundation Barbara Jordan Health Policy Scholars and the Robert Wood Johnson Foundation Health and Society Scholars programs. One noteworthy example of a current training program is the Robert Wood Johnson Foundation Health Policy Research Scholars (HPRS) program, which provides policy and leadership training for doctoral students from underrepresented backgrounds, broadly defined. When asked about the role of HPRS in advancing Black women in health policy, Executive Director Dr. Lydia Isaac stated, "HPRS has a huge role in advancing the role of Black women in health policy because it is providing Black women scholars with the tools to understand how policy is created and be part of and play the policy 'game' or process. My hope is that by providing these tools Black women will have the knowledge, skills and training to transform and fundamentally change the process so that we produce more equitable health policies that support the health and well-being of our communities" (personal communication, 2019).

Continued investment in the educational capital of Black women in health policy and health-services research is critical for advancing the health of Black women and Black communities. Beyond health-workforce development, policies that shape the social determinants of health (e.g., housing, education, childcare) have historically and will continue to make a difference in the health of Black women. In 2017, the Institute for Women's Policy Research issued a report entitled *The Status of Black Women in the United States.* In this report, DuMonthier et al. (2017) laid out six key recommendations as necessary areas of improvement to advance the health of Black women:

1. Strengthening Black women's political participation

2. Supporting employment and increasing earnings for Black women

3. Creating policy infrastructure to support work-life balance

4. Expanding opportunities and reducing poverty among Black women

5. Improving Black women's health and access to health care services

6. Reducing violence against Black women and increasing safety (p. ix)

These outlined priorities reflect how the social conditions of life have previously and continue to impact the health and well-being of Black women and their families. The public policy response to critical issues affecting the health of Black women has been slow but is beginning to emerge. For example, the maternal mortality rate has been rising in the United States over the last several decades, driven in large part by Black women experiencing three to four times the maternal mortality of White women in the United States (Centers for Disease Control and Prevention, 2018). A recent policy response to this crisis involved expanding doula services to be covered by Medicaid in New York state in 2018 (Ferre-Sadurni, 2018). Also essential to advancing the reproductive health of Black women is the continued support and passage of federal legislation like the Preventing Maternal Deaths Act, which establishes state maternal mortality review committees to review incidents of pregnancy-related death and develop recommendations to prevent future deaths (Caffrey, 2018).

To advance the reproductive health of Black women means to incorporate the racial justice frameworks of organizations like SisterSong and Black Mamas Matter Alliance into health policy. Directly tied to the advancement of Black women's reproductive health is the achievement of environmental justice. Black women are much more likely to be exposed to environmental exogenous estrogen compounds and environmental toxicants such as lead, coal ash, and toxic waste (Morello-Frosch & Shenassa, 2006). Consequently, the fight for environmental justice will continue to be a pressing policy issue that affects Black women's health in a variety of domains. Finally, Black women are disproportionately affected by intimate-partner violence in the United States (Sabri et al., 2013). Ensuring the reduction of violence against Black women necessitates continued support and reauthorization of the federal Violence Against Women Act as well as new policy solutions.

Conclusion

Black women are the past, present, and future of health policy in the United States. Black women have fought for fair housing policies, built institutions for social services, and pioneered the development of community health centers. Numerous individual Black women as well as various grassroots organizations led by Black women have left an indelible mark on health policy in the United States. To realize a future that involves the advancement of health of all Black women, deliberate effort must be put into health-policy and health-services-research workforce diversification and development. Historically and currently prescient issues such as reproductive health, environmental justice, and intimate-partner violence will continue to require bold and inventive policy solutions for a brighter future for Black women.

References

Acevedo-Garcia, D., & Lochner, K. A. (2003). Residential segregation and health. In I. Kawachi & L. F. Berman (Eds.), *Neighborhoods and health* (pp. 265–287). Oxford University Press.

Alexander, M. (2012). *The new Jim Crow: Mass incarceration in the age of color-blindness*. New Press.

Artiga, S., & Hinton, E. (2018). Beyond health care: The role of social determinants in promoting health and health equity. *Health, 20*(10), 1–10.

Avery, B (1987). Equal but still not on the same level. *CONTACT* (98), 2–5.

Bassett, M. T. (2016). Beyond berets: The Black Panthers as health activists. *American Journal of Public Health, 106*(10), 1741–1743.

Blount, L., Boyd, T., & Berry, R. (2018). *Black women vote: The 2018 national health policy agenda*. Black Women's Health Imperative.

Caffrey, M. (2018). Preventing Maternal Deaths Act headed to Trump's desk. *AJMC.* Retrieved January 13, 2019, from https://www.ajmc.com/newsroom/preventing-maternal-deaths-act-headed-to-trumps-desk

Carrie Steele-Pitts Home. (n.d.). *Commitment.* Retrieved March 8, 2019, from http://csph.org/commitment/

Centers for Disease Control and Prevention. (2018). *Pregnancy-related deaths.* Retrieved January 13, 2019, from https://www.cdc.gov/reproductivehealth/maternalinfanthealth/pregnancy-relatedmortality.htm

Desmond, M. (2014). *Poor black women are evicted at alarming rates, setting off a chain of hardship.* MacArthur Foundation.

Dietrich, K. N., Krafft, K. M., Bornschein, R. L., Hammond, P. B., Berger, O., Succop, P. A., & Bier, M. (1987). Low-level fetal lead exposure effect on neurobehavioral development in early infancy. *Pediatrics, 80*(5), 721–730.

DuMonthier, A., Childers, C., & Milli, J. (2017). *The status of Black women in the United States.* Institute for Women's Policy Research. https://iwpr.org/publications/status-Black-women-united-states-report/

Edmunds, M., Bezold, C., Fulwood, C. C., Johnson, B., & Tetteh, H. (2015, September). *The future of diversity and inclusion in health services and policy research: A report on the AcademyHealth workforce diversity 2025 roundtable.* Academy Health. https://www.academyhealth.org/publications/2015-09/future-diversity-and-inclusion-health-services-and-policy-research-report

Ferre-Sadurni, L. (2018, April 22). New York to expand use of doulas to reduce childbirth deaths. *New York Times.* https://www.nytimes.com/2018/04/22/nyregion/childbirth-death-doula-medicaid.html

Gillborn, D. (2008). *Racism and education: Coincidence or conspiracy?* Routledge.

Gillespie, Marcia. (1989). *African American women are for reproductive freedom.* Trust Black Women. Retrieved from https://trustblackwomen.org/2011-05-10-03-28-12/publications-a-articles/african-americans-and-abortion-articles/36-african-american-women-are-for-reproductive-freedom

Goetz, E. G. (2013). *New Deal ruins: Race, economic justice, and public housing policy.* Cornell University Press.

Gregory, C. A., & Deb, P. (2015). Does SNAP improve your health? *Food Policy, 50,* 11–19.

Kaiser Family Foundation. (2018, March). *Women's coverage, access, and affordability: Key findings from the 2017 Kaiser women's health survey* [Issue brief].

Koval, P. (2018). *Toxic effects of lead disposal in water: An analysis of TRI facility releases.* CrossWorks Economic Working Papers, Paper 176.

Logan, O. L. (2013). *Motherwit: An Alabama midwife's story.* Untreed Reads.

McGinnis, S., & Moore, J. (2009). The health services research workforce: Current stock. *Health Services Research, 44*(6), 2214–2226.

Mississippi State Board of Health. (1944). *The relocation of the midwife to the state board of health.*

Morabia, A. (2016). Unveiling the Black Panther Party legacy to public health. *American Journal of Public Health, 106*(10), 1732–1733.

Morello-Frosch, R., & Shenassa, E. D. (2006). The environmental 'riskscape' and social inequality: Implications for explaining maternal and child health disparities. *Environmental Health Perspectives, 114*(8), 1150–1153.

Nelson, A. (2011). *Body and soul: The Black Panther Party and the fight against medical discrimination*. University of Minnesota Press.

Nelson, A. (2016). Genuine struggle and care: An interview with Cleo Silvers. *American Journal of Public Health, 106*(10), 1744–1748.

Neverdon-Morton, C. (1989). *Afro-American women of the South and the advancement of the race, 1895–1925*. University of Tennessee Press.

New York City Housing Authority. (2015). *Resident data book summary* [Data set]. Retrieved from https://data.cityofnewyork.us/Housing-Development/NYCHA-Resident-Data-Book-Summary/5r5y-pvs3

Park, P. (2017). *National snapshot: Poverty among women and families, 2016*. National Women's Law Center.

Pittman, P., & Holve, E. (2009). The health services researcher of 2020: A summit to assess the field's workforce needs. *Health Services Research, 44*(6), 2198–2213.

Rabinowitz, H. N. (1974). From exclusion to segregation: Health and welfare services for southern Blacks, 1865–1890. *Social Service Review, 48*(3), 327–354.

Rothstein, R. (2017). *The color of law: A forgotten history of how our government segregated America*. Liveright Publishing.

Rudolph, L., Caplan, J., Ben-Moshe, K., & Dillon, L. (2013). *Health in all policies: A guide for state and local governments*. American Public Health Association / Public Health Institute.

Sabri, B., Bolyard, R., McFadgion, A. L., Stockman, J. K., Lucea, M. B., Callwood, G. B., Coverston, C. R., & Campbell, J. C. (2013). Intimate partner violence, depression, PTSD, and use of mental health resources among ethnically diverse black women. *Social Work in Health Care, 52*(4), 351–369.

Schnittker, J., Massoglia, M., & Uggen, C. (2011). Incarceration and the health of the African American community. *Du Bois Review: Social Science Research on Race, 8*(1), 133–141.

Smith, S. L. (1995). *Sick and tired of being sick and tired: Black women's health activism in America, 1890–1950*. University of Pennsylvania Press.

Sunflower County Health Department, "Sunflower County Annual Reports, 1936–1937" (MDAH, RG 51, Loc 22-25-1, Box 8710, 2031:311–312).

Thorpe v. Housing Authority of the City of Durham, 393 U.S. 268 (1969).

Tonry, M. (2011). *Punishing race: A continuing American dilemma*. Oxford University Press.

Williams, R. Y. (2004). *The politics of public housing: Black women's struggles against urban inequality*. Oxford University Press.

Williams, R. Y. (2009). "Something's wrong down here": Poor black women and urban struggles for democracy. In K. L. Kusmer & J. W. Trotter (Eds.), *African American urban history since World War II*. University of Chicago Press.

Williams, D. R., & Mohammed, S. A. (2009). Discrimination and racial disparities in health: Evidence and needed research. *Journal of Behavioral Medicine, 32*(1), 20–47.

Chapter 3

The Maternal Mortality Crisis in the Black Community

JOVONNI R. SPINNER, SHEILA CARRETTE,
AND JOYLENE JOHN-SOWAH

Background

The World Health Organization (WHO, 2018a) defines maternal mortality as "the death of a woman while pregnant or within 42 days of termination of pregnancy, irrespective of the duration and site of the pregnancy, from any cause related to or aggravated by the pregnancy or its management, but not from accidental or incidental causes." These deaths are divided into two different categories: direct and indirect. While direct obstetric deaths are the result of pregnancy complications related to interventions, omissions, or improper treatment, indirect obstetric deaths result from existing disease, diseases developed during pregnancy, or from diseases that were exacerbated by the pregnancy (WHO, 2012).

In the United States, maternal mortality remains a serious challenge. While it has decreased significantly over the past two decades on a global level (WHO, 2018b), the United States has seen a steady increase in maternal mortality over the same period (Martin & Montagne, 2017a). Despite spending twice as much on health care as other high-income countries (Papanicolas et al., 2018), the United States still has the highest maternal mortality among these nations, making it the most dangerous place to give birth in the developed world (Martin & Montagne, 2017a).

However, this dismal burden is not evenly distributed among mothers of all races in the United States. Black mothers are three to four times more likely to die because of pregnancy-related complications, with 40.0 deaths per 100,000 live births for Black women compared to 12.4 deaths per 100,000 live births for White women and 17.8 deaths per 100,000 live births for women of other races (Centers for Disease Control and Prevention, 2018). These rates are comparable to those of lower-income countries, like Mexico, where poverty rates are much higher (Villarosa, 2018), and stage III and IV obstetric-transition countries (e.g., India, Guatemala, Botswana, Chile, and China), where access to care is not the primary issue but quality of care and appropriate management of complications remain important (Souza, et al., 2014). The disproportionately high rates of maternal mortality among Black women are the primary reason that the United States struggles in comparison to its counterparts (Martin & Montagne, 2017b).

Causes of Maternal Mortality—Biological, Medical, and Environmental

While there are multiple theories and reasons for the maternal mortality disparity, there are a variety of factors that contribute to this imbalance—ranging from biology to the environment. Often, these disparities are compounded by factors that are social determinants of health (e.g., education, neighborhood) and/or systemic issues (e.g., discrimination and implicit racial bias received from medical providers), which can impede or delay care or impact the quality of care received. These issues are intertwined and exacerbate the rising rates of maternal mortality among Black mothers. This section will examine four critical factors: biological causes, social determinants of health, systemic issues, and providers' implicit bias.

Biological Causes

There is a range of biological factors and preexisting medical conditions that can contribute to higher maternal mortality rates among Black women. Among non-Hispanic Black women, the following are the five leading underlying causes of maternal death: (1) cardiomyopathy (14%), (2) cardiovascular and coronary conditions (12.8%), (3) preeclampsia and eclampsia (11.6%), (4) hemorrhage (10.5%), and (5) embolism (9.3%). Together, these represent 58.1% of pregnancy-related deaths among Black women (Building U.S. Capacity to Review and Prevent Maternal Deaths, 2018). In the same report, among non-Hispanic Whites, the following were the top five causes of pregnancy-related death: (1) cardiovascular and coronary conditions (15.5%), (2) hemorrhage (14.4%), (3) infection (13.4%), (4) mental health conditions (11.3%), and (5) cardiomyopathy (10.3%).

These medical conditions can be exacerbated by other chronic illnesses such as hypertension, diabetes, and obesity. For example, hypertension during pregnancy is known to cause life-threatening complications like preeclampsia, and Black women in the United States suffer from a higher incidence of hypertension with an earlier onset of the disease (Lackland, 2014). Further, diabetes, another known cause of pregnancy-related complications, is twice as prevalent among Black women in comparison to their White counterparts (Office of Minority Health, 2016). Additionally, Black women are 1.6 times as likely to be obese than White women, further increasing the risk for pregnancy-related complications (Office of Minority Health, 2017).

The good news is that most of these deaths have been deemed preventable. The nine maternal mortality review committees estimated that over 60 percent of pregnancy-related deaths were preventable, with cardiovascular disease deemed highly preventable and embolism determined to be least preventable. Among the conditions most relevant to Black women, the most preventable conditions are cardiovascular and coronary conditions, followed by hemorrhage. While it is known that preexisting conditions like hypertension, diabetes, and obesity can increase the risk of experiencing these complications during pregnancy and are diagnosed at higher rates among Black women, in many cases, these biological factors are only a small portion of a more extensive and systematic problem (Martin & Montagne, 2017b).

For example, one study evaluated potential contributing factors and identified patient and family factors, provider factors, and systems-of-care factors as the most common factors contributing to maternal mortality (table 3.1). Additionally, it is noted that patient factors are often dependent upon providers and systems of care, and, even more interestingly, community-level factors were very rarely identified as contributing to pregnancy-related mortality in this study. The authors note that, interestingly, this finding aligns with known research that African American maternal mortality is high across all socioeconomic strata; therefore, it is understandable that the community-level factors would be less impactful.

Table 3.1. Contributing Factors to Maternal Mortality in the United States

Cause of death	Provider contribution (%)	Patient contribution (%)	Systems-of-care contribution (%)
Cardiomyopathy	41.4	43.1	27.3
Cardiovascular/coronary conditions	21.7	42.5	20.8
Preeclampsia/eclampsia	51.8	23.2	17.9
Hemorrhage	31.0	26.0	36.0
Embolism	21.7	65.2	13.0

Note. Adapted from the Building U.S. Capacity to Review and Prevent Maternal Deaths (2018) report. Examples of provider issues include implicit bias, lack of knowledge, failure to screen, lack of appropriate referral, delayed diagnosis or treatment, missed diagnosis, ineffective treatments, and failure to seek consultation. Examples of patient factors include chronic conditions (e.g., substance abuse, obesity) and lack of awareness of warning signs and need to seek care. Systems-of-care factors include institutional racism, inadequately trained or unavailable personnel, lack of policies or procedures, and lack of care coordination.

Social Determinants of Health

Social determinants of health are defined as the conditions in which people are born, live, work, play, and age. They impact a person's health status, quality of life, and functioning (Office of Disease Prevention and Health Promotion, 2019) and contribute to premature morbidity and mortality. These conditions include economic stability, neighborhood conditions, education, food, community, social context, and the health-care system, among other factors.

Three determinants—access to care, education attainment, and income—are directly related to the rising maternal mortality rates (Artiga & Hinton, 2018; Nelson et al., 2018). Among women of childbearing age (18–44 years), not having at least a high school diploma accounted for 5.3 percent of maternal deaths (Nelson et al., 2018). Lower educational attainment has also been linked to low health literacy, which in turn may impact the mother's ability to comprehend and use health information, adhere to treatment protocols, or effectively communicate with her provider. Income can also be a barrier to health care because studies have shown that low-income women often forgo medical care because they cannot afford it (Carroll, 2017).

Another factor is access to care, which is often the first step toward obtaining high-quality medical care; both physical access and the cost of services remain barriers for some. One study showed that 4.9 percent of maternal deaths were attributable to receiving fewer than ten prenatal visits (Nelson et al., 2018). With the passage of the Affordable Care Act in 2010, millions of Americans, including Black women, gained access to health-care insurance, which has helped improve maternal outcomes but does not eliminate disparities. Maternal mortality disparities persist for Black women because they have difficulty accessing quality and culturally appropriate care. About half of all states (n = 27) did not expand Medicaid, and women living in these states may remain underinsured or lack insurance altogether, which means they will have challenges accessing prenatal care (Courtemanche et al., 2017). Even Black women with insurance may still have trouble accessing specialty care, mental health services, or patient-centered care that is culturally appropriate, particularly if they live in rural and underserved areas. Many states and the District of Columbia closed facilities because they could not afford to keep the doors open, thus limiting the number of providers available to treat Black women. In DC, two maternity wards were closed in 2018; closure of facilities disrupts continuity of care, thus limiting options for where women can obtain prenatal care and deliver their babies.

Systemic Issues

Black women have a unique lived experience in the United States, stemming from historical abuses during slavery, Jim Crow, and present-day systemic classism, sexism, and racism experienced in all areas of their lives. It has also been found that among African American women the experience of these cumulative stressors can cause a phenomenon identified as "weathering," making them more susceptible to adverse birth outcomes (Jackson et al., 2001). Having to endure years of racism, both overt and covert, has been shown to negatively impact health outcomes stemming from the lack of quality and quantity of care received throughout the medical system (Jackson et al., 2012). The classification of race is a social construct used to identify and group people in a common category and is not based on any genetic or biologic difference (Wren Serbin & Donnelly, 2016). Even though race in itself does not impact health, the racism that results from being treated negatively due to being a certain race can indeed have negative consequences on health outcomes (Wren Serbin & Donnelly, 2016). Outcomes include higher rates of chronic diseases and maternal mortality, even after controlling for socioeconomic status (Lu, 2018, Jackson et al., 2012).

Racism has three levels: institutionalized, personally mediated, and internalized (Jones, 2000). Internalized racism refers to "acceptance by members of the stigmatized races of negative messages about their own abilities and intrinsic worth" (Jones, p. 1213). Personally mediated racism is defined as "differential assumptions about the abilities, motives, and intentions of others according to their race" (Jones, p. 1212). Lastly, institutional racism refers to "differential access to the goods, services, and opportunities of society." Institutional racism is deeply embedded into the bureaucracies and social structures of institutions such as hospitals. Research shows that Black women report being discriminated against during their prenatal visits and receive differential treatment compared to their White counterparts (Wren Serbin & Donnelly, 2016). Black women reported having to deal with "negativity, stereotyping, and assumptions" based on the color of their skin (Wren Serbin & Donnelly, 2016), and much of this negativity stems from providers' implicit bias.

Implicit Bias

Health-care professionals' implicit bias plays a major role in the quality of care that Black women receive in the medical system and refers to the unconscious thoughts and feelings that medical providers may have that impact their ability to deliver high-quality care (Hall et al., 2015). These implicit biases are often automatically activated and influence providers behaviors toward their patients. This is not unique to one group of providers; high levels of implicit bias cut across specialty, level of training, and years of experience (Hall et al., 2015). These biases are often exacerbated when providers are in high-stress situations, distracted, or pressed for time, as in most medical encounters. Under these circumstances, even the most aware health-care provider may not have the capacity to adequately assess and control their biases.

For example, a provider may have an underlying fear of Black people or may automatically think that a White patient is nicer than a Black patient. One study showed that Black and dark-skinned people experience higher rates of implicit bias from their physicians, which significantly impacted the patient-provider interaction, treatment decision, adherence to treatment protocols, and health outcomes in general (Hall et al., 2015).

Implicit bias also includes behaviors like making assumptions about the patient's ability to adhere to a treatment plan, not giving all of the options for the patient to consider, speaking to her in an authoritative, condescending tone, or using negative body language. This can make her feel inferior and sets the tone for her to feel too uncomfortable to ask questions to ensure she completely understands her treatment plans (Hall et al., 2015; Wren Serbin & Donnelly, 2016). One study showed that when a Black adolescent presented for an office exam, the physician automatically made assumptions regarding her lifestyle and assumed she was sexually active instead of taking the time to have an open dialogue about her sexual history (Hall et al., 2015).

Implicit bias can lead to subtle practices like keeping Black women waiting longer for appointments or spending less time during their appointments compared to those of their White counterparts. Studies have documented that, many times, Black women present to the doctor or emergency room with symptoms that are indicative of larger problems and get brushed aside, dismissed, and not taken seriously (Wren Serbin & Donnelly, 2016). The *New York Times* reported in 2018 that one Black mother spoke with her doctor about experiencing unusual headaches and swelling yet was told to take Tylenol. She was not taken seriously although she complained of symptoms throughout her pregnancy, and her chart was not properly notated with her symptoms. She eventually ended up in the emergency room and lost her baby (Villarosa, 2018).

In another case, an affluent, married mother died after giving birth to her second child at a world-renowned medical facility in Los Angeles. Her premature death was due to receiving poor medical care and not being taken seriously, despite having a husband advocating for her. She was visibly having difficulty recovering from childbirth and waited for hours to get medical care, despite being told that the medical team was addressing her concerns. She hemorrhaged to death, which is the fourth leading cause of maternal mortality and could have been prevented if the medical team took her symptoms seriously (Helm, 2018).

These real-world cases exemplify how despite a high socioeconomic status, high levels of education, and access to the best care, Black women are still treated poorly, leading to higher maternal mortality rates (Helm, 2018; Jackson et al., 2001). One study showed that even when controlling for education levels, Black, college-educated women were still more than twice as likely to experience life-threatening complications during pregnancy than White women who did not graduate from high school (New York City Department of Health and Mental Hygiene, 2016). There is mounting research and anecdotal evidence to demonstrate that Black women are being dismissed and not given quality care despite being in visible distress. This continues the cycle of marginalizing Black women and perpetuating the health-disparities cycle.

Recommendations to Improve Care

Reducing maternal mortality rates among Black women is a multifaceted issue that can be solved by using innovative approaches at the individual, community, system, and policy levels.

For example, at the individual level, it is important to improve the patient's knowledge of risk and signs and symptoms of potential complications that should signal the need to call a provider or obtain emergent care. Even though individual-level recommendations were notably absent from the nine-committees study, the use of adjunct community facilitators such as nurse midwives, health educators, and community health workers at the start of pregnancy to guide patient understanding of the process may have potential roles in the effective delivery of education and information or attainment of appropriate care access during the pregnancy period. High-quality evidence to determine the usefulness of these approaches has not yet been obtained. At the community level, expectant mothers should be linked with certified community-based doulas who assist by advocating for the mother, communicating on her behalf, and providing emotional support. Women who use doulas have less stressful births and are two times less likely to have a birth complication (Gruber et al., 2013). To improve patient care at the systems level, medical schools should revise their curricula to include cultural competency training, and physicians should receive subsequent training as part of their licensure to address implicit bias (Betancourt, 2003). Lastly, the United States should adopt progressive paid maternity leave policies comparable to other wealthy nations, which would contribute to better birth outcomes, fewer infant deaths, and longer parental life span (Burtle & Bezruchka, 2016).

Additionally, adequately characterizing the problem by collecting and utilizing high-quality data is another step toward addressing maternal mortality. The use of unified definitions and reporting methods has historically been inconsistent in the United States and remains a problem because it impacts how data are obtained and interpreted. There is a need for a consistent, unified vocabulary when discussing maternal mortality. Additionally, for the collection of data, two major approaches have been generally applied when studying pregnancy-related maternal outcomes in the United States.

The first, the review of maternal mortality reports, is the primary approach in the United States. In these studies, *maternal mortality rate* is defined as maternal deaths per 100,000 live births within one year of birth (Centers for Disease Control and Prevention, 2018). Another term often encountered is *pregnancy-related deaths*, which is defined as deaths causally related to pregnancy or its management that occur during pregnancy or within a year of the end of a pregnancy. These mortality numbers are preferred because the overall number of maternal deaths is relatively low, making it more manageable for comprehensive review and assessment.

The other popular approach, the study of "maternal near-miss cases," is defined as cases among mothers or a woman who nearly died but survived a complication that occurred during pregnancy, childbirth, or within forty-two days of termination of pregnancy (World Health Organization, 2009). This approach is valued because it can directly inform on problems and obstacles occurring in pregnancy management and because the frequency of incidents is much higher than that of maternal mortality, thus the data is more robust. The results of these studies have been applied with positive results in many countries worldwide including several in Europe, Central Asia, Southeast Asia, Latin America, and the Caribbean. A systematic review highlighted that the implementation of the near-miss case review cycle strategies may significantly decrease maternal mortality (odds ratio 0.77, 95% confidence interval 0.61–0.98) in high-burden countries (Lazzarini et al., 2018). We believe that there are findings from this approach that may be applicable to improving the management of maternal mortality among Black women in the United States.

An additional recommendation is to consider requiring facilities to routinely evaluate and report near-miss cases and use disease-based criteria for evaluation of these cases and their potential complications based on the WHO definitions referenced earlier (Nelissen et al., 2013) in the effort to improve standards regarding assessment, diagnosis, and treatment decisions. Disease-based criteria have been shown to be more inclusive in capturing a wider range of potential complications (Nelissen et al., 2013) and can thus potentially provide a toolbox of actions that can be taken to avoid certain complications.

In general, it is felt that identification and appropriate management of women at high risk for labor complications, careful supervision of labor and childbirth, prompt use of effective interventions, and essential newborn care can potentially avert the majority of perinatal maternal and child deaths. While the numbers from the study represent data from only a small proportion of the country (Building U.S. Capacity to Review and Prevent Maternal Deaths, 2018), there is still the opportunity to examine how the knowledge gained from this study can be applied to improve outcomes and determine which approaches may be adaptable to African American mothers. Findings from the nine-committees study resulted in the development of over 193 recommendations for improving maternal mortality and morbidity outcomes, which were subsequently grouped into themes.

Moving forward, these resulting themes can be applied to those factors most relevant and applicable to the leading causes of death among African American women to implement effective interventions, programs, and policies:

- Improve training for providers

- IEnforce (system-level) policies and procedures

- Adopt levels of maternal care to properly triage patients and ensure appropriate level of care determination

- Improve patient-provider communication

- Improve procedures related to communication and coordination between providers

- Improve standards regarding assessment, diagnosis, and treatment decisions

- Improve policies related to patient management, communication and coordination between providers, and language translation

- Improve policies regarding prevention initiatives, including screening procedures and substance-abuse prevention or treatment programs (Building U.S. Capacity to Review and Prevent Maternal Deaths, 2018)

Emerging Evidence

The WHO is compiling evidence through the Better Outcomes in Labor Difficulty (BOLD) project. BOLD is the overarching project, which includes the Simplified, Effective Labor Monitoring-to-Action (SELMA) tool and the Passport for Safer Birth projects. These are prospective studies that plan to capture data to inform the quality of facility-based intrapartum care and accelerate the reduction of intrapartum-related maternal, fetal, and newborn mortality and morbidity. These studies will address the critical impediments in the process of labor care and establishing the desired connection between the health system and the community. This project seeks to achieve this goal through the development of an evidence-based and easy-to-use labor algorithm and innovative tools that create community demand for quality intrapartum care (Souza et al., 2015). SELMA is a subpart of the BOLD initiative and intends to address the complexities of labor monitoring by making sense of the complex information in the form of a labor-care algorithm. It is envisioned that the tool will alleviate the burden of decision-making for health professionals during labor, foster optimal labor management, and optimize task shifting by supporting decision-making of less specialized health professionals (Souza et al., 2015). Both projects are underway, with data being compiled over two years, in studies in underresourced countries (Nigeria and Uganda), with the aim of obtaining publishable results that can be applicable to many countries worldwide.

Conclusion

Despite improvements in every area of public health—ranging from hygiene and nutrition to health care and living conditions—Black women continue to have the worst health outcomes for many preventable diseases, including breast cancer, obesity, and maternal mortality. More than a century after W. E. B. Du Bois first described the racial infant- and maternal-health disparities in his book *The Philadelphia Negro*, this country is still in a public health crisis, plagued by preventable maternal deaths. Surviving childbirth is a human right, and every woman should be entitled to quality medical care. To achieve health equity, more needs to be done through advocacy, policies, and programs that address the underlying root causes of this public health crisis.

References

Artiga, S. & Hinton, E. (2018, May 10). *Beyond health care: The role of social determinants in promoting health and health equity* [Issue brief]. Kaiser

Family Foundation. Retrieved January 12, 2019, from https://www.kff.org/disparities-policy/issue-brief/beyond-health-care-the-role-of-social-determinants-in-promoting-health-and-health-equity/

Betancourt, J. R. (2003). Cross-cultural medical education. *Academic Medicine*, *78*(6), 560–569.

Building U.S. Capacity to Review and Prevent Maternal Deaths. (2018). *Report from nine maternal mortality review committees*. https://reviewtoaction.org/sites/default/files/2021-03/Report%20from%20Nine%20MMRCs%20final_0.pdf

Burtle, A., & Bezruchka, S. (2016). Population health and paid parental leave: What the United States can learn from two decades of research. *Healthcare (Basel, Switzerland)*, *4*(2), 30.

Carroll, A. E. (2017). Why is US maternal mortality rising? *JAMA*, *318*(4), 321.

Centers for Disease Control and Prevention. (2018, August 7). *Pregnancy mortality surveillance system*. Retrieved January 12, 2019, from https://www.cdc.gov/reproductivehealth/maternalinfanthealth/pregnancy-mortality-surveillance-system.htm

Courtemanche, C., Marton, J., Ukert, B., Yelowitz, A., & Zapata, D. (2017). Early impacts of the Affordable Care Act on health insurance coverage in Medicaid expansion and non-expansion states. *Journal of Policy Analysis and Management*, *36*(1), 178–210.

De Savigny, D., & Adam, T. (Eds.). (2009). *Systems thinking for health systems strengthening*. Alliance for Health Policy and Systems Research / World Health Organization.

Gruber, K. J., Cupito, S. H., & Dobson, C. F. (2013). Impact of doulas on healthy birth outcomes. *The Journal of Perinatal Education*, *22*(1), 49–58.

Hall, W. J., Chapman, M. V., Lee, K. M., Merino, Y. M., Thomas, T. W., Payne, B. K., Eng, E., Day, S. H., & Coyne-Beasley, T. (2015). Implicit racial/ethnic bias among health care professionals and its influence on health care outcomes: A systematic review. *American Journal of Public Health*, *105*(12), e60–e76.

Helm, A. (2018, October 19). Yet another beautiful black woman dies in childbirth. *The Root*. Retrieved January 12, 2019, from https://www.theroot.com/kira-johnson-spoke-5-languages-raced-cars-was-daughte-1829862323

Jackson, F. M., Phillips, M. T., Hogue, C. J., & Curry-Owens, T. Y. (2001). Examining the burdens of gendered racism: Implications for pregnancy outcomes among college-educated African American women. *Maternal and Child Health Journal*, *5*, 95–107.

Jackson, F. M., Rowley, D. L., & Owens, T. C. (2012). Contextualized stress, global stress, and depression in well-educated, pregnant, African-American women. *Women's Health Issues*, *22*(3), e329–e336.

Jones, C. P. (2000). Levels of racism: A theoretic framework and a gardener's tale. *American Journal of Public Health*, *90*(8), 1212–1215.

Lackland, D. T. (2014). Racial differences in hypertension: Implications for high blood pressure management. *The American Journal of the Medical Sciences*, 348(2), 135–138.

Lazzerini, M., Ciuch, M., Rusconi, S., & Covi, B. (2018). Facilitators and barriers to the effective implementation of the individual maternal near-miss case reviews in low/middle-income countries: A systematic review of qualitative studies. *BMJ Open*, 8(6), e021281.

Lu, M. C. (2018). Reducing maternal mortality in the United States. *JAMA*, 320(12), 1237.

Martin, N., & Montagne, R. (2017a, May 12). U.S. has the worst rate of maternal deaths in the developed world. *NPR*. https://www.npr.org/2017/05/12/528098789/u-s-has-the-worst-rate-of-maternal-deaths-in-the-developed-world

Martin, N., & Montagne, R. (2017b, December 7). Black mothers keep dying after giving birth. Shalon Irving's story explains why. In *All Things Considered*. NPR. https://www.npr.org/2017/12/07/568948782/Black-mothers-keep-dying-after-giving-birth-shalon-irvings-story-explains-why

Nelissen, E., Mduma, E., Broerse, J., Ersdal, H., Evjen-Olsen, B., van Roosmalen, J., & Stekelenburg, J. (2013). Applicability of the WHO maternal near miss criteria in a low-resource setting. *PLoS ONE*, 8(4), e61248.

Nelson, D. B., Moniz, M. H., & Davis, M. M. (2018). Population-level factors associated with maternal mortality in the United States, 1997–2012. *BMC Public Health*, 18(1).

New York City Department of Health and Mental Hygiene. (2016). *Severe maternal morbidity in New York City, 2008–2012*. https://www1.nyc.gov/assets/doh/downloads/pdf/data/maternal-morbidity-report-08-12.pdf

Office of Disease Prevention and Health Promotion. (2019, January 12). Social determinants of health. *Healthy People 2020*. U.S. Department of Health and Human Services. https://www.healthypeople.gov/2020/topics-objectives/topic/social-determinants-of-health

Office of Minority Health. (2016, July 13). *Diabetes and African Americans*. U.S. Department of Health and Human Services. https://minorityhealth.hhs.gov/omh/browse.aspx?lvl=4&lvlid=18

Office of Minority Health. (2017, August 25). *Obesity and African Americans*. U.S. Department of Health and Human Services. https://minorityhealth.hhs.gov/omh/browse.aspx?lvl=4&lvlid=25

Papanicolas, I., Woskie, L. R., & Jha, A. K. (2018). Health care spending in the United States and other high-income countries. *JAMA*, 319(10), 1024–1039.

Souza, J. P., Tunçalp, Ö., Vogel, J., Bohren, M., Widmer, M., Oladapo, O., Say, L., Gülmezoglu, A. M., & Temmerman, M. (2014). Obstetric transition: The pathway towards ending preventable maternal deaths. *BJOG: An International Journal of Obstetrics & Gynaecology*, 121(Suppl. 1), 1–4.

Souza, J. P., Oladapo, O. T., Bohren, M. A., Mugerwa, K., Fawole, B., Muscovici, L., Alves, D., Perdona, G., Olveira-Ciabati, L., Vogel, J. P., Tunçalp, Ö., Zhang, J., Hofmeyr, J., Bahl, R., Gülmezoglu, A. M., & WHO BOLD Research Group. (2015). The development of a Simplified, Effective, Labour Monitoring-to-Action (SELMA) tool for Better Outcomes in Labour Difficulty (BOLD): Study protocol. *Reproductive Health*, *12*(1), 49.

Villarosa, L. (2018, April 11). Why America's black mothers and babies are in a life-or-death crisis. *New York Times Magazine*. https://www.nytimes.com/2018/04/11/magazine/black-mothers-babies-death-maternal-mortality.html

World Health Organization. (2012). *The WHO Application of ICD-10 to deaths during pregnancy, childbirth and the puerperium: ICD-MM*. http://apps.who.int/iris/bitstream/handle/10665/70929/9789241548458_eng.pdf

World Health Organization. (2018a). *Maternal mortality ratio (per 100 000 live births)*. Retrieved January 8, 2019, from https://www.who.int/healthinfo/statistics/indmaternalmortality/en/

World Health Organization. (2018b, February 16). *Maternal mortality*. https://www.who.int/news-room/fact-sheets/detail/maternal-mortality

Wren Serbin, J., & Donnelly, E. (2016). The impact of racism and midwifery's lack of racial diversity: A literature review. *Journal of Midwifery & Women's Health*, *61*(6), 694–706.

Chapter 4

Promoting Self-Care and Awareness of Stress, the Strong Black Woman Schema, and Mental Health among African American Women

DAKOTA KING-WHITE, KELLY YU-HSIN LIAO, AND ELICE E. ROGERS

"Since their arrival on the shores of the United States, women of African descent have been assaulted by the intersection of racism and sexism" (Walker-Barnes, 2017, p. 43). Due to enduring challenges, African American women face specific stressors that can impact their mental health. However, it is important to consider the various types of stressors when promoting the overall health of these women. It is also imperative for African American women to understand the definition of self-care and ways to support their overall mental health when facing stressors. *Self-care* is defined as being intentional about actions that will promote an overall healthy lifestyle. African American women often overlook their own stressor-related self-care. African American women constantly provide support to others, and by doing so they often neglect their self-care (Walker-Barnes, 2017). Because of this, it is vital for health-care professionals to encourage African American women to own their feelings and to express them (Lashley et al., 2017).

When expressing their emotions, it is vital that African American women get the support needed to not only live but to thrive mentally, emotionally, and physically. Quite often, African American women seek out social support from other African Americans when challenges arise related to sexism and racism (Lashley et al., 2017). Thus, it is also pertinent to have strategies in place that will allow African American women to balance the various activities and stressors they may be facing. According to Woods-Giscombé and Lobel (2008), stress can be categorized into three types—generic stress, race-related stress, and gender-related stress. Special attention is needed to this categorization for African American women because this population faces stressors of all three types, which in turn can impact their mental health and physical health.

Three Types of Stress and Related Impacts on African American Women

African American women may experience stress when they perceive that they are unable to cope with the overwhelming amount of duties and challenges facing them on a daily basis, including racism and sexism. Research has established that more emphasis needs to be placed on helping African American women coping with stress-related factors. However, it is important to understand the various types of stress in order to develop strategies for women to deal effectively with stressors that may impact their overall physical and mental health. Stress has been correlated with many negative health outcomes for African American women (Walker-Barnes, 2017). These health outcomes are often due to stress not being addressed.

There are three common types of stress: acute stress, episodic stress, and chronic stress (American Psychological Association, n.d.; Miller & Smith, 1994). Acute stress is the most common type of stress, and everyone experiences this type of stress. Acute stress normally settles itself within a day or two, and women are normally able to manage these stressors without a specific intervention. Examples of causes of acute stress that women may face on a daily basis are getting kids off to school on time, being late to work or a meeting, or disagreement with a partner. When considering the various types of stress for African American women, the age of the woman must be considered and acknowledged due to specific age-related stressors that they may experience in their lives.

Episodic stress involves a frequent or even endless sense of worry and may manifest in mental and physical symptoms if not addressed. Some symptoms women may experience are headaches, change of appetite, sleep irregularities, and overall experience of depression (Walker-Barnes, 2017). Episodic stress may present from ongoing situations, such as continual conflict with a colleague, the process of aging, or balancing work and family. Finally, chronic stress is constant anxiety that occurs when a person is faced with a long-term stressor over which they perceive having no control or no way of addressing the challenge. Chronic stress can cause a considerable amount of distress that can impact a woman mentally and physically. Chronic stress may present itself due to such things as an illness, job loss, or loss of a loved one.

Due to the various stressors that African American women experience, attention must be given to the specific mental health concerns that they face related to stress. According to the National Alliance on Mental Illness (2019), common mental health disorders among African Americans include but are not limited to major depression, attention deficit hyperactivity disorder, and post-traumatic stress disorder. Black or African American adults with mental illness have lower rates of utilizing mental health services compared to White adults (Substance Abuse and Mental Health Services Administration [SAMSHA], 2015). African American women have reported disproportionately high rates of adverse health conditions, including cardiovascular disease (Thom et al., 2006), obesity (Wang & Beydoun, 2007), adverse birth outcomes (Hamilton et al., 2009), and untreated or mistreated psychological conditions (SAMSHA, 2009). Compared to non-Hispanic Whites, African Americans with any mental illness have lower rates of using mental health services related to prescription medications and outpatient services but higher rates of using inpatient services (SAMSHA, 2015).

Overall, African American women have been found to be less likely than White women to use mental health–care services despite equal or greater need (Brown et al., 2003; Kohn & Hudson, 2002). According to SAMSHA (2015), Black or African American adults with any mental illness have lower rates of pursuing mental health services when compared to non-Hispanic White adults with any mental illness. These services include but are not limited to utilization of prescription drugs and outpatient mental health services (SAMHSA, 2015). Due to these statistics, specific attention must be given to the impact of stress on African American women's mental health.

Impact of Gendered Racism and the Strong Black Woman Schema on African American Women's Mental Health

In American society, African American women experience dual oppression from racism and sexism that influences their emotional well-being and health. Researchers have conceptualized the intersections of racism and sexism experienced by African American women as gendered racism (Essed, 1991; Thomas et al., 2008). Crenshaw (1991), who coined the term *intersectionality*, asserted that the multiple forms of discrimination are interdependent and interlocking and result in unique, not just additive, multiple inequalities.

Gendered Racism

For African American women, the intersection of their racial and gender identities creates unique experiences that are qualitatively different from both women of other racial groups and African American men. For example, they are stereotyped as domestic workers, mammies, promiscuous, angry, and welfare mothers (Collins, 2000; West, 1995). Gendered racism has a deleterious effect among African American women. It has been related to higher levels of psychological distress (Lewis & Neville, 2015; Thomas et al., 2008), greater depressive symptoms (Carr et al., 2014), and more post-traumatic stress symptoms (Woods et al., 2009).

As we talk about African American women, more attention must be given to misogynoir. Oftentimes in the literature, discussions are presented individually about racism and sexism experienced by African American women. According to Ussher (2016), *misogyny* is defined as an overall disgust and intolerance of women and hoping to openly oppress women. However, a recent term, *misogynoir*, has received more attention when it comes to understanding the plight and the challenges of African American women. *Misogynoir* is misogyny focused on African American women where race and gender play a part in how they are treated. This term was coined by Moya Bailey and Trudy (2018). When racism and sexism are talked about pertaining to African American women, these two terms cannot be used in isolation, and misogynoir must be explored to ensure that we are openly supporting African American women and empowering them despite their challenges.

Strong Black Woman Schema

One factor related to race and gender as well as stress and coping among African American women is the Strong Black Woman (SBW) schema (e.g., Beauboeuf-Lafontant, 2009; Hamilton-Mason et al., 2009; Thomas et al., 2004). The SBW schema is a multidimensional construct encompassing traits such as unyielding strength, assumption of multiple roles, self-reliance, emotional suppression, resistance to vulnerability and dependence, determination to succeed, and obligation to help others (e.g., Beauboeuf-Lafontant, 2007; Settles et al., 2008; Woods-Giscombé, 2010). Scholars have described the central tenets of the SBW schema as "strength" and "caregiving" (Beauboeuf-Lafontant, 2007; Woods-Giscombé, 2010). Strength is characterized by the determination to succeed, self-control, independence, and work ethic, while caregiving is exhibited by prioritizing others' needs, being self-sacrificing, and supporting families and communities (e.g., Woods-Giscombé, 2010). Those who endorse the schema persevere in the face of obstacles with limited resources, cope with stress on their own, and provide support without the expectation of reciprocation (Beauboeuf-Lafontant, 2007; Donovan & West, 2015). Indeed, being strong is an important and effective coping strategy that allows African American women to manage life's adversities.

According to the SBW conceptual framework, racism, race, and gender-based oppression, disenfranchisement, and limited resources—during and after legalized slavery in the United States—forced African American women to assume multiple roles (i.e., nurturer and financial provider) and adopt the SBW schema (Beauboeuf-Lafontant, 2003; Harris-Lacewell, 2001; Woods-Giscombé, 2010). The internalization of the SBW schema was necessary for personal, familial, and community survival during slavery (e.g., see Donovan & West, 2015). Although African American women today no longer face slavery, they are confronted with intersectional stressors such as gendered racism. Thus, the SBW schema has been appropriated within the Black communities in response to racialized sexism and derogatory images of Black womanhood (Harrington et al., 2010).

By embracing the SBW schema, African American women could define themselves in a positive light because the schema encompasses many positive attributes and increases self-efficacy for confronting challenges (Harrington et al., 2010). Indeed, many African American women view the SBW schema as central to their self-image (Beauboeuf-Lafontant, 2009). In addition to the aforementioned historical and sociopolitical contextual factors such as racism, gender-related experiences also contribute to the development and maintenance of the SBW schema. These experiences include gender stereotyping, mistreatment or abuse, single motherhood, challenges associated with being a successful and highly educated African American woman, and perceived benefits of the SBW role such as caring for their children and families (Beauboeuf-Lafontant, 2007; Woods-Giscombé, 2010).

African American women are socialized by media, parents, and their communities to internalize and accept the SBW schema (Kerrigan et al., 2007; Stanton et al., 2017). For example, African American women socially indoctrinate their daughters at a young age to be independent and assume multiple roles through conversations, modeling, and vicarious conditioning (Abrams et al., 2014; Staples & Johnson, 1993). In the media, African American female artists also exemplify perseverance, success, self-sufficiency, and self-reliance and serve as role models for other African American women (Henry et al., 2010). Not surprisingly, the SBW schema is found to be a salient image for many African American women (Donovan & West, 2015; Thomas et al., 2004).

The SBW schema has been viewed as both an asset and a liability. African American women perceive adoption of the SBW schema to confer benefits, such as cultivating a positive self-image, a sense of self-efficacy, and a commitment to caring for families (Woods-Giscombé, 2010). In addition, it has helped African American families survive and endure historical hardships (Mullings & Schulz, 2006). However, women who internalize the SBW schema are faced with overwhelming responsibilities that can result in exhaustion (Beauboeuf-Lafontant, 2005). Those women are also expected to minimize any struggles they face, to resist being vulnerable, and to postpone self-care since others' needs are always prioritized (Beauboeuf-Lafontant, 2007; Woods-Giscombé, 2010). Eventually, many African American women realize that the costs of adhering to the SBW schema outweigh its benefits (Woods-Giscombé, 2010). Indeed, the characteristics associated with the SBW schema and African American women's attempts to live up to this ideology of invincibility contribute to the stress that many African American women experience in their daily lives (Black & Peacock, 2011).

Due to the pressure to maintain the image of strength even in the midst of managing their own struggles, embracing the SBW schema can lead to the development of chronic stress among African American women (Woods-Giscombé & Black, 2010). In turn, chronic stress is associated with increased vulnerability for cardiovascular disease, high blood pressure, and increased heart rate (Williams & Cashion, 2008). Harrington et al. (2010) found that African American female trauma survivors were likely to internalize the SBW schema, which in turn promoted emotional inhibition and regulation difficulties, eating for psychological reasons, and eventually binge eating. The internalization of the SBW schema is also associated with depressive and anxious symptoms (Beauboeuf-Lafontant, 2007; Woods-Giscombé, 2010). Further, internalizing the SBW schema can intensify the negative effect of stress on depressive symptoms, suggesting that the schema can exacerbate existing mental health conditions (Donovan & West, 2015).

The SBW schema is also linked to loneliness because its tenets encourage women to not seek assistance and to endure hardships in isolation (Speight et al., 2012). The schema is framed by expectations that women both manage their problems alone and provide self-sacrificial care for others (Abrams et al., 2014). These expectations are likely to have an additive effect on their loneliness. In fact, a study by Woods-Giscombé (2010) found that women who internalized the SBW schema reported that they often feel misunderstood by others and may isolate themselves during periods of stress.

The negative mental health consequences associated with internalizing the SBW schema underscore the importance of the construct. Identifying the mechanisms or the pathways between the SBW schema and health can shed light on which processes should be the target of clinical interventions for women who internalize the schema. For example, the endorsement of the SBW schema might lead to low *self-compassion*, defined as viewing oneself with kindness and nonjudgment in the midst of suffering, recognizing one's suffering as part of a larger movement, and holding one's painful feelings and thoughts in mindful awareness (Neff, 2003). Specifically, those who endorse the SBW schema are likely to have low self-compassion because they are not likely to accept their negative emotions and take care of themselves in difficult times (Neff, 2003). This suggests that cultivating African American women's self-compassion, such as encouraging the use of self-compassion journaling, might help lessen the negative impact of SBW schema endorsement on their mental health.

When working with those who internalize the SBW schema, mental health and other public health professionals must be mindful that these women might underreport symptoms and/or downplay their distress levels, tend to focus on others, and delay seeking help for emotional distress (Thomas et al., 2005; Watson & Hunter, 2015). In addition, Walcott-McQuigg (1995) suggested that consuming excessive food might be a strategy used to relieve suppressed psychological distress in some African American women. This suggests that emotional eating might be a health risk associated with the schema. Mental health and other public health professionals must educate African American women that, while there are benefits associated with the SBW schema, there might also be harmful mental health consequences in trying to live up to this image.

Future studies need to examine the influence of culturally congruent coping strategies on African American women's endorsement of the SBW schema (Greer, 2011). Collective and spiritual coping are two coping strategies that reflect an African-centered worldview that is grounded in a spiritual belief system and emphasizes extended familial kinship bonds (Mattis, 2002). Collective coping involves relying on social networks to cope with stress, while spiritual coping pertains to actions (e.g., praying) that reflect connections with spiritual elements in the universe. Findings from a focus-group study indicated that African American women who internalized the SBW schema identified spirituality as a source of solace and empowerment because it guides them in making appropriate decisions and provides them with the sustenance needed to overcome adversity (Abrams et al., 2014). Additionally, women who internalized the SBW schema were found to use collective and spiritual coping to manage the stress associated with the schema (James, 2015). These findings suggest that these two coping strategies might help women cope with the stress and sense of isolation associated with the SBW schema.

More importantly, the creation and internalization of the SBW schema was a way to cope with multiple oppressive forces like racism, sexism, and classism (Donovan & West, 2015). These oppressions reflect the structural constraints placed on African American women and need to be addressed as a priority. Public education, social policies, and legislation that prevent and decrease these oppressive forces will be of utmost importance to the mental health of African American women. If interventions or changes at the societal level are made, African American women might have less need to embody the SBW schema. Thus, focusing on intervention programs that target gendered racism and classism constitute steps toward the goal of improving the mental health for this vulnerable population.

Additional Strategies to Promote Self-Care and Awareness of Mental Health among African American Women

African American women are extremely powerful and possess attributes that can support them to thrive mentally and physically. Power is often defined by control of others; however, Evans (2017) discusses that African American women can gain this sense of power by having control of themselves. This power is obtained by learning how to embrace oneself and taking time to explore this process (Evans, 2017). When African American women face these various challenges, it is important for them to be aware of their stressors and their overall mental health. Also, it is imperative that mental health and other public health professionals adopt a commitment to self-care that focuses on the whole person through empowering African American women to use their voices. Because of the various demands that African American women face, it is vital that they embrace strategies that promote self-care and mental health awareness, such as the following:

- Realizing the stressors they face in their daily lives and identifying when they are overwhelmed

- Putting themselves first when it comes to self-care and mental health and knowing that this must happen in order to ensure that they remain healthy physically and emotionally

- Finding people who are a part of their support system and utilizing that system when help is needed

- Creating healthy boundaries in all areas of their lives and learning to say no when they need time for themselves

- Empowering them to use their voices to create healthy boundaries in relationships that may be toxic and/or draining

- Giving themselves permission to care for themselves despite what others may say

- Pursuing mental health support when needed and embracing the idea that therapy is a resource that can benefit them emotionally, psychologically and physically

- Embracing healthy approaches to letting go of things that are out of their control

Conclusion

As noted throughout this chapter, African American women face unique challenges that can possibly impact their overall mental health and well-being. These various challenges may cause stress that must not be overlooked by professionals when working with African American women. In response to these stressors, mental health and other health-related practitioners must adopt a commitment to empower women to practice self-care and to use their voices to promote an awareness about mental health and the importance of self-care among African American women. For African American women to thrive mentally and physically, it is important to promote preventative approaches that include the coping strategies and suggestions provided throughout this chapter. In conclusion, it is vital that mental health and other public health professionals continue to advocate and promote the importance of self-care and mental health awareness in a society that can be extremely stressful for African American women.

References

Abrams, J. A., Maxwell, M., Pope, M., & Belgrave, F. Z. (2014). Carrying the world with the grace of a lady and the grit of a warrior: Deepening our understanding of the "Strong Black Woman" schema. *Psychology of Women Quarterly, 38*, 503–518.

American Psychological Association. (n.d.). *Stress: The different kinds of stress.* Retrieved from http://www.apa.org/helpcenter/stress-kinds.aspx

Bailey, M., & Trudy. (2018). On misogynoir: Citation, erasure, and plagiarism. *Feminist Media Studies, 18*(4), 762–768.

Beauboeuf-Lafontant, T. (2003). Strong and large Black women? Exploring relationships between deviant womanhood and weight. *Gender & Society, 17*, 111–121.

Beauboeuf-Lafontant, T. (2005). Keeping up appearances, getting fed up: The embodiment of strength among African American women. *Meridians: Feminism, race, transnationalism, 5*(2), 104–123.

Beauboeuf-Lafontant, T. (2007). You have to show strength: An exploration of gender, race, and depression. *Gender & Society, 21*, 28–51.

Beauboeuf-Lafontant, T. (2009). *Behind the mask of the strong Black woman: Voice and the embodiment of a costly performance.* University of Chicago Press.

Black, A. R., & Peacock, N. (2011). Pleasing the masses: Messages for daily life management in African American women's popular media sources. *American Journal of Public Health, 101*, 144–50.

Brown, C., Abe-Kim, J. S., & Barrio, C. (2003). Depression in ethnically diverse women: Implications for treatment in primary care settings. *Professional Psychology: Research and Practice, 34(1)*, 10–19.

Carr, E. R., Szymanski, D. M., Taha, F., West, L. M., & Kaslow, N. J. (2014). Understanding the link between multiple oppressions and depression among African American women: The role of internalization. *Psychology of Women Quarterly, 38*, 233–245.

Collins, P. H. (2000). *Black feminist thought: Knowledge, consciousness, and the politics of empowerment* (2nd ed.). Routledge.

Crenshaw, K. W. (1991). Mapping the margins: Intersectionality, identity politics, and violence against women of color. *Stanford Law Review, 43*, 1241–1299.

Essed, P. (1991). *Understanding everyday racism: An interdisciplinary theory.* Sage.

Evans, S. (2017). From worthless to wellness: Self-worth, power, and creative survival in memoirs of sexual assault. In S. Y. Evans, K. Bell, & N. K. Burton (Eds.), *Black women's mental health* (pp. 89–121). State University of New York Press.

West, C. M. (1995). Mammy, sapphire, and jezebel: Historical images of Black women and their implications for psychotherapy. *Psychotherapy, 32*, 458–446. doi:10.1037/0033-3204.32.3.458

Greer, T. M. (2011). Coping strategies as moderators of the relationship between race- and gender-based discrimination and psychological symptoms for African American women. *Journal of Black Psychology, 37*, 42–54.

Hamilton, B. E., Martin, J. A., & Ventura, S. J. (2009, March 18). Births: Preliminary data for 2007. *National Vital Statistics Reports, 57*(12). https://www.cdc.gov/nchs/data/nvsr/nvsr57/nvsr57_12.pdf

Hamilton-Mason, J., Hall, J. C., & Everett, J. E. (2009). And some of us are braver: Stress and coping among African American women. *Journal of Human Behavior in the Social Environment, 19*, 463–482.

Harrington, E. F., Crowther, J. H., & Shipherd, J. C. (2010). Trauma, binge eating, and the "strong Black woman." *Journal of Consulting and Clinical Psychology, 78*, 469–479.

Harris-Lacewell, M. (2001). No place to rest: African American political attitudes and the myth of Black women's strength. *Journal of Women Politics & Policy, 23,* 1–33.

Henry, W. J., West, N. M., & Jackson, A. (2010). Hip-hop's influence on the identity development of Black female college students: A literature review. *Journal of College Student Development, 51,* 237–251.

James, E. L. (2015). *The Superwoman Schema and the mediating factors of coping strategies and help-seeking attitudes for depression in African American women* [Unpublished doctoral dissertation]. University of Georgia.

Kerrigan, D., Andrinopoulos, K., Johnson, R., Parham, P., Thomas, T., & Ellen, J. M. (2007). Staying strong: Gender ideologies among African-American adolescents and the implications for HIV/STI prevention. *Journal of Sex Research, 44,* 172–180.

Kohn, L. P., & Hudson, K. M. (2002). Gender, ethnicity and depression: Intersectionality and context in mental health research with African American women. *African American Research Perspectives, 8,* 174–184.

Lashley, M.-B., Marshall, V., & McLaurin-Jones, T. (2017). Looking through the window: Black women's perspectives on mental health and self-care. In S. Y. Evans, K. Bell, & N. K. Burton (Eds.), *Black women's mental health* (pp. 215–229). State University of New York Press.

Lewis, J. A., & Neville, H. A. (2015). Construction and initial validation of the Gendered Racial Microaggressions Scale for Black women. *Journal of Counseling Psychology, 62*(2), 289–302.

Mattis, J. S. (2002). Religion and spirituality in the meaning-making and coping experiences of African American women: A qualitative analysis. *Psychology of Women Quarterly, 4,* 309–321.

Miller, L. H., & Smith, A. D. (1994). *The stress solution: An action plan to manage the stress in your life.* Pocket Books.

Mullings, L., & Schulz, A. J. (2006). Intersectionality and health: An introduction. In A. J. Schulz & L. Mullings (Eds.), *Gender, race, class, & health: Intersectional approaches* (pp. 3–17). Jossey-Bass.

National Alliance on Mental Illness. (2019). *African American mental health.* https://www.nami.org/find-support/diverse-communities/african-americans

Neff, K. D. (2003). Self-compassion: An alternative conceptualization of a healthy attitude toward oneself. *Self and Identity, 2,* 85–101.

Settles, I. H., Pratt-Hyatt, J. S., & Buchanan, N. T. (2008). Through the lens of race: Black and White women's perceptions of womanhood. *Psychology of Women Quarterly, 32,* 454–468.

Speight, S. L., Isom, D. A., & Thomas, A. J. (2012). From Hottentot to Superwoman: Issues of identity and mental health for African American women. In C. Z. Enns & E. N. Williams (Eds.), *The handbook of feminist multicultural counseling psychology* (pp. 115–130). Oxford University Press.

Stanton, A. G., Jerald, M. C., Ward, L. M., & Avery, L. R. (2017). Social media contributions to Strong Black Woman ideal endorsement and Black women's mental health. *Psychology of Women Quarterly, 41,* 465–478.

Staples, R., & Johnson, L. B. (1993). *Black families at the crossroads: Challenges and prospects.* Jossey-Bass.

Substance Abuse and Mental Health Services Administration. (2009). *Results from the 2009 National Survey on Drug Use and Health: Volume I. Summary of national findings.* U.S. Department of Health and Human Services. NSDUH Series H-38A, HHS Publication No. SMA 10-4586Findings.

Substance Abuse and Mental Health Services Administration. (2015). *Racial/ ethnic differences in mental health service use among adults.* https://www.samhsa.gov/data/sites/default/files/MHServicesUseAmongAdults/MHServicesUseAmongAdults.pdf

Thom, T., Haase, N., Rosamond, W., Howard, V. J., Rumsfeld, J., Manolio, T., Zheng, Z. J., Flegal, K., O'Donnell, C., & Kittner, S. (2006). Heart disease and stroke statistics—2006 update: A report from the American Heart Association Statistics Committee and Stroke Statistics Subcommittee. *Circulation, 113,* 85–151.

Thomas, A. J., Speight, S. L., & Witherspoon, K. M. (2005). Internalized oppression among Black women. In J. L. Chin (Ed.), *Psychology of prejudice and discrimination* (Vol. 3, pp. 113–132). Praeger Press.

Thomas, A. J., Witherspoon, K. M., & Speight, S. L. (2004). Toward the development of the Stereotypic Roles for Black Women Scale. *Journal of Black Psychology, 3,* 426–442.

Thomas, A. J., Witherspoon, K. M., & Speight, S. L. (2008). Gendered racism, psychological distress, and coping styles of African American women. *Cultural Diversity and Ethnic Minority Psychology, 14,* 307–314.

Ussher, J. M. (2016). Misogyny. In *The Wiley Blackwell encyclopedia of gender and sexuality studies.* John Wiley & Sons. https://www.researchgate.net/publication/315786004_Misogyny

Walcott-McQuigg, J. A. (1995). The relationship between stress and weight-control behavior in African-American women. *Journal of the National Medical Association, 87*(6), 427–432.

Walker-Barnes, C. (2017). When the bough breaks: The StrongBlackWoman and the ebodiment of stress. In S. Y. Evans, K. Bell, & N. K. Burton (Eds.), *Black women's mental health* (pp. 43–55). State University of New York Press.

Wang, Y., & Beydoun, M. (2007). The obesity epidemic in the United States—gender, age, socioeconomic, racial/ethnic, and geographic characteristics: A systematic review and meta-regression analysis. *Epidemiologic Reviews, 29,* 6–28.

Watson, N. N., & Hunter, C. D. (2015). Anxiety and depression among African American women: The costs of strength and negative attitudes toward psychological help-seeking. *Cultural Diversity and Ethnic Minority Psychology, 21,* 604.

Williams, S. H., & Cashion, A. (2008). Negative affectivity and cardiovascular disease in African American single mothers. *The ABNF Journal: Official Journal of the Association of Black Nursing Faculty in Higher Education, 19*(2), 64–67.

Woods, K. C., Buchanan, N. T., & Settles, I. H. (2009). Sexual harassment across the color line: Experiences and outcomes of cross- versus intraracial sexual harassment among Black women. *Cultural Diversity and Ethnic Minority Psychology, 15*(1), 67–76.

Woods-Giscombé, C. L. (2010). Superwoman schema: African American women's views on stress, strength, and health. *Qualitative Health Research, 20*, 668–683.

Woods-Giscombé, C. L., & Black, A. R. (2010). Mind-body interventions to reduce risk for health disparities related to stress and strength among African American women: The potential of mindfulness-based stress reduction, loving-kindness, and the NTU therapeutic framework. *Complementary Health Practice Review, 15*, 115–131.

Woods-Giscombé, C. L., & Lobel, M. (2008). Race and gender matter: A multi-dimensional approach to conceptualizing and measuring stress in African American women. *Cultural Diversity and Ethnic Minority Psychology, 14*(3), 173–182.

PART II

LOCATE DISPARITY

SECTION OUTLINE: DEANNA J. WATHINGTON

The World Health Organization defines *health* as "a complete state of physical, mental and social well-being and not merely the absence of disease or infirmity."[1] I believe public health is the space, the umbrella, under which all health professionals gather, labor, conduct research, exchange ideas, deliver services, and create effective, innovative solutions.

Practice among an Invisible Population

Indeed, public health practitioners are guided by the core functions of the field—assessment, policy development, and assurance. It is imperative that we collect, analyze, share, and review information about the health of our communities as we work toward achieving improved health status. We must hold steadfast to utilizing scientific knowledge and credible, demonstrated evidence as we lead and contribute to policy and regulatory decision-making to positively impact the health of Americans. And, to fulfill our third function, we commit wholeheartedly to ensuring the provision of necessary and vital services to the populations we serve.

For a number of years, many public health practitioners have begun to view their work (and the outcomes derived from it) through the lens of determinants of health. Historically, research and practice in public health

95

and medicine have focused on causes and cures of disease. Identifying and using the determinants of health as a framework expands our understanding and ability to successfully tackle disease and, most importantly, to shape health within our communities.

Determinants can be social, structural, or environmental in nature. Indeed, we have long recognized that where you are born, live, work, and play have a profound effect on your health and life span—especially if citizens are prevented from accessing or acquiring support, resources, opportunity, and safety. The logical question following from this statement is, Why? If we want the country to be healthy and to prosper, why wouldn't we want to create conditions, practices, and policies that allow every citizen to flourish and live to their fullest potential?

Much evidence now exists concerning many of the determinants of health: education, income level, social status, poverty, early childhood experience, employment/working conditions, chronic stress, racism, discrimination, gender bias, social support, neighborhood, housing, safety, physical environment. In fact, the social and economic factors, physical environment, and health behaviors, as provided in the list above, account for up to 80 percent of our health! In addition, research and practice has consistently found the negative impacts from these factors to be worse among Black women.

Given that health disparities arise, in great part, due to social and economic inequalities and disadvantages, it is all the more imperative to gain an understanding of how those negative experiences can be ameliorated in affected populations by listening to and working with those populations in a systems-thinking and culturally relevant approach.

A number of approaches and screening tools have become available including the Health Leads Social Needs Screening Toolkit, the Accountable Health Communities (AHC) screening tool, WeCare, and the Protocol to Respond to and Assess Patient Assets, Risks, and Experiences (PRAPARE) tool. The AHC screening tool focuses on four major determinants (food insecurity, housing, transportation, and safety), with subsequent questions addressing an additional eight determinant areas (income/resources/financial strain, employment, family/community support, education, physical activity, disabilities, mental health, and substance abuse).

At least one of the tools also inquires about race, ethnicity, and spoken language. While these screenings represent progress in recognizing and attempting to document and address the systemic causes of health inequities, we have much work to do around the beliefs and attitudes that contribute to social control.

This section provides a rich selection of chapters addressing how we as public health practitioners can apply our core functions to acknowledging, addressing, and elevating the health of Black women. Even more importantly, this section is a clear and present reminder that ideology, class structure, practices, stereotypes, beliefs, and language enable societies to rationalize inequality and in doing so render it invisible. The disparate health outcomes of Black women and other communities of color in comparison to the referent population strip away that invisibility and give voice to the facts. If public health and health equity are the framework, where do attitudes and knowledge about Black women fit? Where do prevention and care fit? What are the appropriate skills needed to deliver that care? And what are the pressing questions and afflictions that require action and solutions? These contributions provide rejoinders to those questions—they provide a primer for those who are unaware, a conversation for those currently engaged in the work, and a guide for those in search of next steps.

In the first chapter of the section, Traci N. Bethea and Yvette C. Cozier's contribution, "The Black Women's Health Study: Working Together to Improve the Health of Black Women," provides an introduction to the Black Women's Health Study and summarizes its key findings. Their chapter is, in many ways, a good jumping-off point for the state of Black women's health today, providing crucial context for the volume as a whole. By focusing exclusively on Black women, the Black Women's Health Study and Bethea and Cozier normalize and center this population as subjects of inquiry and importance, a stark contrast from other studies in which Whiteness and (to a lesser extent) maleness entertain center stage.

In "The Swelling Wave of Oppression," Jayme Canty explores the effects of bias and its accompanying societal (economic and political) stigmas on the health of Black queer women. The author notes the depth and breadth of the impact intersectionality and heterosexism have on the health challenges experienced by this population of Black women. Canty also highlights the impact of region and the imperative to more clearly situate race, gender, sexuality, and other aspects of identity within historical and geographic contexts.

Alisa Valentin and Christy Gamble Hines provide a nuanced analysis of the maternal-health-care crisis affecting Black women in rural areas in their chapter, "Rural Black Maternal Health in the Age of Digital Deserts." The authors offer insight as to the maternal-health-care obstacles facing Black women in general and, more specifically, Black women living in rural areas. The authors explore the potential of telehealth for reducing some of the barriers presented by rural isolation as well as challenges to launching this approach. The authors propose policy solutions that can be used to improve the maternal health care for Black rural women.

Author Esther Piervil assesses a highly relevant topic for Black women in "Pouring from a Leaking Cup," wherein she addresses informal family caregiving in the Black community. She writes that caregiving is "perceived as an honorable obligation" while acknowledging it "is often an involuntary choice . . . rarely based on the caregiver's level of preparedness or access to resources and support" (163).

As stated previously, where you are born, live, work and play have a profound effect on your health and life span. In this section we add a little more to that list; we posit that the skin and body you are born in has just as much impact in this society.

In the era of COVID-19, this hypothesis has proven to be true. The significant impact of the novel coronavirus on the health of Black women in this society is an unwavering, persistent, and irrefutable fact. The evidence is as broad as the topics covered by the contributions in this section, beginning with the severe ramifications occurring among Black queer women, including higher rates of loss of employment and income, housing insecurity, a heightened state of health care in jeopardy, and the ever-present realities of racism and violence. COVID is delivering a two-fold effect as Black women face the specter of the pandemic along with the continued need for HIV prevention in our communities. Both viruses evoke stress, anxiety, and fear around the possibility of infection as well as increased morbidity and mortality within the Black population. In addition, social isolation and mental health issues accompany both viruses. Current concerns are also focused on provision of care and treatment and vaccination hesitancy.

Black women serving as caregivers in their families and often in multigenerational settings find that the novel coronavirus poses a threat to the health of their families or suddenly thrusts them into the role of caregiver. Over the course of the pandemic, research and practice have revealed additional sequelae for caregivers themselves. These range from risk of COVID infection to increased depression and anxiety. Stress is the fraying thread weaving through many aspects of the COVID pandemic—

tying together heightened concern about short- and long-term effects on mental and physical health. For Black women, this additive factor joins the daily stress suffered as a result of microaggressions, overt racism, sexism, violence, and bias against intersectionality. This section serves as a clarion call that, even in the midst of this COVID pandemic, we must still address and confront the centuries-long pandemic of structural racism and its harmful effects on health.

E pluribus unum. Out of many, one. A revered quotation; however, the health of Black women, along with other "invisible" populations, stands in the void as evidence that we have not yet achieved this lofty goal. We have a great deal of expertise about what works for us, about how to be culturally appropriate in caring for us, about how to approach us not as a monolithic group or as stereotypes but as the incredibly unique, significant, multilayered population we are. We are challenging the society to be better. Do better. Do better so we can all thrive. Elevating the health status of those with the worst outcomes will only serve to elevate the health status of all citizens. The next section, the longest of the three, focuses on proposed and practiced solutions to naming and locating health inequity. Social justice work requires action in research, communities, agencies, and all quadrants of health-care professions.

Note

1. "Constitution," World Health Organization, https://www.who.int/about/governance/constitution.

Chapter 5

The Black Women's Health Study

Working Together to Improve the Health of Black Women

TRACI N. BETHEA AND YVETTE C. COZIER

Introduction

The Black Women's Health Study (BWHS) was developed to address a lack of research on Black women's health. To date, the vast majority of epidemiologic research on women has been conducted in White populations. Just as it has been assumed that results from men are generalizable to women, results from White women have been assumed to be generalizable to women of color. Additionally, it has been assumed that the socioeconomic trajectories of White women are the same as for women of color despite evidence to the contrary (Williams, 2002). Fortunately, there is a growing recognition of the need for studies of health and illness in specific racial and ethnic groups.

Black women carry a greater burden of morbidity and mortality than White women, with higher rates for virtually every major illness (S. E. Taylor & Holden, 2009). For example, mortality rates are higher for three leading causes of death: heart disease, malignant neoplasms, and cerebrovascular disease. For the most common cancer in women, breast cancer, the incidence in Black women has increased and is now equal to that of White women (DeSantis et al., 2016), while mortality is 39% greater in Black women (DeSantis et al., 2017). Some of the differences in disease incidence and mortality between Black and White women are attributable to differences in socioeconomic status and access to and use of health services, but these factors do not provide an entire explanation (Baquet et al., 1991; O'Keefe et al., 2015; Williams, 2002). For example, preterm delivery is more common among Black women than White women, but the difference is greatest among women with the highest educational levels (Kramer & Hogue, 2009). Factors responsible for these and other observed disparities need to be elucidated and can best be addressed within a study of socioeconomically and geographically diverse Black women. The BWHS addresses this need.

The Black Women's Health Study

Design of the Study

Collection of questionnaire data. The BWHS was established in 1995 when fourteen-page health questionnaires were mailed to subscribers to *Essence* magazine (a general-readership magazine targeted to African American women), friends and relatives of early respondents, and members of the Black Nurses' Foundation and the National Education Association (Rosenberg, Palmer, Rao, & Adams-Campbell, 1999). The women were invited to participate in a long-term follow-up study of the health of African American women. The 1997 questionnaire asked about a participant's race/ethnicity, and 99.6% of respondents identified themselves as Black. Women who did not report being Black were excluded from the cohort. Follow-up has been successful for >80% of potential person-years through the 2015 questionnaire cycle.

The 59,000 women aged 21–69 years at entry with valid residential addresses comprised the BWHS cohort at baseline. The median age at entry was 38 years old, and 80% of participants had completed education beyond high school. Participants were from across the US—Northeast, 28%; South, 30%; Midwest, 23%; West, 19%—with 85% from New York, California, Illinois, Georgia, New Jersey, Virginia, Maryland, Louisiana, South Carolina, Indiana, Massachusetts, and the District of Columbia, and they are followed through postal questionnaires that are mailed every two years. Since 2003, questionnaires have also been provided online on the BWHS website (www.bu.edu/BWHS).

At baseline, BWHS participants provided information on demographics, medical and reproductive history, menopausal status, smoking and alcohol use, physical activity, current weight and weight at age 18, waist and hip circumference, adult height, use of selected medications such as oral contraceptives and female-hormone supplements, diet (via a modified version of the sixty-item Block/National Cancer Institute food frequency questionnaire), and use of medical care. The follow-up questionnaires updated information on several factors (e.g., weight, menopausal status) and obtained information on incident disease and new topics of interest. The 1997 questionnaire included questions on racial/ethnic heritage, experiences of racial discrimination, use of hair relaxers, and exposure to passive smoke at various ages. The 1999 and 2005 questionnaires included the twenty-item Center for Epidemiologic Studies Depression Scale to measure symptoms of depression. The 1999 questionnaire obtained a history of cancer (sites included breast, lung, colon, rectum, ovary, and prostate) in the participant's biological parents, siblings, and children. The 2003 questionnaire had questions about pace of walking and perceptions of health-care quality. The 2005 questionnaire asked about violence victimization across the life span, coping skills, and stress. We have also collected information on sleep disorders, night-shift work, social support, caregiving, hair loss, pregnancy outcomes, dental health, religiosity/spirituality, and self-rated physical and mental health.

Collection of data from other sources. Information on deaths is obtained annually from the National Death Index. Information on incident cancer is obtained from twenty-four state cancer registries located in states in which 95% of participants live. Information on air pollution has been obtained from various publicly accessible sources and linked to participants' residential addresses. Information on neighborhood characteristics, such as the median housing value, has been obtained from US Census data and linked to participants' residential addresses.

Collection of biospecimens. During 2004–2008, 28,000 participants provided saliva samples, which have been used in genetic analyses. During 2013–2017, 13,000 participants provided blood samples, which have been used in genetic analyses and analyses of blood biomarkers. Several thousand participants with cancer have allowed access to their tumor tissue samples, allowing for studies of genetic and other alterations in the tumor tissue.

Input from Black Women

The BWHS has been advised for many years by a scientific advisory board consisting largely of Black women. These advisors have a wide range of expertise and experience, including familiarity with the special health-related and social problems that Black women may face. Study investigators solicit advice on study directions, questionnaire design, and other issues pertinent to interacting with study participants from a participant advisory group of volunteers from among the cohort. Participants often send in comments.

Two Decades and Counting: A Selection of Research Findings from the Black Women's Health Study[1]

At the beginning of the study in 1995, almost all participants had completed high school, and 44% had completed college. More than a third were married or living as married, and 19% lived alone. Forty percent had childcare responsibilities, and 12% helped care for parents or other relatives. Most (82%) had used oral contraceptives, 24% had gone through menopause, and 15% had used female-hormone supplements. Almost one-third of participants ages 40–49 and 38% of participants ages 50–59 had undergone a hysterectomy. Only 16% of participants were current smokers. The most commonly reported medical conditions were uterine fibroids, hypertension, high cholesterol, and diabetes.

This section provides a summary of some of the main findings from BWHS research. While we have published more than 240 scientific manuscripts, the outcomes presented here are of particular relevance for the health of Black women, who disproportionately suffer from preterm birth (MacDorman, 2011), uterine fibroids (Stewart et al., 2017), estrogen receptor–negative breast cancer (Kerlikowske et al., 2017), and a host of other health outcomes compared to White women (Williams, 2002).

Reproductive Health

Birth outcomes. Greater body mass index (BMI), greater waist circumference, and greater waist-to-hip ratio were associated with delayed time to pregnancy (Wise et al., 2013). Working night shifts also delayed time to pregnancy, particularly among older women (Sponholtz et al., 2021). Women who were underweight had a higher risk of both spontaneous and medically induced preterm birth, while women who were obese had a higher risk of medically induced preterm birth (Wise, Palmer, et al., 2010). Women who were overweight when they became pregnant or had excess weight gain during the pregnancy were more likely to have a baby with macrosomia (i.e., a birth weight ≥8.8 lb.; Li, Rosenberg, Palmer, et al., 2013).

Women who were born in the US (compared to women born in other countries) and women who grew up in a predominantly Black neighborhood (compared to women who grew up in a predominantly White neighborhood) were less likely to breastfeed, and those who breastfed did so for a shorter duration (Griswold et al., 2018). Women who reported experiencing unfair treatment on the job breastfed for a shorter time than women who did not report unfair treatment (Griswold et al., 2018).

Uterine fibroids. Higher weight was associated with higher risk of uterine fibroids (benign tumors in the womb; Wise et al., 2005), while late age at menarche, having had children, and late age at first birth were associated with lower risk (Wise et al., 2004). Higher levels of dairy, fruit, and vegetable intakes were associated with lower risk of fibroids (Wise, Radin, et al., 2011; Wise, Radin, et al., 2010), while consumption of foods with a higher glycemic index was associated with higher risk (Radin et al., 2010).

Cancer

Breast cancer. Advances in technology and research have redefined breast cancer as a heterogeneous disease. One classification of different subtypes uses hormone receptor status: estrogen receptor, progesterone receptor, and human epidermal growth factor receptor 2. Breast tumors that are negative for the estrogen receptor (ER–) or are negative for all three of these receptors (i.e., triple negative) are more commonly diagnosed among Black women (Carey et al., 2006). These subtypes often grow more aggressively and can be difficult to treat. Risk factors for breast cancer can differ by subtype. A wide range of potential risk factors for breast cancer have been assessed in the BWHS:

Dietary factors: Neither dietary glycemic load nor glycemic index was related to breast cancer risk (Palmer, Boggs, Adams-Campbell, & Rosenberg, 2008). There was also no association for meat, total fat, saturated fat, total dairy, or low-fat dairy intake (Genkinger et al., 2013). Women who were not overweight or obese who ate a diet characterized by the intake of fruits and vegetables as well as legumes, fish, and poultry (i.e., a prudent dietary pattern) had a lower risk of breast cancer (Agurs-Collins et al., 2009; Boggs et al., 2010).

Body size: Taller height was associated with greater risk of estrogen receptor–positive (ER+) breast cancer, as was early age at menarche (Bertrand, Gerlovin, et al., 2017). Higher BMI at age 18 was associated with a lower risk of breast cancer at age 18, but adult obesity and adult weight gain were associated with higher risk of ER+ postmenopausal breast cancer (Palmer et al., 2007). Abdominal obesity was associated with higher risk of ER– breast cancer only among young women (age <45; Bertrand, Bethea, et al., 2017).

Reproductive factors: Women who had several children were at higher risk of ER– breast cancer than women with fewer children, but the increase was not present among women who breastfed (Palmer et al., 2011; Palmer et al., 2003). Recent use of female-hormone supplements of estrogen with progestin was associated with increased risk of ER+ breast cancer (Rosenberg et al., 2006). Recent use of oral contraceptives (i.e., within the past five years) was associated with an increase in breast cancer risk (Rosenberg et al., 2010). Women who underwent a bilateral oophorectomy, compared to women who had a hysterectomy with ovarian conservation, had a lower risk of ER+ breast cancer (Boggs et al., 2014).

Physical activity: Vigorous physical activity during high school was associated with lower risk of postmenopausal breast cancer (Rosenberg et al., 2014). There were no associations of physical activity at other time periods with breast cancer risk. Sedentary behavior—sitting for long periods of time—was associated with increased risk (Nomura et al., 2016).

Psychosocial factors: Women who reported frequent experiences of perceived racism had a higher risk of breast cancer at younger ages (T. R. Taylor et al., 2007). Experiences of unfair treatment on the job, in housing, and with the police were also associated with a higher risk of breast cancer (T. R. Taylor et al., 2007). Women who reported experiencing physical abuse during adulthood had an increased risk of breast cancer (Wise, Palmer, et al., 2011). There was no association for sexual abuse or physical abuse experienced during childhood or adolescence (Wise, Palmer, et al., 2011).

Other notable findings: Women with a family history of breast cancer were at increased risk of developing breast cancer themselves, particularly if the family member was diagnosed at a young age (Palmer et al., 2009). Higher blood levels of vitamin D were associated with lower risk of breast cancer (Palmer et al., 2016). Type 2 diabetes was associated with higher risk of ER– breast cancer (Palmer et al., 2017). Current and long-duration use of aspirin was associated with reduced risk of breast cancer (Bosco et al., 2011). Risk of breast cancer increased with cigarette smoking that had begun at a young age and continued for many years, and the risk was the same regardless of whether the cigarettes were mentholated (Bethea et al., 2014; Rosenberg, Boggs, et al., 2013). Hair-relaxer use was not associated with breast cancer risk (Rosenberg et al., 2007). Lower neighborhood socioeconomic status was associated with a small increase in risk of ER– breast cancer (Palmer et al., 2012). Being born at a low birth weight or a high birth weight was associated with increased breast cancer risk, as was being born to a mother older than age 35 (Barber et al., 2019). Numerous genetic variants were associated with small increases or decreases in risk of breast cancer—either overall or of certain subtypes.

Other cancers. The incidence of lung cancer is higher among African Americans for reasons that are not currently understood (Schabath et al., 2016). In the BWHS, cigarette smoking is a strong risk factor for lung cancer, and obesity was associated with decreased risk of lung cancer among current smokers (Bethea et al., 2013). Risk of ovarian cancer is lower among Black women than among White women, but ovarian cancer mortality is much higher in Black than White women (Park et al., 2017). In the BWHS, long duration of oral contraceptive use was associated with reduced risk of ovarian cancer (Bethea et al., 2017). Use of postmenopausal female-hormone supplements was associated with increased risk, while childbearing and tubal ligation were associated with decreased risk (Bethea et al., 2017). Long duration of oral contraceptive use was associated with reduced risk of endometrial cancer, while current use of estrogen-only female-hormone supplements was associated with increased risk (Sponholtz et al., 2018). Periodontal disease and tooth loss were associated with increased risk of pancreatic cancer (Gerlovin et al., 2019). Pancreatic cancer is another cancer for which the risk and mortality is higher for African Americans than for Whites (Ashktorab et al., 2017). Further research into pancreatic cancer in the BWHS is ongoing.

Obesity and Cardiometabolic Diseases

Weight gain and obesity. Women with high intakes of hamburgers from fast-food restaurants and of sugar-sweetened beverages gained more weight (Boggs et al., 2013). The risk of becoming obese was lower in women who had high intake of fruits and vegetables and low intake of red meat, processed meats, fried foods, and sweets (Boggs, Palmer, et al., 2011). Women who participated in vigorous exercise or brisk walking gained less weight than inactive women (Rosenberg, Kipping-Ruane, et al., 2013). Women living in urban neighborhoods where the street layout made walking more feasible gained less weight and were less likely to become obese than women living in neighborhoods that were less conducive to walking (Coogan et al., 2011). Childbearing was associated with more weight gain, with the greatest gain occurring after the birth of the first child (Rosenberg et al., 2003). Women who lived in the most deprived neighborhoods had significantly greater weight gain and were more likely to be obese than women who lived in wealthier neighborhoods (Coogan et al., 2010), regardless of their educational attainment or income (Cozier et al., 2014). Both daily experiences of racism and institutional experiences of racism were associated with increased risk of becoming obese (Cozier et al., 2014).

Diabetes. Women with a higher BMI had a higher risk of diabetes, and women with greater waist-to-hip ratio were also at higher risk, regardless of their BMI (Krishnan, Rosenberg, Djousse, et al., 2007). Healthier diets, including those with fewer processed foods, were associated with lower risk. Greater intake of whole grains was associated with lower risk (van Dam et al., 2006). Greater intake of cereal fiber and lower glycemic index were also associated with reduced risk (Krishnan, Rosenberg, Singer, et al., 2007). The incidence of diabetes was higher among women who had high intakes of sugar-sweetened beverages (Palmer, Boggs, Krishnan, et al., 2008), women who had frequent restaurant meals of hamburgers or fried chicken (Krishnan, Coogan, et al., 2010), and women who were inactive and spent long hours sitting and watching television (Krishnan et al., 2009). Women who exercised vigorously on a regular basis had a much lower risk of diabetes than those who were inactive (Krishnan et al., 2009); brisk walking was also associated with lower risk (Krishnan et al., 2009).

Women who were born prematurely or had a low birth weight were at higher risk of developing diabetes as adults (Ruiz-Narváez et al., 2014). Women who had a baby that was born preterm experienced greater risk of diabetes, regardless of whether they were diagnosed with gestational diabetes (James-Todd et al., 2014). Depression was associated with higher diabetes risk (Vimalananda et al., 2014). Both daily experiences of racism and institutional racism were associated with increased risk of developing diabetes in adulthood (Bacon et al., 2017). Women who had worked night shifts for many years had a higher risk of diabetes (Vimalananda et al., 2015). Having a lower income or lower educational attainment or living in a poorer neighborhood was associated with higher risk of diabetes (Krishnan, Cozier, et al., 2010). The findings for air pollution were mixed, with higher levels of ozone being related to increased risk of diabetes and no association for fine particulate matter or nitrogen dioxide (Coogan et al., 2012).

Hypertension. Obesity was associated with increased risk of hypertension (Rosenberg, Palmer, Adams-Campbell, & Rao, 1999). Religious or spiritual coping was associated with decreased risk, while more frequent prayer was associated with increased risk (Cozier et al., 2018). Women who lived in neighborhoods with a higher median housing value had lower risk of hypertension, irrespective of their individual educational attainment or income (Cozier et al., 2007). The findings for air pollution were mixed, with higher levels of ozone being related to increased risk of hypertension and no association observed for fine particulate matter or nitrogen dioxide (Coogan et al., 2012). Expansion of BWHS research to myocardial infarction, stroke, and other cardiovascular conditions is ongoing.

Autoimmune Diseases

Sarcoidosis. Black women are more likely to be diagnosed with sarcoidosis than White women (Dumas et al., 2016). In the BWHS, weight gain and obesity were associated with higher risk of sarcoidosis (Cozier et al., 2015), but reproductive factors were unrelated to risk (Cozier et al., 2012).
Lupus. Lupus tends to affect women of childbearing age and is more prevalent among Black women than White women (Schabath et al., 2016). In the BWHS, there was an increased risk of lupus with cigarette smoking and a decreased risk with moderate alcohol consumption (Cozier et al., 2019b; Formica et al., 2003). Obesity at age 18 was also associated with higher risk, but neither baseline nor recent obesity affected risk (Cozier et al., 2019a).

Mortality

The rate of premature mortality for Black women exceeds that of White women, although the disparity has been decreasing over time (Best et al.,

2018). In an analysis of never smokers, higher BMI was associated with increased risk of death, while large waist circumference was associated with increased mortality only among women who were not obese (Boggs, Rosenberg, et al., 2011). BWHS participants who ate a diet with high intake of whole grains and low intake of red meat experienced a lower risk of mortality, and participants who ate a diet with high intake of red and processed meat experienced increased mortality risk (Boggs et al., 2015). Women with sarcoidosis had a higher risk of mortality, particularly at younger ages (Tukey et al., 2013).

Black women who lived in poorer neighborhoods had a higher risk of all-cause and cancer mortality than women who lived in more affluent neighborhoods, regardless of their educational attainment (Bethea et al., 2016). Among women who did not complete sixteen years of education, living in a neighborhood with a low socioeconomic status was associated with increased risk of cardiovascular mortality (Bethea et al., 2016). For breast cancer, women who had been diagnosed with diabetes were at higher risk of mortality, especially if they had diabetes for five or more years before they were diagnosed with breast cancer (Charlot et al., 2017). Natural menopause before age 40 was associated with greater risk of all-cause and cause-specific mortality, irrespective of smoking status or use of female-hormone supplements (Li, Rosenberg, Wise, et al., 2013).

New Areas of Research in the Black Women's Health Study

We will continue to investigate risk factors such as racial discrimination and outcomes including ER– breast cancer that are critical for Black women's health. In addition, we will explore new research areas and important health topics that become more relevant as the cohort ages. New topics of study are identified through scientific collaborations and literature reviews of emerging hypotheses and other searches of medical and public health research, as well as from suggestions from BWHS participants and the study's external advisory board.

Mammographic Density

Recent evidence suggests that having dense breasts is a risk factor for breast cancer (Boyd et al., 2007; Boyd et al., 2011). Although Black women tend to have denser breasts than White women (McCarthy et al., 2016), few studies have investigated mammographic density among Black women or the association of mammographic density with breast cancer risk by subtype (Ma et al., 2009; Razzaghi et al., 2013; Ursin et al., 2003). To address this lack of information, we are collecting digital mammograms from a subset of BWHS participants. Using computational approaches, we are characterizing mammographic density from the mammogram images. These data will be used to assess risk factors for dense breasts and investigate mammographic density as a risk factor for breast cancer, with particular attention to ER– breast cancer.

Cancer Risk Prediction

Current breast cancer risk prediction models have not performed well at predicting risk of breast cancer for Black women. The models predict risk for breast cancer overall without consideration of subtype. Breast cancer subtype is particularly important for Black women because up to a third of Black breast cancer patients are affected by the aggressive ER– subtype (Carey et al., 2006; DeSantis et al., 2016; Sineshaw et al., 2014). Efforts to use BWHS data to develop and test new models are underway, based on assessing subtypes separately.

Cancer Survivorship

As treatments for cancers improves, it is important to investigate ways to help cancer survivors live the healthiest lives possible. Few studies have included Black cancer survivors in large numbers (Coughlin et al., 2015). The BWHS has begun to evaluate the health effects of treatment, whether treatment was concordant with subtype-specific guidelines, and other factors among women who have been diagnosed with breast cancer. In the future, this work will be extended to other cancer sites.

The Microbiome

The microbial communities on and in human bodies are comprised of trillions of microbial cells, including bacteria, viruses, and fungi. A wealth of evidence from animal models and human patients indicates that the microbiome can affect the host's weight, metabolism, inflammation, and insulin sensitivity as well as susceptibility to obesity, diabetes, inflammatory bowel disease, and other conditions (Althani et al., 2016; Lynch & Pedersen, 2016). Much more research needs to be undertaken in population-based studies. Using biospecimens from saliva samples, the BWHS has begun investigating health outcomes related to species diversity and abundance in the oral microbiome. Because the microbiome can be affected by dietary changes, the use of antibiotics and other medications, and probiotic supplementation, findings may be translatable to interventions for a variety of medical conditions.

Sleep

Black Americans are at higher risk than other racial groups of experiencing sleep problems, such as more fragmented sleep, shorter sleep duration, and poorer sleep quality (Adenekan et al., 2013; Ruiter et al., 2011). The BWHS is examining factors, such as racial discrimination (Bethea et al., 2020), that may be related to sleep duration and to insomnia symptoms. The BWHS's first clinical trial is underway to address treatment of insomnia symptoms using web-based interventions (Patient-Centered Outcomes Research Institute, n.d.).

Aging

In 2017, the median age of BWHS participants was 60 years old, while the oldest participants were 92 years old. The aging of the BWHS cohort over our more than twenty years of follow-up and during future follow-up provides the opportunity to obtain important data about the health of Black women as they age. Areas of interest include urinary incontinence and cognitive function, both of which may be related to comorbid conditions like diabetes.

Issues of Ethics and Informed Consent

In the era of social media and big data, increased sharing of data across studies and on public-access databases is being encouraged and sometimes required by funders such as the National Institutes of Health. Comfort with public disclosure of personal details may vary greatly across populations. At the same time, there is a great need for scientific collaboration and for transformative research. The BWHS is planning research projects to investigate participants' views on data sharing to ensure that data use and collaborations with other investigators are consistent with participants' understanding and informed consent. Other research issues are identification of barriers and facilitators of biospecimen donation. There is a lack of knowledge about the views of underrepresented populations in particular.

Summary

Although some disparities have decreased, Black-White health disparities persist. Only continued attention and effort will ensure that these disparities continue to decline. The BWHS represents an important part of this effort. It is important to note that the BWHS is limited to Black women and therefore cannot directly address racial health disparities through the simultaneous study of Black and White women. Nevertheless, the BWHS represents a socioeconomically and geographically diverse study population that has contributed essential data to help improve public health and clinical care for Black women and to support the policy changes and public investments necessary to sustain those improvements. The motto of the BWHS is "working together to improve the health of Black women," and it is our sincere hope that the dedication of BWHS participants and the contributions of BWHS investigators and staff members are informing, empowering, and changing the lives of Black women.

Coda

December 2019 marked the emergence of the global pandemic caused by SARS-CoV-2 (COVID-19) infection (Zhu et al., 2020). In the US, Black people have experienced disproportionate COVID-19-related morbidity and mortality, due in large part to residence in dense, low-resource communities and employment in occupations with high exposure risk (Snowden & Graaf, 2021). Additionally, individuals with underlying chronic illness are at increased risk of COVID-19 infection, which may further contribute to racial disparities in outcomes. One study found that 33% of Black adults and 27% of White adults were at higher risk of COVID-19 due to having one or more chronic diseases (Raifman & Raifman, 2020). Recent research also suggests that environmental pollution, which disproportionately affects communities of color, may increase risk of coronavirus mortality (Petroni et al., 2020).

To address the impact of coronavirus among Black women, the BWHS COVID-19 Study was initiated in the fall of 2020. A web-based questionnaire assessed participants' experiences related to COVID-19, including diagnostic testing, hospitalization, and the occurrence of selected postinfection health conditions (e.g., heart attack, stroke, peripheral neuropathy). Other questions asked about living arrangements, working conditions, and the economic impact of the pandemic. Over ten thousand

BWHS participants completed questionnaires. Starting with the 2021 questionnaire cycle, COVID-19 infection and related illness will be included in the list of health conditions.

The BWHS has also partnered with other organizations and health studies to form the Coronavirus Pandemic Epidemiology (COPE) consortium. Through the consortium, the BWHS is encouraging participants and their social networks to download a smartphone application that functions as a coronavirus-symptom tracker (https://covid.joinzoe.com/us-2). The app will enable public health professionals and researchers to collect data on the spread of coronavirus infection and symptoms. The overall goal is to identify factors related to coronavirus symptoms and long-term health effects of the infection and its treatment.

Note

1. See *BWHS Publications*, https://www.bu.edu/bwhs/research/publications/.

References

Adenekan, B., Pandey, A., McKenzie, S., Zizi, F., Casimir, G. J., & Jean-Louis, G. (2013). Sleep in America: Role of racial/ethnic differences. *Sleep Medicine Reviews, 17*(4), 255–262.

Agurs-Collins, T., Rosenberg, L., Makambi, K., Palmer, J. R., & Adams-Campbell, L. (2009). Dietary patterns and breast cancer risk in women participating in the Black Women's Health Study. *American Journal of Clinical Nutrition, 90*(3), 621–628.

Althani, A. A., Marei, H. E., Hamdi, W. S., Nasrallah, G. K., El Zowalaty, M. E., Al Khodor, S., Al-Asmakh, M., Abdel-Aziz, H., & Cenciarelli, C. (2016). Human microbiome and its association with health and diseases. *Journal of Cellular Physiology, 231*(8), 1688–1694.

Ashktorab, H., Kupfer, S. S., Brim, H., & Carethers, J. M. (2017). Racial disparity in gastrointestinal cancer risk. *Gastroenterology, 153*(4), 910–923.

Bacon, K. L., Stuver, S. O., Cozier, Y. C., Palmer, J. R., Rosenberg, L., & Ruiz-Narváez, E. A. (2017). Perceived racism and incident diabetes in the Black Women's Health Study. *Diabetologia, 60*(11), 2221–2225.

Baquet, C. R., Horm, J. W., Gibbs, T., & Greenwald, P. (1991). Socioeconomic factors and cancer incidence among blacks and whites. *Journal of the National Cancer Institute, 83*(8), 551–557.

Barber, L. E., Bertrand, K. A., Rosenberg, L., Battaglia, T. A., & Palmer, J. R. (2019). Pre- and perinatal factors and incidence of breast cancer in the Black Women's Health Study. *Cancer Causes &Control, 30*(1), 87–95.

Bertrand, K. A., Bethea, T. N., Adams-Campbell, L. L., Rosenberg, L., & Palmer, J. R. (2017). Differential patterns of risk factors for early-onset breast cancer by ER status in African American women. *Cancer Epidemiology, Biomarkers & Prevention, 26*(2), 270–277.

Bertrand, K. A., Gerlovin, H., Bethea, T. N., & Palmer, J. R. (2017). Pubertal growth and adult height in relation to breast cancer risk in African American women. *International Journal of Cancer, 141*(12), 2462–2470.

Best, A. F., Haozous, E. A., Berrington de Gonzalez, A., Chernyavskiy, P., Freedman, N. D., Hartge, P., Thomas, D., Rosenberg, P. S., & Shiels, M. S. (2018). Premature mortality projections in the USA through 2030: A modelling study. *Lancet Public Health, 3*(8), e374-e384.

Bethea, T. N., Palmer, J. R., Adams-Campbell, L. L., & Rosenberg, L. (2017). A prospective study of reproductive factors and exogenous hormone use in relation to ovarian cancer risk among Black women. *Cancer Causes & Control, 28*(5), 385–391.

Bethea, T. N., Palmer, J. R., Rosenberg, L., & Cozier, Y. C. (2016). Neighborhood socioeconomic status in relation to all-cause, cancer, and cardiovascular mortality in the Black Women's Health Study. *Ethnicity & Disease, 26*(2), 157–164.

Bethea, T. N., Rosenberg, L., Boggs, D. A., & Palmer, J. R. (2014). Menthol cigarettes in relation to breast cancer incidence in African American women. *Cancer Research, 72*(8 Suppl.), Abstract 664.

Bethea, T. N., Rosenberg, L., Charlot, M., O'Connor, G. T., Adams-Campbell, L. L., & Palmer, J. R. (2013). Obesity in relation to lung cancer incidence in African American women. *Cancer Causes & Control, 24*(9), 1695–1703.

Bethea, T. N., Zhou, E. S., Schernhammer, E. S., Castro-Webb, N., Cozier, Y. C., & Rosenberg, L. (2020). Perceived racial discrimination and risk of insomnia among middle-aged and elderly Black women. *Sleep, 43*(1).

Boggs, D. A., Ban, Y., Palmer, J. R., & Rosenberg, L. (2015). Higher diet quality is inversely associated with mortality in African-American women. *Journal of Nutrition, 145*(3), 547–554.

Boggs, D. A., Palmer, J. R., & Rosenberg, L. (2014). Bilateral oophorectomy and risk of cancer in African American women. *Cancer Causes Control, 25*(4), 507–513.

Boggs, D. A., Palmer, J. R., Spiegelman, D., Stampfer, M. J., Adams-Campbell, L. L., & Rosenberg, L. (2011). Dietary patterns and 14-y weight gain in African American women. *American Journal of Clinical Nutrition, 94*(1), 86–94.

Boggs, D. A., Palmer, J. R., Wise, L. A., Spiegelman, D., Stampfer, M. J., Adams-Campbell, L. L., & Rosenberg, L. (2010). Fruit and vegetable intake in relation to risk of breast cancer in the Black Women's Health Study. *American Journal of Epidemiology*, *172*(11), 1268–1279.

Boggs, D. A., Rosenberg, L., Coogan, P. F., Makambi, K. H., Adams-Campbell, L. L., & Palmer, J. R. (2013). Restaurant foods, sugar-sweetened soft drinks, and obesity risk among young African American women. *Ethnicity & Disease*, *23*(4), 445–451.

Boggs, D. A., Rosenberg, L., Cozier, Y. C., Wise, L. A., Coogan, P. F., Ruiz-Narváez, E. A., & Palmer, J. R. (2011). General and abdominal obesity and risk of death among Black women. *New England Journal of Medicine*, *365*(10), 901–908.

Bosco, J. L., Palmer, J. R., Boggs, D. A., Hatch, E. E., & Rosenberg, L. (2011). Regular aspirin use and breast cancer risk in US Black women. *Cancer Causes & Control*, *22*(11), 1553–1561.

Boyd, N. F., Guo, H., Martin, L. J., Sun, L., Stone, J., Fishell, E., Jong, R. A., Hislop, G., Chiarelli, A., Minkin, S., & Yaffe, M. J. (2007). Mammographic density and the risk and detection of breast cancer. *New England Journal of Medicine*, *356*(3), 227–236.

Boyd, N. F., Martin, L. J., Yaffe, M. J., & Minkin, S. (2011). Mammographic density and breast cancer risk: Current understanding and future prospects. *Breast Cancer Research*, *13*(6), 223.

Carey, L. A., Perou, C. M., Livasy, C. A., Dressler, L. G., Cowan, D., Conway, K., Karaca, G., Troester, M. A., Tse, C. K., Edmiston, S., Deming, S. L., Geradts, J., Cheang, M. C., Nielsen, T. O., Moorman, P. G., Earp, H. S., &Millikan, R. C. (2006). Race, breast cancer subtypes, and survival in the Carolina Breast Cancer Study. *JAMA*, *295*(21), 2492–2502.

Charlot, M., Castro-Webb, N., Bethea, T. N., Bertrand, K., Boggs, D. A., Denis, G. V., Adams-Campbell, L. L., Rosenberg, L., & Palmer, J. R. (2017). Diabetes and breast cancer mortality in Black women. *Cancer Causes & Control*, *28*(1), 61–67.

Conte, C. J. (2018, December 18). *Black Women's Health Study: Publications*. Retrieved from www.bu.edu/bwhs/research/publications

Coogan, P. F., Cozier, Y. C., Krishnan, S., Wise, L. A., Adams-Campbell, L. L., Rosenberg, L., & Palmer, J. R. (2010). Neighborhood socioeconomic status in relation to 10-year weight gain in the Black Women's Health Study. *Obesity (Silver Spring)*, *18*(10), 2064–2065.

Coogan, P. F., White, L. F., Evans, S. R., Adler, T. J., Hathaway, K. M., Palmer, J. R., & Rosenberg, L. (2011). Longitudinal assessment of urban form and weight gain in African-American women. *American Journal of Preventative Medicine*, *40*(4), 411–418.

Coogan, P. F., White, L. F., Jerrett, M., Brook, R. D., Su, J. G., Seto, E., Burnett, R., Palmer, J. R., & Rosenberg, L. (2012). Air pollution and incidence of hypertension and diabetes mellitus in black women living in Los Angeles. *Circulation*, *125*(6), 767–772.

Coughlin, S. S., Yoo, W., Whitehead, M. S., & Smith, S. A. (2015). Advancing breast cancer survivorship among African-American women. *Breast Cancer Research and Treatment, 153*(2), 253–261.

Cozier, Y. C., Barbhaiya, M., Castro-Webb, N., Conte, C., Tedeschi, S., Leatherwood, C., Costenbader, K. H., & Rosenberg, L. (2019a). A prospective study of obesity and risk of systemic lupus erythematosus (SLE) among Black women. *Seminars in Arthritis and Rheumatism, 48*(6), 1030–1034.

Cozier, Y. C., Barbhaiya, M., Castro-Webb, N., Conte, C., Tedeschi, S. K., Leatherwood, C., Costenbader, K. H., & Rosenberg, L. (2019b). Relationship of cigarette smoking and alcohol consumption to incidence of systemic lupus erythematosus in the Black Women's Health Study. *Arthritis Care & Research, 71*(5), 671–677.

Cozier, Y. C., Berman, J. S., Palmer, J. R., Boggs, D. A., Wise, L. A., & Rosenberg, L. (2012). Reproductive and hormonal factors in relation to incidence of sarcoidosis in US Black women: The Black Women's Health Study. *American Journal of Epidemiology, 176*(7), 635–641.

Cozier, Y. C., Coogan, P. F., Govender, P., Berman, J. S., Palmer, J. R., & Rosenberg, L. (2015). Obesity and weight gain in relation to incidence of sarcoidosis in US Black women: Data from the Black Women's Health Study. *Chest, 147*(4), 1086–1093.

Cozier, Y. C., Palmer, J. R., Horton, N. J., Fredman, L., Wise, L. A., & Rosenberg, L. (2007). Relation between neighborhood median housing value and hypertension risk among Black women in the United States. *American Journal of Public Health, 97*(4), 718–724.

Cozier, Y. C., Yu, J., Coogan, P. F., Bethea, T. N., Rosenberg, L., & Palmer, J. R. (2014). Racism, segregation, and risk of obesity in the Black Women's Health Study. *American Journal of Epidemiology, 179*(7), 875–883.

Cozier, Y. C., Yu, J., Wise, L. A., VanderWeele, T. J., Balboni, T. A., Argentieri, M. A., Rosenberg, L., Palmer, J. R., & Shields, A. E. (2018). Religious and spiritual coping and risk of incident hypertension in the Black Women's Health Study. *Annals of Behavioral Medicine, 52*(12), 989–998.

DeSantis, C. E., Fedewa, S. A., Goding Sauer, A., Kramer, J. L., Smith, R. A., & Jemal, A. (2016). Breast cancer statistics, 2015: Convergence of incidence rates between Black and white women. *CA: A Cancer Journal for Clinicians, 66*(1), 31–42.

DeSantis, C. E., Ma, J., Goding Sauer, A., Newman, L. A., & Jemal, A. (2017). Breast cancer statistics, 2017, racial disparity in mortality by state. *CA: A Cancer Journal for Clinicians, 67*(6), 439–448.

Dumas, O., Abramovitz, L., Wiley, A. S., Cozier, Y. C., & Camargo, C. A., Jr. (2016). Epidemiology of sarcoidosis in a prospective cohort study of U.S. women. *Annals of the American Thoracic Society, 13*(1), 67–71.

Formica, M. K., Palmer, J. R., Rosenberg, L., & McAlindon, T. E. (2003). Smoking, alcohol consumption, and risk of systemic lupus erythematosus in the Black Women's Health Study. *Journal of Rheumatology, 30*(6), 1222–1226.

Genkinger, J. M., Makambi, K. H., Palmer, J. R., Rosenberg, L., & Adams-Campbell, L. L. (2013). Consumption of dairy and meat in relation to breast cancer risk in the Black Women's Health Study. *Cancer Causes & Control, 24*(4), 675–684.

Gerlovin, H., Michaud, D. S., Cozier, Y. C., & Palmer, J. R. (2019). Oral health in relation to pancreatic cancer risk in African American women. *Cancer Epidemiology, Biomarkers & Prevention, 28*(4), 675–679.

Griswold, M. K., Crawford, S. L., Perry, D. J., Person, S. D., Rosenberg, L., Cozier, Y. C., & Palmer, J. R. (2018). Experiences of racism and breastfeeding initiation and duration among first-time mothers of the Black Women's Health Study. *Journal of Racial and Ethnic Health Disparities, 5*(6), 1180–1191.

James-Todd, T., Wise, L., Boggs, D., Rich-Edwards, J., Rosenberg, L., & Palmer, J. (2014). Preterm birth and subsequent risk of type 2 diabetes in Black women. *Epidemiology, 25*(6), 805–810.

Kerlikowske, K., Gard, C. C., Tice, J. A., Ziv, E., Cummings, S. R., Miglioretti, D. L., & Breast Cancer Surveillance Consortium. (2017). Risk factors that increase risk of estrogen receptor–positive and –negative breast cancer. *Journal of the National Cancer Institute, 109*(5).

Kramer, M. R., & Hogue, C. R. (2009). What causes racial disparities in very preterm birth? A biosocial perspective. *Epidemiologic Reviews, 31*, 84–98.

Krishnan, S., Coogan, P. F., Boggs, D. A., Rosenberg, L., & Palmer, J. R. (2010). Consumption of restaurant foods and incidence of type 2 diabetes in African American women. *American Journal of Clinical Nutrition, 91*(2), 465–471.

Krishnan, S., Cozier, Y. C., Rosenberg, L., & Palmer, J. R. (2010). Socioeconomic status and incidence of type 2 diabetes: results from the Black Women's Health Study. *American Journal of Epidemiology, 171*(5), 564–570.

Krishnan, S., Rosenberg, L., Djousse, L., Cupples, L. A., & Palmer, J. R. (2007). Overall and central obesity and risk of type 2 diabetes in U.S. Black women. *Obesity (Silver Spring), 15*(7), 1860–1866.

Krishnan, S., Rosenberg, L., & Palmer, J. R. (2009). Physical activity and television watching in relation to risk of type 2 diabetes: The Black Women's Health Study. *American Journal of Epidemiology, 169*(4), 428–434.

Krishnan, S., Rosenberg, L., Singer, M., Hu, F. B., Djousse, L., Cupples, L. A., & Palmer, J. R. (2007). Glycemic index, glycemic load, and cereal fiber intake and risk of type 2 diabetes in US Black women. *Archives of Internal Medicine, 167*(21), 2304–2309.

Li, S., Rosenberg, L., Palmer, J. R., Phillips, G. S., Heffner, L. J., & Wise, L. A. (2013). Central adiposity and other anthropometric factors in relation to risk of macrosomia in an African American population. *Obesity (Silver Spring)*, *21*(1), 178–184.

Li, S., Rosenberg, L., Wise, L. A., Boggs, D. A., LaValley, M., & Palmer, J. R. (2013). Age at natural menopause in relation to all-cause and cause-specific mortality in a follow-up study of US Black women. *Maturitas*, *75*(3), 246–252.

Lynch, S. V., & Pedersen, O. (2016). The human intestinal microbiome in health and disease. *New England Journal of Medicine*, *375*(24), 2369–2379.

Ma, H., Luo, J., Press, M. F., Wang, Y., Bernstein, L., & Ursin, G. (2009). Is there a difference in the association between percent mammographic density and subtypes of breast cancer? Luminal A and triple-negative breast cancer. *Cancer Epidemiology, Biomarkers & Prevention*, *18*(2), 479–485.

MacDorman, M. F. (2011). Race and ethnic disparities in fetal mortality, preterm birth, and infant mortality in the United States: An overview. *Seminars in Perinatology*, *35*(4), 200–208.

McCarthy, A. M., Keller, B. M., Pantalone, L. M., Hsieh, M. K., Synnestvedt, M., Conant, E. F., Armstrong, K., & Kontos, D. (2016). Racial differences in quantitative measures of area and volumetric breast density. *Journal of the National Cancer Institute*, *108*(10).

Nomura, S. J., Dash, C., Rosenberg, L., Palmer, J., & Adams-Campbell, L. L. (2016). Sedentary time and breast cancer incidence in African American women. *Cancer Causes & Control*, *27*(10), 1239–1252.

O'Keefe, E. B., Meltzer, J. P., & Bethea, T. N. (2015). Health disparities and cancer: Racial disparities in cancer mortality in the United States, 2000–2010. *Frontiers in Public Health*, *3*, 51.

Palmer, J. R., Adams-Campbell, L. L., Boggs, D. A., Wise, L. A., & Rosenberg, L. (2007). A prospective study of body size and breast cancer in Black women. *Cancer Epidemiology, Biomarkers & Prevention*, *16*(9), 1795–1802.

Palmer, J. R., Boggs, D. A., Adams-Campbell, L. L., & Rosenberg, L. (2008). Glycemic index, sweets, and breast cancer risk in the Black Women's Health Study [Abstract]. *American Journal of Epidemiology*, *167*(Suppl.), S235.

Palmer, J. R., Boggs, D. A., Adams-Campbell, L. L., & Rosenberg, L. (2009). Family history of cancer and risk of breast cancer in the Black Women's Health Study. *Cancer Causes & Control*, *20*(9), 1733–1737.

Palmer, J. R., Boggs, D. A., Krishnan, S., Hu, F. B., Singer, M., & Rosenberg, L. (2008). Sugar-sweetened beverages and incidence of type 2 diabetes mellitus in African American women. *Archives of Internal Medicine*, *168*(14), 1487–1492.

Palmer, J. R., Boggs, D. A., Wise, L. A., Adams-Campbell, L. L., & Rosenberg, L. (2012). Individual and neighborhood socioeconomic status in relation to breast cancer incidence in African-American women. *American Journal of Epidemiology*, *176*(12), 1141–1146.

Palmer, J. R., Boggs, D. A., Wise, L. A., Ambrosone, C. B., Adams-Campbell, L. L., & Rosenberg, L. (2011). Parity and lactation in relation to estrogen receptor negative breast cancer in African American women. *Cancer Epidemiology, Biomarkers & Prevention*, 20(9), 1883–1891.

Palmer, J. R., Castro-Webb, N., Bertrand, K., Bethea, T. N., & Denis, G. V. (2017). Type II diabetes and incidence of estrogen receptor negative breast cancer in African American women. *Cancer Research*, 77(22), 6462–6469.

Palmer, J. R., Gerlovin, H., Bethea, T. N., Bertrand, K. A., Holick, M. F., Ruiz-Narváez, E. N., Wise, L. A., Haddad, S. A., Adams-Campbell, L. L., Kaufman, H. W., Rosenberg, L., & Cozier, Y. C. (2016). Predicted 25-hydroxyvitamin D in relation to incidence of breast cancer in a large cohort of African American women. *Breast Cancer Research*, 18(1), 86.

Palmer, J. R., Wise, L. A., Horton, N. J., Adams-Campbell, L. L., & Rosenberg, L. (2003). Dual effect of parity on breast cancer risk in African-American women. *Journal of the National Cancer Institute*, 95(6), 478–483.

Park, H. K., Ruterbusch, J. J., & Cote, M. L. (2017). Recent trends in ovarian cancer incidence and relative survival in the United States by race/ethnicity and histologic subtypes. *Cancer Epidemiology, Biomarkers & Prevention*, 26(10), 1511–1518.

Patient-Centered Outcomes Research Institute. (n.d.). *Comparing ways to treat insomnia among black women*. Retrieved January 15, 2019, from https://www.pcori.org/research-results/2017/comparing-ways-treat-insomnia-among-black-women

Petroni, M., Hill, D., Younes, L., Barkman, L., Howard, S., Howell, I. B., Mirowsky, J., & Collins, M. B. (2020). Hazardous air pollutant exposure as a contributing factor to COVID-19 mortality in the United States. *Environmental Research Letters*, 15(9), Article 0940a9.

Radin, R. G., Palmer, J. R., Rosenberg, L., Kumanyika, S. K., & Wise, L. A. (2010). Dietary glycemic index and load in relation to risk of uterine leiomyomata in the Black Women's Health Study. *American Journal of Clinical Nutrition*, 91(5), 1281–1288.

Raifman, M. A., & Raifman, J. R. (2020). Disparities in the population at risk of severe illness from COVID-19 by race/ethnicity and income. *American Journal of Preventative Medicine*, 59(1): 137–139.

Razzaghi, H., Troester, M. A., Gierach, G. L., Olshan, A. F., Yankaskas, B. C., & Millikan, R. C. (2013). Association between mammographic density and basal-like and luminal A breast cancer subtypes. *Breast Cancer Research*, 15(5), R76.

Rosenberg, L., Boggs, D. A., Adams-Campbell, L. L., & Palmer, J. R. (2007). Hair relaxers not associated with breast cancer risk: Evidence from the Black Women's Health Study. *Cancer Epidemiology, Biomarkers & Prevention*, 16(5), 1035–1037.

Rosenberg, L., Boggs, D. A., Bethea, T. N., Wise, L. A., Adams-Campbell, L. L., & Palmer, J. R. (2013). A prospective study of smoking and breast cancer risk among African-American women. *Cancer Causes & Control, 24*(12), 2207–2215.

Rosenberg, L., Boggs, D. A., Wise, L. A., Adams-Campbell, L. L., & Palmer, J. R. (2010). Oral contraceptive use and estrogen/progesterone receptor-negative breast cancer among African American women. *Cancer Epidemiology, Biomarkers & Prevention, 19*(8), 2073–2079.

Rosenberg, L., Kipping-Ruane, K. L., Boggs, D. A., & Palmer, J. R. (2013). Physical activity and the incidence of obesity in young African-American women. *American Journal of Preventative Medicine, 45*(3), 262–268.

Rosenberg, L., Palmer, J. R., Adams-Campbell, L. L., & Rao, R. S. (1999). Obesity and hypertension among college-educated Black women in the United States. *Journal of Human Hypertension, 13*(4), 237–241.

Rosenberg, L., Palmer, J. R., Bethea, T. N., Ban, Y., Kipping-Ruane, K., & Adams-Campbell, L. L. (2014). A prospective study of physical activity and breast cancer incidence in African-American women. *Cancer Epidemiology, Biomarkers & Prevention, 23*(11), 2522–2531.

Rosenberg, L., Palmer, J. R., Rao, R. S., & Adams-Campbell, L. L. (1999). Risk factors for coronary heart disease in African American women. *American Journal of Epidemiology, 150*(9), 904–909.

Rosenberg, L., Palmer, J. R., Wise, L. A., & Adams-Campbell, L. L. (2006). A prospective study of female hormone use and breast cancer among Black women. *Archives of Internal Medicine, 166*(7), 760–765.

Rosenberg, L., Palmer, J. R., Wise, L. A., Horton, N. J., Kumanyika, S. K., & Adams-Campbell, L. L. (2003). A prospective study of the effect of childbearing on weight gain in African-American women. *Obesity Research, 11*(12), 1526–1535.

Ruiter, M. E., Decoster, J., Jacobs, L., & Lichstein, K. L. (2011). Normal sleep in African-Americans and Caucasian-Americans: A meta-analysis. *Sleep Medicine, 12*(3), 209–214.

Ruiz-Narváez, E. A., Palmer, J. R., Gerlovin, H., Wise, L. A., Vimalananda, V. G., Rosenzweig, J. L., & Rosenberg, L. (2014). Birth weight and risk of type 2 diabetes in the Black Women's Health Study: Does adult BMI play a mediating role? *Diabetes Care, 37*(9), 2572–2578.

Schabath, M. B., Cress, D., & Munoz-Antonia, T. (2016). Racial and Ethnic Differences in the Epidemiology and Genomics of Lung Cancer. *Cancer Control, 23*(4), 338–346.

Sineshaw, H. M., Gaudet, M., Ward, E. M., Flanders, W. D., DeSantis, C., Lin, C. C., & Jemal, A. (2014). Association of race/ethnicity, socioeconomic status, and breast cancer subtypes in the National Cancer Data Base (2010–2011). *Breast Cancer Research and Treatment, 145*(3), 753–763.

Snowden, L. R., & Graaf, G. (2021). COVID-19, social determinants past, present, and future, and African Americans' health. *Journal of Racial and Ethnic Health Disparities*, 8(1):12–20.

Sponholtz, T. R., Bethea, T. N., Ruiz-Narváez, E. A., Boynton-Jarrett, R., Palmer, J. R., Rosenberg, L., & Wise, L. A. (2021). Night shift work and fecundability in late reproductive-aged African American women. *Journal of Women's Health*, 30(1), 137–144.

Sponholtz, T. R., Wise, L. A., Hatch, E. E., Palmer, J. R., Rosenberg, L., & Adams-Campbell, L. L. (2018). Exogenous hormone use and endometrial cancer in U.S. Black women. *Cancer Epidemiology, Biomarkers & Prevention*, 27(5), 558–565.

Stewart, E. A., Cookson, C. L., Gandolfo, R. A., & Schulze-Rath, R. (2017). Epidemiology of uterine fibroids: A systematic review. *BJOG*, 124(10), 1501–1512.

Taylor, S. E., & Holden, K. B. (2009). The health status of Black women. In R. L. Braithwaite, S. E. Taylor, & H. M. Treadwell (Eds.), *Health issues in the Black community* (3rd ed., pp. 55–71). Jossey-Bass.

Taylor, T. R., Williams, C. D., Makambi, K. H., Mouton, C., Harrell, J. P., Cozier, Y., Palmer, J. R., Rosenberg, L., & Adams-Campbell, L. L. (2007). Racial discrimination and breast cancer incidence in US Black women: the Black Women's Health Study. *American Journal of Epidemiology*, 166(1), 46–54.

Tukey, M. H., Berman, J. S., Boggs, D. A., White, L. F., Rosenberg, L., & Cozier, Y. C. (2013). Mortality among African American women with sarcoidosis: Data from the Black Women's Health Study. *Sarcoidosis Vasculitis and Diffuse Lung Disease*, 30(2), 128–133.

Ursin, G., Ma, H., Wu, A. H., Bernstein, L., Salane, M., Parisky, Y. R., Astrahan, M., Siozon, C. C., & Pike, M. C. (2003). Mammographic density and breast cancer in three ethnic groups. *Cancer Epidemiology, Biomarkers & Prevention*, 12(4), 332–338.

van Dam, R. M., Hu, F. B., Rosenberg, L., Krishnan, S., & Palmer, J. R. (2006). Dietary calcium and magnesium, major food sources, and risk of type 2 diabetes in U.S. Black women. *Diabetes Care*, 29(10), 2238–2243.

Vimalananda, V. G., Palmer, J. R., Gerlovin, H., Wise, L. A., Rosenzweig, J. L., Rosenberg, L., & Ruiz-Narváez, E. A. (2014). Depressive symptoms, antidepressant use, and the incidence of diabetes in the Black Women's Health Study. *Diabetes Care*, 37(8), 2211–2217.

Vimalananda, V. G., Palmer, J. R., Gerlovin, H., Wise, L. A., Rosenzweig, J. L., Rosenberg, L., & Ruiz-Narváez, E. A. (2015). Night-shift work and incident diabetes among African-American women. *Diabetologia*, 58(4), 699–706.

Williams, D. R. (2002). Racial/ethnic variations in women's health: The social embeddedness of health. *American Journal of Public Health*, 92(4), 588–597.

Wise, L. A., Palmer, J. R., Boggs, D. A., Adams-Campbell, L. L., & Rosenberg, L. (2011). Abuse victimization and risk of breast cancer in the Black Women's Health Study (corrected). *Cancer Causes & Control*, 22(4), 659–669.

Wise, L. A., Palmer, J. R., Harlow, B. L., Spiegelman, D., Stewart, E. A., Adams-Campbell, L. L., & Rosenberg, L. (2004). Reproductive factors, hormonal contraception, and risk of uterine leiomyomata in African-American women: A prospective study. *American Journal of Epidemiology, 159*(2), 113–123.

Wise, L. A., Palmer, J. R., Heffner, L. J., & Rosenberg, L. (2010). Prepregnancy body size, gestational weight gain, and risk of preterm birth in African-American women. *Epidemiology, 21*(2), 243–252.

Wise, L. A., Palmer, J. R., & Rosenberg, L. (2013). Body size and time-to-pregnancy in black women. *Human Reproduction, 28*(10), 2856–2864.

Wise, L. A., Palmer, J. R., Spiegelman, D., Harlow, B. L., Stewart, E. A., Adams-Campbell, L. L., & Rosenberg, L. (2005). Influence of body size and body fat distribution on risk of uterine leiomyomata in U.S. Black women. *Epidemiology, 16*(3), 346–354.

Wise, L. A., Radin, R. G., Palmer, J. R., Kumanyika, S. K., Boggs, D. A., & Rosenberg, L. (2011). Intake of fruit, vegetables, and carotenoids in relation to risk of uterine leiomyomata. *American Journal of Clinical Nutrition, 94*(6), 1620–1631.

Wise, L. A., Radin, R. G., Palmer, J. R., Kumanyika, S. K., & Rosenberg, L. (2010). A prospective study of dairy intake and risk of uterine leiomyomata. *American Journal of Epidemiology, 171*(2), 221–232.

Zhu, N., Zhang, D., Wang, W., Li, X., Yang, B., Song, J., Zhao, X., Huang, B., Shi, W., Lu, R., Niu, P., Zhan, F., Ma, X., Wang, D., Xu, W., Wu, G., Gao, G. F., Tan, W.; China Novel Coronavirus Investigating and Research Team. (2020). A novel coronavirus from patients with pneumonia in China, 2019. *New England Journal of Medicine, 382*(8), 727–733.

Chapter 6

The Swelling Wave of Oppression

An Intersectional Study to Evaluate Health Challenges of Self-Identified Black Queer Women in the American South

JAYME CANTY

With several documented works on Black women as a demographic group, questions are still evolving regarding their health status. As a whole, Black women living in the United States are particularly vulnerable to life-altering health problems, which include but are not limited to HIV/AIDS, heart disease, breast cancer, infant mortality, obesity, and substance abuse. However, the Black female experience is not monolithic but composed of a myriad of identities that are not limited to race and gender, such as Black queer women. According to Kimberly Arriola, Christina Borba, and Winifred Thompson, Black queer women experience social stigmas associated with sexual orientation. Arriola et al. (2007) argue that this additional hurdle of sexual marginalization may cause Black queer women to experience poorer health than their heterosexual counterparts. In comparison to Black heterosexual women, Black queer women are less likely to seek preventative health services, less likely to have health insurance, more likely to experience obesity, and more likely to engage in alcohol and tobacco use. Further, Black queer women have shorter life expectancies, higher rates of heart disease, and lower physical activity (Ramsey et al., 2010).

Unfortunately, there are limited studies or theoretical frameworks within the public health field that focus specifically on this population. While studies are starting to uncover the health challenges of Black queer women, there is not much of an explanation for why this population encounters certain health difficulties. Research on the health challenges of lesbian or queer women primarily focuses on White women. Because studies on women's physical health are limited to the realm of obstetrics and gynecology, they often define women's health care in terms of their relationships with men, thus marginalizing White lesbian women (Rosser, 1993). The understanding of Black women's health relies on the experiences of Black heterosexual women (Welch, 2003). The growing public health research focusing on Black queer persons focuses primarily on HIV diagnosis and prevention in Black gay men (Peterson & Jones, 2009). Black queer women are often overlooked within the public health community, subsumed under "sexual-minority women" or "queer women of color" (Mays et al., 2002). Several articles may focus on queer persons but rarely give special attention to specific queer communities of color (Bowen et al., 2008; Boehmer et al., 2007). It appears as though many public health scholars focus primarily on Black gay men but place Black queer women alongside other queer women or with Black heterosexual women, rarely giving them special consideration.

Black queer women are often overlooked and rarely investigated within the public health realm. Public health scholars have uncovered some health challenges queer persons of color experience but rarely investigate their root causes or recognize how specific intersectional identities within certain geographic locations impact health status. This article aims to reposition southern Black queer women from the margin to the center of public health studies to determine what obstacles within the American South lead to their health challenges. Furthermore, this work addresses the need to utilize the intersectional approach in evaluating the health disparities southern Black queer women encounter. This public health approach opens the door for uncovering the reasons Black queer women are more susceptible to health difficulties in comparison to their heterosexual sisters.

The Necessity of Using an Intersectional Approach to Uncover the Health Challenges of Southern Black Queer Women

This work employed an intersectional approach to health disparities instead of the biomedical lens to health because Black queer women cannot separate their sexuality from their race, gender, class, and geographic location (Canty, 2017). All of these identities intersect with one another and provide an inclusive, complex perspective to the world around these individuals. Geographic location constitutes an additional identity label that affects the lives of those on the sexual margin. Previous public health research on queer persons of color or Black women has employed more of a biomedical approach to determine what health challenges they face.

The biomedical lens answers the question of *how* persons acquire certain health challenges and disparities, while the intersectional approach tries to answer *why* certain persons are vulnerable to certain health ailments. The intersectional approach opens the door for a multidimensional analysis and its influence upon the daily lives of individuals with overlapping identities (Canty, 2017). The intersectional approach provides public health scholars the opportunity to view personal identity from a multifaceted perspective that considers race, gender, and class as more than biological markers. Instead, these elements are representative of the intersectional identity. Additionally, this approach investigates how intersectional identities are not simply a personal investigation; it exposes the ways macro and micro systems as well as power systems impact one's lived experiences.

Intersectionality itself is the study of multilayered identities creating a new identity. It does not take an additive approach of including multiple identities arbitrarily; instead, intersectionality creates interlocking and overlapping identities that rely on one another to determine one's identity overall. All of these identities intersect with one another and provide an inclusive, complex perspective on the world around the individual. The intersectional approach opens the door for how intersectional identity manifests within one's life. Southern Black queer women fit within this paradigm because their intersectional identities represent an internal identity practice as well as an evaluation of external systems of power, particularly as it relates to heterosexism and homophobia within the American South. This public health approach opens the door to investigating the ways the American South becomes an identity marker that could ultimately impact the health challenges of already marginalized populations.

Even with the intersectional approach, there are limited theoretical frameworks to help address the health challenges Black queer women face (Canty, 2017). Black queer women's health is often subsumed under the issues of Black women. Previous intersectional approaches to Black women's health have included social and economic systems that hinder overall health status and the macro- and micro-level stressors Black women face daily (Mullings, 2002; Geronimus, 2001). While intersectional theoretical frameworks such as Sojourner Syndrome and the weathering theory offer powerful explanatory tools to account for the health challenges of Black women, the tools only include the intersectional identities of race, class, and gender. Realities of sexuality within a certain geographic location provide an additional stressor for Black queer women, which manifests in their health status. For Black queer women, these intersectional theories provide a partial explanation for their health disparities. I introduce the "swelling wave of oppression" theory as an intersectional model to explain why Black queer women are more vulnerable to health challenges compared to Black heterosexual women (Canty, 2017). While this theory of the "swelling wave" appears similar to intersectionality, it inherits different components.

New Intersectional Framework: The Swelling Wave of Oppression

This study proposes a new model that is inclusive of sexuality and geographic location as additional explanatory tools to already existing theories of intersectional identity (Mullings, 2002; Geronimus, 2001). The swelling wave theory provides an intersectional lens for evaluating how social and economic experiences could impact the health challenges of Black queer women. Unlike the biomedical approach to health research, the intersectional approach addresses how systems of oppression on both the macro and micro levels impact one's health status. The biomedical approach focuses more on the behavioral aspect of health but disregards how multilayered identities can influence an individual's health outcome (Weber & Parra-Medina, 2003). The intersectional approach to health provides an opportunity for humanists and social scientists to evaluate individuals' behavior as well as the social and environmental factors that contribute to their overall health status.

While this discussion may not directly address all the health outcomes that can occur, this theory and the intersectional approach shed light on the social and economic challenges that impede one's health. This research started as an attempt to evaluate what social, economic, and political challenges influence the health status of Black queer and heterosexual women in the American South. This theory is grounded on the data provided, which focused primarily on social and economic factors that influenced health outcomes, not necessarily determining what those health outcomes were. The theory also infers that one must evaluate an individual's experience in order to understand the possible health outcomes that can occur. This study employed the intersectional approach, extending the research beyond the biomedical realm to determine what factors contribute to the health challenges of Black queer women.

Environmental science research shows that there is a "swell" effect on ocean waves when air energies mix with bodies of water, such as oceans, seas, or lakes. Water swells are derived from a series of water waves, mostly multiple storm waves, and distant water systems. Prior to the swell, the body of water is at rest. Once the body of water comes into contact with friction, such as an object thrown into the body of water or wind energies, the body of water moves from its original location to another. The swelling occurs when multiple water waves move away from the original source, causing larger water movements and energies. The stronger the winds at the source area, the bigger the swell and the further it will travel. The wind waves accelerate in speed as they combine and merge with other waves.

Depending on the energy of the air, waves can be very large or small. The more energy in the air, the larger the wave, and the less energy in the air, the smaller the wave. The larger waves are more likely to create swells, where they travel at faster speeds and farther distances and often merge with other waves. The swelling wave is not easily recognized by the average viewer unless they are looking for it. In many instances, the swelling ocean wave looks similar to locally produced wave formations. On the surface, local and swell waves share like characteristics, but individuals searching for the swell waves will recognize the differences between swell and local waves. Typically, environmental scientists apply mathematics and physics to explain this phenomenon. The swelling wave theory can also be applied to humanistic and social science research.

Certain components distinguish the experiences of Black queer women from those of Black heterosexual women, such as the stress associated with sexuality and heterosexism Black queer women experience in the America South. Black queer women are more likely to view sexual orientation as a stressor in comparison to Black heterosexual women in the American South (Canty, 2017). In fact, Southern Black queer women rank sexual orientation as a significant identity stressor on a level similar to race, class, and gender (Canty, 2017). One of the main reasons Southern

Black queer women view sexual orientation as a stressor is due to the heterosexism experienced in the American South.

Jung and Smith (1993) describe *heterosexism* as a "reasoned system of bias regarding sexual orientation. It denotes prejudice in favor of heterosexual people and connotes prejudice against bisexual and, especially, homosexual people" (p. 13). Just like racism and sexism, heterosexism is a daily reality for Black queer women in various social spaces such as with family and at church, two social spaces that many Black persons in the American South encounter more. Encountering heterosexism in various social areas in the American South reemphasizes Black queer women's marginalized status. Yet the notion of heterosexism in the American South must include the *assumption* of heterosexuality within social and economic spaces. In the American South, heterosexuality is preferred and assumed because it aligns with the religious doctrines that are manifested within any Southern state, particularly in rural spaces. Black queer women in the American South not only deal with being Black women in the South but must also deal with exaggerated heterosexism based on this geographic location. This assumption of heterosexuality forms an additional energy in the swell wave for Southern Black queer women.

When an individual is in the ocean, they quickly recognize the different intensities of the waves. They prepare themselves for the waves coming toward them. Without this awareness to combat the waves, an individual continues to drown without much relief. Similarly, Southern Black queer women recognize and find ways to prepare themselves for waves of oppression. Without the appropriate assistance or preparation, one can drown under the waves of oppression they face. This theory suggests that Black queer women are not adequately prepared for the waves of oppression related to heterosexism in the American South. Black queer women may be more equipped to deal with the waves of oppressions based on race, class, and gender but struggle with preparing for the waves of oppression related to their sexual orientation (Canty, 2017). This lack of preparation causes Black queer women to become more vulnerable to health challenges in comparison to their heterosexual peers. While Black women as a whole experience drowning, this theory argues that Southern Black queer women are more likely to drown based on their experiences with their sexual identities in the American South. Several factors cause southern Black queer women to metaphorically drown under these swell waves: complexities associated with vacillating queer identity, the realities of the Christian Black church, limited lessons from maternal figures, limited social support networks, and economic obstacles associated with queer identity.

Complexities of Vacillating Black Queer Identity

For Southern Black queer women, identity and gender presentation play a significant role in the creation of the swell wave. Southern Black queer women are attached to their Blackness while also in constant realization of their sexual orientation within the Black community. This population recognizes that their social identity creates a marginalization within the larger LGBTQIA+ community due to their race as well as within the Black community as a result of their sexuality. In many cases, Southern Black queer women emphasize how their identity vacillates based on who they are with at any given time. They are considered "the gay one" within the Black community while simultaneously labeled as "the Black one" in LGBTQIA+ communities. Masculine-identified queer women ("studs") report being perceived as queer first and Black women second, whereas cisgender queer women ("femmes") are more likely to identify themselves as Black women first, then queer. This vacillating identity causes studs to be more visible within the White queer and Black heterosexual communities because they "wear" their sexualities. Likewise, femmes are less visible within the White queer and Black communities because their feminine presentation leads to the assumption of heterosexual identity.

This complex, vacillating identity impacts Black queer women's inter-actions within various social institutions, such as family and church. These social spaces are significant in the lives of all Black persons, especially in the American South. Consequently, Black queer women are relegated to a metaphorical closet in these spaces as a result of their vacillating identities, where they remain invisible in the Black community based on their sexuality and in the LGBTQIA+ community based on their race. This vacillating identity, assumption of heterosexual identity, and marginalization in several communities causes them to drown under the waves of heterosexism.

Realities of Sexuality within the Christian Black Church in the American South

The Southern Christian Black church (hereafter referred to as "the Church") is the foundational social institution. It is not by happenstance that the American South is known as the Bible Belt. This name reflects the large population of Protestant religious organizations and the evolution of the evangelical revivalism that developed in the American South during the antebellum era. Unlike other regions in the United States, the American South has a unique history associated with the Protestant religion and the Church as a result of the Civil War (Harvey, 2015; Raboteau, 1978). The Church became a safe space for enslaved Africans because many of these White Southern churches started to include enslaved African populations (Harvey, 2015). As a result of the Civil War, the Church then became an autonomous organization for formerly enslaved Africans in the South, evolving for generations as a space of political autonomy, educational attainment, and economic prosperity for Black people in America.

The Church is a multifaceted space that indoctrinates many Black persons, regardless of sexuality. It became the space that provided formal education for Blacks, economic assistance, social interactions, and political affiliations. The Church is more than a religious place to worship; it was an institution of socialization that continues to socialize Black persons about Southern culture and ideologies (Harvey, 2015). Some of these ideologies include inequalities associated with gender and sexuality. For Black queer women, the Church becomes the first social institution, outside of family, where they are introduced to homophobia, limited gender constructions, and the politics of respectability through dress and appearance. Without these heteronormative gender presentations intact, an individual may be ostracized within the Church community. Because of the Church, Southern Black queer women experience additional pressures to conform to religious virtues associated with femininity. If a stud chooses not to embody femininity through dress or behavior, she may be subject to scrutiny, or even contempt. The Church can be a safe haven for cisgender, heterosexual Black persons in the American South but serves as an obstacle for Black queer women. This obstacle amplifies the wave, causing them to drown without adequate support or preparation.

Limited Lessons from Maternal Figures

Black maternal figures provide Black women with the preparation necessary to survive and balance in the swell waves, and they pass down methods of coping against multiple waves of oppression through measures of health prevention. The knowledge from maternal figures serves as a model for Black female health. Even if Black heterosexual women do not go to the doctor often, there is an understanding that a Black woman *should* seek preventive health care to improve their overall health status. Though the knowledge from previous generations may not always be advantageous, it is still information necessary for Black women's survival and equips Black women for the waves oppression they may encounter. Black heterosexual women may find means to cope with the stress of either trying to emulate their maternal figures or improve their lives so they do not perpetuate the same negative health behaviors and outcomes of their maternal figures. Metaphorically, Black heterosexual women are the better-equipped swimmers who can combat the hefty waves of oppression because of the generational knowledge they have received from maternal figures.

Consequently, Black queer women remain vulnerable to further health ailments because they do not necessarily receive this information from maternal figures. Black heterosexual women are more likely to credit their maternal figures for providing them with knowledge regarding preventive health care (Canty, 2017). Because of the social and economic challenges Southern Black queer women face, they may not use their maternal figures as models for health because they provide limited tools for their survival. While Southern Black queer women may be equipped to deal with issues of race, gender, and class within social, economic, and political structures, they may not be able to ascertain how to combat issues associated with heterosexism. This limited generational preparation for combatting the heterosexist wave of oppression can increase the likelihood of Southern Black queer women drowning in the waves of oppression overall. This limited knowledge from maternal figures may shed light on their inability to combat certain waves of oppression, causing them to be vulnerable to health challenges.

Limited Social Support Networks

The limited availability of social support networks causes Black queer women to be vulnerable to the waves of oppression. Families are significant social support networks and socialization agents. Black queer women may receive limited support from their families because they cannot fully disclose their lifestyles within their heteronormative families. Often, Black queer women do not disclose specifics of their personal lives to their families because the families may not be able to provide emotional support for the problems they face in terms of sexuality. Southern Black queer women find stress from their familial relationships as a result of their sexual orientation. This obstacle causes an additional strain, adding to waves of oppressions faced.

Because Southern Black queer women find limited support from their biological families, they are more likely to seek support from sources outside of family to alleviate tensions that may arise from their sexual orientation. For Black queer women, their significant others, friends, and mentors are more essential as support systems, while family and church are secondary. These social outlets alleviate the mental and emotional stress they experience from dealing with their biological families. With limited support from the Church, family, and some friends, Black queer women may find it a challenge to confront their waves of oppression. Black queer women recognize the difficulty of creating their own safety nets before they encounter the waves of oppression. Without this assistance, they may drown under the waves.

Economic Strains to Queer Identity

The social experiences of Southern Black queer women often manifest within the economic realm as well. Similar to other Black female populations, Southern Black queer women experience financial hardships associated with limited generational knowledge of finances and burdens associated with being the sole breadwinners of families. Limitations via economic hardships among Black women lead directly to their poor health statuses (Canty, 2017). If one cannot afford basic health care, then they cannot receive the preventive treatment necessary for maintaining wellness. Regardless of sexuality, preventive healthcare is considered a luxury for Southern Black women because they are typically responsible for the financial burdens of their families. This financial burden may cause additional health strains due to the "strong Black woman" persona many Black women adopt as a means of survival (Mullings, 2002).

Southern Black queer women's economic strain occurs also within the workplace, related to queer visibility. The concept of passing becomes an obstacle within the workplace as Southern Black queer women attempt to exist in a space that assumes heterosexuality. Typically, the notion of passing relates to Black persons with lighter complexion or mixed ancestry who may pass for another ethnic or racial group in order to gain social mobility. Passing in this sense extends to sexual identity as well. Gender presentation often correlates to the ability to pass as heterosexual.

For example, cisgender queer women can pass for heterosexual women because their physical appearance and behavior align with the pervasive, albeit limited, social constructions of femininity and womanhood. The person who performs their biologically assigned gender may receive some benefits. This presentation of gender and passing for heterosexual often determines how Southern Black queer women are treated at work. For femmes, passing becomes a shield of survival in the workplace in the South, while the workplace acts as a space of daily discomfort for studs (Canty, 2017). At work, Black queer women are constantly "coming out" to coworkers through daily small talk. Discussions at the water cooler or in the break room can become a daily traumatic experience for some Black queer women who are not visibly queer or out at their places of employment. Queer persons of color living in the South may not be out at their workplaces due to fear of judgment and even termination.

Conclusion

The swelling wave of oppression theory suggests that Black women are different and therefore deal with social and economic issues differently. Given this knowledge, public health and humanity scholars can start addressing Black women similar to the way the environmental scientist examines the swell and local waves. While there are many similarities among Black women, the differences that exist create larger waves of oppression. This research is not meant to create a dichotomy between the two populations of Black women examined in this study. Instead, it invites public health scholars and medical experts to pay closer attention to the differences between these two populations of Black women and how these differences cause variations in the health challenges they face. With the knowledge of these different lived experiences and the stressors that come with them, public health scholarship can start to find larger problems that connect all marginalized populations. This swelling wave framework sets the stage for evaluating how Southern Black queer women view their daily experiences and its influence on their overall health statuses.

The swelling wave theory arises from an intersectional lens but varies from intersectionality itself. Intersectionality is an *interracial* aspect, describing how one experiences gender differently based on other identity markers such as race, ethnicity, and gender expression. Intersectionality critically responds to the white mainstream feminist notion that experiences with gender are monolithic and forces gender scholars to recognize that racial and ethnic identities change the way gender is played out. Intersectionality evolved into a theory that focuses on the multilayered differences within gender identity. It is not an additive approach to identity but instead relies on the idea that gender identity is mixed with other identities, creating a new identity. Intersectionality also relies on the analysis of macro and micro systems of oppression. The swelling wave theory is an *intraracial* model looking at differences that exist within marginalized communities. Because this study was based on a comparative analysis within a specific racial and gender community, it does not necessarily align with what is traditionally viewed as intersectionality because it recognizes differences within racially marginalized communities. While this model relies heavily on the notion of intersectionality for the purpose of determining the significance of differences and varying experiences with oppression, it focuses on differences that exist within marginalized communities themselves. It opens the door for evaluating how other identities, such as transgender, gender-nonbinary, and bisexual identities, impact one's health challenges. This model can be used as a foundation for other queer and transgender persons of color to evaluate what lived experiences impact their health status.

The theory also suggests that an individual's personal experiences may yield their overall health status. The experiences of Southern Black women, both heterosexual and queer, are unique and open the discussion about their health challenges. Intersectional and public health scholars cannot discuss the health status of marginalized communities without addressing the social, economic, and political obstacles they encounter in their lives. While other intersectional theories investigate the challenges Black women face in terms of racism, sexism, and classism, the swelling wave of oppression model further reiterates how Black queer women's daily experiences with sexual identity shed light on their health challenges. In order for public health researchers and health-care professionals to tackle solutions to Black women's health, they cannot treat Black women as a monolithic group. The experiences of Black queer women challenge public health scholars not to fall into the one-pill-fits-all remedy. Each identity variation requires a different prescription.

Societal norms vary based on geographic location, which can impact the health challenges Black women face. There should be closer attention paid to the impact of geographic location in the daily lives of Black women, because it may expose the differences in their daily experiences and the obstacles they encounter in seeking medical attention. The American South creates a unique experience for several marginalized populations, particularly as it relates to the impact of religious institutions upon economic and political spaces. The geographic location of the American South impacts the complexities with navigating sexual identity. Further investigation needs to be placed upon the ways the American South impacts the health challenges of Southern Black queer women and the ways that the American South acts as an intersectional identity marker. Researchers must deconstruct what this location means for Black queer women.

Public health and intersectional scholars cannot have one all-encompassing conversation about Black women because the experiences of Black women vary based on several additional identity markers, such as sexuality and geographic location. Black queer women challenge the conventional notion that there is a monolithic experience to being a Black woman and living in the American South. Exposing the experiences of these marginalized women becomes the starting point to finding a solution to the obstacles that impede their health.

References

Arriola, K. R. J., Borba, C. P. C., & Thompson, W. W. (2007). The health status of black women: Breaking through the glass ceiling. *Black Women, Gender, and Families*, 1(2), 1–23.

Boehmer, U., Bowen, D. J., & Bauer, G. R. (2007). Overweight and obesity in sexual-minority women: Evidence from population-based data. *American Journal of Public Health*, 97(6), 1134–1140.

Bowen, D. J., Balsam, K. F., & Ender, S. R. (2008). A review of obesity issues in sexual minority women. *Obesity (Silver Spring)*, 16(2), 221–228.

Canty, J. N. (2017). *The "swelling wave of oppression": An intersectional approach to the health challenges of Black heterosexual and Black queer women in the American South* [Doctoral dissertation, Clark Atlanta University]. ProQuest Dissertations and Theses.

Geronimus, A. T. (2001). Understanding and eliminating racial inequalities in women's health in the United States: The role of the weathering conceptual framework. *Journal of the American Medical Women's Association*, 56(4), 133–150.

Harvey, P. (2015). Race, culture, and religion in the American South. In J. Barton (Ed.), *Oxford research encyclopedia of religion*, Oxford University Press.

Jung, P. B., & Smith, R. F. (1993). *Heterosexism: An ethical challenge*. State University of New York Press.

Mays, V. M., Yancey, A. K., Cochran, S. D., Weber, M., & Fielding, J. E. (2002). Heterogeneity of health disparities among African American, Hispanic, and Asian American women: Unrecognized influences of sexual orientation. *American Journal of Public Health, 92*(4), 632–639.

Mullings, L. (2002). The Sojourner Syndrome: Race, class, and gender in health and illness. *Voices, 6*(1), 32–36.

Peterson, J. L., & Jones, K. T. (2009). HIV prevention for Black men who have sex with men in the United States. *American Journal of Public Health, 99*(6), 976–980.

Raboteau, A. J. (1978). *Slave religion: The "invisible institution" in the antebellum South.* Oxford University Press.

Ramsey, F., Hill, M. J., & Kellam, C. (2010). *Black Lesbians matter: An examination of the unique experiences, perspectives, and priorities of the Black Lesbian community.* Zuna Institute.

Rosser, S. V. (1993). Ignored, overlooked, or subsumed: Research on lesbian health and health care. *National Women's Studies Association Journal, 5*(2), 183–203.

Weber, L., & Parra-Medina, D. (2003). Intersectionality and women's health: Charting a path to eliminating health disparities. *Advances in Gender Research, 7*, 181–230.

Welch, M. (2003). Care of Blacks and African Americans. In J. Bigsby (Ed.), *Cross-cultural medicine* (pp. 29–59), American College of Physicians Press.

Chapter 7

Rural Black Maternal Health in the Age of Digital Deserts

ALISA VALENTIN AND CHRISTY M. GAMBLE

As the first Black woman in the United States to become the gubernatorial candidate for a major political party, Stacey Abrams campaigned on a progressive platform in 2018 that included reforming Georgia's health-care system in order to improve and expand health-care access for all Georgians. During a 2018 interview with Oprah Winfrey, Abrams was asked to address the high maternal mortality rate in Georgia and stated,

> Let's understand: Georgia has the highest maternal mortality rate in the nation. More women die within a year of giving childbirth in Georgia than any other state because we don't have access to doctors. We have 79 counties that do not have an OB-GYN. We have 64 counties without a pediatrician. We have women who give birth, and the first time they see a doctor is at the hospital, and that's assuming they can get there, because there are nine counties without . . . doctors. (NBC News, 2018, 35:45)

Georgia has 159 counties, which means nearly half of the counties in the state are without physicians who specialize in childbirth and prenatal and postpartum care. Newkirk (2018) cited several structural reasons why Georgia was experiencing this crisis, including the closure of labor and delivery units and even entire hospitals. The problem is exacerbated by the long distances that women must then travel to seek maternal health care. According to Gary Hart, "If you want to go to an OB/GYN, depending on where you live in the country, you may have to go 200 miles" (Warshaw, 2017). The economic and financial strains for women seeking health care are significant: a woman would, in some instances, have her job security threatened after being forced to miss a full day of work just to keep an appointment with her obstetrician (Warshaw, 2017). And while maternal mortality is an issue that spans across Georgia, and the United States, it impacts Black women at a higher rate than White women. "To black women in Georgia, the stakes of the debate over health-care access are no less than life or death," said Vann Newkirk (2018).

In 2020, the world was forever changed by the emergence of the novel coronavirus (also known as COVID-19), which became a global pandemic. The pandemic quickly exacerbated existing health and technological disparities, leaving marginalized communities of color as well as rural communities bearing the brunt of the negative impacts of the virus. Existing systemic health disparities, such as higher rates of obesity and hypertension, placed many rural residents at risk of contracting COVID-19 and potentially having a more severe reaction to the virus. In addition, social inequities, such as the lack of access to primary and specialty care as well as little to no affordable, reliable broadband internet access, also increased the risk of contracting or developing severe COVID-19. These long-standing inequities compounded to widen the health disparity gap experienced by rural residents, particularly rural Black residents.

As a result of the rapid spread of the highly contagious and deadly COVID-19 and the numerous executive orders issued by governors and mayors, the health-care system altered the way it delivered health care to all patients. During the pandemic, health systems and other medical facilities transitioned to the remote provision of care, utilizing telehealth platforms for the screening of patients and the treatment of patients with nonurgent complaints to protect health-care providers, staff, and patients.

Prior to the pandemic, states had very restrictive policies regarding the use of telehealth and reimbursement for its services. As a result, many hospital systems and providers did not use telehealth platforms to deliver health care. However, the pandemic led to many states relaxing previous regulations around reimbursement, privacy, and consent to encourage the use of telehealth to prevent the onset and spread of COVID-19.

Because the transition to telehealth during the pandemic resulted in the continued delivery of health-care services while protecting both providers and patients, there is real potential for this telecommunications tool to result in the reduction and elimination of health disparities. However, due to the digital divide—"where some individuals and communities lack the technical devices and/or broadband systems internet access needed for telehealth"—many marginalized communities of color and rural communities have not been able to enjoy the benefits associated with the access to telehealth (Hill & Burroughs, 2020).

In a fast-developing technological era, it is inexcusable and immoral that the health inequities experienced by rural communities, and particularly Black women in rural communities, continue to persist and grow unchecked, particularly after the COVID-19 pandemic shined a spotlight on these inequities. It is imperative that inclusive policies are developed and implemented to protect all communities, regardless of race, geographic location, or socioeconomic status. One solution to eliminating the health inequities experienced by rural Black women is the unfettered access to telehealth by ensuring marginalized communities of color have access to reliable, affordable broadband. This chapter will provide an analysis of the maternal health crisis Black women in rural areas continue to experience and propose policy solutions that can be implemented to improve maternal health care for Black women who reside in rural communities.

Understanding Black Maternal Health

An issue that was once considered to be an epidemic in developing countries—maternal mortality and morbidity—has increasingly become a problem in the United States. The US maternal mortality rate has more than doubled between 1990 and 2013 (Agrawal, 2015). Black women are especially hard hit, disproportionately suffering or dying from mostly preventable pregnancy-related complications compared to women of other racial and ethnic backgrounds. This alarming disparity has persisted for decades and continues to increase (Martin & Montagne, 2017). In the US, Black women are dying, on average, at three to four times the rate of White women (Creanga et al., 2017), and in some places, such as New

York City, Black women are twelve times more likely to suffer maternal death compared to White women (Martin & Montagne, 2017). These statistics hold true across education, income, class, and other socioeconomic factors (Martin & Montagne, 2017).

The research on the risk factors for negative birth outcomes—including advanced maternal age, poor health, low income, and a lack of prenatal care, to name a few—is clear (Murray, 2019). However, Black women who are of normal weight, receive prenatal care, and live in upper-class neighborhoods still experience higher maternal mortality and morbidity rates compared to White women who are overweight or obese, do not receive prenatal care, and live in low-income neighborhoods. Black women also have higher rates of cesarean sections compared to White women and are two times more likely to be readmitted in the month after the surgery (Martin & Montagne, 2017). They are also twice as likely to experience perinatal mood disorders, which are linked to poor maternal health outcomes, but are half as likely to receive mental health treatment and counseling as White women (Martin & Montagne, 2017; Taylor & Gamble, 2017).

The root of the problem is systemic racism and gendered and racial discrimination that Black women routinely experience, not only within the health-care system but within every system that intersects with their daily lives. The concept of "weathering," which describes the impact of the chronic stress that Black women and other marginalized women of color experience due to racism, sexism, and other stressors, illustrates the main reason why Black American women continue to experience a rise in maternal mortality and morbidity rates (Geronimus, 1992). Despite progress since the civil rights movement, Black Americans have continued to suffer from unequal access to quality education, healthy food, affordable and stable housing, comprehensive health care, equal pay and wealth, and accommodating transportation (Stanford Center on Poverty and Inequality, 2017; White, 2015). These stressors are the product of systemic disenfranchisement that has over the years resulted in incredible physical and mental toxic stress for Black women, which negatively impacts women's health, including pregnancy outcomes. While the US has not officially listed racism as a risk factor that leads to poor maternal health outcomes for Black women, the evidence overwhelmingly supports this conclusion (Alhusen et al., 2016; Crear-Perry, 2018).

One of the most significant stressors for many Black women is the barrier to accessing affordable, quality, comprehensive, equitable, and patient-centered health care. It is an unfortunate fact that Black women are more likely to be uninsured and low income, and as a result they are more likely to be enrolled in Medicaid (Gamble & Taylor, 2017). For many low-income women, especially those living in states that have not expanded Medicaid under the Patient Protection and Affordable Care Act, also known as the Affordable Care Act or ACA, becoming pregnant makes them eligible to enroll in Medicaid and receive vital prenatal and some postpartum care. However, due to the time it takes to enroll upon confirming pregnancy status, these women are more likely to initiate prenatal care later in the pregnancy (Martin & Montagne, 2017). They may also be left without coverage during the most crucial postpartum period. All of these experiences can negatively impact the health of mother and child as well as lead to the onset of maternal mood disorders such as depression and anxiety (Gamble & Taylor, 2017).

In addition, the adverse experiences of Black women within the health-care system are amplified by implicit biases and covert and overt racism exhibited by health-care providers, medical protocols, and hospital systems. Research has shown that hospitals that predominantly care for Black patients—"Black-serving hospitals"—offer poorer quality of care, which results in worse health outcomes (Waldman, 2017; Ly et al., 2010). As it relates to maternal health, mothers were more likely to suffer serious pregnancy-related complications at Black-serving hospitals than non-Black-serving hospitals (Waldman, 2017). And research has shown that when Black women gave birth at the same hospitals as White women, their risk of pregnancy complications were cut in half. Moreover, Black women were more likely to report being discriminated against when they visited a physician or clinic, especially during childbirth hospital stays (*Discrimination in America*, 2017; Declercq et al., 2013).

Rural Maternal Health

If there is one part of the country that has been significantly impacted by high maternal mortality and morbidity rates, it is rural America. After analyzing the Centers for Disease Control and Prevention mortality data, *Scientific American* found that the maternal mortality rate in large metropolitan areas was 18.2 per 100,000 live births, but in most rural areas the rate was 29.4 (Maron, 2017). Between 2004 and 2014, 179 rural counties stopped offering in-county hospital-based obstetric services, and that is in addition to the 898 counties that never offered in-county obstetric services to begin with (Hung, Kozhimannil, et al., 2017). A significant number of rural hospitals continue to remain vulnerable to closures due to the tight operating budgets and financial margins under which they operate (Maron, 2017). The practice of obstetrics and gynecology (OB-GYN) is one of the first units that rural hospitals eliminate because of the high operating cost associated with childbirth (Maron, 2017). Besides the cost to the hospital, there are other reasons used to justify hospital closures in rural areas, such as that rural residents are more likely (1) to have a low income, so there is an increased likelihood that the mother will be covered by Medicaid, which reimburses physicians at a lower rate compared to private insurance; (2) to be less healthy, so there is an increased need for specialty providers to be on-site to provide emergency care; and (3) to be older, so there is a decreased likelihood of a high volume of births to financially justify keeping maternity wards in hospitals (Maron, 2017).

Even though discussions of rural America tend to focus on White people, it is important to note that more than ten million people of color live in rural U.S. communities—one in five rural residents is a person of color, with 40 percent identifying as Black (Kozhimannil, 2017). As the disappearance of obstetric care becomes commonplace in rural America, it has led to a maternity care crisis that is disproportionately impacting rural Black mothers. Research has shown that the strongest predictor of whether a rural community has available obstetric care or would lose this care over the following decade was the percentage of Black residents in that community—the higher the percentage of Black women of reproductive age, the more likely the county was to lack or lose access to obstetric care (Hung, Henning-Smith, et al., 2017). Since January 2010, at least 138 rural hospitals have closed in thirty-seven states, and the majority of these hospital closures have occured in predominantly Black and Latinx communities (NC Rural Health Research Program, 2021). For example, in Alabama, a hospital serving what was known as its "poorest and most rural county" was closed, a county where 72 percent of the residents were Black, resulting in residents having to travel at least fifty minutes for health-care services (Warshaw, 2017). In Alabama and Georgia, states with a high population of rural Black Americans, the impact of the loss of obstetric care is being realized by the community, and Black female physicians have tried to fill the gap by providing this care to high-risk women living in Black communities who have been traveling farther distances to receive quality obstetric care services (Kozhimannil, 2017; Marquez, 2017).

Telehealth: A Tool to Improve Health Outcomes in Rural Communities

Five years after former US president Barack H. Obama signed the ACA into law, the National Advisory Committee on Rural Health and Human Services (2015) stated, "Telehealth has the potential to be an important tool in health care delivery system reform and [the committee] believes the technology can help rural areas take advantage of the ACA's focus on *improving access to care, enhancing quality, and reducing costs*" (p. 2, emphasis added). Although the ACA has repeatedly been under attack in Congress and in the federal courts, this statement by the committee remains true in the twenty-first century. The three pillars listed by the committee speak to the need for telehealth in rural communities.

There are several reasons why it is difficult to recruit ob-gyns to work in rural areas, including that these areas do not offer the same lifestyles as major metropolitan cities and that physicians in rural areas are typically overworked due to the lack of ob-gyns, making the decision to join the rural physician workforce daunting and less compelling. In acknowledging this barrier to recruiting physicians to care for rural patients, it is important to use innovative breakthroughs to develop new solutions. One solution that can resolve the issue of physical proximity is virtual proximity, namely telehealth. Telehealth is similar in concept to telemedicine, but it includes a vast array of remote health-care services that go beyond those traditionally delivered by physicians to, oftentimes, deliver educational or supportive services, whereas telemedicine is used primarily by physicians to provide medical, diagnostic, treatment-related, and health-monitoring services to patients remotely (Federal Communications Commission [FCC], n.d.).

In addition to assisting with recruiting additional physicians to care for rural patients, telehealth also has the ability to enhance quality of care. As stated previously, rural practitioners, especially ob-gyns, are overworked. Some physicians see between thirty and forty patients in a day and take on several twenty-four-hour shifts (Newkirk, 2018). This heavy workload could lead to "rushed or poor care" (Brody, 2018). Telehealth could alleviate these workloads because this technological advancement has the ability to both "[recruit] and [retain] more providers in rural areas, as a virtual network of professional peers can reduce rural practitioner isolation and burnout" (National Advisory Committee on Rural Health and Human Services, 2015, p.4). There are also innovative remote tools that could allow patients to communicate with providers in various ways, such as via video conference, instant messages, or text messages. This may allow time for patients to ask thoughtful questions and receive health-care instructions they can consistently refer back to as needed in between physical visits and prevent patients from having to travel to and from appointments.

As is the case with broadband infrastructure, there is an economic case for deploying telehealth services. There is evidence that telehealth "lowers health care costs, while improving access and quality of care" (American Hospital Association, 2016, p.1). Additionally, the majority of Medicaid programs cover some sort of telehealth services, which is important for rural communities because "Medicaid . . . cover[s] nearly one in four (24%) nonelderly individuals in rural areas" (Foutz et al., 2017).

The coronavirus pandemic revealed to the medical community as well as patients the ability of telehealth to "bridge communication gaps, allow for the continuation of care and reduce patient and clinical exposure to the coronavirus" (Hirko et al., 2020).

While telehealth has the potential to reduce and, eventually, eliminate health disparities, ongoing barriers such as the lack of access to reliable, affordable broadband could prevent this technological tool from becoming a viable alternative to traditional in-person medical care for millions of people across the United States. As it relates to rural areas, it is clear that policies must be implemented to ensure rural patients have access to primary and speciality care as hospitals continue to shutter. Advancements in technology allow for telehealth to be a transformational way to assist marginalized patients of color in rural areas; however, affordable, reliable broadband must be prioritized across these communities.

Broadband Access and Adoption in Rural Communities of Color

Throughout the COVID-19 pandemic, many activities that would typically take place in person were moved online so people could continue learning, working, and managing these aspects of their lives from the safety of their homes. Unfortunately, the pandemic exacerbated many of the gaps in broadband access and left individuals and families with few methods to access connectivity. Social-distancing requirements and building closures meant people without home broadband could no longer get connected from anchor institutions and public places such as libraries, neighborhood service centers, and schools. Some with mobile-only connections had to navigate online daily life with restrictive data caps, while others were forced to drive to parking lots of local restaurants to access Wi-Fi. The national crisis demonstrated with greater clarity that millions of Americans are unable to operate in a remote or even hybrid virtual world as a result of the digital divide.

The term *digital divide* was developed by Larry Irving, who was the first Black American to be inducted into the Internet Hall of Fame (*Larry Irving*, 2019). During the Clinton administration, Irving was the assistant secretary of commerce for communications and information and administrator of the National Telecommunications and Information Administration. Throughout his work in the 1990s, Irving and his colleagues produced empirical research on the digital divide and defined the then-nascent phenomenon as "the divide between those with access to new technologies and those without" (Irving, 1999). Although Irving's research was conducted more than two decades prior to the COVID-19 public health crisis, the same technological inequities persisted: low-income households, rural households, and marginalized people of color (particularly those from Black, Latinx, and Indigenous communities) remain on the wrong side of the digital divide.

Policy makers, researchers, and organizers continue to advocate for digital inclusion policies that address the full scope of the digital divide. The National Digital Inclusion Alliance (n.d.) defines *digital inclusion* as follows:

> Digital Inclusion refers to the activities necessary to ensure that all individuals and communities, including the most disadvantaged, have access to and use of Information and Communication Technologies (ICTs). This includes 5 elements: 1) affordable, robust broadband internet service; 2) internet-enabled devices that meet the needs of the user; 3) access to digital literacy training; 4) quality technical support; and 5) applications and online content designed to enable and encourage self-sufficiency, participation and collaboration. Digital Inclusion must evolve

as technology advances. Digital Inclusion requires intentional strategies and investments to reduce and eliminate historical, institutional and structural barriers to access and use technology.

Without access to affordable broadband, the devices needed to navigate the internet, and the skills needed to ensure one is able to use the internet, there are immediate and dire consequences for the ability to access tele-health services, government resources, and economic opportunities. While the COVID-19 pandemic put a momentary spotlight on the issue, this served as a reminder that there has always been an urgent need to bridge the digital divide across the United States, particularly in communities that were hardest hit by the compounding public health and economic crisis—Black, Latinx, and Indigenous communities.

Prior to the COVID-19 pandemic, the former FCC commissioner and acting chairwoman Mignon Clyburn, who was the first Black woman to hold these positions at the Commission, consistently discussed afford-ability as a major obstacle to broadband adoption. In 2017, when the FCC was hyperfocused on building out broadband to unserved communities, Commissioner Clyburn also noted how the affordability barrier was one that could impact millions of Americans who simultaneously lack access to health care. She stated, "And for those living in areas where connectivity is widely available, affordability is too often a major barrier to access. This is simply unacceptable. It cannot be allowed to continue, because if we couple this with the millions of people who lack access to high-quality health care services, we have a clinical crisis on our hands" (Clyburn, 2017). Commissioner Clyburn, a South Carolina native, advocated for increased broadband access and adoption in rural areas of the United States, particularly in communities that experienced persistent poverty, because she believed health, economic, and connectivity disparities were closely tied. In addition, she recognized an important pillar of digital inclusion: households need broadband to be both accessible and affordable.

The affordability barrier to broadband is persistent in marginalized communities of color. In 2019, Pew Research found substantial disparities in broadband adoption across Black and Latinx communities. In 2021, 29 percent of Black adults and 35 percent of Latinx adults reported that they did not have a home broadband connection (Atske & Perrin, 2021). Also, 31 percent of Black adults and 33 percent of Latinx adults reported that they did not own a desktop or laptop computer while simultaneously reporting they were more dependent on mobile devices to access the internet (Atske & Perrin, 2021).

Additionally, a 2016 study by Free Press, a grassroots advocacy organization focused on media reform, found that several factors led to the systemic exclusion of communities of color in the digital age. In this report, *Digital Denied*, it was argued that much of the connectivity disparities that persisted in communities of color were the result of income inequality. For example, this study found that "only 49 percent of households with annual family incomes below $20,000 have internet in the home, compared to nearly 90 percent of households with incomes above $100,000" (Turner, 2016, p. 25). This is a significant issue for Black, Latinx, and Indigenous communities in rural areas because these groups have historically experienced poverty levels at higher rates than White rural communities, which impacts their ability to afford a broadband connection (Valentin, 2018).

The 2016 Free Press study also found that marginalized people of color were more likely to have only one internet service provider (ISP) option in their respective communities, which is the result of "structural discrimination [that] exacerbates market failures" (Turner, 2016, p. 14). When only one ISP is available to consumers in a specific geographic region, that sole company has the ability to charge higher rates than they would arguably charge if there were other competitors in that wired-broadband market (Turner, 2016). This issue then compounds with the issue of income inequality because it makes broadband less affordable, specifically in communities with significant populations of people of color.

Despite affordability and other barriers to connectivity that remain, it is clear that access to broadband can no longer be viewed as a luxury. Broadband remains a necessity not only to access telehealth services but to even ensure one has health-care coverage. For example, in Arkansas, a state with a 17 percent poverty rate that has also consistently ranked as one of the least connected states, Medicaid recipients were required to log their working hours online every month in order to continue receiving Medicaid benefits (Holder, 2018). In January 2019, it was reported that 18,000 Arkansas residents lost their Medicaid coverage due to the inability to adhere to the newly implemented work requirements that mandated beneficiaries report their qualified work hours (Hardy, 2019). This situation was worsened by individuals' lack of access to robust, affordable broadband, which was needed to effectively log those hours.

It should also be noted that the FCC's decision to repeal its 2015 Open Internet Order, commonly referred to as net neutrality, has the potential to impact the innovation of telehealth and mobile health apps and could have adverse impacts on the ability of marginalized communities of color to access health-care services (Gamble & Scurato, 2017a, 2017b). The three bright line rules of net neutrality are no blocking, no throttling, and no paid prioritization of content on the internet. The FCC's 2015 net neutrality rules ensured that all internet users would be able to access all content online without interferences from their ISP. The subsequent repeal of the 2015 Open Internet Order means that the FCC lacks authority to investigate discriminatory practices by ISPs such as digital redlining, predatory data caps, and hidden fees. If a strong net-neutrality framework combined with FCC authority over broadband is not reinstated, these practices can disproportionately impede marginalized people of color from accessing robust broadband services.

As stated in "Understanding Black Maternal Health" above, structural inequities are what have led to disparities in broadband access and adoption in rural communities of color. Policy makers cannot leave it simply to the market to fix itself. Large telecommunications companies will continue to build out upgraded broadband technologies in areas they deem most profitable. It is necessary for Congress and the federal agencies of jurisdiction to work collaboratively with state and local governments to take an approach to broadband deployment similar to that taken with electricity. In other words, regardless of the cost and profit, reliable, affordable broadband should be deployed across this country because it is a necessary tool that impacts almost every aspect of our lives. Connecting the unconnected and underconnected through broadband will allow all people, regardless of their geographic location, income level, or race, to fully participate in modern society, with the outcome of also reducing disparities in Black maternal health.

Proposed Solutions for Addressing Rural Black Maternal Health

While there have been several proposed solutions to address the historic rise in maternal deaths in the United States, none of them adequately addressed the unique epidemic experienced by Black mothers. There is a need to address the inconsistent practices within the obstetrics field, develop a national database of maternal deaths, create state maternal-mortality review boards, and ensure close coordination of antenatal and primary care (Agrawal, 2015). But Black mothers also need solutions that address the root causes of their pregnancy-related complications: inequities in social factors and the implicit bias and systemic racism within the health-care system.

Medicaid has traditionally been the payer for the majority of births in the US; it is also the largest payer for births by Black and Latinx women. In 2018, Medicaid paid for 65 percent of births for Black women. Prior to the pandemic, only nineteen state Medicaid programs reimbursed for telehealth services delivered to their beneficiaries, but during the COVID-19 pandemic payment for telehealth services was expanded to all fifty states and the District of Columbia. Even though the OB-GYN field is considered a "high touch" field, maternal telehealth was quickly adopted within the field to offer prenatal and postpartum care.

Black women need unfettered access to trusted providers who consistently offer high-quality, affordable, comprehensive, equitable, and culturally appropriate health care. This includes universal access to doulas, specifically doulas of color. Doulas are trained nonmedical professionals who provide labor, birth, and postpartum support in the form of emotional, physical, and informational support (Gruber et al., 2013). Doulas of color have long been respected and valued within the Black community. Their practices date back to the precolonization era in African communities, when Black birth workers were viewed as spiritual healers and family-planning counselors (Jett, 2017). These doula practices continued during slavery, with many Black birth workers attending the births of not just Black women but also White women, and during the Jim Crow era, when Black women were forced to deliver their babies at home after hospitals denied them access due to their race (Jett, 2017; Ollove, 2017).

While research has shown that doula-assisted mothers are less likely to have low-birth-weight babies and birth complications and are more likely to breastfeed compared to mothers without this support, in 2012, only 6 percent of pregnant women received supportive care from a doula (Gruber et al., 2013; Hodnett et al., 2012; Declercq et al., 2013). The low percentage of use of doulas is likely due to the fact that doula services have not been covered by insurance and cost at least $1,000 out of pocket, which puts this service out of reach for many low-income women who are more likely to be enrolled in Medicaid, which has not covered doula services (Bobrow, 2018). Several cities have created or have been interested in adopting doula training programs, but it has a minimal impact when the option does not exist for all pregnant women (Ollove, 2017).

Doulas, specifically doulas of color, can address several of the issues mentioned within this chapter that contribute to the disparate maternal outcomes experienced by Black women by offering trusted, empowering, and culturally sensitive care while also advocating for equitable, comprehensive, quality, and patient-centered medical care. Doulas would provide the vital care needed to not only decrease the US maternal mortality rate but also eliminate the maternal mortality and morbidity disparity between Black and White women, especially in rural areas.

Additionally, having access to pregnancy and childbirth information informs the expectations and experiences of pregnant women (Martin et al., 2013). Misinformation or a lack of information can cause a woman to overreact to normal pregnancy situations or forgo necessary treatment, potentially leading to the experience of trauma and a "psychologically negative birth experience" and increasing the risk of developing a perinatal mood disorder (Martin et al., 2013). This is why access to trusted sources of information, particularly those online, is so important.

A national survey of postpartum women found that mothers, especially first-time mothers, viewed information provided by a maternity care provider, childbirth education classes, pregnancy and childbirth websites and apps, and general medical or health websites as "very valuable" and trustworthy during their pregnancies (Declercq et al., 2013). In addition, the women reported high rates of usage of devices with internet connections at least once a week to access information about pregnancy and childbirth (Declercq et al., 2013). Given the benefits that access to pregnancy and childbirth information provide for women during their pregnancy, access to online sources of information is a key solution for improving Black maternal health outcomes.

Likewise, telehealth has the opportunity to provide pregnant women with access to experts who can provide vital pregnancy and childbirth information and answer women's questions. It is an affordable and efficient means to removing barriers to accessing accurate health-care information from a credible and trusted professional. The numerous benefits of telemedicine for hospitals and patients—decreased appointment waiting and travel times, increased specialty and urban hospital collaborations, and increased hospital savings—have resulted in the increased adoption of the technology by rural hospitals (Ripton & Winkler, 2016).

For rural Black women, telehealth could provide the pre- and postnatal care, including mental health counseling, that is a necessity during and after pregnancy in the midst of widespread obstetric shortages. It could also provide expanded access to supportive health-care professionals, such as doulas, who could offer quality and culturally appropriate health care tailored to the lived experiences of each patient. For a population dealing with long commutes and dwindling access to maternity care, telehealth can help patients keep critical and vital prenatal and postpartum appointments. But certain policy changes have to be in place to realize these benefits. Policy makers must make permanent any changes to telehealth policies that occurred during the COVID-19 pandemic, which allowed medical providers in all fifty states and the District of Columbia to offer telehealth services to patients.

Telehealth services must come with payment parity, meaning they should be reimbursed at the same rate as in-person health-care services. Moreover, telehealth policies must expand the types of providers who can be reimbursed for services beyond the traditional medical providers to include maternity support providers such as doulas, midwives, and lactation consultants, to name a few. In addition, policies must expand the types of services that are critical to populations that suffer disproportionately from maternal mortality and morbidity (e.g., mental health counseling, lactation coaching, doula support, home visiting, childbirth and parenting courses).

Policy makers should consider these changes to long-standing tele-health policies to ensure equitable access to maternal telehealth, which could eliminate health inequities experienced by rural residents and marginalized communities of color.

Broadband Deployment and Affordability Policy Recommendations

There are several recommendations for policy makers to improve broadband access and adoption in rural communities of color, which could protect Black women's maternal health. Inclusive policies that should be implemented to ensure marginalized communities can access broadband include adequate and equitable allocation of federal funds, removal of barriers to deployment, legislation to support competition, and long-term governmental solutions to address broadband adoption in low-income communities.

Congress should pass legislation that creates and sustains digitally inclusive communities with competitive markets. With increased competition among broadband providers, prices often decrease, which makes broadband more affordable for all communities in that market. Additionally, marginalized communities of color and low-income communities are impacted by unjust, discriminatory deployment of upgraded infrastructure, a concept that is widely referred to as digital redlining. Legislation must prohibit digital redlining to ensure marginalized communities of color and low-income communities are equitably served.

Additionally, Congress should work to remove barriers to broadband deployment that can drive down deployment costs. One way this can be done is through congressional support for "dig once" policies. Dig once policies "mandate the installation of fiber conduits during federally funded highway projects" (Brodkin, 2017). According to Brodkin (2017), these conduits can make it cheaper and easier to install fiber after the completion of road construction, which can help mitigate economic challenges of building out in certain communities. Similarly, the FCC manages and administers the Universal Service Fund (USF), which comprises several programs designed to reduce disparities in connectivity.

One USF program, known as the High Cost program, provides funding to carriers to deploy networks in rural areas. The FCC administers billions of dollars of funds through this program, but by the time the networks are deployed they may not meet the modern-day connectivity needs of communities as made evident by the COVID-19 pandemic. The FCC should require providers who receive High Cost funding to build out high-speed broadband above the Commission's current definition of 25 Mbps (download) /3 Mbps (upload) in order to future-proof the networks that were built using these limited funds. Additionally, the Commission should require carriers who receive USF dollars to offer an affordable option so low-income households in rural areas can adopt broadband once it arrives in their communities.

The federal government must also implement and expand policies that offset the cost of broadband for low-income households. The FCC's Lifeline program was established during the Reagan administration to ensure low-income households could access communications services (mainly telephone services during that era). In response to the Hurricane Katrina crisis, the Lifeline program was expanded to cover wireless services. Most recently, under President Obama, the FCC expanded Lifeline to cover broadband services as well. As of 2021, Lifeline remains severely undersubscribed, with approximately a 20 percent participation rate despite the economic and public health crises. Over the course of the pandemic, there were calls from policy makers on Capitol Hill and the FCC to ensure there was increased coordination between the Commission and other federal agencies that administered programs that make households eligible for the Commission's subsidy program (such as the United States Department of Agriculture, which administers the Supplemental Nutrition Assistance Program) so more consumers are notified of their eligibility to receive free or discounted communications services.

It is imperative that the FCC take steps to better promote participation in this program to the over thirty million eligible households. Also, in 2021, the minimum service standards for Lifeline-supported services were 4.5 GB of data and 1,000 minutes per month at 3G speeds (FCC, 2021a). The FCC should update the Lifeline program so carriers can provide meaningful connectivity to low-income households with an appropriate subsidy, which has stalled at $9.25 per month for over a decade, as of 2021.

During the COVID-19 pandemic, a new affordability program was created. Congress passed the Consolidated Appropriations Act in December 2020, which directed the FCC to establish the Emergency Broadband Benefit program. In February 2021, the Commission voted unanimously to establish the $3.2 billion program, which would provide qualifying households with discounts of up to $50 a month for broadband service and discounts of up to $75 a month if the household was located on tribal lands (FCC, 2021b). Additionally, through this emergency program, eligible households would receive a one-time discount of up to $100 on the purchase of a computer or tablet. At the time of publication, this program was less than sixty days away from being available to consumers; it has the potential to transform the lives of marginalized people of color across America, including Black mothers in rural communities. If successful, this program could serve as a blueprint for how this country could address broadband affordability in the future. It is important for advocates in both the health and telecommunications spaces to continue to push for the preservation of bold programs that help low-income people across the United States access affordable broadband.

It should also be noted that the FCC launched a $200 million COVID-19 Telehealth Program through funds appropriated by Congress in the Coronavirus Aid, Relief, and Economic Security (CARES) Act "to help health care providers provide connected care services to patients at their homes or mobile locations in response to the COVID-19 pandemic" (FCC, 2020, p. 4). Additionally, through the aforementioned Consolidated Appropriations Act, an additional $249.5 million in funding was provided to the FCC for this telehealth program. The Commission expanded administrative responsibilities to the Universal Service Administrative

Company so that the second round of the program could be swiftly implemented. Through this program, health-care providers across the country would have additional funds for tablet computers, telemedicine carts, network upgrades, mobile hotspots, and remote patient-monitoring systems. This program has the potential to assist health-care providers in properly monitoring Black mothers in rural communities throughout the nation. Congress and the FCC should continue these efforts to support those who have historically been marginalized in our health-care and communications systems.

These are a few of the many policy recommendations that could be used to deploy affordable, reliable broadband to more communities, thus creating a route to accessible health care for Black women and their families through the use of telehealth. These policy recommendations should be implemented in conjunction with the previously listed health-care policy recommendations in order to improve the Black maternal mortality and morbidity rates in this country, specifically in rural communities.

Conclusion

Black women in the United States face not only a trifecta of systemic discrimination due to their race, gender, and socioeconomic status but also discrimination based on additional intersectional identites they hold (e.g., geography, sexuality). When these layers of discrimination are applied to varying industries that are increasingly interdependent, such as maternal health in rural communities, there are adverse effects for marginalized women of color. Future research should examine the intersection of rural broadband, Black maternal health, and telehealth services. Furthermore, additional advocacy work must be done to create and support policies at all levels of the government and industry to better protect the maternal health of rural Black women. This is necessary in order to ensure that rural Black mothers can live happy, healthy, and thriving lives.

References

Agrawal, P. (2015). Maternal mortality and morbidity in the United States of America. *Bulletin of the World Health Organization*, 93(3), 135.

Alhusen, J. L., Bower, K., Epstein, E., & Sharps, P. (2016). Racial discrimination and adverse birth outcomes: An integrative review. *Journal of Midwifery and Women's Health*, 61(6), 707–720.

American Hospital Association. (2016). *Telehealth: Helping hospitals deliver cost-effective care*. https://www.aha.org/system/files/content/16/16Telehealth-issuebrief.pdf

Atske, S., & Perrin, A. (2021). *Home broadband adoption, computer ownership vary by race, ethnicity in the U.S.* Pew Research Center. https://www.pewresearch.org/fact-tank/2021/07/16/home-broadband-adoption-computer-ownership-vary-by-race-ethnicity-in-the-u-s/

Bobrow, E. (2018, August 28). What it's like to be a doula for women of color. *The Cut*. https://www.thecut.com/2018/08/what-its-like-to-be-a-doula-for-women-of-color.html

Brodkin, J. (2017, March 22). "Dig once" bill could bring fiber Internet to much of the US. *Ars Technica*. https://arstechnica.com/information-technology/2017/03/nationwide-fiber-proposed-law-could-add-broadband-to-road-projects/

Brody, B. (2018, November 14). The ob-gyn shortage is real—and it might impact your care. *Glamour*. https://www.glamour.com/story/ob-gyn-shortage

Clyburn, M. (2017, March 30). *Remarks of FCC Commissioner Mignon L. Clyburn (as prepared): 5th Annual Telehealth Summit of South Carolina*. https://www.fcc.gov/document/commissioner-clyburn-remarks-5th-annual-sc-telehealth-summit

Creanga, A. A., Syverson, C., Seek, K., & Callaghan, W. M. (2017). Pregnancy-related mortality in the United States, 2011–2013. *Obstetrics & Gynecology*, 130(2), 366–373.

Crear-Perry, J. (2018, April 11). Race isn't a risk factor in maternal health. Racism is. *Rewire News Group*. https://rewire.news/article/2018/04/11/maternal-health-replace-race-with-racism/

Declercq, E., Sakala, C., Corry, M. P., Applebaum, S., & Herrlich, A. (2013). *Listening to mothers III Pregnancy and Birth: report of the third national U.S. survey of women's childbearing experiences*. Childbirth Connection. http://transform.childbirthconnection.org/wp-content/uploads/2013/06/LTM-III_Pregnancy-and-Birth.pdf

Discrimination in America: Experiences and views of American women. (2017, December). NPR / Robert Wood Johnson Foundation / Harvard T. H. Chan School of Public Health. https://www.rwjf.org/content/dam/farm/reports/surveys_and_polls/2017/rwjf441994

Federal Communications Commission. (n.d.). *Telehealth, telemedicine and telecare: What's what?* https://www.fcc.gov/general/telehealth-telemedicine-and-telecare-whats-what

Federal Communications Commission. (2020, April 2). *Promoting telehealth for low-income consumers; COVID-19 Telehealth Program* (Report no. FCC-

20-44). https://www.fcc.gov/document/fcc-fights-covid-19-200m-adopts-long-term-connected-care-study

Federal Communications Commission. (2021a, July 30). *Wireline Competition Bureau announces update Lifeline minimum service standards and indexed budget amount.* https://docs.fcc.gov/public/attachments/DA-21-930A1.pdf

Federal Communications Commission. (2021b, September). *Emergency Broadband Benefit Program.* https://www.fcc.gov/emergency-broadband-benefit-program

Foutz, J., Artiga, S., & Garfield, R. (2017, April). *The role of Medicaid in rural America.* Henry J. Kaiser Family Foundation. https://www.kff.org/medicaid/issue-brief/the-role-of-medicaid-in-rural-america/

Gamble, C. M. & Taylor, J. (2017). *Maternity care under ACA repeal: Implications for Black women's maternal health.* Center for American Progress. https://www.americanprogress.org/issues/women/reports/2017/08/07/437116/maternity-care-aca-repeal/

Gamble, C. M. & Scurato, C. (2017a, May 16). Rolling back net neutrality would hurt minorities and low-income families. *The Hill.* https://thehill.com/blogs/pundits-blog/healthcare/333581-rolling-back-net-neutrality-would-hurt-minorities-and-low

Gamble, C. M. & Scurato, C. (2017b, December 13). Repealing net neutrality would reduce access to critical health services. *The Hill.* https://thehill.com/opinion/healthcare/364714-repealing-net-neutrality-would-reduce-access-to-critical-health-services

Geronimus, A. T. (1992). The weathering hypothesis and the health of African-American women and infants: Evidence and speculations. *Ethnicity & Disease, 2*(3), 207–221.

Gruber, K. J., Cupito, S. H., & Dobson, C. F. (2013). Impact of doulas on healthy birth outcomes. *The Journal of Perinatal Education, 22*(1), 49–58.

Hardy, B. (2019, June 23). Study: Arkansas Medicaid work requirement did not boost employment. *Times Record.* https://www.swtimes.com/news/20190623/study-arkansas-medicaid-work-requirement-did-not-boost-employment

Hill, I., & Burroughs, E. (2020). *Maternal telehealth has expanded dramatically during the COVID-19 pandemic: Equity concerns and promising approaches.* Urban Institute. https://www.urban.org/sites/default/files/103126/maternal-telehealth-has-expanded-dramatically-during-the-covid-19-pandemic.pdf

Hirko, K. A., Kerver, J. M., Ford, S., Szafranski, C., Beckett, J., Kitchen, C., & Wendling, A. L. (2020). Telehealth in response to the COVID-19 pandemic: Implications for rural health disparities. *Journal of the American Medical Informatics Association, 27*(11), 1816–1818.

Hodnett, E. D., Gates, S., Hofmeyr, G. J., Sakala, C., & Weston, J. (2012). Continuous support for women during childbirth. *Cochrane Database of Systematic Reviews.*

Holder, S. (2018, August 21). In Arkansas, "digital redlining" could leave thousands without health care. *Bloomberg CityLab*. https://www.citylab.com/equity/2018/08/arkansas-medicaid-work-requirements-online-reporting/567589/

Hung, P., Henning-Smith, C. E., Casey, M. M., & Kozhimannil, K. (2017). Access to obstetric services in rural counties still declining, with 9 percent losing services, 2004–14. *Health Affairs, 36*(9), 1663–1671.

Hung, P., Kozhimannil, K., Henning-Smith, C., & Casey, M. (2017, April). *Closure of hospital obstetric services disproportionately affects less-populated rural counties*. University of Minnesota Rural Health Research Center. http://rhrc.umn.edu/wp-content/files_mf/1491501904UMRHRCOBclosuresPolicyBrief.pdf

Irving, L. (1999). Introduction. *Falling through the net: Defining the digital divide*. National Telecommunications and Information Administration. https://www.ntia.doc.gov/legacy/ntiahome/fttn99/introduction.html

Jett, M. (2017, March 17). *A brief history of black midwifery in the US*. Doula Trainings International. https://doulatrainingsinternational.com/brief-history-Black-midwifery-us/

Kozhimannil, K. B. (2017, September 5). Role of racial and geographical bias in rural maternity care. *AJMC*. https://www.ajmc.com/contributor/katy-b-kozhimannil-phd-mpa/2017/09/role-of-racial-and-geographical-bias-in-rural-maternity-care

Larry Irving. (2019). Internet Hall of Fame. https://www.internethalloffame.org/inductees/larry-irving

Ly, D. P., Lopez, L., Isaac, T., & Jha, A. K. (2010). How do Black-serving hospitals perform on patient safety indicators? Implications for national reporting and pay-for-performance. *Medical Care, 48*(2), 1133–1137.

Maron, D. F. (2017, February 15). Maternal health care is disappearing in rural America. *Scientific American*. https://www.scientificamerican.com/article/maternal-health-care-is-disappearing-in-rural-america/

Martin, D. K., Bulmer, S. M., & Pettker, C. (2013). Childbirth expectations and sources of information among low- and moderate-income nulliparous pregnant women. *The Journal of Perinatal Education, 22*(2), 103–112.

Martin, N., & Montagne, R. (2017, December 7). Black mothers keep dying after giving birth. Shalon Irving's story explains why. In *All Things Considered*. NPR. https://www.npr.org/2017/12/07/568948782/Black-mothers-keep-dying-after-giving-birth-shalon-irvings-story-expains-why

Marquez, J. R. (2017, July 12). In much of rural Georgia, maternal health-care is disappearing. *Atlanta*. https://www.atlantamagazine.com/health/rural-georgia-maternal-healthcare-disappearing-joy-baker/

Murray, D. (2019, January 11). Maternal mortality rate, causes, and prevention. *Verywell Family*. https://www.verywellfamily.com/maternal-mortality-rate-causes-and-prevention-4163653

National Advisory Committee on Rural Health and Human Services. (2015, March). *Telehealth in rural America: Policy brief March 2015.* https://www.hrsa.gov/advisorycommittees/rural/publications/telehealthmarch2015.pdf

National Digital Inclusion Alliance. (n.d.). *Definitions.* https://www.digitalinclusion.org/definitions/

NBC News. (2018, Nov. 1). *Watch live: Oprah campaigns with Georgia Democrat Stacey Abrams* [Video]. YouTube. https://www.youtube.com/watch?v=oW9gL9nV8QI&t=2146s

NC Rural Health Research Program. (n.d.). *Rural hospital closures.* Cecil G. Sheps Center for Health Services Research. Retrieved September 2021 from https://www.shepscenter.unc.edu/programs-projects/rural-health/rural-hospital-closures/

Newkirk, V. R., II. (2018, November 2). Stacey Abrams's prescription for a maternal-health crisis. *The Atlantic.* https://www.theatlantic.com/politics/archive/2018/11/stacey-abrams-and-georgias-maternal-health-crisis/574687/

Ollove, M. (2017, September 25). Cities turn to doulas to give black babies a better chance at survival. *Washington Post.* https://www.washingtonpost.com/national/health-science/cities-turn-to-doulas-to-give-black-babies-a-better-chance-at-survival/2017/09/22/07420956-8363-11e7-ab27-1a21a8e006ab_story.html

Ripton, J. T., & Winkler, C. S. (2016). How telemedicine is transforming treatment in rural communities. *Becker's Health IT & CIO Report.* https://www.beckershospitalreview.com/healthcare-information-technology/how-telemedicine-is-transforming-treatment-in-rural-communities.html

Stanford Center on Poverty and Inequality. (2017). State of the union 2017: The poverty and inequality report. Special issue, *Pathways Magazine.* https://inequality.stanford.edu/sites/default/files/Pathways_SOTU_2017.pdf

Taylor, J., & Gamble, C. M. (2017). *Suffering in silence: Mood disorders among pregnant postpartum women of color.* Center for American Progress. https://www.americanprogress.org/issues/women/reports/2017/11/17/443051/suffering-in-silence/

Turner, S. D. (2016, December). *Digital denied: The impact of systemic racial discrimination on home-internet adoption.* Free Press. https://www.freepress.net/sites/default/files/legacy-policy/digital_denied_free_press_report_december_2016.pdf

Valentin, A. (2018, October 19). Why rural communities of color are left behind: A call for intersectional demographic broadband data. *Public Knowledge.* https://www.publicknowledge.org/news-blog/blogs/why-rural-communities-of-color-are-left-behind-a-call-for-intersectional-demographic-broadband-data

Waldman, A. (2017). How hospitals are failing Black mothers. *ProPublica.* https://www.propublica.org/article/how-hospitals-are-failing-Black-mothers

Warshaw, R. (2017, October 31). Health disparities affect millions in rural U.S. communities. *AAMCNews*. https://news.aamc.org/patient-care/article/health-disparities-affect-millions-rural-us-commun/

White, G. B. (2015, May 16). Stranded: How America's failing public transportation increases inequality. *The Atlantic*. https://www.theatlantic.com/business/archive/2015/05/stranded-how-americas-failing-public-transportation-increases-inequality/39349/

Chapter 8

Pouring from a Leaking Cup

Informal Family Caregivers in the Black Community

ESTHER PIERVIL

In the Black community, the family unit provides the original blueprint for navigating the Black experience and meeting expectations therein—essentially serving as a template and filter for the expression of cultural norms, i.e., family roles, gender norms, traditions, beliefs, and rules for interacting within specific cultures and across extended kin networks in the community (Kane, 2000; Dilworth-Anderson, 2001; Mendenhall et al., 2017). A manifestation of this collective community worldview can be observed in the frequency and normality of informal family caregiving across kin networks. Classically perceived as an honorable obligation, the decision to become a family caregiver in the Black community is often an involuntary choice, an almost instinctive compulsion to do the right thing. It is a decision that is rarely based on the caregiver's level of preparedness or access to resources and support (Dilworth-Anderson, 2001; Giarelli et al., 2003; Piervil et al., 2018).

The most recent appraisals of informal caregiving in the United States indicate an estimated 65 million Americans aged eighteen and older reported providing care to a chronically ill or disabled family member (National Alliance for Caregiving & AARP Public Policy Institute, 2015).

In the literature, informal family caregivers are generally defined as individuals that provide unpaid care to a relative for an extended period of time. More explicitly, Schulz and Quittner (1998) defined caregiving as "extraordinary care (i.e., tasks that exceed the bounds of what is normative or usual for a parental, sibling, or spousal relationship) involving significant expenditures of time and energy often for months or years, requiring the performance of tasks that may be physically demanding and unpleasant."

Economic Value and Impact of Caregiver Support

The economic value of family caregivers has continued to grow over time. In 2009, family caregivers in the United States provided an estimated $450 billion of unpaid labor each year (National Family Caregivers Association & Family Caregiver Alliance, 2006; Feinberg et al., 2011). Like most phenomena in the US, rates of caregiving and caregiver outcomes vary by race, ethnicity, gender, and country of origin (Aranda & Knight, 1997; Ho et al., 2009; Pharr et al., 2014). In a national sample of elderly adults, 44 percent of Latino respondents and 34 percent of Black respondents were reported to have received home-based family caregiving compared to 25 percent of non-Hispanic White respondents (Weis et al., 2005). Trivedi et al. (2014) reported that the average caregiver was fifty-five years old and female. Women were more likely to report providing twenty hours of care or more to a family member; those who identified as family caregivers were 2.5 times more likely than noncaregivers to live in poverty and 5 times more likely to receive Supplemental Security Income.

In 2016, 78 percent of caregivers incurred out-of-pocket expenses as a result of caregiving. Pinquart and Sörensen (2005) reported that, compared to non-Hispanic White respondents, ethnic minorities had lower socioeconomic status and were more likely to receive care from family and friends; congruously, a statement by the National Alliance for Caregiving and AARP (2015) reported that, across race and ethnicity, financial strain measured by out-of-pocket spending was highest among Hispanic/Latino and African American caregivers, who spent an average of 44 percent and 34 percent of their income as a result of caregiving activities, respectively, compared to 14 percent of out-of-pocket spending among White caregivers. Notably, while African American caregivers reported having worse physical health than White caregivers in the sample, they also reported lower levels of caregiver burden and depression, despite reporting higher levels of poverty and financial strain (Pinquart & Sörensen, 2005). This misalliance of strained circumstance and perceived well-being aligns with the work of Terrie Williams in her book *Black Pain: It Just Looks Like We're Not Hurting* (2009), where she explains the phenomena of Black women committed to "passing for normal." Bell (2017) expands on this concept and highlights a host of disparities, unhealthy habits, negative stereotypes, and detrimental behaviors within groups of women as symptoms of larger fractures in Black women's mental health. As Black women find themselves increasingly taking on the role of caregiver and for longer periods of time, it becomes necessary to explore their experiences more meticulously, toward a better understanding of needs, barriers to support, and implications for public health practice and research initiatives.

Informal Family Caregivers across the Prostate Cancer Continuum of Care

Prostate cancer (CaP) is a serious public health issue in the Black community. Disparities in the incidence and prevalence of morbidity and mortality related to CaP in this community have been well documented (Ries et al., 2000; 2016; Jemal et al., 2017; U.S. Cancer Statistics Working Group, 2017). As a result, there has been a steady push to increase early detection of CaP in older Black men. Recent advances in technology and the impetus to increase early detection of CaP in older Black men have resulted in significant increases in rates of survival among this vulnerable population. As survival rates increase, the incidence and duration of family caregiving also increases. Compounding this problem, research indicates there is an association between caregiving and negative health outcomes, increasing the disproportionate burden of disease and hardship in the Black community. Thus, this study sought to better understand the caregiving experience of family caregivers in the Black community across the CaP continuum of care. Specific aims of this research were to classify needs and support preferences of CaP caregivers at various stages of caregiving.

Methodology

Qualitative data were collected using constructivist grounded theory methodology to explore the CaP caregiving experience in the Black community. To ensure quality and rigor, this research aimed to incorporate a dimension of reflexivity throughout the research process (Koch & Harrington, 1998).

Rapport was established with the population of interest as a result of continued participation in activities and events associated with the Florida Minority Cancer Research and Training Center (MiCaRT). In 2016 a series of informal focus groups were conducted at the MiCaRT community town-hall forum with a purposive sample of self-identified CaP advocates who reported providing care for a family member diagnosed with CaP in the past seven years. Initial research questions sought to understand key concepts that were central to the caregiving experience in the Black community. Sample questions included the following: What is the role of the caregiver in the CaP process? How has the CaP experience impacted your well-being? Were you prepared to be a caregiver? Memos and notes from the focus groups were coded to reveal key themes that were used to inform topic areas for the development of a population-specific semistructured interview guide for use among informal CaP caregivers during individual face-to-face interview sessions in the north–north central region of Florida.

The semistructured interview guide, approved by the institutional review board, initially consisted of twenty-six items and was modified throughout the study process as new insights from the community of interest were identified.

Inclusion criteria for participants were as follows: self-identified as an informal caregiver of a Black man with history of CaP and eighteen years of age or older. Interviews were conducted with twelve self-identified CaP caregivers. Characterized by an iterative process for developing meaning and generating theory, the grounded theory methodology was used as a systematic approach to identify concepts and develop theory that is grounded in data (Strauss & Corbin, 1994; Charmaz, 2006). Facilitation of interviews was guided by Kvale's interview criteria and therefore sought to create the most conducive setting for participants to feel comfortable to respond and share their understanding of the CaP experience based on their own perspectives and lived experiences (Kvale, 1996). Recruitment took place through a variety of community venues, such as UF Health Shands Hospital, Health Street community engagement programming, local churches, the Florida MiCaRT center, and other community advocacy organizations in the north–north central region of Florida.

Purposive sampling was used to guide early stages of data collection gathering information from individuals most knowledgeable about this community. Later stages of data collection employed theoretical sampling techniques to address gaps identified in the data, modify questions, refine participant recruitment, and clarify uncertainties in the analysis. Recruitment ended when saturation was reached (i.e., nothing new emerged from subsequent participant interviews).

Data collection and analysis were conducted concurrently. Interviews were audio recorded and transcribed by a professional transcription service. In addition, transcripts were verified by the principal investigator to ensure accuracy. NVivo software was used to code transcripts and organize codes into larger themes. Emerging themes and constructs were used to develop a substantive theory to inform a model of the critical aspects of CaP caregiving in the Black community. Where possible, this study aimed to establish both rigor and credibility of interviews by adhering to the thirty-two-item COREQ (consolidated criteria for reporting qualitative research; Tong et al., 2007); dimensions of reflexivity (Koch & Harrington, 1998) were also incorporated throughout the research process to promote complete and transparent reporting.

Reflexivity Statement

As a Black, Haitian American female scholar, I have a special interest in addressing the disproportionate suffering related to chronic disease in the Black community. The disproportionate rate of morbidity and mortality related to prostate cancer among Black men and the resulting increase in family caregiving is especially disconcerting from a personal perspective, given that I self-identify as the daughter, sister, and niece of multiple Black men. Having served as a family caregiver myself, I interpret this problem to be an issue that is detrimental to the ethnic-minority community as a whole, increasing economic challenges and other hardships already experienced at disproportionate rates in this community. In addition, my understanding of social and behavioral science theories related to health and health promotion has been informed by my background in behavioral science, health policy, and community health. As a researcher, I bring this theoretical knowledge, in addition to my own personal lived experience, to my identification and understanding of social phenomena.

Findings

Participant ages ranged from 47 to 71 years. Caregivers in this sample self-identified as spouses, adult children, and other family relatives. Data related to needs and support preferences were categorized into three primary themes: (1) population-specific programming, (2) accessible support services, and (3) educational resources. A discussion of emerging themes follows. A key strength of the qualitative approach, in most instances, direct quotes are given in conjunction with each theme for their ability to provide a voice for special populations and aid in the dissemination of marginalized perspectives of disenfranchised groups whose needs are often excluded from academic literature (Creswell, 2009).

Population-Specific Programming

Participants in this group indicated there was a need for culturally sensitive programming that considers caregiver support preferences related to facilitation of services in order to increase credibility and trustworthiness. Further, participants specified the importance of integrating faith-based components throughout support programs offered for this community. In addition to support preferences and faith-based components, participants also mentioned the need for age-appropriate and relationship-specific support programs.

Support Preferences

Caregiver narratives. Participants in this sample indicated that facilitation of support programs by individuals with firsthand experience was essential to establishing trust and building rapport in this community. Specifically, participants expressed the need for a facilitator that would be able to relate to the caregiving experience and contribute to the collective caregiver narrative based on firsthand experience. One participant stated,

> Probably someone that have experience, because if you have not experienced it, how can you come before someone and tell someone you should do this when you haven't lived through it? . . . So, it would have to be someone that have already experienced, that have that knowledge, and not coming from a book perspective, where they read all this information in a book and now they can share. It would have to be someone that really knows about being a caregiver.

Another participant echoed this sentiment with even more emphasis, recalling the frustration experienced after receiving sympathy instead of empathy and having to listen to "blasé" words of encouragement that made her feel like the facilitator was not being sincere or authentic, stating,

> 'Cause people say "I understand," but "_____ no, you don't understand." . . . Don't tell me you understand, because, unless you've been there when he was puking, and the pain, and all these meds, and cleaning them up and trying to build on this man, that you've invested a life . . . "You don't understand a DAMN thing! Don't tell me you understand."

Cultural concordance. Racial and ethnic match were also cited as a preference for facilitators of caregiver support groups. Participants indicated that it was easier to gain rapport with someone who shared a similar cultural background. However, in the case of prostate cancer, having firsthand experience was viewed as a more vital facilitator characteristic. While not as significant as firsthand experience as a caregiver, cultural aspects were still an important support need and preference. One participant mentioned, "The doctors, the few doctors that we were referred to for various stages and everything that he was going through, none of them looked like us."

Unbiased providers. In addition to caregiver narratives and racial/ethnic concordance, caregivers also mentioned a preference for nonmedically trained support facilitators, again citing the significance of firsthand experience. When probed about facilitator preferences, one caregiver responded, "Not the physician. Maybe another person that has gone through it, with some questions to ask, to kind of help them to see the way they need to be thinking. . . . So that people can see that this is not a doctor; it's not somebody that works for the drug company or whatever." Several participants shared this sentiment and felt that medical providers themselves were biased. Participants expressed that they preferred not to receive support from medical providers or other clinically trained support staff that may be influenced by pharmaceutical companies or using procedures that would benefit the hospital. Participants indicated that they were more in favor of staff that seemed neutral and trained to provide information without bias.

Faith-Based Components

The integration of faith-based components into support programs, in combination with scientifically sound information or evidence-based recommendations, was also a theme that emerged repeatedly in the data. One participant shared, "I'm so glad now that the churches are becoming more involved, but I think we need tools for them," while another participant stated the importance of the church in everyday life: "When we in trouble . . . the church is our first refuge. I don't know about you. But the people I know and the circles I run, when something happens, we get on the phone and we call our pastors."

Age-Appropriate and Relationship-Specific Components

Caregivers in this sample indicated the need for support programming that was age appropriate. Participants shared that the process of providing care occurred at various stages in life and their needs changed based on age and relationship to the person to whom they were providing care. Related older caregivers indicated the need for support that was catered to children as a means of helping children in the family understand what was happening in terms that they could understand. One caregiver stated, "We tried to shield our girls as much as possible, but I just don't feel it's the way to do that either. I think, now knowing what I know today, I think we would have incorporated them more . . . maybe found material that were related on a child level, that they can understand."

In addition to age-appropriate material, caregivers stated that there was a need for support programming that offered relationship-specific components, as the experience would be different for an adult child as opposed to the experience of a spouse.

Accessible Support Services

Nonspiritual Counseling

The need for counseling services was mentioned repeatedly throughout the interviews. Caregivers reported feeling forgotten and perceived support services to be provided as an afterthought. One participant stated, "Nobody seems to really care about the caregiver, to tell you the truth. They care about the patient but not about the caregiver."

Caregivers felt that support programs should incorporate support programs designed to help caregivers and patients navigate the process of sharing the CaP diagnosis with family and friends. In addition to sharing the diagnosis, caregivers indicated a need for professional counseling service in addition to the spiritual support that was offered by the church. One participant stated,

> Yeah, I would go to him and say, "I'm so tired and I just don't know how much I'm going to be able to take." He didn't get it. Like he'd say "you need to pray more. You need to lean on God more. You need to tell God," . . . and all of those things, like I say, are awesome. But the physical me, the mental me, not the spiritual me, needed somebody, maybe with some counseling experience, to come and deal with that feeling of frustration, that feeling of coping, the need to cope, I think, a 1-800 number. I mean, that's a little impersonal, informal, but just having that counselor, that person that you can go in and vent to, I think would have made the world [of difference] 'cause that would've been an outlet, instead of having just to keep it all in and put on this face, we put on this look of "oh, I'm fine. I'm great. Everything's gonna be fine."

Fatalism

Cancer fatalism was also a major theme discussed by the caregivers in this group. Caregivers shared that men in the Black community were extremely intimidated and fearful of cancer. One participant stated,

> I have to be honest. I think I was more in tune to what the doctor was saying than he was. He began to start talking about, "Who's gonna walk my daughters down the aisle? Who's gonna help my wife, you know, care for our family?" So he took on that macho persona, and all I could share was, "Honey, this is about you. Right now, it's about you. We need you to be healthy and we will be fine."

Conversely, another participant shared that cancer fatalism was a personal fear that caused additional stress and worry, saying, "The first thing I thought of was 'I don't wanna lose him' . . . 'cause you know when they say the big C, then the big D coming, as they say."

Educational Resources

Educational needs were also reported to be a significant need in this sample of caregivers. Participants reported having received subpar information and explanations from doctors and other medical staff. One participant stated, "Considering that, 'oh, I got a booklet.' I think one of the doctors gave me a trifold that just explained where the prostate gland was. I'm like, 'Really?' But nothing really, besides the little note, you know, when you go up to the hospital and they print out the paper when they discharging you."

Participants also emphasized the need for digestible information and materials provided on various platforms and related to all aspects of care and potential negative side effects or common occurrences across the CaP care continuum: "[It would be better] if the material can be tailored in such a way that it gives enough information but they're not overloaded like the internet does."

Other respondents echoed this sentiment and expressed the need for information in an express format targeting key points for the caregiver related to expectations and preparedness: "Maybe they need to have, like—and I don't know if it's already there—once they have patient pamphlets or whatever, what will happen, what the patient is to expect. Then they have to have a section, 'As a caregiver, this is how you can help this patient.'"

Training related to physical aspects of caregiving was also a theme identified by caregivers in this group. Caregivers indicated that they were not prepared to provide care and that typically it was incumbent upon them to make sense of medical devices and other clinical aspects of providing care. One participant stated, "No. I wasn't prepared. I just learned on my own from day to day just to do it. I mean, it just come natural. . . . It wasn't anyone there to say 'well be on the lookout for these symptoms,' or, you know, what you can do just in case this occur. I really wasn't prepared for it; it just happened."

Discussion and Implications for Public Health Practice and Research

Evidence from the academic literature suggests that caregiver support is a key element in cancer survivorship and engagement with health-care systems (Blanchard et al., 2005; Webb et al., 2006; Lepore et al., 2012; Piervil et al., 2018). In the face of continuous provider shortages and limited access to quality care, informal family caregiving should not be diminished. There is great value in family caregiving networks in the Black community, and caregivers have a significant impact on the lifestyle and health-seeking behaviors of men in the Black community (Piervil et al., 2018). Additionally, preliminary research has shown that participation in programs focused on education and support can have a positive impact on caregiver health (Zarit et al., 1999). Thus, public health interventions should seek to adopt a curriculum that covers concepts such as soldiering, passing for normal, the myth of the strong Black woman, and other detrimental symptoms of poor health, in conjunction with providing resources and circumventing systemic issues in the care continuum. This study had minor limitations. Among them were small sample size and limited generalizability to a larger population due to the unique nature of the sample.

Conclusion

The goal of this research was to identify key aspects—as defined by and with significant input from the community affected—of intervention designs necessary to optimize health promotion programs for vulnerable ethnic-minority populations toward improved health outcomes and well-being in this community. While statistically overburdened with diminishing health in the face of adversity and continued disparities in health equity, Black women continue to pour into their families and communities unconditional support and informal caregiving.

It is said that you cannot pour from an empty cup; this research suggests that, despite the resilience and resourcefulness frequently used to describe Black women and their ability to "fill their own cups," without systemic support and a focus on population-specific needs, as Black women work to fortify their own health and to strengthen their community's resources they are inevitably stuck in a system that leads to a quicker depletion of their own personal resources and health stock. Unfortunately, as is often the case, Black women eventually find themselves pouring from a leaking cup. Future research should focus on finding evidence-based best practices for incorporating the caregiver in the CaP care continuum. In addition, public health interventions should seek to collaborate with trusted community institutions, such as the church and local minority-owned small businesses, to incorporate professional counseling with more traditional, faith-based, and culturally accepted and/or normalized coping strategies.

References

American Cancer Society. (2016). *Cancer facts and figures for African Americans 2016–2018*.

Aranda, M. P., & Knight, B. G. (1997). The influence of ethnicity and culture on the caregiver stress and coping process: A socio-cultural review and analysis. *Gerontologist, 37*, 342–354.

Bell, K. (2017). Sisters on sisters: Inner peace from the Black woman mental health professional perspective. In S. Y. Evans, K. Bell, & N. Burton (Eds.), *Black women's mental health: Balancing strength and vulnerability* (pp. 23–41). State University of New York Press.

Blanchard, K., Proverbs-Singh, T., Katner, A., Lifsey, D., Pollard, S., & Rayford, W. (2005). Knowledge, attitudes and beliefs of women about the importance of prostate cancer screening. *Journal of the National Medical Association, 97*(10), 1378–1385.

Charmaz, K. (2006). *Constructing grounded theory* (2nd ed.). Sage.

Creswell, J. W. (2009). *Research design: Qualitative, quantitative, and mixed methods* (3rd ed.). Sage.

Dilworth-Anderson, P. (2001). Extended kin networks in Black families. In A. J. Walker, M. Manoogian-O'Dell, L. A. McGraw, & D. L. G. White (Eds.), *Families in later life: Connections and transitions* (pp. 104–106). Pine Forge Press.

Feinberg, L., Reinhard, S. C., Houser, A., & Choula, R. (2011). *Valuing the invaluable: 2011 update: The growing contributions and costs of family caregiving*. AARP Public Policy Institute.

Giarelli, E., McCorkle, R., & Monturo, C. (2003). Caring for a spouse after prostate surgery: The preparedness needs of wives. *Journal of Family Nursing, 9*(4), 453–485.

Ho, S. C., Chan, A., Woo, J., Chong, P., & Sham, A. (2009). Impact of caregiving on health and quality of life: A comparative population-based study of caregivers for elderly persons and noncaregivers. *The Journals of Gerontology: Series A, 64*(8), 873–879.

Jemal, A., Ward, E. M., Johnson, C. J., Cronin, K. A., Ma, J., Ryerson, A. B., Mariotto, A., Lake, A. J., Wilson, R., Sherman, R. L., Anderson, R. N., Henley, S. J., Kohler, B. A., Penberthy, L., Feuer, E. J., & Weir, H. K. (2017). Annual report to the nation on the status of cancer, 1975–2014, featuring survival. *JNCI: Journal of the National Cancer Institute, 109*(9). https://doi.org/10.1093/jnci/djx030

Kane, C. M. (2000). African American family dynamics as perceived by family members. *Journal of Black Studies, 30*(5), 691–702.

Koch, T., & Harrington, A. (1998). Reconceptualizing rigour: The case for reflexivity. *Journal of Advanced Nursing, 28*, 882–890.

Kvale, S. (1996). *InterViews: An introduction to qualitative research interviewing.* Sage.

Lepore, S. J., Wolf, R. L., Basch, C. E., Godfrey, M., McGinty, E., Shmukler, C., Ullman, R., Thomas, N., & Weinrich, S. (2012). Informed decision making about prostate cancer testing in predominantly immigrant black men: A randomized controlled trial. *Annals of Behavioral Medicine, 44*(3), 320–330.

Mendenhall, R., Henderson, L., & Scott, B. M. (2017). African American mothers' parenting in the midst of violence and fear: Finding meaning and transcendence. In S. Y. Evans, K. Bell, & N. K. Burton (Eds.), *Black women's mental health: Balancing strength and vulnerability* (pp. 183–197). State University of New York Press.

National Alliance for Caregiving & AARP Public Policy Institute. (2015). *Caregiving in the U.S.* http://www.caregiving.org/caregiving2015/

National Family Caregivers Association & Family Caregiver Alliance. (2006). *Prevalence, hours and economic value of family caregiving, updated state-by-state analysis of 2004 national estimates by Peter S. Arno, PhD.*

Pharr, J. R., Francis, C. D., Terry, C., & Clark, M. C. (2014). Culture, caregiving, and health: Exploring the influence of culture on family caregiver experiences. *International Scholarly Research Notices, 2014,* 1–8.

Piervil, E., Odedina, F., & Young, M. E. (2018). The role and influence of prostate cancer caregivers across the care continuum. *Health Promotion Practice, 20*(3), 436–444.

Pinquart, M., & Sörensen, S. (2005). Ethnic differences in stressors, resources, and psychological outcomes of family caregiving: A meta-analysis. *The Gerontologist, 45*(1), 90–106.

Ries, L. A. G., Eisner, M. P., Kosary, C. L., Hankey, B. F., Miller, B. A., Clegg, L., Mariotto, A., Fay, M. P., Feuer, E. J., & Edwards, B. K. (Eds.). (2003). *SEER cancer statistics review, 1975–2000.* National Cancer Institute. http://seer.cancer.gov/csr/1975_2000/

Schulz, R., & Quittner, A. L. (1998). Caregiving through the life-span: An overview and future directions. *Health Psychol.* 17: 107–111.

Strauss, A., & Corbin, J. (1994). Grounded theory methodology: An overview.

Tong, A., Sainsbury, P., & Craig, J. (2007). Consolidated criteria for reporting qualitative research (COREQ): A 32-item checklist for interviews and focus groups. *International Journal for Quality in Health Care, 19*(6), 349–357.

Trivedi, R., Beaver, K., Bouldin, E. D., Eugenio, E., Zeliadt, S. B., Nelson, K., Rosland, A.-M., Szarka, J. G., & Piette, J. D. (2014). Characteristics and well-being of informal caregivers: Results from a nationally-representative US survey. *Chronic Illness, 10*(3), 167–179.

U.S. Cancer Statistics Working Group. (2017). *United States cancer statistics: 1999–2014 incidence and mortality web-based report.* U.S. Department of

Health and Human Services, Centers for Disease Control and Prevention and National Cancer Institute.

Webb, C. R., Kronheim, L., Williams, J. E., & Hartman, T. J. (2006). An evaluation of the knowledge, attitudes, and beliefs of African-American men and their female significant others regarding prostate cancer screening. *Ethnicity & Disease, 16*(1), 234–238.

Weiss, C. O., Gonzalez, H. M., Kabeto, M. U., & Langa, K. M. (2005). Differences in amount of informal care received by non-Hispanic whites and latinos in a nationally representative sample of older Americans. *Journal of the American Geriatrics Society, 53*(1), 146–151.

Zarit, S., Gaugler, J. & Jarrott, S. (1999). Useful services for families: Research findings and directions. *International Journal of Geriatric Psychiatry, 14,* 165–181.

PART III

ACT FOR CHANGE

SECTION OUTLINE: SARITA K. DAVIS

The concept of Sankofa is central to advancing the agenda of Black women in public health. *Sankofa* is a symbol used by the Akan people of Ghana. This image is generally depicted as a bird taking a step forward with its head turned back to hold an egg. It expresses the importance of reaching back to knowledge gained in the past and bringing it into the present in order to make positive progress. In the context of Black women and public health, *Sankofa* means learning from our history in order to serve the needs of our future. Chapters in this third section offer insights about planning and training issues related to Black women and public health. While this content resides at the end of the book, it is critical to moving forward.

In the first chapter of this section, Jenny Douglas recognizes the contributions of Black women to addressing racial inequalities in the field of public health in the United Kingdom. Douglas creates a historical timeline that illustrates a chronology and typology of contributions of Black women in the UK in the twentieth century, including public health education, research, and activism. Douglas attempts to fill in the blanks of Black women's erasure from the annals of public health history and to demonstrate how her work in the field is part of a long tradition.

Building on the Douglas narrative of Black women's contributions to best practices in public health, Mandy Hill, Ndidiamaka N. Amutah-Onukagha, Charlene A. Flash, Kelli Joiner, Folake Olayinka, and

Bisola Ojikutu tackle the low utilization rate among Black women of HIV prevention services in general and oral pre-exposure prophylaxis (PrEP) in particular. This pertinent presentation of the research versus the realities faced in practice results in relevant recommendations concerning future implementation strategies and working to broaden access to PrEP and offers a specific example of how intersectional understanding is required to root out harmful or ineffective systemic practices.

In another pertinent professional intervention, Andrea Anderson, Judy Washington, and Joedrecka S. Brown Speights eloquently lay out the importance of mentoring Black women in public health and the medical professions. As physicians themselves, the authors reflect on the positive effects mentoring had on their individual well-being as students as well as on their careers. In guiding us through some daunting data on the health disparities faced by Black women in society, the authors make the case that the increased presence of Black women in public health and US medical schools could increase culturally responsive health-service delivery and help to reduce disparities. While detailing the downward trend of Black women seeking degrees in public health, the authors also draw attention to the declining number of Black women faculty members in the field as well. Finally, the authors conclude that anyone can mentor by simply offering words of encouragement.

As Byllye Avery indicated, "we all do public health." The next two chapters elevate examples of community-based and community-driven public health practitioners and uncover further evidence of historical social justice work that must be studied in order to build effective approaches. In their chapter, Portia A. Jackson Preston, Leslie Bronner, and Yvonne Bronner examine the significant topic of "Stress and Black Women's Health" with provision of key strategies for future policy and practice. Taken together, the King-White et al. chapter and the Jackson Preston et al. chapter truly speak to the striking impact stress, particularly chronic stress from race-, gender-, and class-based factors, has on Black women's health.

While yoga and its practice in the US has been coded White, affluent, female, and thin, Tamara Y. Jeffries, Santiba D. Campbell, and Yasmeen J. Long remind us that Alice Coltrane was not only a seminal figure in the introduction of yoga to the US; her yogic journey prompted her to introduce a more holistic version of its practice into Black communities intentionally designed to help them heal and overcome various traumas, both historical and contemporary as well as personal and political. The chapter raises the question, Given yoga's healing potential, why did its practice in Black communities not expand significantly in the latter portion of the twentieth century? Why has Alice Coltrane / Swamini Turiyasangitananda been largely erased from the history of yoga's spread within the US? What role did her identities as Black and female play in that erasure? And how might Black communities re-embrace yoga given its healing potential? This story, like the recent work by Stephanie Evans to uncover the yogic legacy of prominent figures like Rosa Parks, has deep implications for how public health workers approach communities and how assumptions about practices like yoga must be reexamined.[1]

Part memoir and part empirical research, in the closing chapter, I explore the utility of subjective inquiry in conducting research with Black women in public health. I describe the dominant research paradigm used in public health and its limitations in addressing the layered and nuanced needs of Black women. I offer a short list of disciplines that use subjective inquiry to illustrate the utility of the practice in other disciplines. Finally, I offer personal and professional examples of how subjective inquiry has informed my practice and research.

Note

1. Evans, S. Y. (2019, June 21). Black women's historical wellness: History as a tool in culturally competent mental health services. *Association of Black Women Historians*. http://abwh.org/2019/06/21/Black-womens-historical-wellness-history-as-a-tool-in-culturally-competent-mental-health-services/

Chapter 9

Black Women and Public Health in the UK

JENNY DOUGLAS

I was appointed as a district health promotion manager in West Birmingham in the West Midlands in the UK in September 1984, where I was one of a very small number of Black health promotion managers in the whole of the UK. I established and developed a health promotion department in an area of Birmingham with a very diverse and multicultural population. At the time of my appointment, health education departments were being renamed health promotion departments, and the work of the departments was being refocused from behavior-change approaches to addressing inequalities in health. The World Health Organization (WHO, 1981) had developed the Health for All by the Year 2000 initiative, and there were thirty-eight targets focused on reducing inequalities in health. This heralded a need to move beyond health education, which focused on giving advice on healthy lifestyles and educating about health.

Introduction: The Development of
Public Health Organizations in the UK

Health education in the UK can be traced back to the nineteenth century. Women volunteers visited poor women in their homes to try to educate them about hygiene, healthy living, and domestic management. The Manchester and Salford Ladies Health Society was formed as the

Ladies Sanitary Reform Association in 1867 (Dingwall, 1977) under the sponsorship of an all-male Manchester and Salford Sanitary Association, which was founded in 1852. The men focused on lectures and delivering literature and placards to mills and factories, while the women visited homes and advised on hygiene in the home and childcare. It has been argued that this was the basis of health visiting.

The first paid health visitor was appointed in 1867 to assist the women volunteer visitors. This was followed by the development of the role of health education officers in the early twentieth century who were part of the local-authority public health departments. Health education services were also part of local authorities in the 1970s and became part of area health authorities with the reorganization in 1974. A further reorganization in 1984 created district health authorities, and large health education services in some areas were split up and moved into district health authorities.

Relationship between Health Education and Health Promotion in the Mid-1980s

Although the origins of health promotion are much debated, Catford (2007) argues that the term *health promotion* was increasingly used in the 1980s by public health activists who were dissatisfied with health education and disease prevention and the biomedical focus of public health, with its emphasis on individual behavior change. The Ottawa Charter (WHO, 1986) was arguably the genesis of health promotion. The Ottawa Charter for Health Promotion emerged from the First International Conference on Health Promotion held in Ottawa, Canada, November 17–21, 1986. In the years following the Ottawa Charter, there was an expansion in health promotion both as a profession and as a field of practice in the UK.

The Ottawa Charter marked a move from health education to health promotion in the mid-1980s. Slowly, most health education departments were renamed health promotion departments, although many critics questioned whether there was any change in the type of work that was undertaken by the department and argued that it was still very much influenced by health education rather than health promotion principles and approaches. At this point consultants in public health and district medical officers were medically trained and qualified. Health promotion units were often located within public health departments. Health promotion specialists came from a wide range of professional backgrounds, but many had been teachers or nurses.

Postgraduate courses in health promotion were developed; one of the first courses was established in 1972 at Leeds Polytechnic (now Leeds Beckett University), initially in health education but changed to health promotion in the mid-1980s. Across the UK, health promotion specialists emerged from the existing health education officers, and the late 1980s witnessed the establishment of a professional group called health promotion specialists. Health promotion units were established as part of health services in major cities, where they were charged with developing health promotion programs for populations that were becoming increasingly diverse following postwar migration from the Caribbean, the Indian subcontinent, and Africa.

Relationship between Health Promotion and Public Health in the 1990s to 2000s

The relationship of health promotion to public health received considerable attention in the 1990s to 2000s (Douglas, 2009). During the period of the Conservative government under the leadership of Margaret Thatcher (1979 to 1990), public health was kept on the agenda by a group of nonmedical public health activists, many of whom were health promotion specialists. The concept of health inequalities was not recognized by Margaret Thatcher, who only recognized "variations in health," despite the fact that the UK was a signatory to the World Health Organization's Health for All strategy, and hence there was a return to an emphasis on individual behavior change and away from developing public health strategies that focused on social, economic, and political factors that affected health.

With the election of a Labour government under the leadership of Tony Blair in 1997, there was a renewed emphasis on addressing inequalities in health. The politics of public health and health promotion are complex and contradictory. However, as public health rose higher on the political agenda, health promotion specialists seemed to disappear, renamed as public health practitioners and public health specialists. The political focus of health promotion strategies had a major influence on the now renamed New Public Health.

There was keen debate about the boundaries between public health and health promotion. MacDonald (1998) stated that "the principles and content of modern health promotion . . . are identical to those of the new public health" (p. 28). Fighting for a territory that was rapidly changing, some health promotion specialists chose to call themselves public health practitioners, arguing that health promotion (through the development of healthy public policies) was one of the main areas of public health. A multidisciplinary public health function was proposed. The *Report of the Chief Medical Officer's Project to Strengthen the Public Health Function* stated that "the aim is a strong, effective, sustainable and multidisciplinary public health function which is in good shape to underpin the delivery of the NHS Plan and to improve health and reduce inequalities" (Department of Health, 2001, p. 43).

The emphasis on developing a wider multidisciplinary public health approach met with some resistance in certain quarters where there was an adherence to a more medical model of public health. What was clear was the need for a well-skilled multidisciplinary public health workforce that was able to work in partnership with a range of organizations in both formal and informal settings to promote public health.

Black Women and Public Health in the UK

Throughout the latter half of the twentieth century and into the twenty-first century, Black women across the UK have been involved in campaigning for change, setting up Black women's groups to challenge inappropriate, racist, and ethnocentric practices within the National Health Service (NHS). In the post–World War II period, African Caribbean women migrated to the UK in the 1950s to work in the newly established NHS. Employed in public health work as nurses, health visitors, midwives, and community health workers, the majority of these women experienced racism and discrimination that impacted their ability to progress into senior managerial roles in the NHS (Beishon et al., 1995).

While working and enabling change with the NHS, Black nurses were active in their local communities and churches, establishing and contributing to a range of voluntary organizations. The activism of these Black women has largely remained undocumented. However, for many Black people access to medical health care remains an important and overriding concern, and Black women continue to organize for change and improve public health.

Nineteenth-Century Involvement of Black Women in Public Health: Mary Seacole

One of the earliest documented contributions of a Black woman to public health in the UK is that of Mary Seacole. Born in Jamaica around 1805, Mary Seacole applied to the British authorities to be sent as an army nurse to join the war effort in the Crimean War in 1854 (Dabydeen et al., 2007). After sailing to London in the autumn of 1854, she was rejected and not allowed to join the army nurses. Alarmed by the discriminatory treatment she received, she refused to accept the rejection, and she sailed to Balaklava in February 1855, setting up a "British hotel" where she tended the sick and wounded.

Mary Seacole returned to the UK and was the first African Caribbean woman in Britain to publish an autobiography in 1857 (see Seacole, 1857). The pioneering work of Mary Seacole was recognized with a statue, which was unveiled in London in 2016, after a twelve-year campaign to raise funding. Following Mary Seacole's work, there was no more documented involvement of Black women in public health in the UK until the 1950s.

Postwar Migration of Caribbean Nurses

Although the Black presence in Britain can be traced to Roman times (Fryer, 1984), the emergence of a significant Black population did not occur until the post–World War II era. In the late 1940s, 1950s, and 1960s, called the Windrush era, Black people migrated from the English-speaking Caribbean—mainly Barbados, Trinidad, St. Lucia, and Jamaica—and were recruited to work in the NHS, which was established in 1948. Black women worked as nurses, auxiliaries, and cleaners. While academic literature has focused on the racism and discrimination that these women experienced, there has been little acknowledgment or documentation of the substantial contribution that these women made to public health (Douglas, 2019). In the 1960s and later, many African nurses migrated from Nigeria, Ghana, Malawi, and other African countries to work as nurses in the NHS because of a shortage of UK nurses.

As well as working in the NHS, many nurses were also involved in their churches and communities developing health promotion initiatives and strategies to challenge racist and ethnocentric health services (Douglas, 2019).

Health Promotion Specialists

Despite the need to develop health promotion programs and initiatives with Black, Asian, and minority ethnic communities (the term *Black, Asian, and minority ethnic communities* refers to people from Africa; the Caribbean; the Indian subcontinent—India, Pakistan, and Bangladesh; China; and other ethnic groups) that addressed health inequalities experienced by those communities, there were relatively few Black health promotion specialists or health promotion managers employed by health services even though there was development and expansion of the field of health promotion.

My first task on appointment as a district health promotion manager in West Birmingham was not only to draw together epidemiological information that existed on the health of the population but also to identify the issues that local people believed were important to their health. This involved undertaking research to ascertain health concerns before developing appropriate health promotion programs in conjunction with local communities (Douglas, 1995, 1996).

One of the major areas of concern that emerged nationally was that of nutrition education. The Department of Health developed the Stop Rickets Campaign in 1981 to inform Asian families of the high incidence of rickets and osteomalacia among the Asian population due to Vitamin D deficiency (Bahl, 1981). While it was extremely important to focus on a major health concern of Asian communities, there was no focus on nutrition in Caribbean communities. There was no research on the nutrition and dietary practices of Caribbean communities in the UK. I obtained funding from the Inner City Partnership program to undertake research on the dietary practices of Caribbean young mothers in Birmingham (Kemm et al., 1986, 1987; Douglas, 1987).

I had the opportunity to visit the Caribbean during the tenure of a traveling fellowship to examine approaches to health and nutrition education in Jamaica, Barbados, and Trinidad. This enabled me to develop culturally relevant health promotion material in the form of a training resource on Caribbean food and diet for health workers and other professionals who were giving dietary advice to members of the Caribbean community (Douglas, 1987).

During my travel fellowship, I was introduced to the work of the World Health Organization and the Health for All strategy (WHO, 1981). The Health for All principles, based upon notions of community development, community participation, and empowerment and the key principles of the Ottawa Charter for Health Promotion (WHO, 1986), informed the health promotion programs and initiatives I developed. However, despite WHO's emphasis on addressing inequalities in health in Europe, nowhere was any reference made to Black and minority ethnic communities in Europe and the impact of racial discrimination on their health. WHO still does not adopt an intersectional approach to public health.

In 1988, I became director of health promotion in the neighboring borough of Sandwell. In this role, I was able to obtain external funding for a number of research and development initiatives on the health needs of Black and minority ethnic communities (Douglas, 1996). One of the major initiatives was the Smethwick Heart Action Research Project (SHARP; Douglas, 1996), which was funded by the Health Education Council from 1991 to 1994. It aimed to identify risk factors for Black and minority ethnic communities in Smethwick in relation to coronary heart disease and stroke and to examine social, economic, and political factors that affected their health as well as the effects of racism and racial discrimination. As an action research project, it developed a range of health promotion programs and initiatives based upon the needs identified by the SHARP survey respondents.

I have argued that, in the main, health promotion programs and strategies "did not acknowledge inequalities in health in relation to poverty, class, culture or gender" (Douglas, 1995, p. 75). I further argued that health promotion programs developed by most health promotion units "had not involved Black and minority ethnic communities, groups or individuals in their conceptualisation, development or implementation" (p. 75). Through SHARP, Black and minority ethnic communities were involved in every stage of the development of health promotion programs: in their planning, implementation, and evaluation.

Black Women Health Activists

The women's health movement emerged in the 1960s and 1970s as part of the second-wave feminist movement. This movement urged women to take control of their health and their bodies and to make the personal the political. With a focus on reproductive health and empowerment, the women's health movement demanded appropriate health services for and by women. At the forefront of this movement was the Boston Women's Collective and their groundbreaking book *Our Bodies, Ourselves*, the feminist health-care handbook. *Our Bodies, Ourselves* was first published commercially in 1973 and sold over 4 million copies (Davis, 2007).

However, many Black women felt that the women's health movement did not reflect the concerns and experiences of Black women.

Black women established their own women's health groups across the UK to discuss issues that concerned Black women in relation to reproductive rights. Although a research study documenting the health activism of Black women in the UK is lacking, existing documentation points to Black women's health groups having been established in many UK towns and cities—for example, London (Brixton and Southall), Birmingham, Manchester, Coventry, Liverpool, and Cardiff (Sudbury, 1998). The Brixton Black Women's Group was formed in 1973 to discuss Black women's experience of racialized and gendered oppression (Bryan et al., 1985).

One of their major campaigns was a campaign to stop the use of the injectable contraceptive Depo-Provera, which was being administered to White working-class women and Black and minority ethnic women without their knowledge or consent in NHS hospitals across the UK (Brent Community Health Council, 1981). The campaign was effective, and the pharmaceutical company was not granted a license for the long-term use of Depo-Provera. Black women organized other effective campaigns around the development of sickle cell and thalassemia centers and services and the development of appropriate mental health services.

There are enduring inequities in Black women's health and well-being in the UK, in relation to diabetes, hypertension, mental health, breast cancer, and maternal mortality and morbidity (Douglas, 2018). The 2018 MBRRACE-UK report stated that "there are striking inequalities: Black women are five times and Asian women two times more likely to die as a result of complications in pregnancy than white women and urgent research and action to understand these disparities is needed" (Knight et al., 2018). Despite the recognition that urgent research was needed, there is still a gap in the public health evidence available to understand why Black women are at greater risk of maternal mortality. There is a need for research studies involving and led by Black women.

Research Projects, Black Health Researchers, and Black Women Public Health Specialists

While there are a few Black women undertaking research to examine the health needs of Black communities, such researchers are quite disparate and isolated. To this end, we established a Black Women's Health and Wellbeing Research Network at the Open University (www.open.ac.uk/Black-womens-health-and-wellbeing).

The aim of the network is to provide a space for Black women researchers to discuss their research and to exchange knowledge with other researchers, practitioners, policy makers, community workers, and Black lay women. The network organized a conference on Black Women's Health and Wellbeing in 2011 (which resulted in a special issue of the journal *Critical Public Health* [Douglas & Watson, 2013]), featuring articles on health promotion, Black women and mental health, Black women and body image, and Black women and physical activity.

There are relatively few Black women public health specialists, some from a medical background and some from a multidisciplinary public health background. Even fewer have become directors of public health. The UK Public Health Register is an independent, dedicated regulator for public health professionals in the United Kingdom. It is a voluntary register of public health specialists and practitioners. There are currently only twenty-one Black female practitioner registrants and seventeen Black female specialist registrants on the UK Public Health Register (P. Sull, personal communication, January 31, 2019). This does not reflect the number of Black women currently employed in the NHS who are involved in public health work.

The experiences of Black women public health doctors mirror very much the experiences of Black women academics (Douglas, 2017), who experience daily microaggressions and receive little or no support from managers and limited opportunities for personal and professional development. These Black women have often had to seek their own opportunities for personal and professional development, and at their own expense. Many of these women felt that they were working in isolation with little support. However, Black women public health doctors highlighted the importance of workshops and spaces where they were able to meet with other Black women to discuss their day-to-day experiences and develop networks and alliances. Often working in multiethnic, multicultural, and multiracial locations, these Black women made it a priority to address inequities in health experienced by Black, Asian, and minority ethnic communities by developing public health and health promotion initiatives that were relevant to the populations in the locations in which they were working.

Conclusion: Recommendations for Future Work in Research, Policy, and Practice

This chapter aims to give an overview of Black women working in public health in the UK and to address the historical erasure of Black women's contribution to public health in the UK. The health activism of Black women in the UK has received little academic attention, and further research is required to address this and to make visible the work and contribution that Black women public health practitioners and public health specialists have made to public health. There are an increasing number of Black women involved in researching Black women's health and a growing number of organizations involved in addressing policy and practice in relation to the health of Black communities in the UK. However, urgent attention and action is required to address widening inequities in health—for example, maternal mortality. This is one of the major concerns of the current time for Black women.

A recent report published in November 2018, stated that Black women are five times more likely to die from complications of pregnancy and childbirth than White women (Knight et al., 2018). Black women, midwives, and doulas have worked to address this by establishing organizations such as Mimosa Midwives and Abuela Doulas, who run doula preparation courses, a Wisdom of Abuelas course, a cultural competency course, and a reproductive justice retreat (see abueladoulas.co.uk). In addition, the Five X More campaign established a petition to lobby the government, which attracted 187,000 signatures. As stated by Schulz and Mullings (2006), "health disparities based on race/racism, class and gender/sexism are matters of life and death" (p. 3), and nowhere is this more true than in relation to maternal mortality.

COVID-19 has disproportionately affected the lives of Black women in the USA and in the UK. Black women are more likely to have died and been hospitalized than their White female counterparts for a variety of complex and interrelated reasons (Harewood, 2021). First, a large percentage of Black women in the UK are employed in the NHS as nurses. Many Black nurses felt that they were working on the front line in hospitals, without adequate personal protective equipment to protect them from exposure to COVID-19, and they often felt unable to discuss their concerns with their line managers or departmental managers. Some Black nurses felt that they were more likely to be asked to work in unsafe environments than their White colleagues. In addition to being put at greater risk of exposure to COVID-19, Black nurses, health workers, auxiliaries, and cleaners often have underlying health conditions and comorbidities such as hypertension, diabetes, and liver conditions. Furthermore, Black communities in the UK are often forced into inner-city areas where they are exposed to traffic pollution and other environmental hazards and dense housing.

The experience of Black communities with COVID-19 has demonstrated long-standing health inequities on both sides of the Atlantic. I have consistently highlighted these in health promotion literature (Douglas, 1995, 1996, 2017, 2018, 2019) and more recently in a BBC documentary (Harewood, 2021). As we develop future public health strategies and policies, there is a need to adopt intersectional approaches that recognize racialized, gendered, and classed experiences of Black women. While Black women need culturally relevant and specific health promotion public resources and advice, there is a need for culturally safe health services that ensure that Black women do not experience racially discriminatory or disadvantageous treatment. There is a need for more Black women in public health to shape the development of relevant and appropriate services and to set and lead the research agenda on health inequalities.

Black women's contribution to public health has been ignored and erased. In this chapter I have documented some of the ways in which Black women have influenced public health and improved the health of Black communities through their organization and activism. I have, through telling my history in public health, demonstrated that public health cannot be divorced from a Black feminist and an intersectional lens. If we are to fully understand the factors that influence the health of Black communities and develop policies and practices that address inequities in health, we must develop and utilize intersectional conceptual frameworks for public health. This has been laid bare by the disproportionate impact that COVID-19 has had on Black communities in the UK and the USA.

References

Bahl, Veena. (1981). Stop Rickets campaign. *Nutrition & Food Science, 81*(3), 2–5.

Beishon, S., Virdee, S., & Hagell, A. (1995). *Nursing in a multi-ethnic NHS.* Policy Studies Institute.

Brent Community Health Council. (1981). *Black people and the health service.*

Bryan, B., Dadzie, S., & Scafe, S. (1985). *The heart of the race: Black women's lives in Britain.* Virago.

Catford, J. (2007) Ottawa 1986: The fulcrum of global health development. *Promotion and Education, 14*(6, Suppl. 2), 6–7.

Dabydeen, D., Gilmore, J., & Jones, C. (2007). *The Oxford Companion to Black British History*. Oxford University Press.

Davis, K. (2007). *The making of* Our Bodies, Ourselves: *How feminism travels across borders*. Duke University Press.

Department of Health. (2001) *The report of the chief medical officer's project to strengthen the public health function*. London.

Dingwall, R. (1977). Collectivism, regionalism and feminism: Health visiting and British social policy 1850-1975. *Journal of Social Policy*, 6(3), 291–315.

Douglas, J. (1987). *Caribbean food and diet*. National Extension College for Training in Health and Race.

Douglas, J. (1995) Developing anti-racist health promotion strategies. In R. Bunton, S. Nettleton, & R. Burrows (Eds.), *The sociology of health promotion: Critical analyses of consumption, lifestyle and risk* (pp. 70–77). Routledge.

Douglas, J. (1996) Developing with Black and minority ethnic communities, health promotion strategies which address social inequalities. In P. Bywaters & E. McLeod (Eds.), *Working for equality in health* (pp. 179–196). Routledge.

Douglas, J. (2009). The rise of modern multidisciplinary public health. In J. Douglas, S. Earle, S. Handsley, L. Jones, C. E. Lloyd, & S. Spurr (Eds.), *A reader in promoting public health: Challenge and controversy* (2nd ed., pp. 9–14). Sage / Open University.

Douglas, J., & Watson, N. (2013). Editorial: Resistance, resilience and renewal: The health and well-being of black women in the Atlantic Diaspora—developing an intersectional approach. *Critical Public Health*, 23(1), 1–5.

Douglas, J. (2017). The struggle to find a voice on Black women's health: From the personal to the political. In D. Gabriel & S. A. Tate (Eds.), *Inside the Ivory Tower: Narratives of women of colour surviving and thriving in British academia* (pp. 91–107). Trentham Books.

Douglas, J. (2018). The politics of Black women's health in the UK: Intersections of "race," class, and gender in policy, practice, and research. In N. Alexander-Floyd & J. Jordan-Zachery (Eds.), *Black women and politics: Demanding citizenship, challenging power, and seeking justice* (pp. 49–68). State University of New York Press.

Douglas, J. (2019) Black women's activism and organisation in public health—struggles and strategies for better health and wellbeing. *Caribbean Review of Gender Studies*, (13), 51–68.

Fryer, P. (1984). *Staying power: The history of black people in Britain*. Humanities Press International.

Harewood, D. (Host). (2021, March 2). *Why is Covid killing people of colour?* [Documentary]. BBC One.

Kemm, J. R., Douglas, J., & Sylvester, V. (1986). A survey of infant feeding practice by Afro-Caribbean mothers in Birmingham. *Proceedings of the Nutrition Society*, 45(3), 87a.

Kemm, J. R., Douglas, J., & Sylvester, V. (1987). Eating patterns of Afro-Caribbean mothers in Birmingham. *Proceedings of the Nutrition Society, 46*(2), 100A.

Knight, M., Bunch, K., Tuffnell, D., Jayakody, H., Shakespeare, J., Kotnis, R., Kenyon, S., & Kurinczuk, J. J. (Eds.). (2018). *Saving lives, improving mothers' care: Lessons learned to inform maternity care from the UK and Ireland Confidential Enquiries into Maternal Deaths and Morbidity 2014–16*. MBRRACE-UK.

MacDonald, T. H. (1998) *Rethinking health promotion: A global approach*. Routledge.

Seacole, M. (1857). *Wonderful adventures of Mrs Seacole in many lands*. James Blackwood.

Shulz, A. J., & Mullings, L. (2006). *Gender, race, class, and health: Intersectional approaches*. Jossey-Bass.

Sudbury, J. (1998). *Other kinds of dreams: Black women's organisation and the politics of transformation*. Routledge.

World Health Organization. (1981). *Global strategy for health for all by the year 2000*. Geneva.

World Health Organization. (1986). *Ottawa Charter for Health Promotion*. Geneva.

Chapter 10

Enhancing Clinical Practice to Include Biomedical HIV Prevention for Black Women

MANDY HILL, NDIDIAMAKA N. AMUTAH-ONUKAGHA,
CHARLENE A. FLASH, KELLI JOINER, FOLAKE OLAYINKA,
AND BISOLA OJIKUTU

The addition of clinical practice guidelines for biomedical HIV-prevention services for women to routine clinical practice will optimize HIV-preventive care (Institute of Medicine, 2011; Shekelle, 2018). This strategy will significantly impact Black women, who have higher rates of HIV diagnosis than women of any other racial group in the United States (Centers for Disease Control and Prevention [CDC], n.d.-c). Though effective, evidence-based, behavioral, and biomedical HIV-prevention interventions exist, engagement in and uptake of these strategies among Black women is low (Wu et al., 2017). Nevertheless, inclusion of these strategies within routine clinical practice for Black women will improve the persistent racial and ethnic disparities in HIV incidence, whereas failure to include biomedical HIV-prevention strategies within clinical practice fuels persistent racial and ethnic disparities in HIV incidence. In this chapter, we explore the history of HIV prevention among Black women and outline strategies to successfully integrate biomedical HIV prevention into clinical practice.

History

HIV Incidence among Black Women

According to 2014 CDC data, Black women have the highest rate of HIV diagnoses among all women, with an annual rate of 50.8 new HIV infections per 100,000 women, compared to 15.8 per 100,00 Hispanic women and 7.7 per 100,000 White women (CDC, n.d.-b; Texas Department of State Health Services HIV/STD Program, 2016). From 2010 to 2014, the HIV diagnosis rate among Black women decreased (McCree et al., 2017). However, factors such as poverty, discrimination, stigma, engagement in survival and transactional sex, and normative sexual behaviors that promote HIV risk (e.g., tolerance of infidelity and sexual concurrency) continue to contribute to the high HIV incidence among Black women (Adimora et al., 2002; Adimora et al., 2006; Dunkle et al., 2010; Hill, Andrews, et al., 2018; Hill et al., 2016; Hill et al., 2017; Morris & Kretzschmar, 1997). Uptake of effective biomedical HIV-prevention strategies could potentially decrease the rate of new infections among this disproportionately impacted group (CDC, n.d.-b, n.d.-c; Adimora et al., 2006; Heumann, 2018; Huang et al., 2018; Smith et al., 2018).

Strategies to Reduce HIV Incidence among Black Women

Developing a strategic approach to reducing HIV incidence among Black women necessitates a clear and thorough understanding of the benefits and risks of potential HIV-prevention approaches. History has demonstrated that the use of vaccinations to combat the spread of disease is a safe and efficient way to eradicate a global virus like HIV (Bekker et al., 2012). However, no vaccine has been shown to have high enough efficacy to warrant use outside a clinical trial setting (Hsu & O'Connell, 2017). Thus, an HIV vaccine as a lead HIV-prevention strategy is not yet advised or viable. Other biomedical interventions have been widely tested and evaluated (Bekker et al., 2012; Flash et al., 2014; Heumann, 2018). Current recommendations for biomedical prevention among women include oral pre-exposure prophylaxis (PrEP), oral post-exposure prophylaxis (PEP), and treatment as prevention (TasP) (Heumann, 2018). PrEP involves the ongoing use of antiretroviral drugs traditionally used to treat HIV infection, such as coformulated tenofovir disoproxil fumarate (TDF) and emtricitabine (FTC), to prevent HIV transmission (Blumenthal et al., 2015;

Heffron et al., 2017; Huang et al., 2018; Velloza & Heffron, 2017). The Food and Drug Administration (FDA) has approved the combination of TDF and FTC in the US for use as PrEP. Despite demonstrated efficacy among men, women, and people who inject drugs, there has been limited uptake among women.

PrEP Efficacy to Date

Though oral PrEP efficacy among men who have sex with men (MSM) who are at high risk for HIV infection has received considerable attention, published efficacy data on PrEP among women lacks uniformity and requires refinement (Janes et al., 2018; Mayer & Ramjee, 2015). A series of meta-analyses of oral TDF/FTC effectiveness included five randomized placebo-controlled trials that included women; they demonstrated varying levels of efficacy (Fonner et al., 2016; Hanscom et al., 2016). Findings showed that with high levels of adherence (75 percent), oral PrEP is estimated to be effective in women. In a randomized controlled trial of oral PrEP in heterosexual women, participants who were given TDF showed no reduction in HIV acquisition, which led to an early halt of the study (Fransen et al., 2017; Wynne et al., 2018). Further investigation revealed poor adherence drove poor efficacy. An oral PrEP trial including women who use injection drugs showed a 48.9 percent reduction in HIV incidence (Choopanya et al., 2013). Oral PrEP achieves high efficacy in women when levels of adherence to a PrEP regimen are high; however, those with low PrEP adherence demonstrate low efficacy (Escudero et al., 2015; Koss et al., 2018). Limited research via clinical trials in women has taken place to date, and PrEP is not always included in clinical practice for Black women. This clinical norm is a disservice to Black women who could benefit from PrEP.

In addition to oral PrEP, the vaginal ring provides a simple and long-acting way of administering antiretroviral therapy for HIV prevention (Baeten et al., 2016). Vaginal rings for HIV prevention in women have proven safe and efficacious, with a lower rate of HIV transmission among women randomized to the dapivirine as compared to the placebo (Nel, van Niekerk, et al., 2016). In a small placebo-controlled trial, women randomized (2:1) to receive vaginal rings containing dapivirine had less chance of contracting HIV as compared to those receiving the placebo (Nel, Bekker, et al., 2016; Nel, van Niekerk, et al., 2016). In another, single-arm, placebo-controlled randomized trial conducted among 2,629 women, the dapirivine ring successfully reduced the risk of HIV transmission among participants (Baeten et al., 2016).

A third biomedical HIV-prevention strategy utilizes a topical gel applied directly to the site of sexual exposure. Like the dapivirine ring, the topical gel has the potential to effectively deliver higher local protective concentrations of drug to the cervix, vagina, and/or rectum than oral PrEP (Marrazzo, 2018). Due to the highly variable and exceptional mutation rate of HIV, scientists are challenged with creating a topical therapy that would be highly efficacious with every HIV strain (Traore et al., 2018). Topical vaginal or rectal preventive therapy may offer women who are challenged by daily oral-medication adherence with a plausible, safe, and effective alternative HIV-prevention therapy. In women who were adherent to the topical application regimen, vaginal tenofovir gel provided modest protection against HIV infection (Heumann, 2018). Topical therapy may provide alternative dosing strategies that may facilitate adherence and provide alternatives to people who cannot tolerate or do not prefer oral medication. Although no gel is currently FDA approved, microbicide trials are underway, and a gel is a potential future delivery system for PrEP. Nonetheless, some Black women who voice theoretical interest in PrEP uptake describe reservations about gel inconvenience and potential side effects for themselves and partners (Auerbach et al., 2015).

The minimal uptake of PrEP as an effective intervention among Black women, the population of women that are most at risk for HIV and would benefit most from PrEP (Smith et al., 2018), is fueled by the varying accessibility of PrEP to women of different socioeconomic backgrounds. In order to visualize this issue, a socioecological framework can be used to comprehensively examine the significant barriers that stimulate disparities of PrEP uptake among Black women. These barriers can be better identified by delving into the unique experiences of Black women in the US.

Facilitators of and Barriers to PrEP Uptake for Black Women

Although PrEP is a viable HIV-prevention strategy for Black women in the US who are at disproportionate risk for HIV despite existing prevention tools, there is a need to invest in the facilitators of and mitigate the barriers to PrEP uptake among them. Particularly, among women living in poverty in high-HIV-incidence settings (Hodder et al., 2013), high prevalence of HIV in their sexual networks puts these women at excess risk for HIV even when they have few sexual partners. Fear of perceptions of unfaithfulness, low socioeconomic and educational status, and desire to conceive contribute to low condom use (Aral et al., 2008; Hallfors et al., 2007; Seth et al., 2010; Wingood & DiClemente, 2000). These factors may also impair PrEP uptake (Flash et al., 2014).

The social-ecological model explores the interaction between individual, relationship, community, and societal factors (CDC, n.d.-d). On a societal level, the mistrust of medical institutions may serve as a barrier to uptake of medical advances such as PrEP among Black women (Cargill & Stone, 2005; Cuevas, 2013; Gamble, 1997). For many Black women, historical and contemporary discrimination and racism have likely increased their level of distrust of the health-care system (Auerbach et al., 2015; Gamble, 1997). On a structural level, PrEP may be less accessible in neighborhoods with higher populations of Black individuals (Ojikutu et al., 2018, 2019). In some cases, an impoverished condition alongside competing survival needs contributes to low PrEP uptake (Auerbach et al., 2015; Wingood et al., 2013). Lack of access to health care or not having a regular source of health care is a significant contributor to low willingness to use PrEP (Ojikutu et al., 2018, 2019). Currently, it's unclear if low-income women can afford the estimated cost of over $10,000 per year for PrEP uptake in the absence of access to the widely available patient assistance programs (Flash et al., 2017; Gilead, n.d.-a, n.d.-b, n.d.-c). Although the cost of PrEP for low-income individuals may be covered by commercial patient assistance programs, the cost of clinician evaluation and labs may still represent a potential cost barrier (Flash et al., 2017).

On an individual level, we cannot assume that the experiences of MSM and international populations with PrEP will predict PrEP uptake among women in the US. Black women's misgivings about PrEP efficacy may inhibit uptake. Fears of PrEP uptake, as articulated by some Black women in Auerbach et al.'s (2015) qualitative focus group, in part stems from a lack of standard training on cultural competency and sensitivity among health-care providers when educating their Black female patients in a way that resonates these patients. Only 10 percent of the women who described structural barriers to PrEP had a working knowledge of PrEP, and those that knew of PrEP were unaware of the potential use of PrEP among women (Auerbach et al., 2015). Some of these women believed that the lack of information on PrEP was influenced by the social devaluation of Black women (Auerbach et al., 2015; Auerbach et al., 2012; Flash et al., 2017; Flash et al., 2014). Other qualitative inquiries among Black women identified a need for provider education, given their preference for primary care providers (PCPs) as PrEP educators and prescribers. Screening for PrEP eligibility can foster improved discourse on sexual health (Auerbach et al., 2015). Collectively, this implies that more support is needed to make this effective preventive measure available to Black women who are at the most risk for an HIV diagnosis as compared to other women.

In order to limit HIV transmission among women, future work should identify and address barriers to and facilitators of PrEP access among Black women in primary care settings as well as educate and motivate patients to request PrEP if appropriate, as patient request has been described as a potential driver of PrEP prescribing (Krakower et al., 2014). HIV-preventive systems should uniquely consider the socioeconomic background of all patients, including Black women. This requires financial commitment and culturally sensitive preventive measures that apply to a diverse group of Black women from various social levels and backgrounds.

Practice

The Practice of HIV Prevention through Behavioral Interventions

Behavioral interventions with targeted behavior-change strategies through risk reduction and adoption of preventive practices are complementary HIV-prevention strategies that predate the advent of PrEP (DiClemente & Wingood, 1995; DiClemente et al., 2004; DiClemente et al., 2010). The disproportionate impact of HIV/AIDS on Black women warrants the development of effective strategies to prevent HIV incidence, detect HIV early, and ensure that adequate prevention options exist (Amutah, 2012). The comprehensive approach of assessing theoretical, behavioral, and intervention-imposed influences on sexual decision-making was sufficiently intensive and appropriately targeted to promote behavior change (Horvath et al., 2012).

The work of noted interventions, particularly effective behavioral interventions, has driven the HIV/STI-prevention field for decades (Collins et al., 2006; Horvath et al., 2012). More recently, CDC (n.d.-a) has identified a set of high-impact HIV prevention (HIP) interventions that are cost effective and scalable and target high-risk populations. However, few HIP interventions specifically target Black women. Community-based organizations that implement these interventions can receive capacity-building support, training, and funding through state departments of public health (Purcell et al., 2016). Use of theory-based interventions, particularly those using theories focusing on psychosocial constructs such as attitudes, beliefs, perceived behavioral control, social norms, and intentions, pertaining to the theory of planned behavior and reasoned action, have proven to be successful at HIV/STI prevention (Dworkin et al., 2009; Ehrhardt et al., 2002; El-Bassel et al., 2003; Wingood et al., 2004). However, a comprehensive theoretical approach for Black women is needed to discover culturally relevant factors that are likely to influence sexual decision-making and PrEP uptake. To fully examine prevention of HIV in Black women, the contextualized role of sexual decision-making and the impact it has on PrEP uptake and consistent utilization cannot be overstated.

Changing HIV Prevention to Include PrEP

Today, the targeted behavior in HIV prevention focuses on PrEP uptake and consistent condom use among individuals at significant risk for HIV. Unfortunately, PrEP has not been well integrated into clinical practice. Many PCPs are unaware of its efficacy in reducing HIV transmission and are not prescribing PrEP. In addition, at-risk patients are not aware of this effective HIV-prevention strategy (Auerbach et al., 2015). Though pervasive in the LGBT community, PrEP discourse among heterosexual women is limited.

The potential benefit to Black women of successful use of strategies to improve PrEP uptake rates is not yet actualized (Ojikutu et al., 2018, 2019; Rendina et al., 2017; Shrestha et al., 2016). As HIV continues to disproportionately impact women of color, additional research is needed to optimize HIV-preventive care to help women remain HIV negative (Amutah, 2012). To date, PrEP uptake among women in the US, irrespective of race or ethnicity, has been low (Smith et al., 2018), despite almost 500,000 women having a PrEP indication based on a host of risk factors (Lambert, 2018). PrEP uptake data has been limited in the US (Smith et al., 2018), and few studies examine PrEP adoption among women. Black women in particular continue to be underrepresented in PrEP research and PrEP implementation efforts in real-world settings, despite higher risks of HIV acquisition as compared to other groups of women (Auerbach et al., 2015; Lambert, 2018).

Salient Findings Demonstrating Feasibility of PrEP for Black Women

Several pilot studies have been completed and are underway to better establish the acceptability of PrEP as a leading HIV-prevention method for Black women. In a study including Black women ages 18–29 years who engaged in condomless sex and substance use, 69 percent of them were willing to use PrEP after participating in a survey designed to increase willingness for PrEP uptake (Hill, Stotts, & Heads, 2018). In a separate focus-group study, inner-city Black women ages 18–50 years revealed an interest in taking PrEP, preferably in the form of a pill (Flash et al., 2014).

In another research study, an online survey was administered to 855 Black men and women (mean age 33 years) to explore willingness to use PrEP, which found that 26 percent of participants were willing to use PrEP (Ojikutu et al., 2019). Other studies have noted that awareness of PrEP was limited among Black women in the US and that many women were interested in and willing to use PrEP once they knew more about it (Auerbach et al., 2015). Specifically, Black women were reported to have an increased willingness to adopt PrEP if it was recommended to them by a friend or one of their health-care providers (Auerbach et al., 2015; Wingood et al., 2013).

Future research regarding biobehavioral and biomedical strategies and ancillary interventions can promote uptake and adherence among Black women. Additionally, a focus on the barriers (such as stigma and being unaware of HIV risks) and the facilitators (such as receiving PrEP knowledge from a friend or trusted provider) to PrEP uptake and utilization in real-world settings is timely and necessary. Integrated models are needed to investigate the lived experiences of women that include an examination of the individual, familial, contextual, and environmental considerations that contribute to the utilization of PrEP.

Planning

PrEP and Primary Care

Although HIV specialists have more experience with antiretroviral therapy than PCPs do, they are less likely to encounter women at risk for HIV. Conversely, PCPs express concerns regarding time needed to assess sexual risk and want additional training on antiretroviral therapy (Krakower et al., 2014). Provider barriers to PrEP provision include concerns about effectiveness outside of clinical trials due to suboptimal adherence, the burden of clinical monitoring, medication cost, and inability to identify patients who might benefit. For women, this challenge is heightened as their risk assessment involves inquiry about partner risk factors that may or may not be apparent to the woman being assessed (Aaron et al., 2018). Nonetheless, successful demonstration projects in the US exhibit real-world feasibility (Flash et al., 2018).

Few studies have explored barriers to and facilitators of PrEP implementation among PCPs for at-risk Black women. Limited inquiry by PCPs about issues of sexual health (Tao et al., 2000), relationship status, and social factors such as injection drug use and sex work may impair recognition of PrEP-appropriate patients (Young et al., 2014). Just as contraceptive counseling by PCPs influences adoption of contraception use by patients (Tao et al., 2000), HIV prevention counseling may influence PrEP uptake. Medical mistrust, perceived lack of risk, and stigma can also hinder uptake of HIV-prevention measures and testing even among women who have access to care or a willing prescriber (Haley & Justman, 2013).

Implementation Strategies for PrEP

Successful implementation should include patients as potential drivers of demand, equip providers with knowledge and skills, and address contextual barriers. Suggested PrEP implementation strategies in the literature include educational interventions, user-friendly guideline summaries, peer testimonials, brief evidence-based risk-assessment tools, adherence interventions (Krakower & Mayer, 2012; Krakower et al., 2014), and measures to assist patients in discussing PrEP with providers (Krakower & Mayer, 2012). Negative perceptions can be addressed through provider education. Capitalizing on perceived facilitators such as encountering patients who request PrEP, positive peer norms, and CDC guidance also advances implementation. The World Health Organization (WHO) calls for real-world approaches that are sensitive to the needs, preferences, and social norms of at-risk women. WHO favors prevention services that can be adapted to existing health services supported by provider training materials and practical screening tools (WHO, 2015).

Regional differences in PrEP-prescribing patterns are evident even among places of early adoption such as San Francisco and New York (Blumenthal et al., 2015), highlighting the need for locally specific implementation efforts. Multifaceted strategies that are context and culture specific are needed (Pettifor et al., 2015).

As additional preventive oral medications, topical microbicides, and other alternative delivery systems and alternative drugs emerge, implementation strategies addressing barriers and facilitating integration of HIV-preventive strategies into existing health-care structures are needed. Ideal strategies will identify vulnerable patients, cross-train staff, and integrate sexual health and HIV prevention into routine care (Flash et al., 2012).

PrEP Access in Diverse Settings

In addition to the traditional primary care setting, alternative sites of PrEP access include sexually transmitted disease (STD) clinics, community health centers, emergency departments, community-based organizations, and online and brick-and-mortar pharmacies. Each of these models has promising elements, whether it be the STD clinic staff members trained in sexual health counseling, social workers referring patients to PrEP clinics during emergency department visits, or the reach of community-based organizations and pharmacies outside of traditional care-delivery locations for potential PrEP users not already linked to care (Mayer et al., 2018). At present, most of these models prioritize men for PrEP uptake. More research is needed to determine how alternative HIV preventive care models can be tailored to the needs of women in general and Black women in particular.

Conclusion

Research validating the safety and efficacy of varied delivery methods of PrEP to women demonstrates the capacity of scientists to inform clinical practice in a way that would effectively integrate biomedical HIV prevention for women into clinical practice. Thousands of articles loudly proclaim that the public health threat to sexually active women is dangerous as women represent half of all new HIV diagnoses globally (Flash et al., 2017). Stakeholders at every level of the health-care spectrum have an ethical duty to meet the public health need of the populations they serve. Black women constitute a key part of that patient population. Changes to clinical practice to address HIV prevention for Black women who are more at risk for HIV than other women are needed and warranted. Targeted efforts for HIV prevention among Black women in clinical practice settings can promote health equity and narrow racial and gender-based health disparities.

References

Aaron, E., Blum, C., Seidman, D., Hoyt, M. J., Simone, J., Sullivan, M., & Smith, D. K. (2018). Optimizing delivery of HIV preexposure prophylaxis for women in the United States. *AIDS Patient Care and STDs, 32*(1), 16–23.

Adimora, A. A., Schoenbach, V. J., Bonas, D. M., Martinson, F. E., Donaldson, K. H., & Stancil, T. R. (2002). Concurrent sexual partnerships among women in the United States. *Epidemiology, 13*(3), 320–327.

Adimora, A. A., Schoenbach, V. J., & Doherty, I. A. (2006). HIV and African Americans in the southern United States: Sexual networks and social context. *Sexually Transmitted Diseases, 33*(7 Suppl.), S39–S45.

Amutah, N. (2012). African American women: The face of HIV/AIDS. *The Qualitative Report, 47*(92), 1–15.

Aral, S. O., Adimora, A. A., & Fenton, K. A. (2008). Understanding and responding to disparities in HIV and other sexually transmitted infections in African Americans. *Lancet, 372*(9635), 337–340.

Auerbach, J. D. Banyan, A, and Riordan, M. (2012). *Will and should women in the U.S. use PrEP? Findings from a focus group study of at-risk HIV negative women in Oakland, Memphis, San Diego, and Washington, DC.* AIDS United. http://www.avac.org/sites/default/files/u3/shouldWomenUSusePrEP.pdf

Auerbach, J. D., Kinsky, S., Brown, G., & Charles, V. (2015). Knowledge, attitudes, and likelihood of pre-exposure prophylaxis (PrEP) use among US women at risk of acquiring HIV. *AIDS Patient Care and STDs, 29*(2), 102–110.

Baeten, J. M., Palanee-Phillips, T., Brown, E. R., Schwartz, K., Soto-Torres, L. E., Govender, V., Mgodi, N. M., Matovu Kiweewa, F., Nair, G., Mhlanga, F., Siva, S., Bekker, L.-G., Jeenarain, N., Gaffoor, Z., Martinson, F., Makanani, B., Pather, A., Naidoo, L., Husnik, M., . . . & MTN-020–ASPIRE Study Team. (2016). Use of a vaginal ring containing dapivirine for HIV-1 prevention in women. *New England Journal of Medicine, 375*(22), 2121–2132.

Bekker, L. G., Beyrer, C., & Quinn, T. C. (2012). Behavioral and biomedical combination strategies for HIV prevention. *Cold Spring Harbor Perspectives in Medicine, 2*(8).

Blumenthal, J., Jain, S., Krakower, D., Sun, X., Young, J., Mayer, K., Haubrich, R., & CCTG 598 Team. (2015). Knowledge is power! Increased provider knowledge scores regarding pre-exposure prophylaxis (PrEP) are associated with higher rates of PrEP prescription and future intent to prescribe PrEP. *AIDS and Behavior, 19*(5), 802–810.

Cargill, V. A., & Stone, V. E. (2005). HIV/AIDS: A minority health issue. *Medical Clinics of North America, 89*(4), 895–912.

Centers for Disease Control and Prevention. (n.d.-a). *Effective interventions: HIV prevention that works*. Retrieved 2018 from https://effectiveinterventions.cdc.gov/

Centers for Disease Control and Prevention. (n.d.-b). *HIV among women*. Retrieved 2016 from https://www.cdc.gov/hiv/group/gender/women/index.html

Centers for Disease Control and Prevention. (n.d.-c). *HIV and African American women*. Retrieved 2015 from https://www.cdc.gov/healthcommunication/toolstemplates/entertainmented/tips/hivwomen.html

Centers for Disease Control and Prevention. (n.d.-d). *The social-ecological model: A framework for prevention*. Retrieved 2018 from https://www.cdc.gov/violenceprevention/about/social-ecologicalmodel.html

Choopanya, K., Martin, M., Suntharasamai, P., Sangkum, U., Mock, P. A., Leethochawalit, M., Chiamwongpaet, S., Kitisin, P., Natrujirote, P., Kittimunkong, S., Chuachoowong, R., Gvetadze, R. J., McNicholl, J. M., Paxton, L. A., Curlin, M. E., Hendrix, C. W., Vanichseni, S., & Bangkok Tenofovir Study Group. (2013). Antiretroviral prophylaxis for HIV infection in injecting drug users in Bangkok, Thailand (the Bangkok Tenofovir Study): A randomised, double-blind, placebo-controlled phase 3 trial. *Lancet, 381*(9883), 2083–2090.

Collins, C., Harshbarger, C., Sawyer, R., & Hamdallah, M. (2006). The Diffusion of Effective Behavioral Interventions project: Development, implementation, and lessons learned. *AIDS Education and Prevention, 18*(4 Suppl. A), 5–20.

Cuevas, A. G. (2013). *Exploring four barriers experienced by African Americans in healthcare: Perceived discrimination, medical mistrust, race discordance, and poor communication* [Master's thesis]. Portland State University.

DiClemente, R. J., & Wingood, G. M. (1995). A randomized controlled trial of an HIV sexual risk-reduction intervention for young African-American women. *JAMA, 274*(16), 1271–1276.

DiClemente, R. J., Wingood, G. M., Harrington, K. F., Lang, D. L., Davies, S. L., Hook, E. W., III, Oh, M. K., Crosby, R. A., Hertzberg, V. S., Gordon, A. B., Hardin, J. W., Parker, S., & Robillard, A. (2004). Efficacy of an HIV prevention intervention for African American adolescent girls: A randomized controlled trial. *JAMA, 292*(2), 171–179.

DiClemente, R. J., Wingood, G. M., Rose, E., Sales, J. M., & Crosby, R. A. (2010). Evaluation of an HIV/STD sexual risk-reduction intervention for pregnant African American adolescents attending a prenatal clinic in an urban public hospital: preliminary evidence of efficacy. *Journal of Pediatric and Adolescent Gynecology, 23*(1), 32–38.

Dunkle, K. L., Wingood, G. M., Camp, C. M., & DiClemente, R. J. (2010). Economically motivated relationships and transactional sex among unmarried

African American and white women: Results from a U.S. national telephone survey. *Public Health Reports, 125*(Suppl. 4), 90–100.

Dworkin, S. L., Fullilove, R. E., & Peacock, D. (2009). Are HIV/AIDS prevention interventions for heterosexually active men in the United States gender-specific? *American Journal of Public Health, 99*(6), 981–984.

Ehrhardt, A. A., Exner, T. M., Hoffman, S., Silberman, I., Leu, C. S., Miller, S., & Levin, B. (2002). A gender-specific HIV/STD risk reduction intervention for women in a health care setting: Short- and long-term results of a randomized clinical trial. *AIDS Care, 14*(2), 147–161.

El-Bassel, N., Witte, S. S., Gilbert, L., Wu, E., Chang, M., Hill, J., & Steinglass, P. (2003). The efficacy of a relationship-based HIV/STD prevention program for heterosexual couples. *American Journal of Public Health, 93*(6), 963–969.

Escudero, D. J., Kerr, T., Wood, E., Nguyen, P., Lurie, M. N., Sued, O., & Marshall, B. D. (2015). Acceptability of HIV pre-exposure prophylaxis (PrEP) among people who inject drugs (PWID) in a Canadian setting. *AIDS and Behavior, 19*(5), 752–757.

Flash, C., Krakower, D., & Mayer, K. H. (2012). The promise of antiretrovirals for HIV prevention. *Current Infectious Disease Reports, 14*(2), 185–193.

Flash, C. A., Adegboyega, O. O., Yu, X., Avalos, C., Johnson, S., Mayer, K. H., & Giordano, T. P. (2018). Correlates of linkage to HIV preexposure prophylaxis among HIV-testing clients. *Journal of Acquired Immune Deficiency Syndromes, 77*(4), 365–372.

Flash, C. A., Dale, S. K., & Krakower, D. S. (2017). Pre-exposure prophylaxis for HIV prevention in women: Current perspectives. *International Journal of Women's Health, 9*, 391–401.

Flash, C. A., Stone, V. E., Mitty, J. A., Mimiaga, M. J., Hall, K. T., Krakower, D., & Mayer, K. H. (2014). Perspectives on HIV prevention among urban Black women: A potential role for HIV pre-exposure prophylaxis. *AIDS Patient Care and STDS, 28*(12), 635–642.

Fonner, V. A., Dalglish, S. L., Kennedy, C. E., Baggaley, R., O'Reilly, K. R., Koechlin, F. M., Rodolph, M., Hodges-Mameletzis, I., & Grant, R. M. (2016). Effectiveness and safety of oral HIV preexposure prophylaxis for all populations. *AIDS, 30*(12), 1973–1983.

Fransen, K., de Baetselier, I., Rammutla, E., Ahmed, K., Owino, F., Agingu, W., Venter, G., Deese, J., Van Damme, L., Crucitti, T., & FEMPrEP Study Group. (2017). Detection of new HIV infections in a multicentre HIV antiretroviral pre-exposure prophylaxis trial. *Journal of Clinical Virology, 93*, 76–80.

Gamble, V. N. (1997). Under the shadow of Tuskegee: African Americans and health care. *American Journal of Public Health, 87*(11), 1773–1778.

Gilead. (n.d.-a). *Gilead patient assistance programs.* Retrieved 2017 from http://www.gilead.com/responsibility/us-patient-access

Gilead. (n.d.-b). *Welcome to the Gilead Advancing Access® co-pay program.* Retrieved 2017 from https://www.gileadadvancingaccess.com/copay-coupon-card

Gilead. (n.d.-c). *What it takes to start TRUVADA for PrEP.* Truvada. Retrieved 2017 from https://start.truvada.com/starting-truvada

Haley, D. F., & Justman, J. E. (2013). The HIV epidemic among women in the United States: A persistent puzzle. *Journal of Women's Health, 22*(9), 715–717.

Hallfors, D. D., Iritani, B. J., Miller, W. C., & Bauer, D. J. (2007). Sexual and drug behavior patterns and HIV and STD racial disparities: The need for new directions. *American Journal of Public Health, 97*(1), 125–132.

Hanscom, B., Janes, H. E., Guarino, P. D., Huang, Y., Brown, E. R., Chen, Y. Q., Hammer, S. M., Gilbert, P. B., & Donnell, D. J. (2016). Brief report: Preventing HIV-1 infection in women using oral preexposure prophylaxis: A meta-analysis of current evidence. *Journal of Acquired Immune Deficiency Syndromes, 73*(5), 606–608.

Heffron, R., McClelland, R. S., Balkus, J. E., Celum, C., Cohen, C. R., Mugo, N., Bukusi, E., Donnell, D., Lingappa, J., Kiarie, J., Fiedler, T., Munch, M., Fredricks, D. N., Baeten, J. M., & Partners PrEP Study Team. (2017). Efficacy of oral pre-exposure prophylaxis (PrEP) for HIV among women with abnormal vaginal microbiota: a post-hoc analysis of the randomised, placebo-controlled Partners PrEP Study. *Lancet HIV, 4*(10), e449–e456.

Heumann, C. L. (2018). Biomedical approaches to HIV prevention in women. *Current Infectious Disease Reports, 20*(6), 11.

Hill, M., Andrews, S., Granado, M., Nielsen, E., & Grimes, R. (2018). Just: An indicator of minimized value of the sexual act. *HIV and AIDS Research Journal, 1*(2), 1–9.

Hill, M., Granado, M., & Stotts, A. (2016). Theoretical implications of gender, power, and sexual scripts for HIV prevention programs aimed at young, substance-using African-American women. *Journal of Racial and Ethnic Health Disparities, 4*(6), 1175–1180.

Hill, M., Granado, M., Villarreal, Y., Fuega, J., Robinson, D., & Stotts, A. (2017). Predictors of sexual scripts among young, sexually-active, substance-using African American women. *Journal of AIDS and Clinical Research, 8*(1), 655.

Hill, M., Stotts, A., and Heads, A. (2018). *An evaluation of whether an intervention coupled with a referral to a PrEP clinic from the emergency department increases PrEP uptake* [Paper presentation]. 11th Annual Conference on the Science of Dissemination and Implementation, Washington, DC.

Hodder, S. L., Justman, J., Hughes, J. P., Wang, J., Haley, D. F., Adimora, A. A., Del Rio, C., Golin, C. E., Kuo, I., Rompalo, A., Soto-Torres, L., Mannheimer, S. B., Johnson-Lewis, L., Eshleman, S. H., El-Sadr, W. M., HIV Prevention Trials Network 064, & Women's HIV SeroIncidence Study Team. (2013). HIV acquisition among women from selected areas of the United States: A cohort study. *Annals of Internal Medicine, 158*(1), 10–18.

Horvath, K. J., Nygaard, K., Danilenko, G. P., Goknur, S., Michael Oakes, J., & Simon Rosser, B. R. (2012). Strategies to retain participants in a long-term HIV prevention randomized controlled trial: Lessons from the MINTS-II Study. *AIDS and Behavior, 16*(2), 469–479.

Hsu, D. C., & O'Connell, R. J. (2017). Progress in HIV vaccine development. *Human Vaccines & Immunotherapeutics, 13*(5), 1018–1030.

Huang, Y. A., Zhu, W., Smith, D. K., Harris, N., & Hoover, K. W. (2018). HIV preexposure prophylaxis, by race and ethnicity—United States, 2014–2016. *MMWR: Morbidity and Mortality Weekly Report, 67*(41), 1147–1150.

Institute of Medicine. (2011). *Clinical practice guidelines we can trust.* National Academies Press.

Janes, H., Corey, L., Ramjee, G., Carpp, L. N., Lombard, C., Cohen, M. S., Gilbert, P. B., & Gray, G. E. (2018). Weighing the evidence of efficacy of oral PrEP for HIV prevention in women in southern Africa. *AIDS Research and Human Retroviruses, 34*(8), 645–656.

Koss, C. A., Liu, A. Y., Castillo-Mancilla, J., Bacchetti, P., McHugh, C., Kuncze, K., Morrow, M., Louie, A., Seifert, S., Okochi, H., MaWhinney, S., Gandhi, M., & Anderson, P. L. (2018). Similar tenofovir hair concentrations in men and women after directly observed dosing of tenofovir disoproxil fumarate/emtricitabine: Implications for preexposure prophylaxis adherence monitoring. *AIDS, 32*(15), 2189–2194.

Krakower, D., & Mayer, K. H. (2012). Engaging healthcare providers to implement HIV pre-exposure prophylaxis. *Current Opinion in HIV and AIDS, 7*(6), 593–599.

Krakower, D., Ware, N., Mitty, J. A., Maloney, K., & Mayer, K. H. (2014). HIV providers' perceived barriers and facilitators to implementing pre-exposure prophylaxis in care settings: A qualitative study. *AIDS and Behavior, 18*(9), 1712–1721.

Lambert, C. M. J., Amico, K., Mugavero, M., & Elopre, L. (2018). Women to prevent HIV: An integrated theoretical framework to PrEP Black women in the United States. *Journal of the Association of Nurses in AIDS Care, 29*(6), 835–848.

Marrazzo, J. M. (2018). Biomedical prevention of HIV in women: Challenges and approaches, with particular reference to the vaginal microbiome. *Transactions of the American Clinical and Climatological Association, 129*, 63–73.

Mayer, K. H., Chan, P. A., R. Patel, R., Flash, C. A., & Krakower, D. S. (2018). Evolving models and ongoing challenges for HIV preexposure prophylaxis implementation in the United States. *Journal of Acquired Immune Deficiency Syndromes, 77*(2), 119–127.

Mayer, K. H., & Ramjee, G. (2015). The current status of the use of oral medication to prevent HIV transmission. *Current Opinion in HIV and AIDS, 10*(4), 226–232.

McCree, D. H., Sutton, M., Bradley, E., & Harris, N. (2017). Changes in the disparity of HIV diagnosis rates among Black women—United States, 2010–2014. *MMWR: Morbidity and Mortality Weekly Report, 66*(4), 104–106.

Morris, M., & Kretzschmar, M. (1997). Concurrent partnerships and the spread of HIV. *AIDS, 11*(5), 641–648.

Nel, A., Bekker, L. G., Bukusi, E., Hellstrm, E., Kotze, P., Louw, C., Martinson, F., Masenga, G., Montgomery, E., Ndaba, N., van der Straten, A., van Niekerk, N., & Woodsong, C. (2016). Safety, acceptability and adherence of dapivirine vaginal ring in a microbicide clinical trial conducted in multiple countries in sub-Saharan Africa. *PloS One, 11*(3), e0147743.

Nel, A., van Niekerk, N., Kapiga, S., Bekker, L. G., Gama, C., Gill, K., Kamali, A., Kotze, P., Louw, C., Mabude, Z., Miti, N., Kusemererwa, S., Tempelman, H., Carstens, H., Devlin, B., Isaacs, M., Malherbe, M., Mans, W., Nuttall, J., . . . & Ring Study Team. (2016). Safety and efficacy of a dapivirine vaginal ring for HIV prevention in women. *New England Journal of Medicine, 375*(22), 2133–2143.

Ojikutu, B. O., Bogart, L. M., Higgins-Biddle, M., Dale, S. K., Allen, W., Dominique, T., & Mayer, K. H. (2018). Facilitators and barriers to pre-exposure prophylaxis (PrEP) use among Black individuals in the United States: Results from the National Survey on HIV in the Black Community (NSHBC). *AIDS and Behavior, 22*(11), 3576–3587.

Ojikutu, B. O., Bogart, L. M., Mayer, K. H., Stopka, T. J., Sullivan, P. S., & Ransome, Y. (2019). Spatial access and willingness to use pre-exposure prophylaxis (PrEP) among Black/African-American individuals in the United States. *JMIR Public Health and Surveillance, 5*(1), e12405.

Pettifor, A., Nguyen, N. L., Celum, C., Cowan, F. M., Go, V., & Hightow-Weidman, L. (2015). Tailored combination prevention packages and PrEP for young key populations. *Journal of the International AIDS Society, 18*(2 Suppl. 1), 19434.

Purcell, D. W., McCray, E., & Mermin, J. (2016). The shift to high-impact HIV prevention by health departments in the United States. *Public Health Reports, 131*(1), 7–10.

Rendina, H. J., Whitfield, T. H., Grov, C., Starks, T. J., & Parsons, J. T. (2017). Distinguishing hypothetical willingness from behavioral intentions to initiate HIV pre-exposure prophylaxis (PrEP): Findings from a large cohort of gay and bisexual men in the U.S. *Social Science and Medicine, 172*, 115–123.

Seth, P., Raiford, J. L., Robinson, L. S., Wingood, G. M., & DiClemente, R. J. (2010). Intimate partner violence and other partner-related factors: Correlates of sexually transmissible infections and risky sexual behaviours among young adult African American women. *Sex Health, 7*(1), 25–30.

Shekelle, P. G. (2018). Clinical practice guidelines: What's next? *JAMA, 320*(8), 757–758.

Shrestha, R., Altice, F. L., Huedo-Medina, T. B., Karki, P., & Copenhaver, M. (2016). Willingness to use pre-exposure prophylaxis (PrEP): An empirical test of the information-motivation-behavioral skills (IMB) model among high-risk drug users in treatment. *AIDS and Behavior, 21*(5), 1299–1308.

Smith, D. K., Van Handel, M., & Grey, J. (2018). Estimates of adults with indications for HIV pre-exposure prophylaxis by jurisdiction, transmission risk group, and race/ethnicity, United States, 2015. *Annals of Epidemiology, 28*(12), 850–857.e9.

Tao, G., Irwin, K. L., & Kassler, W. J. (2000). Missed opportunities to assess sexually transmitted diseases in U.S. adults during routine medical checkups. *American Journal of Preventive Medicine, 18*(2), 109–114.

Texas Department of State Health Services HIV/STD Program. (2016, April). *HIV/STD health disparities in Texas.* https://www.dshs.texas.gov/hivstd/info/edmat/HealthDisparities.pdf

Traore, Y. L., Chen, Y., & Ho, E. A. (2018). Current state of microbicide development. *Clinical Pharmacology and Therapeutics, 104*(6), 1074–1081.

Velloza, J., & Heffron, R. (2017). The vaginal microbiome and its potential to impact efficacy of HIV pre-exposure prophylaxis for women. *Current HIV/AIDS Reports, 14*(5), 153–160.

Wingood, G. M., & DiClemente, R. J. (2000). Application of the theory of gender and power to examine HIV-related exposures, risk factors, and effective interventions for women. *Health Education and Behavior, 27*(5), 539–565.

Wingood, G. M., DiClemente, R. J., Mikhail, I., Lang, D. L., McCree, D. H., Davies, S. L., Hardin, J. W., Hook, E. W., III, & Saag, M. (2004). A randomized controlled trial to reduce HIV transmission risk behaviors and sexually transmitted diseases among women living with HIV: The WiLLOW Program. *Journal of Acquired Immune Deficiency Syndromes, 37*(Suppl. 2), S58–S67.

Wingood, G. M., Dunkle, K., Camp, C., Patel, S., Painter, J. E., Rubtsova, A., & DiClemente, R. J. (2013). Racial differences and correlates of potential adoption of preexposure prophylaxis: Results of a national survey. *Journal of Acquired Immune Deficiency Syndromes, 63*(Suppl. 1), S95–S101.

World Health Organization. (2015). *WHO technical update on pre-exposure prophylaxis (PrEP).* http://www.who.int/hiv/pub/prep/prep-technical-update-2015/en/

Wu, H., Mendoza, M. C., Huang, Y. A., Hayes, T., Smith, D. K., & Hoover, K. W. (2017). Uptake of HIV preexposure prophylaxis among commercially insured persons—United States, 2010–2014. *Clinical Infectious Diseases, 64*(2), 144–149.

Wynne, J., Muwawu, R., Mubiru, M. C., Kamira, B., Kemigisha, D., Nakyanzi, T., Kabwigu, S., Nakabiito, C., & Kiweewa Matovu, F. (2018). Maximizing participant retention in a phase 2B HIV prevention trial in Kampala, Uganda: The MTN-003 (VOICE) Study. *HIV Clinical Trials, 19*(5), 1–7.

Young, I., Flowers, P., & McDaid, L. M. (2014). Barriers to uptake and use of pre-exposure prophylaxis (PrEP) among communities most affected by HIV in the UK: Findings from a qualitative study in Scotland. *BMJ Open, 4*(11), e005717.

Chapter 11

Am I My Sister's Mentor?

Why Mentoring Underrepresented Minority Medical and Public Health Faculty Can Improve the Health of Black Women

ANDREA ANDERSON, JUDY WASHINGTON,
AND JOEDRECKA S. BROWN SPEIGHTS

Personal Reflection of Dr. Anderson

When I was a freshman in college in the early nineties, a friend of my mother's sent me a card that I received in my student mailbox one brisk November morning. That was a time when email was relatively new and college students were still excited to receive pen-and-paper mail. Ms. Thomas, as I affectionately knew her, was an "auntie" figure to me, a long-term friend and colleague of my mother Marilyn, who had seen me grow up, attending my school performances, giving me encouraging compliments when I was an awkward preteen, and keeping up on my school progress through my always-supportive and loving mother.

I was a Black student from New York, a science major, who like many others had been something of a standout at my local high school. Now, here I was tentatively making my way at a challenging New England Ivy League university where not many looked like me. On the cover of the card was a beautiful Black woman wearing a long cloak-like garment that appeared to be made of traditional African kente cloth. She was pictured from the back with her arm shrouding a younger, smaller female figure. Below the pair in simple text was written,

> I, too,
> Have moved along
> This path you follow.
> There is no easy way.
> Here is my strength.
> Here is my counsel.

I remember standing in the busy student mail room holding that card. The clamor and hustle of the students surrounding me quieted in my consciousness, and I immediately felt strengthened to read those words. It was like they reached out to me, standing tall and clear, almost defiant in stark contrast against the white cardstock. I walked out into that New England morning toward the library or the chemistry lab, or whatever I had planned, with a feeling of renewed calm and purpose, a drive to go on, and, more importantly, a belief that I could.

In retrospect, I realize that the feeling that enveloped me that morning long ago is called resilience and what I had just experienced was one of my first memories of mentorship. As I reflect on my journey as a physician, I am reminded that mentorship was crucial to my personal well-being and, ultimately, to the completion of my preparation and training to practice patient-centered medicine and my ability to impact the health and wellness of others, including Black women.

The State of Black Women

According to the World Health Organization (1946), *health* can be defined as "a state of complete physical, mental and social well-being and not merely the absence of disease or infirmity." Unfortunately, not all population groups have the same experience of health. Generally, inequalities in health outcomes are a result of lack of opportunities for health improvement, exposures to stressors, historical and modern-day injustices, and lack of access to quality health care including preventive care over time (Phelan et al.,

2010). Differences in health-care outcomes are of multifactorial etiology and influenced by institutional, provider, and patient factors.

In 2002, the Institute of Medicine found the system of health care including provider bias to be a key contributor to health disparities—unfair differences in health outcomes—of minority populations including Black women (Smedley et al., 2002; Green et al., 2010). Health and health care are just some of the determinants of well-being. Additionally, the natural and built environment, economic opportunity and stability, social and community context, and education contribute to the health of individuals and populations (Office of Disease Prevention and Health Promotion, n.d.). According to a recent study by the Center for American Progress (Guerra, 2013), Black women experience health disparities at a higher rate than many other groups.

The health of Black women is influenced by structural and systematic barriers including racism, toxic stress including violence, limited access to quality health care and education, and elements that influence well-being like social, cultural, political, economic, and other environmental factors as well as a person's biology and behavioral choices. These inequities traverse socioeconomic lines and have a direct impact on individual and public health outcomes. Some of the statistics of the inequities that we can impact are as follows (Guerra, 2013):

Economic

- The US gender-based wage gap is particularly damaging for Black women. As of 2014, for Black women who worked full time, year round, the median annual earnings were 64 percent of what they were for White men. Black women in the US who work full time and year round are typically paid 63 cents for every dollar paid to White, non-Hispanic men. (United States Census Bureau, 2017). In some states this is as low as 49 cents per dollar earned by their White male counterparts (National Partnership for Women and Families, 2018).

- Eighty percent of Black women in the US are the sole or primary breadwinners of their families (McGirt, 2017).

- Black women in the US and their children with low incomes are evicted at alarmingly high rates, leading to a cascade of hardships. In disadvantaged neighborhoods, eviction is to women what incarceration is to men: incarceration locks Black men up, while evictions lock Black women out (Desmond, 2014).

Health

- Hypertension, or elevated blood pressure, is more prevalent among Black women than any other group of women. This contributes to elevated rates of and deaths from heart disease, stroke, and kidney disease among Black women (Guerra, 2013).

- While White women are more likely to develop breast cancer, Black women have higher overall mortality rates from breast cancer. Every year, an average of five Black women per day die from complications of breast cancer (Guerra, 2013).

- Black women have higher rates of human papillomavirus, or HPV, and cervical cancer, with mortality rates two to three times those of White women. The rate at which Black American women are dying from the disease is comparable to that of women in many poor and developing nations (Guerra, 2013).

- Black women experience unintended pregnancies at three times the rate of White women. These rates may reflect the access to care and family-planning services available to these women (Guerra, 2013).

- Black women are four times more likely to die from pregnancy-related causes, such as embolism and pregnancy-related hypertension, than any other racial group. These statistics are collected for pregnant women or women one year out from having a baby. These disparities are seen even after correcting for things like socioeconomic status and education (Guerra, 2013).

- Black women have the highest rates of premature births and infant mortality and are more likely to have infants with low or very low birth weights. Black infants are more than 2.4 times more likely than White infants to die in their first year of life (Guerra, 2013).

These disparities are daunting and may signal a crisis among Black women and, subsequently, Black communities. A multifactorial approach is needed that includes the input of all societal sectors with a view toward progress.

Although disparities are persistent and pervasive, these disparities can vary by community, and pockets of progress are seen in some areas, like infant mortality. For example, Brown Speights et al., in their 2017 analysis in the *American Journal of Public Health* of state-level progress in reducing the Black infant mortality gap, astutely observed that several states demonstrated trends toward more equitable health outcomes. They proposed a positive message that there is hope as seen in these pockets of progress. The investigators encouraged a more positive focus on what certain outliers are doing right and avoiding a sense of the inevitability of our inability to decrease or eliminate health disparities (Brown Speights, Goldfarb, et al., 2017; Rust et al., 2012). Likewise, we need to ask ourselves what the best practices are that are capitalizing on the resiliency of populations experiencing health disparities, in this case Black women, and working to right the ship.

One of these best practices is the need to both teach and produce a diverse, culturally sensitive health-care workforce to care for these populations to encourage a continued trend toward decreasing health disparities. Numerous studies have shown the Black and Hispanic physicians are more likely to care for underserved populations such as Black women and other racial minorities—populations who are more likely to experience economic and health-outcome disparities (Saha et al., 2000; S. Laditka & J. Laditka, 2002; J. N. Laditka, 2004). For example, Marrast et al. (2014) demonstrated that physicians who come from racial and ethnic populations that are underrepresented in medicine (URM) care for 53.5 percent of non-White patients and 70.4 percent of non-English-speaking patients. In comparing data from the past quarter century, it still rings true that minority populations play a vital role in the improvement of access to care and health outcomes for racial minorities, namely Black women. Furthermore, improved patient outcomes in primary care have also been linked to improvements in physician diversity (S. Laditka & J. Laditka, 2002).

These data suggest that these physicians and health-care providers are perhaps more able, more willing, or both to tackle the complexities of health care from clinical, cultural, socioeconomic, and emotional lenses (Freudenberg et al., 2015). These data in no way support some sort of postmodern resegregation of the health-care delivery system wherein only Black doctors care for Black patients. Nor do they aim to undermine the efforts of our White colleagues in caring for non-White communities. The data simply suggest that real attention should be paid to the factors that aid in the production of this crucial workforce whose members are more likely to care for populations who suffer health disparities at higher numbers, like Black women.

The case for Black women and public health must include a discussion of the need for increased faculty diversity at US medical schools and schools of public health. Lett et al. (2018) detail the importance of diversity in the medical workforce in their recent analysis of the concerning trend of declining racial and ethnic diversity in clinical academic medicine. The conclusion here is the health of the nation and its most vulnerable populations is inextricably linked to recruiting and producing a diverse health-care workforce. We would argue that, as a nation, we cannot achieve health equity without a systematic approach to increasing the diversity of the health-care workforce.

Intentional recruitment and retention of a diverse health-care workforce is linked to recruiting and maintaining a diverse faculty in academic medicine and public health institutes of higher learning. This case is reflected by the Diversity 3.0 initiative proposed in 2010 by the Association of American Medical Colleges (AAMC), which emphasized that diversity and inclusion in academic medicine are in of themselves important for addressing health disparities (J. N. Laditka, 2004; Nivet, 2015). Similarly, we must consider the need to also focus emphasis on schools of public health, where the drivers of health equity research and programs are incubated. Furthermore, private institutions use more public funds but have less-diverse student bodies and faculties. Public schools train a higher percentage of Black and Hispanic students but have less funding.

We need to push for equal access to research dollars and free up public institution faculty members to engage in research (Freudenberg et al., 2015). Medical institutions with diverse faculties are often better equipped to address the needs of marginalized patients, specifically though research and primary care. They are also often more suited for training the next generation of physicians to practice culturally relevant medicine (King et al., 2004).

A Closer Look at Public Health and Primary Care

The state of Black women's health can benefit most, perhaps, from improved access to primary care. The American Academy of Family Physicians (AAFP, n.d.) defines *primary care* as that care provided by "physicians specifically trained for and skilled in comprehensive, first contact, and continuing care for persons with any undiagnosed sign, symptom, or health concern (the 'undifferentiated' patient) not limited by problem origin (biological, behavioral, or social), organ system, or diagnosis."

In addition to treating illness, primary care includes health promotion and maintenance, disease prevention, patient education, and counseling in a variety of health-care settings. Primary care physicians are advocates for the patient in coordinating the cost-effective use of the entire health-care system to benefit the patient. Finally, and perhaps most importantly, "primary care promotes effective communication" with patients and encourages the role of the patient as a "partner in health care" (AAFP, n.d.). A primary care physician is a trained specialist in family medicine, internal medicine, OB-GYN, or pediatrics who takes continuing responsibility for providing the patient's comprehensive care, often providing care services to a defined population of patients. The style of primary care practice is such that the personal primary care physician serves as the entry point for substantially all the patient's medical and health-care needs. Many of the health disparities affecting Black women can be directly benefited from improving the access to and the quality of primary care received by these women.

There is now a growing interest for primary care and public health providers to collaborate to address and improve access to care for vulnerable populations. Recent work by Pratt et al. (2018) showed that barriers such as addressing scarce resources, changes to health-care billing, and demands on provider time pose a systemic problem. One approach is to have interdisciplinary teams in the primary care office. Still, barriers such as a "lack of shared priorities and mutual awareness" exist because of the lack of education (Pratt et al., 2018). Centers for Disease Control and Prevention, through its Academic Partnerships to Improve Health, is encouraging collaboration between public health, medical, and nursing institutions to develop educational curricula and hands-on experiences for students in the primary care setting to teach the skills needed (CDC, n.d.).

The Current Numbers

Increasingly, diversity has been embraced as a core value and fundamental priority across medical education in recent years. The benefits of diverse and inclusive medical schools are increasingly understood by senior administrators, faculty members, and students alike (AAMC, 2009). Medical school leaders are incorporating diversity and inclusion into their institution-wide assessments and strategic planning. While this trend is encouraging, it needs to be supported and reinforced on many levels to continue to ensure a positive move toward a health-care workforce that reflects the cultural diversity as seen in the population of health-care consumers.

Currently, according to the AAMC (n.d.), there are over 90,000 students enrolled in the 171 medical schools in the US and its territories. During the 2018–19 school year, 6,510 students identified or were identified by their schools as Black of African American. This number represents approximately 6.7 percent of the current US medical student population (AAMC, n.d.). Of note, the diminishing numbers of Black men currently enrolled in US medical schools is a part of a disturbing new trend highlighted in the eye-opening 2015 AAMC report on the state of Black men in US medical education. The report uncovered that the current number of Black men currently enrolled in medical school was actually lower than the number enrolled decades before in 1978. The report analyzed this concerning trend and highlighted strategies for reversal (AAMC, 2015).

Faculty diversity has important implications for medical student diversity. Again, we can look to the AAMC for this publicly available data compiled annually in the *Faculty Roster*, an annual report that tracks numbers and certain trends among US medical school faculty (AAMC, 2017). When we break the numbers down by gender, the trends are even more apparent. We see that the number of faculty members who identify as Black or African American reported by US medical schools equals about 5,746, or approximately 3.3 percent of the total numbers of US medical faculty members, and Black or African American women make up slightly more than half of the number of Black faculty members. With the exception of students studying at the medical schools of historically Black colleges and universities (HBCUs), many Black medical students in the US might anecdotally be able to count the number of Black faculty members they encountered in the preclinical and clinical years of their medical school training on their fingers.

While we are impressed by the overall gains that have been made in faculty diversity, research shows that Black and Hispanic individuals are even more underrepresented in the medical school faculty in 2016 than in 1990 at the assistant, associate, and full professor levels among US clinical faculty in nearly all specialties. One exception, however, is the field of obstetrics and gynecology, where Black women were represented at levels on par with the US census at the assistant professor level and the trend was toward greater representation at the associate and full professor levels (Fisher et al., 2017.

Faculty diversity is closely linked to student diversity, cultural competence of graduates, and an inclusive climate on campus (Lautenberger et al., 2016). Faculty racial, ethnic, and gender diversity helps to ensure a more comprehensive research agenda, improves patient care, and is an institutional driver of excellence (AAMC, 2019). Medical students of color are more likely to highly rate faculty diversity when deciding what medical school to attend. The AAMC-administered Matriculating Student Questionnaire allows investigators to explore differences in student medical school choice based on race and ethnicity. Data from 2012 show that many students from racial backgrounds traditionally underrepresented in medicine (URM) who matriculated into medical school that year valued the existence of programs geared toward minority or disadvantaged students. In addition, most of these students reported that a diverse faculty and student body were "positive" or "very positive" factors in their decision to attend a school (Xierali et al., 2016). It seems like diversity begets diversity. However, while racial diversity in the faculty of US medical schools has shown a promising and historic increase, the levels still fall woefully short of matching those of the US population.

Where Have All the Faculty Members Gone?

If we have made the case that faculty diversity influences diversity among medical career students and subsequently patient outcomes specifically among Black and other vulnerable populations, then two questions arise:

1. Why do academic medical faculty members want to leave academia?

2. What efforts have proven effective for recruiting and supporting URM medical school faculty members?

URM faculty members face several difficulties that influence their attrition from academic medicine. These difficulties include but are not limited to isolation, stereotyping, racism, and a lack of mentorship. Losing faculty members, specifically women and faculty members of color, is of grave concern. One study estimated the cost of faculty attrition to account for 5 percent of the entire academic medical center annual budget. Jackson et al. (2019) found that among public health graduates, despite increases in the number of Black doctoral graduates over time, commensurate increases in the proportion of Black graduates who had accepted an academic position at the time of graduation were not seen. Campbell and Rodríguez (2013) estimated that there is an 80 percent overlap of the reasons for minority students' departure from undergraduate education and reasons for minority faculty members' difficulties in remaining in academic medicine. These include but are not limited to

1. Isolation

2. Stereotyping (or racism)

3. Lack of mentorship

4. Financial struggles

5. Lack of advisement or support

6. Low institutional expectations

7. Career and professional advancement

8. Low salaries when compared to private practice or other full-time clinical jobs

9. Chairman/departmental leadership issues

Cropsey et al. (2008) concurred, finding that among women and URM faculty the top three reasons for faculty attrition are lack of professional advancement, low salary, and leadership issues. The ranking of these reasons varied slightly across racial and gender groups, with women and minority faculty also citing personal reasons for leaving. Students of color on average come from lower socioeconomic backgrounds when starting medical school and graduate with more debt overall (Cropsey et al., 2008; Rodríguez et al., 2014). On average they then need to contribute a higher percentage of their salaries to pay off high medical school debt (Rodríguez & Campbell, 2014). Jackson et al. (2019), in looking at data from public health graduates, found a "positive association between doctoral graduates from underrepresented minority groups who received full tuition remission as doctoral students and accepted an academic position" (p. 70).

This consideration coupled with the others mentioned factor heavily into graduates' decision to enter and stay in academic medicine, which in general offers lower financial compensation than the private sector. Overall, studies indicate that URM faculty members are less likely to be promoted to associate professor or to full professor when compared with White faculty members. Even when controlling for possible confounders, including productivity and seniority, these trends are still seen. These faculty members are also more likely to report wanting to leave academic medicine in the next five years when compared with their White counterparts (Palepu et al., 2000).

By virtue of their small numbers in departments and on campuses, Black women and other URM faculty members are vulnerable to isolation within their academic communities. Women of color may experience bias in the workplace because of their intersecting identities as both racial and ethnic minorities and women. The AAMC, in their 2016 overview of female full-time medical school faculty of color, found that these women face additional challenges in the "double bind"—that is, they have two identities that experience marginalization (Lautenberger et al., 2016; Ong et al., 2011). Women faculty members make up more than one-third of the full-time faculty workforce. In addition to helping to attract and train culturally competent URM students who will often go on to treat Black women in substantial numbers, the presence of Black and URM faculty members is significant in many ways. Medical and public health school faculty members sit on committees and governing bodies that make major administrative decisions.

The impact of a more diverse faculty can influence things from admission and retention of students to curricular content decisions to outreach programs and high school and college pipeline programs. Some students can face academic difficulty in medical school because of a number of factors including feelings of isolation, high academic loads, and demanding schedules. Having a faculty adviser or dean who looks like you can be a legitimating presence—something of a figurative buoy to hold onto. As in all aspects of life, representation matters. It is important for Black students to see faces that look like them at the helm of leadership and teaching at their university as a tool for retention and subsequent graduation. As mentioned above, these students are likely to be the ones to go on to treat communities of color and potentially impact the statistics mentioned at the outset of this chapter (Campbell & Rodríguez, 2014). These students are also the pool from which future medical and public health academicians would be drawn, thus continuing the cycle.

Why Mentoring Matters

Voytko and Lakoski (2019) detail several reasons that mentorship is important:

1. To attract, retain and engage high performers

2. To swiftly acculturate new members

3. To foster a collaborative environment

4. To increase stability and productivity

5. To promote diversity of thought and style

6. To develop leadership talent

7. To extend one's professional contributions

Several studies clamor for a call to action for both undergraduate and academic medical institutions to increase the recruitment and retention of URM students and faculty. We know that mentorship is vital to academic success in that it promotes retention and encourages vitality or resilience. A systematic review by Rodríguez, Campbell, Fogarty, and Williams (2014) found that faculty development programs in "15 different institutions showed mentoring and faculty development for minority faculty could increase retention, academic productivity, and promotion rates" for URM faculty (p. 100). Through their review of 548 studies, the researchers highlighted best practices and underscored the potential effect these mentoring programs can have on the recruitment and retention of URM faculty.

Best practices of successful programs include support for teaching, clinical, and research skills; decreasing clinical expectations to facilitate scholarly activity; providing seed money for projects; and use of on- and off-site mentors. One notable program gave promotional weight to community service and faculty participation in pipeline programs (Rodríguez et al., 2014). This is significant, as many URM faculty are often pulled to participate in these programs or to sit on multiple committees within the university. While noteworthy and important, these activities, the "Black tax" or "minority tax," if you will, can take away time from research and resultant scholarly publications, which are often regarded heavily in promotion decisions to associate and/or full professor. Giving equal weight to these other important activities like community service, mentoring, and advising of URM students and student groups can give a more accurate view of URM faculty members' time and value to the university. Similarly, mentoring received by URM doctoral students with research or teaching assistantships is likely a factor in helping to prepare them for success on the academic job market regardless of race. While further research is needed, the role of mentoring cannot be underestimated as a key factor in the recruitment of graduates into academic careers (Jackson et al., 2019; Guevara et al., 2013; Rodríguez et al., 2014; Nunez-Smith et al., 2012).

One example of an innovative URM faculty mentoring program is Quality Mentorship through STFM, which grew as the brainchild of the groups on Latino Faculty and Minority and Multicultural Health of the Society of Teachers of Family Medicine (STFM; Brown Speights, Figueroa, et al., 2017). STFM is a national organization started in 1967 that represents over 5,000 family physicians who educate medical students and residents in the 171 medical schools and 600 family medicine training programs throughout the country. The program paired junior URM family medicine faculty members with seasoned mentors who themselves are URM or are URM-sympathetic. This program is innovative in its approach in that uses long-distance mentoring through an academic society to impact local academic and national success, supports mentors through an advisory group, and uses qualitative and quantitative methods to gain best practices for program design and implementation. The program has partnered with other like-minded organizations and expanded to a campaign focusing on funding programs that support medical students and residents going into academic medicine as well as junior URM faculty members.

I cannot express my gratitude for being a part of this program. The mentoring has helped me to be more intentional about my career and has helped me to see ways that I can continue with my academic career for the long term. Having a mentor who "gets it"—that I can bounce ideas off and even ask the smallest questions has been invaluable for my career peace of mind. My mentor reminds me of small things I can do to prepare myself for promotion and to remain active with

*academic scholarship and publications—this is the "currency" if you
will of academic medicine.*

—Assistant professor and Quality Mentorship mentee

*As one of the mentors, I found mentees and colleagues that continue
to blow me away with their commitment to academic medicine despite
the challenges they face.*

—Associate professor and Quality Mentorship mentor

Conclusion

The situation of Black women and public health is admittedly daunting. The
tapestry of these inequalities and disparities is densely woven with a four-
hundred-year-old thread of discrimination and strife. Black women are the
teachers, caretakers, and drivers of our society who often, out of necessity,
place their health-care needs last. When considering the social determinants of health, this can be a recipe for increased morbidity and mortality
among Black women. Though we realize that Black women are resilient and
possess a broad repertoire of assets to mitigate these negative life factors,
we must ask ourselves, Who cares for the caretaker? Who is more likely
to research and document these disparities and sound the call for change?
Often, Black physicians and allied public health professionals partnering
with Black communities are one part of the solution. Increasing diversity
in academic medicine and public health is an important step, though not
the only step, toward reaching health equity for underserved communities,
including Black women (Marrast et al., 2014; Emery et al., 2018).

US medical schools, schools of public health, and related institutes
of higher health-care education are the fount from where we look to
draw a culturally competent, clinically excellent health-care workforce.
They are whence we draw the ones who will stand in the gap and care
for our mothers, sisters, daughters, grandmas, and sister friends. As such,
there is a need to look critically at who is teaching this workforce. We
can address these concerns through better public and private institution
partnerships, pushing for accountability of how public funds are used,
increasing research, and increasing diversity among faculties. We need
to increase financial support for faculty and research training. Who is
training the doctors and researchers of today and tomorrow? Who trained

that doctor to notice that your grandmother missed her mammogram or that your mother's weight is creeping up, placing her at risk for diabetes? Who gave that doctor the insight that your aunt's missed visits may represent a fear of missing a day's portion of the paycheck with which she supports an entire family? Who trained that doctor to have a frank conversation with your daughter about her sexual health and how to avoid an unintended pregnancy? Who cautioned that young ob-gyn or family physician to vigilantly watch for pregnancy complications in a Black first-time mother? Who helped that doctor to maintain the perspective that your friend's noncompliance may be a mask for the eviscerating sting of depression? Who mentored that MPH candidate to continue her research project on health disparities affecting Black women?

Numerous studies have shown repeatedly that Black medical faculty members are instrumental in attracting, supporting, and training Black physician students who will then go on to care for these populations (Marrast et al., 2014; Saha et al., 2000; Zhang et al., 2015; Pololi et al., 2010; Rodríguez & Campbell, 2016, 2013; Xierali et al., 2016; Rodríguez et al., 2015). Thus, we need a concerted effort to support and increase the numbers of faculty members of color and, specifically with regard to this article, Black women faculty members to a percentage reflective of the population. These faculty members need to be supported, and barriers to retention need to be examined and addressed. Established mentoring programs are one way to support Black faculty members and contribute to continuing the pipeline of Black men and women being admitted to medical school and graduating to enter the health-care research and delivery workforce.

The unprecedented effects of 2020 highlighted the impact of mentoring for Black medical educators and the direct impact on public health outcomes of Black women. The year 2020 brought what many have referred to as the triple pandemic for African Americans. The killing of George Floyd and the global protests that ensued forced many institutions and organizations into a racial reckoning, and many realized the need to examine their policies toward justice, diversity, equity, and inclusion. At the same time, the COVID-19 global pandemic laid bare the health-outcome disparities and economic impact caused by years of structural racism. Blacks, especially Black women, have been disproportionately affected by all aspects of the COVID-19 pandemic, including but not limited to mortality and morbidity, economic impact through job loss, educational disparities revealed by access to remote learning for children, and the digital divide.

Throughout this, Black educators bonded together to provide support to each other by discussing the impact of COVID-19 at their home institutions. Many were asked to step into leadership positions to assist their institutions with a response to the racial protests and a review of curricular and institutional policies. As mothers, physicians, and public health educators, many had to carry on in this public position while continuing to care for patients directly and indirectly impacted by the ravages of COVID-19. Black health providers and educators felt compelled to address COVID-19 pandemic disparities including disproportionate vaccine distribution through education, clinical service, and scholarship on the front lines. We were called on by the larger community, by White colleagues, and by our personal families and contacts to serve as the voice of reason and knowledge while personally dealing with the effects of racism and health disparities in our own lives.

The pressures of the minority tax compelled us to balance the personal impact of systemic racism and COVID-19 with the responsibility of bringing that lived experience to the table and serving in leadership roles in our communities and institutions. Against this backdrop, the authors assert the continued need for mentoring Black physicians and public health leaders to continue to increase the numbers of Black health academics, with the ultimate goal of impacting health disparities and health outcomes for Black women. The times are too dire, and the need is too great. The time to act is now.

～

On a personal note, as a young Black family physician and medical educator, I think back to that card I received as a young undergraduate student that cold November New England morning. I think of the many cloaks that I have been shrouded under to get to this point in my career and those who continue to guide me and many others like me on this path. As you reflect on this reading, I, along with my mentors and coauthors, encourage you to think of who wrapped their cloak around you and said, "Let's walk together." Picture their face. Remember how their encouragement and counsel made you feel. Then, more importantly, take a moment to consider, Around whose shoulders have you shared your cloak?

—Dr. Andrea Anderson

References

American Academy of Family Physicians. (n.d.). *Primary care*. Retrieved January 2019 from https://www.aafp.org/about/policies/all/primary-care.html

Association of American Medical Colleges. (n.d.). *FACTS: Applicants, matriculants, enrollment, graduates, MD-PhD, and residency applicants data* [Data set]. Retrieved January 2019 from https://www.aamc.org/data/facts/enrollmentgraduate

Association of American Medical Colleges. (2015) *Altering the course: Black males in medicine.*

Association of American of Medical Colleges. (2017). *Faculty roster reports 2017.* Retrieved January 2019 from https://www.aamc.org/download/486128/data/17table8.pdf

Association of American Medical Colleges. (2009). *Striving towards excellence: Faculty diversity in medical education.* AAMC Diversity, Policy, and Programs.

Association of American Medical Colleges. (2004) Underrepresented in medicine definition-initiatives-AAMC [internet].

Brown Speights, J. S., Figueroa, E., Figueroa, E., & Washington, J. (2017). Quality mentorship through STFM. *Annals of Family Medicine, 15*(6), 588–589.

Brown Speights, J. S., Goldfarb, S. S., Wells, B. A., Beitsch, L., Levine, R. S., & Rust, G. (2017) State-level progress in reducing the Black-White infant mortality gap, United States, 1999–2013. *American Journal of Public Health, 107*(5),775–782.

Campbell, K. M., & Rodríguez, J. E. (2013). Minority faculty face challenges similar to those of minority college students [Letter to the editor]. *Academic Medicine, 88*(8), 1056–1057.

Campbell, K. M., & Rodríguez, J. E. (2014). Can increasing minority faculty lead to increasing the workforce for underserved and minority populations? [Letter to the editor]. *Academic Medicine, 89*(8), 1094–1095.

Centers for Disease Control and Prevention. (n.d.). *Academic Partnerships to Improve Health (APIH)*. Retrieved January 2019 from https://www.cdc.gov/ophss/csels/dsepd/academic-partnerships/overview.html

Cropsey, K. L., Masho, S. W., Shiang, R., Sikka, V., Kornstein, S. G., Hampton, C. L., & Committee on the Status of Women and Minorities, Virginia Commonwealth University School of Medicine, Medical College of Virginia Campus. (2008). Why do faculty leave? Reasons for attrition of women and minority faculty from a medical school: Four-year results. *Journal of Women's Health, 17*(7), 1111–1118.

Desmond, M. (2014) *How housing matters: Poor black women are evicted at alarming rates, setting off a chain of hardship.* MacArthur Foundation. https://www.

macfound.org/media/files/HHM_Research_Brief_-_Poor_Black_Women_ Are_Evicted_at_Alarming_Rates.pdf

Emery, C. R., Boatright, D., & Culbreath, K. (2018) Stat! An action plan for replacing the broken system of recruitment and retention of underrepresented minorities in medicine [Discussion paper]. *NAM Perspectives.* National Academy of Medicine.

Fisher, Z. E., Rodríguez, J. E., & Campbell, K. M. (2017). A review of tenure for black, Latino, and Native American faculty in academic medicine. *Southern Medical Journal, 110*(1), 11–17.

Freudenberg, N., Klitzman, S., Diamond, C., & El-Mohandes, A. (2015). Keeping the "public" in schools of public health. *American Journal of Public Health, 105*(Suppl 1), S119–S124.

Green, A. R., Carney, D. R., Pallin, D. J., Ngo, L. H., Raymond, K. L., Iezzoni, L. I., & Banaji, M. R. (2007). Implict bias among physicians and its prediction of thrombolysis decisions for black and white patients. *Journal of General Internal Medicine, 22*(9), 1231–1238.

Guerra, M. (2013, November 7). *Fact sheet: The state of African American women in the United States.* Center for American Progress. https://www.american progress.org/issues/race/reports/2013/11/07/79165/fact-sheet-the-state-of-african-american-women-in-the-united-states/

Guevara, J., Adanga, E., Avakame, E., & Carthon, M. (2013). Minority faculty development programs and underrepresented minority faculty representation at US medical schools. *JAMA, 310*(21), 2297–2304.

Jackson, J. R., Holmes, A. M., Golembiewski, E., Brown-Podgorski, B. L., & Menachemi, N. (2019). Graduation and academic placement of underrepresented racial/ethnic minority doctoral recipients in public health disciplines, United States, 2003–2015. *Public Health Reports, 134*(1), 63–71.

King, T. E., Dickenson, T. A, Dubose, T. D., Flack, J. M., Hellmann, D. B., & Pamies, D. B. (2004). The case for diversity in academic internal medicine. *American Journal of Medicine, 116*(4), 284–289.

Laditka, J. N. (2004). Physician supply, physician diversity, and outcomes of primary health care for older persons in the United States. *Health Place, 10*(3), 231–244.

Laditka, S., & Laditka, J. (2002). Physician supply and diversity and access to primary health care [Abstract]. *The Gerontologist, 42*(I.1), 352.

Lautenberger, D., Moses, A., & Castillo-Page, L. C. (2016). An overview of women full-time medical school faculty of color. *AAMC Analysis in Brief, 16*(4), 1–2.

Lett, L., Koniaris, L., Orji, W., Sebro, R., & Koniaris, L. (2018). Declining racial and ethnic representation in clinical academic medicine: A longitudinal study of 16 US medical specialties. *PLOS ONE, 13*(11), e0207274.

Marrast, L., Zallman, L., Woolhandler, S., Bor, D., & McCormick, D. (2014). Minority physicians' role in the care of underserved patients: Diversifying the physician workforce may be key in addressing health disparities [Report]. *JAMA Internal Medicine, 174*(2), 289–291.

McGirt, E. (2017, June 8). The state of black women in the U.S. *Fortune.* http://fortune.com/2017/06/08/the-state-of-Black-women-in-the-u-s/

National Partnership for Women and Families. (2018, April). *Fact sheet: Black women and the wage gap.* Retrieved January 2019 from http://www.nationalpartnership.org/our-work/resources/workplace/fair-pay/african-american-women-wage-gap.pdf

Nivet, M. A. (2015) A Diversity 3.0 update: Are we moving the needle? *Academic Medicine, 90*(12), 1591–1593.

Nunez-Smith, M., Ciarleglio, M., Sandoval-Schaefer, T., Elumn, J., Castillo-Page, L., Peduzzi, P., & Bradley, E. (2012). Institutional variation in the promotion of racial/ethnic minority faculty at US medical schools. *American Journal of Public Health, 102*(5), 852–858.

Office of Disease Prevention and Health Promotion. (n.d.). *Healthy People 2020.* Retrieved January 2019 from https://www.healthypeople.gov

Ong, M., Wright, C., Espinosa, L. L., & Orfield, G. (2011) Inside the double bind: A synthesis of empirical research on undergraduate and graduate women of color in science, technology, engineering, and mathematics. *Harvard Educational Review, 81*(2), 171–208.

Palepu, L., Carr, H., Friedman, S., Ash, A., & Moskowitz, A. (2000). Specialty choices, compensation, and career satisfaction of underrepresented minority faculty in academic medicine. *Academic Medicine, 75*(2), 157–160.

Phelan, J. C., Link, B. G., & Tehranifar, P. (2010). Social conditions as fundamental causes of health inequalities: Theory, evidence, and policy implications. *Journal of Health and Social Behavior, 51*(Suppl.), S28–S40.

Pololi, L., Cooper, L. A., & Carr, P. (2010). Race, disadvantage and faculty experiences in academic medicine. *Journal of General Internal Medicine, 25*(12), 1363–1369.

Pratt, R., Gyllstrom, B., Gearin, K., Lange, C., Hahn, D., Baldwin, L.-M., & Zahner, S. (2018). Identifying barriers to collaboration between primary care and public health: Experiences at the local level. *Public Health Reports, 133*(3), 311–317.

Rodríguez, J. E., & Campbell, K. M. (2013). Ways to guarantee minority faculty will quit academic medicine [Letter to the editor]. *Academic Medicine, 88*(11), 1591–1591.

Rodríguez, J. E., & Campbell, K. M. (2014a). Minority faculty pay a higher proportion of their earnings to student debt [Letter to the editor]. *Academic Medicine, 89*(3), 371–372.

Rodríguez, J. E., Campbell, K. M., & Mouratidis, R. W. (2014b). Where are the rest of us? Improving representation of minority faculty in academic medicine. *Southern Medical Journal, 107*(12), 739–744.

Rodríguez, J. E., Campbell, K. M., Fogarty, J. P., & Williams, R. L. (2014c). Under-represented minority faculty in academic medicine: A systematic review of URM faculty development. *Family Medicine, 46*(2), 100–104.

Rodríguez, J. E., & Campbell, K. M. (2016). Is academic medicine sabotaging its own diversity efforts? [Letter to the editor]. *Academic Medicine, 91*(8), 1036–1037.

Rodríguez, J. E., Campbell, K. M., & Adelson, W. J. (2015). Poor representation of Blacks, Latinos, and Native Americans in medicine. *Family Medicine, 47*(4), 259–263.

Rust, G., Levine, R. S., Fry-Johnson, Y., Baltrus, P., Ye, J., & Mack, D. (2012). Paths to success: Optimal and equitable health outcomes for all. *Journal of Health Care for the Poor and Underserved, 23*(2, Suppl.), 7–19.

Saha, S., Taggart, S., Komaromy, M., & Bindman, A. (2000). Do patients choose physicians of their own race? To provide the kind of care consumers want, medical schools might be able to justify using race as an admissions criterion. *Health Affairs, 19*(4), 76–83.

Smedley, B. D., Stith, A. Y., & Nelson, A. R. (Eds.). (2002). *Unequal treatment: Confronting racial and ethnic disparities in health care.* National Academies Press.

United States Census Bureau. (2017). *PINC-05: Work experience—People 15 years old and over, by total money earnings, age, race, Hispanic origin, sex, and disability status* [2016 data set]. Retrieved January 2019 from https://www.census.gov/data/tables/time-series/demo/income-poverty/cps-pinc/pinc-05.2016.html

Voytko, M. L., & Lakoski, J. M. (2019). *GWIMS mentoring women toolkit for mentees: Mentoring for your academic career success.* Association of American Medical Colleges. https://www.aamc.org/members/gwims/toolkit/343518/toolkithometsr.html

World Health Organization. (1946). *Constitution of the World Health Organization.* https://www.who.int/governance/eb/who_constitution_en.pdf

Xierali, I. M., Fair, M. A., & Nivet, M. A. (2016). Faculty diversity in U.S. medical schools: Progress and gaps co-exist. *AAMC Analysis in Brief, 16*(6).

Zhang, K., Xierali, I., Castillo-Page, L., Nivet, M., & Schoolcraft Conrad, S. (2015). Students' top factors in selecting medical schools. *Academic Medicine, 90*(5), 693–693.

Chapter 12

Stress and Black Women's Health

Origins, Coping Strategies, and Implications for Policy and Practice

PORTIA A. JACKSON PRESTON, LESLIE BRONNER, AND YVONNE BRONNER

Stress, while often invisible to the naked eye, has an enormous impact on the physical and emotional health of Black women. Historically, pressures have forced Black women to be strong, self-sufficient, and resilient while taking a toll on their well-being. This is seen in a greater prevalence of stress-related diseases among Black women compared to White women: 54 percent higher for obesity (National Center for Health Statistics [NCHS], 2018c), 33 percent higher for hypertension (NCHS, 2018b), and 46 percent higher for diabetes (NCHS, 2018a). This chapter defines stress by describing its physical and psychological effects, discusses social determinants of health (SDOH) and health equity using the life-course framework, and highlights current theories explaining stress's impact on the health of Black women. It concludes by addressing evidence-based strategies to mitigate stress and proposing recommendations for policy and practice.

Stress: Definition and Physiology

Stress can be defined as "the physiologic demand placed on the body when one must adapt, cope or adjust" (Nevid & Rathus, 2007). The nature of stress can be physical (e.g., climbing stairs or fighting off an infection) or psychological (e.g., worrying about an upcoming test or meeting financial obligations). Stress is felt when one's appraisal of the demands presented by a situation are greater than the resources available to meet those needs. The extent to which a situation is perceived as stressful is dependent on an individual's assessment (Lazarus & Folkman, 1984; Mason, 1975).

Once an event is appraised as stressful, the body tries to meet the physiological demands needed to maintain bodily functions and return to homeostasis (McEwen, 1998; McEwen & Gianaros, 2010). When a threat is acute, the body activates the hypothalamic-pituitary-adrenal axis, and a signal received by the adrenal gland secretes epinephrine and cortisol as a part of the "fight or flight" response (Fricchione & Iykovic, 2016). Epinephrine release leads to an increase in heart and respiratory rates to prepare the person to address the immediate demand. Cortisol secretion stimulates the liver to increase the production of blood glucose, facilitates the breakdown of fats and proteins to be converted into usable energy, increases blood pressure to ensure oxygen and nutrients get to the parts of the body that need them, and decreases nonessential functions (e.g., digestive and reproductive systems). Cortisol is also responsible for providing the regulatory mechanism to shut down the stress response system when the threat has resolved and homeostasis is restored.

This process becomes problematic when the stress response system is repeatedly activated or prolonged, as is the case with chronic stress. This can cause damage to the stress response system, impacting one's sensitivity to external threats (i.e., lowering the threshold to activate the threat system) and resulting in an inability to turn the system off when the threat has subsided (Fricchione & Iykovic, 2016). The physiologic effect of wear and tear on the body that occurs as a result is referred to as allostatic load (McEwen, 1998).

There are several negative consequences of chronic stress. An excess of epinephrine leads to elevated heart rate and, over time, hypertension and cardiovascular disease (Fricchione & Iykovic, 2016). Excess cortisol leads to suppressed immune function and increased susceptibility to infections, blockage of insulin receptors (increasing the risk of diabetes), and an increase in fat storage in the abdomen (increasing the risk of obesity and inflammation).

In addition, oxidative stress occurs when the body is experiencing chronic stress and increased oxygen consumption is needed to increase energy production (Fricchione & Iykovic, 2016). Free radicals, the toxic byproducts of oxygen metabolism, can damage cell structures and subsequently impact functioning. Finally, individuals may respond to stress by engaging in maladaptive coping, which includes unhealthy behaviors such as smoking, drug and alcohol abuse, and overeating.

Black Women and Stress: Cultural and Social Context

With a foundational understanding of stress, we turn our attention to the SDOH—"the conditions in which people are born, grow, live, work and age" (World Health Organization [WHO], n.d.-a)—and the relationship to health inequity—"the avoidable, unfair, or remediable differences among groups of people" (WHO, n.d.-b)—due to historical racism leading to social and economic disadvantage. The life-course framework, used in maternal and child health, shows that each person is subjected to risk and protective factors from birth that impact their health status throughout the life course (Lu & Halfon, 2013). According to this framework, the family that one is born into can either impart to or deny an individual financial, social, and emotional resources that serve as protective factors and increase the prognosis for a healthy life.

Over the years, public health researchers have increasingly focused on the SDOH such as socioeconomic status (SES), the physical environment, employment, social support networks, and access to health care as important factors contributing to health disparities for Black women (Solar & Irwin, 2007). For example, many studies demonstrate the relationship between health and SES (Adler et al., 1994; Paeratakul et al., 2002; Taylor & Seeman, 1999). Individuals with higher income generally have access to better education and neighborhoods and report higher health status than those who live in poverty.

Research on adverse childhood experiences (ACEs) indicates children who experience multiple ACEs have increased risk of poor health and achievement as adults, contributing to health inequity. These negative outcomes are increased in the presence of low SES (Metzler et al., 2017). Research also shows that socioenvironmental context can have an enduring effect on subsequent generations that is avoidable and remediable (Provencal & Binder, 2015; Shannon, 2013). The theory of intergenerational transmission of stress explains that stress experienced by parents can impact "physical, behavioral, and cognitive outcomes" in children (Bowers & Yehuda, 2016, p. 232). In addition, parental exposure to racial segregation can influence neighborhood attainment (Pais, 2017), while neighborhood poverty can have a negative impact on cognitive ability in subsequent generations (Sharkey & Elwert, 2011).

Because of a long-standing history of race- and gender-based discriminatory practices toward Black women in the US (institutionalized, personally mediated, or internalized [Jones, 2000]), even those who are born into the most optimal social context experience poorer health outcomes when compared to their White peers. For example, Black women with advanced educational status were 1.82 times more likely to experience infant mortality outcomes than White women who had not graduated from high school (Schoendorf et al., 1992). Due in part to racism and health inequity, this gap in infant mortality widens with increased education (Smith et al., 2018).

The negative impact of stress emanates from what Deborah King (1988) refers to as multiple jeopardies based on membership in marginalized race, gender, and class subgroups. Historically, the Sojourner Syndrome, named for the former slave abolitionist Sojourner Truth, posits that the intersecting effects of race, class, and gender are important risk factors, partially explaining higher rates of morbidity and mortality among Black women (Mullings, 2005). Women who are marginalized by other social characteristics, such as sexual orientation, face additional stress (Bowleg et al., 2003).

Frameworks Exploring Stress Coping in Black Women

Increased attention in research has shifted to the development of multidisciplinary frameworks that explain how the "strength" of Black women, often seen as a mechanism of survival and a symbol of pride, negatively impacts Black women's health. Beauboeuf-Lafontant (2009) warns against this glorification, contending that "invocations and practices of strength overlook the fact that Black women are subordinated within race, class, and gender hierarchies" (p. 7). She advocates against research that addresses power structures that institutionalize discrimination requiring Black women to be strong, which compromises their humanity and well-being.

Two frameworks that are helpful for understanding the negative health impact of this archetype are the Superwoman Schema (SWS), based on qualitative research conducted by Woods-Giscombé (2010), and the Strong Black Woman Script (SBW-S), based on a content analysis conducted by Black and Peacock (2011). The SWS defines the Superwoman role as a set of perceived responsibilities imparted to Black women via cultural and societal messaging and familial expectations, such as exhibiting strength while suppressing emotion and prioritizing the needs of others over their own (Woods-Giscombé, 2010). Benefits of this role include preservation of self, family, and community, while liabilities include relationship strain and negative stress-coping behavior. A recent study found that while certain dimensions of the SWS were protective of one's health, other dimensions further exacerbated the relationship between racial discrimination and allostatic load (Allen et al., 2019).

Themes of the SBW-S identified as having a negative impact on health and well-being included putting the needs of others ahead of oneself, executing responsibilities without help from others, suppression of one's emotions, and neglecting to engage in self-care (Black & Peacock, 2011). However, participants cited positive alternatives to the SBW-S, such as asking for help, prioritizing self-care, and expressing one's emotions. Other studies have shown evidence of Black women modifying the role to fit their needs or rejecting aspects they found constraining (Nelson et al., 2016).

Coping Strategies

In considering the development of interventions to promote positive stress coping, it is important to acknowledge the role of systemic change, and that perceptions of stress and coping practices employed by Black women are varied. Recent research has found that self-care helped to mitigate the effect of stress on health among Black women (Adkins-Jackson et al., 2019). Helpful practices to manage stress include cognitive strategies, mindfulness, physical activity, and healthy eating behaviors.

Cognitive Behavioral Therapy

Stress creates challenges by placing demands on the body and via the consequences of how the body responds to such demands. Appraisal of a situation is a complex cognitive task that starts with an internal working model about self, others, and the world, generating expectations (called schemas) about social interactions (APA Working Group on Stress and Health Disparities, 2017). As stated in the previous section, Black women have internalized messages, which are developed based on early experiences of interactions with primary caregivers, that are hypothesized to perpetuate the negative impact of the SDOH on disease development. These attachment relationships form the basis of how individuals experience the world, interpret events, and subsequently experience stress. While these schemas can change throughout the life course, they become harder to change as individuals age.

Cognitive behavioral therapy was developed to help individuals change the way they think and behave. Due to stigma, Black men and women are less likely than Whites to seek therapy and are more likely to receive poor-quality therapy when they do obtain it; thus they are also more likely to leave therapy prematurely (González et al., 2010; Cooper et al., 2003). Research indicates that culturally adapted treatments and interventions can increase behavioral therapy's effectiveness (Griner & Smith, 2006), showing improvements in stress-related outcomes among Black female participants (Kohn et al., 2002; Ward & Brown, 2015). While more research needs to be conducted with Black women to identify their specific needs, therapy can be a helpful resource for stress management.

Mindfulness

Mindfulness can be a helpful intervention for Black women to decrease activation of the stress response system over time (Woods-Giscombé & Black, 2010). Jon Kabat-Zinn (2013) describes mindfulness as a way to ground oneself in the present moment by focusing attention on what one is experiencing internally and externally. Mindfulness-based stress reduction (MBSR) and mindful self-compassion are examples of structured eight-week programs shown to be effective in reducing stress and improving health outcomes (Grossman et al., 2004; Neff & Germer, 2013). Mindfulness-based interventions focusing on healthy eating and physical activity can also be effective in reducing cardiovascular risk (Fulwiler et al., 2015; Jordan et al., 2014; Loucks et al., 2015). The cost of formal mindfulness programs can pose a challenge. However, there are an increasing number of free resources available to support wellness, including Palouse Mindfulness (an eight-week online MBSR program) and meditation apps such as Shine (which centers the experiences of women of color) and Insight Timer.

While there is a paucity of research conducted with Black women, evidence to date indicates an openness to mindfulness-based interventions when mindfulness materials are culturally relevant, do not conflict with spiritual beliefs, and employ the utility of instructors of color (Woods-Giscombé & Black, 2010; Woods-Giscombé & Gaylord, 2014). One example of mindfulness-based programming designed to be responsive to the needs of people of color is Mindfulness for the People, which offers racial resilience training (https://mindfulnessforthepeople.org/).

Physical Activity

Physical activity is associated with lower levels of perceived stress in working adults (Aldana et al., 1996) and fewer reported symptoms of anxiety and depression (Dunn et al., 2001). In order to realize these health benefits, experts recommend 150–300 minutes per week of moderate-intensity activity (e.g., brisk walking) or 75–150 minutes of vigorous activity (e.g., running or jogging), along with at least two days of muscle-strengthening activities (U.S. Department of Health and Human Services, 2018). Barriers to physical activity for Black women include lack of time, space, motivation, energy, childcare, a companion to exercise with, or a safe environment to exercise in (Nies et al., 1999). Strategies that can facilitate physical activity among Black women include a body-positive approach that highlights mental and physical benefits as opposed to weight loss (Wilcox et al., 2002) and identification of activities that can be incorporated into one's daily routine (Nies et al., 1999). Short bouts of exercise at home or in organizational settings (e.g., work sites, churches) can help increase the likelihood of sustainability and improved health status (Barr-Anderson et al., 2011; Bramante et al., 2018).

Healthy Eating

Exposure to stress is associated with an increased desire to consume food—especially nutrient-poor comfort foods (Groesz et al., 2012)—and can result in disordered eating in Black women (Woods-Giscombé, 2010). US dietary guidelines promote prioritizing nutrient-dense foods in one's diet, such as vegetables, whole fruit, and whole grains, while limiting food and beverages high in added sugar, saturated fat, sodium, and alcohol (U.S. Department of Agriculture & U.S. Department of Health and Human Services, 2020). Barriers to healthy eating among Black women include limited time for meal planning and preparation (Doldren & Webb, 2012). Several studies have indicated that the combination of weight loss interventions with stress management (Cox et al., 2013) or mindfulness components (Chung et al., 2016) can be more effective in achieving weight loss and maintenance than focusing on weight loss alone. It is important to note that the relationship between low access to nutritious foods and obesity risk is strongest among Black women living in high-poverty, predominantly Black neighborhoods (Gailey & Bruckner, 2019).

Implications for Policy and Practice

While this chapter focused mainly on strategies at the individual level, we will close by identifying interventions and policies that can help to reach socioeconomically diverse and vulnerable populations:

1. Social determinants of health (SDOH)

    a. Incorporate the SDOH into legislation focused on remediating health inequities, including

        i. neighborhood safety—install adequate lighting, limit the number of liquor stores, and address blight (e.g., empty lots, boarded-up housing);

        ii. healthy eating—incentivize the construction of healthy, affordable food outlets in food deserts; and

        iii. physical activity—improve the built environment to facilitate activity with exercise equipment, sidewalks, and bike paths.

2. Cognitive behavioral therapy and mindfulness

    a. Train health-care providers to speak with patients about identifying stressors and design appropriate interventions to mitigate stress and promote positive stress-coping behaviors.

    b. Ensure content is culturally tailored and that the pacing and cost of therapy and programming are feasible.

    c. Increase racial concordance by training more practitioners of color, especially in underserved areas with large minority populations.

    d. Address issues of access by advocating for increased insurance coverage of therapy visits and mindfulness programs.

e. To expand access to these services, train community health workers to collaborate with health-care practitioners to meet the needs of a more socioeconomically diverse population.

f. Conduct further research focusing on therapy, mindfulness, and health outcomes for Black women.

3. Physical activity

a. Encourage short bouts of exercise in organizational settings where Black women gather, such as work sites and churches.

b. Provide culturally tailored physical activity programming that emphasizes mindfulness, stress management, and the mental and physical benefits of activity.

4. Healthy eating

a. Incorporate mindfulness and stress-management practices as a part of healthy eating.

b. Increase access to and affordability of healthy food in underserved areas.

Stress can influence health not only through the demands placed on an individual but also by how the body responds to such demands. Due to inequities in access to resources, Black women are disproportionately predisposed to adverse health outcomes, and through negative internalized messages the impact can be much greater than for other population groups. The strategies we have listed here can help to empower Black women in their efforts to redefine their own narratives of strength to take control of their health.

References

Adkins-Jackson, P. B., Turner-Musa, T., & Chester, C. (2019). The path to better health for black women: Predicting self-care and exploring its mediating effects on stress and health. *Inquiry, 56*, 1–8.

Adler, N., Boyce, T., Chesney, M., Cohen, S., Folkman, S., Kahn, R., & Syme, S. L. (1994). Socioeconomic status and health: The challenge of the gradient. *American Psychologist, 49*(1), 15–24.

Aldana, S. G., Sutton, L. D., Jacobson, B. H., & Quirk, M. G. (1996). Relationships between leisure time physical activity and perceived stress. *Perceptual and Motor Skills, 82*(1), 315–321.

Allen, A. M., Wang, Y., Chae, D. H., Price, M. M., Powell, W., Steed, T. C., Black, A. R., Dhabhar, F. S., Marquez-Magaña, L., & Woods-Giscombe, C. L. (2019). Racial discrimination, the superwoman schema, and allostatic load: Exploring an integrative stress-coping model among African American women. *Annals of the New York Academy of Sciences, 1457*(1), 104–127.

APA Working Group on Stress and Health Disparitites. (2017). *Stress and health disparities: Contexts, mechanisms, and interventions among racial/ethnic minority and low socioeconomic status populations.* American Psychological Association. https://www.apa.org/pi/health-disparities/resources/stress-report.pdf

Barr-Anderson, D. J., AuYoung, M., Whitt-Glover, M. C., Glenn, B. A., & Yancey, A. K. (2011). Integration of short bouts of physical activity into organizational routine: A systematic review of the literature. *American Journal of Preventive Medicine, 40*(1), 76–93.

Beauboeuf-Lafontant, T. (2009). *Behind the mask of the strong black woman: Voice and the embodiment of a costly performance.* Temple University Press.

Black, A. R., & Peacock, N. (2011). Pleasing the masses: Messages for daily life management in African American women's popular media sources. *American Journal of Public Health, 101*(1), 144–150.

Bowers, M. E., & Yehuda, R. (2016). Intergenerational transmission of stress in humans. *Neuropsychopharmacology, 41*(1), 232–244.

Bowleg, L., Huang, J., Brooks, K., Black, A., & Burkholder, G. (2003). Triple jeopardy and beyond: Multiple minority stress and resilience among black lesbians. *Journal of Lesbian Studies, 7*(4), 87–108.

Bramante, C. T., King, M. M., Story, M., Whitt-Glover, M. C., & Barr-Anderson, D. J. (2018). Worksite physical activity breaks: Perspectives on feasibility of implementation. *Work, 59*(4), 491–499.

Chung, S., Zhu, S., Friedmann, E., Kelleher, C., Kozlovsky, A., Macfarlane, K. W., Tkaczuk, K. H. R., Ryan, A. S., & Griffith, K. A. (2016). Weight loss with mindful eating in African American women following treatment for breast cancer: A longitudinal study. *Supportive Care in Cancer, 24*(4), 1875–1881.

Cooper, L. A., Gonzales, J. J., Gallo, J. J., Rost, K. M., Meredith, L. S., Rubenstein, L. V., Wang, N.-Y., & Ford, D. E. (2003). The acceptability of treatment for depression among African-American, Hispanic, and white primary care patients. *Medical Care, 41*(4), 479–489.

Cox, T. L., Krukowski, R., Love, S. J., Eddings, K., DiCarlo, M., Chang, J. Y., Prewitt, T. E., & West, D. S. (2013). Stress management–augmented behavioral weight loss intervention for African American women: A pilot, randomized controlled trial. *Health Education & Behavior, 40*(1), 78–87.

Doldren, M., & Webb, F. (2012). Facilitators of and barriers to healthy eating and physical activity for Black women: A focus group study in Florida, USA. *Critical Public Health, 23*(1), 32–38.

Dunn, A. L., Trivedi, M. H., & O'Neal, H. A. (2001). Physical activity dose-response effects on outcomes of depression and anxiety. *Medicine and Science in Sports and Exercise, 33*(6, Suppl.), S587–S597.

Fricchione, G., & Iykovic, Y. (2016). *The science of stress: Living under pressure.* University of Chicago Press.

Fulwiler, C., Brewer, J. A., Sinnott, S., & Loucks, E. B. (2015). Mindfulness-based interventions for weight loss and CVD risk management. *Current Cardiovascular Risk Reports, 9*(10), 46.

Gailey, S., & Bruckner, T. A. (2019). Obesity among black women in food deserts: An "omnibus" test of differential risk. *SSM—Population Health, 7*, Article 100363.

González, H. M., Vega, W. A., Williams, D. R., Tarraf, W., West, B. T., & Neighbors, H. W. (2010). Depression care in the United States. *Archives of General Psychiatry, 67*(1), 37–46.

Griner, D., & Smith, T. B. (2006). Culturally adapted mental health intervention: A meta-analytic review. *Psychotherapy (Chic.), 43*(4), 531–548.

Groesz, L. M., McCoy, S., Carl, J., Saslow, L., Stewart, J., Adler, N., Laraia, B., & Epel, E. (2012). What is eating you? Stress and the drive to eat. *Appetite, 58*(2), 717–721.

Grossman, P., Niemann, L., Schmidt, S., & Walach, H. (2004). Mindfulness-based stress reduction and health benefits: A meta-analysis. *Journal of Psychosomatic Research, 57*(1), 35–43.

Jones, C. P. (2000). Levels of racism: A theoretic framework and a gardener's tale. *American Journal of Public Health, 90*(8), 1212–1215.

Jordan, C. H., Wang, W., Donatoni, L., & Meier, B. P. (2014). Mindful eating: Trait and state mindfulness predict healthier eating behavior. *Personality and Individual Differences, 68*, 107–111.

Kabat-Zinn, J. (2013). *Full catastrophe living: Using the wisdom of your body and mind to face stress, pain, and illness* (Rev. ed.). Bantam Books.

King, D. (1988). Multiple jeopardy, multiple consciousness: The context of a Black feminist ideology. *Signs, 14*(1), 42–72.

Kohn, L. P., Oden, T., Muñoz, R. F., Robinson, A., & Leavitt, D. (2002). Adapted cognitive behavioral group therapy for depressed low-income African American women. *Community Mental Health Journal, 38*(6), 497–504.

Lazarus, R. S., & Folkman, S. (1984). The stress concept in the life sciences. In R. Lazarus & S. Folkman, *Stress, appraisal, and coping* (pp. 1–21). Springer.

Loucks, E. B., Britton, W. B., Howe, C. J., Eaton, C. B., & Buka, S. L. (2015). Positive associations of dispositional mindfulness with cardiovascular health: The New England Family Study. *International Journal of Behavioral Medicine, 22*(4), 540–550.

Lu, M., & Halfon, N. (2013). Racial and ethnic disparities in birth outcomes: A life-course perspective. *Maternal and Child Health Journal, 7*(1), 13–30.

Mason, J. W. (1975). A historical view of the stress field. *Journal of Human Stress, 1*(2), 22–36.

McEwen, B. S. (1998). Stress, adaptation, and disease: Allostasis and allostatic load. *Annals of the New York Academy of Sciences, 840*(1), 33–44.

McEwen, B. S., & Gianaros, P. J. (2010). Central role of the brain in stress and adaptation: Links to socioeconomic status, health, and disease. *Annals of the New York Academy of Sciences, 1186*, 190–222.

Metzler, M., Merrick, M. T., Klevens, J., Ports, K. A., & Ford, D. C. (2017). Adverse childhood experiences and life opportunities: Shifting the narrative. *Child and Youth Services Review, 72*, 141–149.

Mullings, L. (2005). Resistance and resilience: The Sojourner Syndrome and the social context of reproduction in central Harlem. *Transforming Anthropology, 13*(2), 79–91.

National Center for Health Statistics. (2018a). *Crude percentages of diabetes for adults aged 18 and over, United States, 2018* [Data set]. National Health Interview Survey. Retrieved from https://www.cdc.gov/nchs/nhis/ADULTS/www/index.htm

National Center for Health Statistics. (2018b). *Crude percentages of hypertension for adults aged 18 and over, United States, 2018* [Data set]. National Health Interview Survey. Retrieved from https://www.cdc.gov/nchs/nhis/ADULTS/www/index.htm

National Center for Health Statistics. (2018c). *Crude percentages of obesity for adults aged 18 and over, United States, 2018* [Data set]. National Health Interview Survey. Retrieved from https://www.cdc.gov/nchs/nhis/ADULTS/www/index.htm

Neff, K. D., & Germer, C. K. (2013). A pilot study and randomized controlled trial of the mindful self-compassion program. *Journal of Clinical Psychology, 69*(1), 28–44.

Nelson, T., Cardemil, E. V, & Adeoye, C. T. (2016). Rethinking strength: Black women's perceptions of the "Strong Black Woman" role. *Psychology of Women Quarterly, 40*(4), 551–563.

Nevid, J. S., & Rathus, S. A. (2007). *Psychology and the challenges of life: Adjustment in the new millennium* (10th ed.). John Wiley & Sons.

Nies, M. A., Vollman, M., & Cook, T. (1999). African American women's experiences with physical activity in their daily lives. *Public Health Nursing, 16*(1), 23–36.

Paeratakul, S., Lovejoy, J., Ryan, D., & Bray, G. (2002). The relation of gender, race and socioeconomic status to obesity and obesity comorbidities in a sample of US adults. *International Journal of Obesity and Related Metabolic Disorders, 26*(9), 1205–1210.

Pais, J. (2017). Intergenerational neighborhood attainment and the legacy of racial residential segregation: A causal mediation analysis. *Demography, 54*(4), 1221–1250.

Provencal, N., & Binder, E. (2015). The effects of early life stress on the epigenome: From the womb to adulthood and even before. *Experimental Neurology, 268,* 10–20.

Schoendorf, K., Hogue, C., Kleinman, J., & Rowley, D. (1992). Mortality among infants of black as compared with white college-educated parents. *New England Journal of Medicine, 326*(23), 1522–1526.

Shannon, S. (2013). Inheriting racist disparities in health: Epigenetics and the transgenerational effects of white racism. *Critical Philosophy of Race, 1*(2), 190–218.

Sharkey, P., & Elwert, F. (2011). The legacy of disadvantage: Multigenerational neighborhood effects on cognitive ability. *American Journal of Sociology, 116*(6), 1934–1981.

Smith, I. Z., Bentley-Edwards, K. L., El-Amin, S., & Darity, W., Jr. (2018, March). *Fighting at birth: Eradicating the black-white infant mortality gap.* Duke University's Samuel DuBois Cook Center on Social Equity and Insight Center for Community Economic Development. https://socialequity.duke.edu/wp-content/uploads/2019/12/Eradicating-Black-Infant-Mortality-March-2018.pdf

Solar, O., & Irwin, A. (2007). *A conceptual framework for action on the social determinants of health.* World Health Organization Commission on Social Determinants of Health.

Taylor, S. E., & Seeman, T. E. (1999). Psychosocial resources and the SES-health relationship. *Annals of the New York Academy of Sciences, 896,* 210–225.

U.S. Department of Agriculture & U.S. Department of Health and Human Services. (2020, December). *Dietary guidelines for Americans, 2020–2025* (9th ed.). https://www.dietaryguidelines.gov/sites/default/files/2020-12/Dietary_Guidelines_for_Americans_2020-2025.pdf.

U.S. Department of Health and Human Services. (2018). *Physical activity guidelines for Americans* (2nd ed.). https://health.gov/sites/default/files/2019-09/Physical_Activity_Guidelines_2nd_edition.pdf

Ward, E. C., & Brown, R. L. (2015). A culturally adapted depression intervention for African American adults experiencing depression: Oh happy day. *American Journal of Orthopsychiatry, 85*(1), 11–22.

Wilcox, S., Richter, D. L., Henderson, K. A., Greaney, M. L., & Ainsworth, B. E. (2002). Perceptions of physical activity and personal barriers and enablers in African-American women. *Ethnicity & Disease, 12*(3), 353–362.

Woods-Giscombé, C. L. (2010). Superwoman Schema: African American women's views on stress, strength, and health. *Qualitative Health Research, 4*(164), 668–683.

Woods-Giscombé, C. L., & Black, A. R. (2010). Mind-body interventions to reduce risk for health disparities related to stress and strength among African American women: The potential of mindfulness-based stress reduction, loving-kindness, and the NTU therapeutic framework. *Complementary Health Practice Review, 15*(3), 115–131.

Woods-Giscombé, C. L., & Gaylord, S. A. (2014). The cultural relevance of mindfulness meditation as a health intervention for African Americans: Implications for reducing stress-related health disparities. *Journal of Holistic Nursing, 32*(3), 147–160.

World Health Organization. (n.d.-a). *Gender, equity and human rights: Social determinants of health.* https://www.who.int/gender-equity-rights/understanding/sdh-definition/en/

World Health Organization. (n.d.-b). *Health systems: Equity.* https://www.who.int/healthsystems/topics/equity/en/

Chapter 13

Alice Coltrane Turiyasangitananda's Yogic Journey

Creativity, Community, and Caretaking

TAMARA Y. JEFFRIES, SANTIBA D. CAMPBELL,
AND YASMEEN J. LONG

Often when people hear the word *yoga* the image that comes to mind is that of a lithe, moneyed White woman bending and twisting herself into impossible contortions. This image is rooted in the history of yoga in the West: from the first arrival of Indian yoga gurus in the United States, American yoga students were "largely female, affluent, and invested in American metaphysical religion" (Deslippe, 2018, p. 5). Not much seems to have changed more than a hundred years later, as media representation of yoga in the United States continues to suggest that its practitioners are thin, educated, upper-middle class, White, and female (Razmjou et al., 2017). One study that examined the physical appearance of yoga-magazine models found that most were White, thin, and lean. Other races, body sizes, and body shapes were unrepresented (Webb et al., 2017). It might be more accurate to say that the current yoga community *appears* to consist of a narrow demographic *because* of the limited representation of it within the media.

Research statistics offer little more diversity than media images. It is difficult to find a current, accurate estimate of yoga practitioners disaggregated by race or ethnicity. An International Association of Yoga Therapists compilation of yoga demographic statistics includes only one study referencing race (Lamb, 2006). Because yoga-specific demographic studies fail to include statistics on race or ethnicity, it appears that yoga practitioners are predominantly White; Black and brown yogis are rendered virtually invisible. However, Black people have been part of the yoga community for decades as students, practitioners, and teachers seeking and sharing the physical, mental, and spiritual benefits of the practice.

Among the earliest and most notable of these teachers was jazz pianist and harpist Alice Coltrane. As the widow of jazz legend John Coltrane, she was an unlikely guru, but her complex and prophetic journey to yoga foreshadowed the modern evolution and proliferation of yoga practice in the Black community and its use as a means of enhancing health and well-being among Black practitioners.

Ashtanga: The Eight-Fold Path

While the word *yoga* today is commonly associated with balance and stretching exercises, Alice Coltrane and her contemporaries studied it as a science and philosophy that promotes physical, mental, and emotional health (SikhNet, 2007). The bending, twisting physical postures (asana) are only one of eight elements that make up the system of yoga. The other parts of this lifestyle system include ethical life choices, personal practices, breathing exercises, sensory control, concentration, meditation, and union with higher consciousness (Brems et al., 2016). There is also any number of yoga schools, philosophies, and practice lineages. This chapter acknowledges that yoga is a diverse tradition that defies rigid definitions (Jain, 2014). For purposes of establishing a description here, our use of the term *yoga* refers to a holistic life practice that intentionally incorporates all eight limbs of yoga and acknowledges the historical origins and evolution of the practice. This definition aligns with Alice Coltrane's focus on the devotional and meditative aspects of yoga practice, and with an approach called "whole yoga," used as a method for making yoga accessible to African American students (Jeffries & Campbell, 2018).

Paschimottanasana: Stretch to the West

The first significant American encounter with a yogic philosophy was in 1893, when Swami Vivekananda traveled from India to the World Congress of Religions in Chicago, to spread the word about Vedanta, a philosophical system based on ancient Indian sacred texts.

Yoga had a renaissance after World War I, coinciding with the Harlem Renaissance of the 1920s and piquing the interest of progressive Black artists and thinkers. In 1926, Paramahansa Yogananda, the author of *Autobiography of a Yogi*, came to the United States as a delegate to the International Congress of Religious Liberals. When he learned that Black people wouldn't be allowed to attend a lecture he gave in Washington, DC, he offered a special session specifically for them (Long, 2016).

The post-civil-rights era saw another surge of interest among Black people embracing yoga, with the practice spreading among Black athletes and celebrities. In September 1975, *Ebony* magazine published a feature on African Americans who had embraced yoga and meditation titled "Yoga: Something for Everyone—Blacks Are Joining the Quest for Peace" (Long, 2016).

Alice and John Coltrane, as well as Sonny Rollins, Vishnu Wood, and others in the jazz world, were ahead of that 1970s yoga surge. By the early 1960s, Christian-bred John had already delved into the study of Eastern philosophy and other faiths, including Hindu mysticism (Taylor, 2009). He read the works of Yogananda and Krishnamurti and engaged in daily meditation practices, which he shared with Alice (Berkman, 2010). By the time yoga was popular enough among Black people to warrant the *Ebony* article, it had been almost ten years since John's death, and Alice had become fully committed to yogic life. She was well into her journey to become a visionary leader, founding a Vedantic study center and an ashram, and becoming a beloved spiritual teacher and healer (Lee, 1982).

Tapasya: Through the Fire

When John died in 1967, he and Alice had been together for only four years. She was now a thirty-year-old widow raising four children on her own, but she continued to compose and perform, carrying on his spiritual and musical legacy but also maintaining her artistic development (Berkman,

2010). Alice recorded four albums between 1968 and 1970. In this, she demonstrated the Black woman's legendary (and sometimes debilitating) ability to keep going in the face of painful conditions. She may have been trying to use her music as a creative outlet to help moderate grief.

After John's death, Alice went into an intense period of prayer, seeking union with the Divine, which is one of the goals of yoga. In her memoir *Monument Eternal* (1978), she wrote, "I felt the deepest transcendental longing to realize the Supreme Lord. This longing within the depths of my heart was soon acknowledged" (Berkman, 2010, p. 64). She describes receiving a direct call from God during meditation, a moment that marked the beginning of a new phase of spiritual reawakening for her.

Alice entered a spiritual process called *tapasya*, or cleansing by fire, an intense period of austerity, asceticism, and spiritual trial (Lee, 1982). She heeded the voice that compelled her to cut her hair, meditated for hours, and fasted until she weighed less than one hundred pounds. She withdrew from daily activities and communication, even from her children (Adams, 2016).

Berkman (2010) suggests that Alice may have been experiencing deep depression or psychosis, but Alice herself later described it as a period of purification, strengthening, and consciousness-raising—a necessary precursor to becoming a spiritual leader. Her perspective is not unlike women who, when emerging from a period of mental health breakdown, speak of their recovery as a personally transformative experience (Lafrance, 2009).

It was during this time that her musician friend Vishnu Wood took her to meet Swami Satchidananda, the "Woodstock guru," in the hope that the guru's messages would lift her spirits. Not long after reaching the swami, she began to emerge from the *tapasya* experience. She developed a close bond with Satchidananda and relied on him for spiritual insight. In 1970, she traveled with him to India to study, tour, perform, and learn new musical traditions. When she returned, she took the spiritual name Turiya and moved to northern California, where she founded the Vedantic Center for the study, teaching, and contemplation of the Vedas, among the world's oldest known scriptures (Taylor, 2009).

It was not until 1976 that she felt called to become a swamini, or spiritual teacher. Divine revelation gave her a mission, described her preparation process, and even bestowed her a new name: Swamini Turiyasangitananda, translated from Sanskrit as the Transcendental Lord's highest song of bliss.

Svasthya: Pathways to Health

Black people's lack of engagement with the Western medical system is often the focus of discussion concerning Black health. Literature about Black people's interaction with the health-care system would suggest that Black people are less likely to seek medical treatment because of distrust of doctors, racial bias, lack of insurance, lack of health education, and other factors. The overall implication is that Black people are disengaged in health care, which is offered as a reason why African Americans have higher mortality rates for illnesses such as heart disease, stroke, cancer, diabetes, HIV, and others (Office of Minority Health, 2019).

Black people's apprehension about the medical system has existed for years, and not without reason. Black people have endured abuse in health-care and medical-research settings, being subjected to unnecessary surgeries and invasive medical procedures and being used as subjects for medical experimentation. Black women, in particular, were subjects of experimental methods, including the use of untested contraceptive techniques and involuntary sterilization (Washington, 2006). When Black bodies were not being preyed upon, they were being turned away, untreated, from White-only hospitals and health facilities.

However, what may appear to be a disengagement with the health-care system does not necessarily represent a disengagement with health care. Black women's engagement in the health care of their families and their community dates back to slavery and the prewar period. According to Rosser (2009), during the postwar period, Black women became the creators and managers of their self-care: they often served as lay midwives and as primary care providers for the community, and they were leaders in shaping their community's and individual health-care needs.

Historically, Black women's care may have relied upon kitchen-made decoctions, nourishing teas and foods, the application of balms and salves, laying on of hands, and, as reinforcement for all of the above, prayer for health. These are methods we would now call complementary and alternative medicine, herbal and nutritional treatments, body-based therapies, and psycho-spiritual practices, with approximately 67 percent of African Americans using them today (Barner et al., 2010).

Alice Coltrane used alternative methods of healing to provide health care for herself and her community. According to her biographers, she used her music and spiritual healing methods to ensure efficient health care well outside the Western medical model. In *Portrait of Devotion*, Adams (2016) documents more than twenty narratives of people who came to Turiyasangitananda with back pain, heart conditions, infertility, cancer, injuries, and other physical and mental ailments. The healing process included prayer, the recitation of mantras, and often an offering. Sometimes Turiyasangitananda would "lay on hands"; at other times, she would gesture in the direction of an injury or direct energy toward it. Some "patients" were sent away with instructions for how to support their healing over time; others felt an immediate improvement. Through Swamini's intervention, many injuries, which individuals have endured for years, were often healed in a moment (Adams, 2016).

Bhajans: The Power of Music

Studies suggest that music can reduce both physical and mental health issues (*Music and health*, 2011). But even before there were empirical studies to support it, Alice believed in the healing power of music. "In India, there is a Name of God known as Nadabrahma. It means God as sound. God is sound," she told Susan Taylor (2009) in an interview for *Essence* magazine. If she could expose people to the sound of God by wrapping them in it through her voice and her instruments, she believed that they could be healed. Sharing music with her followers became the focus of her musicianship.

When she moved to California and started the Vedantic study center, people came for *Satsang* (community worship) not only to study and hear her teaching but also to sing the *bhajans* (chants) that she composed or adapted from traditional Hindu hymns. Listening to recordings from that time, one can hear that the songs took on the cultural flavor infused by Alice's history playing gospel and jazz as a teen in Detroit as well as the vocal style of her followers, most of whom were Black.

She played daily at the ashram, where the *bhajans* were a central part of the worship services. Every few years, she issued a recording of her chants that was made available to devotees and the public. The ultimate goal of the music was to heal people through meditative sound. Coltrane believed that chanting was a form of meditation that helped calm and focused the mind and that the music that followers engaged in on the Sunday *Satsang* (worship service) contributed to their well-being. "Chanting is a healing force for good in our world," she said (Berkman, 2010).

Sangha: The Beloved Community

Turiyasangitananda moved the Vedantic Center to Southern California and operated it out of a building near her home. In 1982, she was called to build an ashram where more people could come to gather, worship, retreat, and serve the community. Some of her followers lived at the Sai Anantam Ashram on a 46-acre property in the Santa Monica mountains; others drove in for weekly services. Most were Black, middle-class, educated adults, though there were European Americans and Asian Americans (Berkman, 2010). Interestingly, this demographic aligns with the complementary medicine users described by Barner and colleagues (2010).

It had been John Coltrane's dream to create a center dedicated to music and devotion, but the ashram's organization and direction were entirely Swamini Alice Coltrane Turiyasangitananda, yet another example of her contribution to the health of her devotees. Indeed, the importance of community cannot be overlooked in the promotion of public health. According to Umberson and Montez (2010), social relationships, in both quantity and quality, affect mental health, health behavior, physical health, and mortality risk. Their research found being involved with formal social groups such as a religious community has a definite impact on health. Community members may influence one another's health behaviors in both positive and negative ways, but having regular, supportive, positive interactions with others reduces the allostatic load—that is, the wear and tear on the body that leads to a variety of illnesses and chronic conditions.

In many Black communities, faith-based organizations take responsibility for overseeing the health and well-being of their constituents. These organizations pay great attention to the implication of spirituality on health outcomes for people within that community (Toms et al., 2001). This supports the notion that spiritual practices are essential elements in the health and well-being of Black communities.

Bhakti: For the Love of the Guru

Berkman (2010) notes that the majority of Turiyasangitananda's followers were Black, a significant point given that yoga and its related practices had not attracted a proportionate number of Black people as practitioners. Turiyasangitananda's ability to attract followers of color may have been because her presence as a Black woman made the ashram and the Vedantic Center more welcoming to them.

Research has shown that health-care providers reveal their implicit and explicit biases toward Black people, which, in turn, may lead to racial disparities in health care and treatment decisions; such penchants are displayed more during interactions between White health-care providers and Black patients (Cooper et al., 2012). Public health research has demonstrated the connection between the quality of health care and the health-care provider's race or ethnicity; patients of color report that they receive better interpersonal care when their provider is of a concordant race or ethnicity (Saha et al., 2003). Implicit and explicit bias and race concordance, as demonstrated in health care, may result in a similar experience in the yoga teacher–student relationship. For example, non-race-concordant yoga teachers may inhibit a Black women's participation and engagement in yoga for its health benefits or as a routine health practice for maintaining wellness and self-care.

Barr-Anderson (2016) acknowledges that the identity of a teacher can have an impact on how well students or followers can absorb the benefits of the teaching. In her study of yoga's effectiveness as a health benefit for Black women, she controlled for the "comfort factor" by making sure teachers were Black. Jeffries and Campbell (2018) refer to this as "the teacher effect." The premise is that students' ability to reap the benefits of a mind-body practice such as yoga may be influenced by how well they can relax and how comfortable they feel about participating fully. The presence and demeanor of the yoga teacher could negatively impact the experience. What Jeffries refers to as "whole yoga," in which students engage all eight limbs of yoga, invites students to practice in a way that can sometimes be emotionally challenging, so yoga students need to be able to practice in an environment that provides a measure of comfort and a sense of safety. The extent to which people can fully participate may influence how much benefit they receive from the practice.

Because she was already well known from her music career and association with John, it may have been easier for Alice Coltrane Turiyasangitananda to motivate the trust of followers. Being a child of the church and a woman of jazz traditions rooted in Black culture may have allowed her to translate the yogic concepts into terms that were more comfortable for her followers. For example, she acknowledged and referred to Jesus and his teachings in her talks, creating a bridge between Western/Christian spiritual traditions and the Hindu-based spiritual practice (Taylor,

2009). This is a crucial consideration for yoga leaders whose students may be unfamiliar or uncomfortable with the Hindu-centric aspects of yoga practice.

Avatar: A Guide for the Future

The current yoga boom is driven in part by the narrative that yoga has significant healing benefits for everything from sinus infections to sciatica. While this cure-all message has long been pushed in popular media and among yoga devotees, it is now being investigated and supported by empirical data. Cramer and colleagues (2016) examined the positive impact of yoga for disease prevention and the improvement of immune function. Many studies have indicated that yoga is an efficient treatment for specific health conditions.

Nevertheless, research is needed to determine yoga's effectiveness for the health and wellness of Black people. Evans (2016) stated that researchers who document yoga's popularity in the United States likely underestimate the fullness of its impact if they do not include data from communities of color. Those examining yoga's health impact must ensure that yoga studies are racially diverse, and they must design studies that focus on participants of color.

Initial steps to explore the current participation and impact of yoga among Black women are being taken in the beginning stages of research. Early reports suggest Black women who introduce a yoga practice into their schedules experience weight loss and stress reduction (Barr-Anderson, 2016). Tenfelde and colleagues (2018) have conducted focus groups to understand better how Black women think about mind-body therapies like yoga and how to introduce them to communities of color to address stress and enhance coping.

Jeffries and Campbell are studying the factors that make a yoga practice culturally accessible for Black practitioners. By introducing a yoga course for college credit at a historically Black college for women and offering various contemplative practice activities on campus, they have gained an understanding of the cultural competency component that is often missing from yoga spaces (i.e., attention to the diversity of religion, body type, accessibility, etc.). Jeffries and Campbell are furthering their studies by addressing the differences between teaching yoga as a primarily physical exercise versus a whole-yoga practice that includes all eight limbs of yoga. Future strategies include the development of an intervention study to investigate the impact of yoga on Black women. Contemplative practices may decrease the negative effect on one's physical and psychological well-being. Yoga may moderate behavioral and physical health outcomes for Black women.

All of these studies, as well as the observed growth of yoga in the Black community, have been presaged by Alice Coltrane Turiyasangitananda's work. She defined yogic practice in her image as an African American woman by including Black music traditions in her teaching, cultivating a culturally aware practice that embraced the Indian roots of yoga but decoded and recoded them for a Black community, and offering spiritual spaces that attracted people of color who sought the mental and physical health benefits cultivated in community. Her ability to build and sustain these institutions of worship attests to her vision; her ability to maintain a devoted following attests to her influence. Ultimately, her legacy will be in the number of people whom she touched, influenced, inspired, and healed.

Coda: The Fire This Time

On a spring evening in 2020, as the setting sun gleams on the White House and makes a candle of the Washington monument, people roll out yoga mats in the middle of the street perpendicular to Pennsylvania Avenue. Under their feet, the name of the street is painted in huge, yellow letters. This is Black Lives Matter Plaza.

For weeks before and after, people take to the streets in Washington, DC, and in every state in the union, protesting the murder of George Floyd by police in Minneapolis. In anguish and anger over another violent loss of life, they raise fists and signs and voices, demanding the acknowledgment of Black humanity. These protests coincide with the global COVID-19 pandemic that is killing thousands in hot spots popping up nationwide. Data show that Black people are disproportionately affected by this lurking virus; public health experts know that this is a result of the collision between the virus and systemic racism.

In the midst of these painful crises, it might seem incongruous to gather for yoga, a practice that is still so strongly associated with privilege, wealth, blissful leisure, and whiteness. But yoga is being claimed and reclaimed by Black and brown people for the benefit of Black and brown lives. It is a healing practice for body and mind—asserted throughout history and affirmed by modern medical research. If Black lives matter, that has to include Black health and wellness. And so, across the country, "yoga for Black lives" events pop up in parks and in virtual spaces, a complement to the marches.

There is the spirit of Alice Coltrane Turiyasangitananda in these actions. She was a role model not only for survival but for thriving in the face of adversity, for hearing the heart's calling and following it, no matter how difficult or unusual the journey. She showed that no matter what happens in our lives—no matter how many fires we face—we must insist on living fully and wholly.

References

Adams, S. C. (2016). *Portrait of devotion: The spiritual life of Alice Coltrane Swamini Turiyasangitananda*. Shankari C. Adams.

Barner, J. C., Bohman, T. M., Brown, C. M., & Richards, K. M. (2010). Use of complementary and alternative medicine for treatment among African-Americans: A multivariate analysis. *Research in Social and Administrative Pharmacy*, 6(3), 196–208. https://doi.org/10.1016/j.sapharm.2009.08.001

Barr-Anderson, D. (2016, September 30). Unlocking the health benefits of yoga for African American women. *CEHD Vision 2020*. https://cehdvision2020. umn.edu/blog/health-benefits-yoga/

Berkman, F. J. (2010). *Monument eternal: The music of Alice Coltrane*. Wesleyan University Press.

Brems, C., Colgan, D., Freeman, H., Freitas, J., Justice, L., Shean, M., & Sulenes, K. (2016). Elements of yogic practice: Perceptions of students in healthcare programs. *International Journal of Yoga*, 9(2), 121–129. https://doi.org/10.4103/0973-6131.183710

Coltrane-Turiyasangitananda, A. (1978). *Monument eternal*. Vedantic Book Press.

Cooper, L. A., Roter, D. L., Carson, K. A., Beach, M. C., Sabin, J. A., Greenwald, A. G., & Inui, T. S. (2012). The associations of clinicians' implicit attitudes about race with medical visit communication and patient ratings of interpersonal care. *American Journal of Public Health*, 102(5), 979–987. https://doi.org/10.2105/AJPH.2011.300558

Cramer, H., Ward, L., Steel, A., Lauche, R., Dobos, G., & Zhang, Y. (2016). Prevalence, patterns, and predictors of yoga use: Results of a U.S. nationally representative survey. *American Journal of Preventive Medicine*, 50(2), 230–235. https://doi.org/10.1016/j.amepre.2015.07.037

Deslippe, P. (2018). The Swami circuit: Mapping the terrain of early American yoga. *Journal of Yoga Studies*, *1*, 5–44. https://journalofyogastudies.org/index. php/JoYS/article/view/2018.v1.Deslippe.TheSwamiCircuit

Evans, S. Y. (2016). Yoga in 42 African American women's memoirs reveal hidden tradition of health [Letter to the editor]. *International Journal of Yoga*, *9*(1), 85. https://doi.org/10.4103/0973-6131.171709

Jain, A. R. (2014). *Selling yoga: From counterculture to pop culture*. Oxford University Press.

Jeffries, T. Y., & Campbell, S. D. (2018, November). *Free their minds: How yoga and mindfulness can help depressed students succeed* [Conference presentation]. 25th National HBCU Faculty Development Network Conference, Jackson Marriott Hotel, Jackson, MS, United States.

Lafrance, M. (2009). *Women and depression: Recovery and resistance*. Routledge.

Lamb, T. (2006). *Yoga statistics and demographics*. International Association of Yoga Therapists. https://c.ymcdn.com/sites/iayt.site-ym.com/resource/resmgr/ bibliographies-members/stats.pdf

Lee, V. (1982, December). The spiritual journey of Alice Coltrane. *Yoga Journal*, 39–40.

Long, J. (Producer and director). (2016, August 29). *The uncommon yogi: A history of blacks and yoga in the U.S.* [Video]. YouTube. https://www.youtube.com/ watch?v=xQqSdB9PD38

Music and health. (2011, July). Harvard Health Publishing. https://www.health. harvard.edu/staying-healthy/music-and-health

Office of Minority Health. (2019). *Minority population profiles: Black/African Americans*. U.S. Department of Health and Human Services. https://www. minorityhealth.hhs.gov/omh/browse.aspx?lvl=3&lvlid=61

Razmjou, E., Freeman, H., & Vladagina, N. (2017, February). Yoga and popular media: Helping or hurting? *Public Health Post*. https://www.publichealthpost. org/research/yoga-popular-media-helping-hurting/

Rosser, S. V. (Ed.). (2009). *Diversity and women's health*. Johns Hopkins University Press.

Saha, S., Arbelaez, J. J., & Cooper, L. A. (2003). Patient-physician relationships and racial disparities in the quality of health care. *American Journal of Public Health*, *93*(10), 1713–1719. https://doi.org/10.2105/AJPH.93.10.1713

SikhNet. (2007). *A thousand mile journey* (Directed and produced by H. Lyle) [Video]. YouTube. https://www.youtube.com/watch?v=hvervoPlRlo#action=share

Taylor, S. (2009, December). A love supreme with Alice Coltrane. *Essence*. https:// www.essence.com/news/a-love-supreme-with-alice-coltrane/

Tenfelde, S. M., Hatchett, L., & Saban, K. L. (2018). "Maybe black girls do yoga": A focus group study with predominantly low-income African-American women. *Complementary Therapies in Medicine*, *40*, 230–235. https://doi. org/10.1016/j.ctim.2017.11.017

Toms, F., Lloyd, C. L., Carter-Edwards, L., & Ellison, C. (2011). Improving health and healthcare advocacy through engagement: A faith-based community view. *Practical Matters, 4,* 1–13. http://practicalmattersjournal.org/wp-content/uploads/2015/09/11_Improving_Health.pdf

Umberson, D., & Montez, J. K. (2010). Social relationships and health: A flashpoint for health policy. *Journal of Health and Social Behavior, 51,* 5–66. https://doi.org/10.1177/0022146510383501

Washington, H. A. (2006). *Medical apartheid: The dark history of medical experimentation on black Americans from colonial times to the present.* Harlem Moon / Broadway Books.

Webb, J. B., Vinoski, E. R., Warren-Findlow, J., Padro, M. P., Burris, E. N., & Suddreth, E. M. (2017). Is the "yoga bod" the new skinny? A comparative content analysis of mainstream yoga lifestyle magazine covers. *Body Image, 20,* 87–98.

Chapter 14

When Black Scholars Embrace Ourselves in Our Research, We Reclaim Our Power

SARITA K. DAVIS

There are some esteem issues that come with the assault of being colonized and being dominated and being marginalized. But we have to push through those and embrace and immerse ourselves in the stunningness that is us. You have to get on that one [wo]man boat and go out into the raging storm until you get to the break of a new day. You have to get to the point where it's like this is *not* truth, and consequently it is no longer going to be *my* truth. And now I'm going to embrace the power of who I am and where I'm from.

—Danai Gurira

Introduction

I selected the above quote from the actress and writer Danai Gurira (qtd. in Griffiths, 2018) because it embodies the world of research from a colonized perspective and the necessity of finding and embracing one's own truth. The multiple truths we seek to understand cannot be authentically understood using the interpretive frameworks and methodologies we were trained to use in westernized institutions of higher education (Ogbu, 1978; Reviere, 2001; Smith, 2012). As a trained program evaluator and social worker, I have evaluated many human services interventions and conducted research in a variety of disciplines including but not limited to education, environmental health, mental health, religious studies, social work, and public health. More specifically, over the past fifteen years, I have conducted research in the area of HIV-prevention education targeting Black women.

The gold standard of research practiced in many of these disciplines I named still demands positivist approaches that promote the notion of a singular truth or reality (Smith, 2012). However, in my professional experience, I have come to realize that traditional approaches to inquiry don't typically yield the liberating outcomes that are urgently needed by the people whose lives I try to serve through my research—people who are living on the margins of society. Fortunately, there are some emerging interpretive frameworks in the social sciences committed to issues of social justice, equity, nonviolence, peace, and universal human rights (Denzin & Lincoln, 2011). These interpretive frameworks, paradigms, or beliefs that researchers bring into their process guide the practice of research. These interpretive frameworks are informed by the lived experiences of people via their history and culture. Consequently, they yield subjective forms of research. My intention in this chapter is twofold. First, to advocate for more subjective forms of practice and research in public health. Second, to encourage scholars to incorporate personal, professional, cultural, and historical lenses in their analyses of health issues affecting Black women.

The following section begins with an examination of the methodological approaches typically used in public health research. I compare these methods of inquiry against those used in disciplines that privilege subjective methodologies. In the next, I use my own HIV research and my personal life story and cultural and historical knowledge to illustrate the value of using more subjective forms of research. The final section consists of a discussion about a transformative Black women's HIV conference I attended in 2017, where I experienced the collective power of Black women leaning into our subjective knowledge and finding healing and liberation.

Public Health versus Other Disciplinary Methodologies

Knowledge construction in the discipline of public health is deeply rooted in the positivist paradigm, which is closely associated with quantitative science. Positivism is a philosophical theory that states knowing can only come from what can be quantified and observed using the five senses (i.e., hearing, touch, sight, smell, and taste). By this definition, all other ways of constructing knowledge are unreliable. Positivism applies the principles of research in the natural sciences to the study of social phenomena. At its core, it is a reductionist philosophy that intends to downsize social phenomena into small, measurable bits of information. Numeric measures are central to the positivist social scientific approach to research. Positivism is a paradigm that posits that human qualities can be quantified (Vogt, 1999). Positivism assumes that there is a singular truth, which can only be discerned through experimentation.

Consequently, the bias toward quantification of knowledge is not widely embraced by cultural and gender studies and is viewed as Euro-centric due to its connection to positivism (Asante, 1990; Reviere, 2001). For example, we can only know if an intervention is effective by compar-ing the results of a treatment and control group. The difference between the two groups is evidence of the effect. While public health research is slowly evolving to embrace more subjective forms of inquiry, the domi-nant research paradigm skews toward positivism (Guest & Namey, 2015; Oliffe & Greaves, 2012).

Let me be clear: there have been and continue to be Black female scholars in the field of public health advocating for culturally informed approaches for addressing the complicated history of Black female sexuality and its relationship to HIV among Black women—from the pioneering scholarship of Gail E. Wyatt (1997; Wyatt et al., 2004) on Black female sexuality; to Faye Belgrave et al. (1997, 2000) and Gina Wingood et al. (Wingood & DiClemente, 2000; Wingood et al., 2004), who concluded that cultural paradigms are central to improving HIV outcomes among Black girls; to, finally, Prather et al. (2006, 2018), who argued that history and culture are requisite components of HIV-prevention education for Black girls and women. While these Black warrior women scholars con-tinue to raise their individual voices through their research, we have yet to experience a paradigm shift that calls the researcher to stand in their subjectivity, triage their historical knowledge and cultural experience to conjure solutions that meet the needs of Black women.

The use of subjective forms of research is not a novel concept. Schol-ars in various disciplines have advocated for these forms of knowledge construction for over thirty years (S. K. Davis et al., 2010; D.-A. Davis & Craven, 2011; Few et al., 2003; McClauren, 2001; Reviere, 2001; Smith,

2012; Tillman, 2002), especially in the fields of anthropology, ethnic studies, sociology, and gender and sexuality studies. The following list is not meant to be exhaustive but rather illustrative, to offer case examples that highlight the utility of subjective forms of inquiry in research.

Within the discipline of anthropology, a group of Black feminist anthropologists have developed their own canon that is simultaneously theoretical and political. These practitioners intentionally seek to deconstruct the institutional racism and sexism that have marked the discipline. Black feminist anthropologists posit that by making the complex intersection of gender, race, class, and sexuality the foundational component of their scholarship scholars gain a different and deeper understanding of how Black women's lives (including that of the researcher) are influenced by structural forces (McClauren, 2001). According to Harrison (1995),

> Black feminist anthropology is defined by its embrace of ideological, methodological, and theoretical diversity among its followers. This is largely because those Black women who dare proclaim themselves feminists lean on the tenets of feminism alongside those of anthropology and embrace an intellectual repertoire that includes women's studies, African American studies, ethnic studies, and African, Caribbean, and Latin American studies. They also embrace the critiques, ideas, metaphors, wisdom, and grounded theories of organic intellectuals in the form of preachers, community activists, street-corner philosophers, and beauty shop therapists alike, who are eloquent about the way in which scholarship has rendered them victims, symbols of poverty, or people without histories. (p. 50)

Some of the subjective forms of inquiry practiced by Black female anthropologists include forays into the fields of folklore (Hurston, 2018), autoethnography (Harrison, 1995), and feminist ethnography (D.-A. Davis & Craven, 2011). It is within the context of social justice that Black female anthropologists continue to encourage the production of racial/sexual/feminist knowledge as a process inseparable from praxis, placing Black female anthropology firmly within a liberating context.

Another area where subjective inquiry is practiced is in Africana studies. Cultural relevance and the identity and social location of the researcher have been debated since the establishment of this discipline (Gould, 1981; Ogbu, 1978). Some scholars argue that researchers of color are more able to bridge the gap among cultural nuances because of their shared understanding of African realities. For example, Madison (1992) says that researchers who have minimal contact with other African-descended groups, regardless of ethnicity, may not be the most suitable to decide whether a particular intervention is appropriate for meeting their needs.

Ultimately, the insider/outsider dilemma must be taken seriously if we are to move beyond superficial connections of race, class, and gender. If transformation is truly the goal of any inclusive paradigm, then the lives and experiences of marginalized groups must be placed at the core of the research context (Mertens, 1999). Consequently, the only way to ensure that relevant African perspectives are included in the problem identification and formulation phase is to center the research agenda in the lived experience of African American communities.

An Afrocentric perspective, as it relates to being well grounded in a people's understanding, insists that the researcher have an affinity with, knowledge of, and respect for the history, culture, and knowledge of African-descendant people. This does not preclude non-African group members from conducting culturally competent research; however, the research agenda must serve the interest of the African-descendant persons of study. According to Kershaw (2004), we should ask some or all of the following questions when defining the research question and the antecedents and outcomes concerning a people's life experiences and life chances: "How do they understand relevant historical and contemporary phenomena related to the question? How have their attitudes and behaviors been shaped and misshaped by this phenomenon? What are the factors that they see as being important? How do we know? Where are their words? When are they speaking? Where is their voice?"

Afrocentricity, conceptualized by Molefi Asante (1987), was designed to engage in subjective analysis targeting Black communities. Afrocentrism asserts that Black scholars have the right and responsibility to describe reality from their own perspectives. The ultimate goal of the scholar is to seek balance (Ma'at) and a productive work (Nommo). In her 2001 article "Toward an Afrocentric Research Methodology," Ruth Reviere builds on the concept of Afrocentry in research by adding the following five Afrocentric canons: (1) the research must be grounded in the experiences of the community being studied (Ukweli), (2) objectivity does not exist

(Utulivu), (3) the duty of the researcher is to create harmony in the research context (Uhaki), (4) the research must privilege the maintenance of the community (Ujamaa), and (5) the research process must be fair to all participants (Kujitoa).

By challenging the traditional Eurocentric premise embedded in Western research, scholars are able to put African models and values at the center of the inquiry (Asante, 1990). According to Asante, this process allows scholars to critique the rules governing Eurocentric inquiry that prevent accurate explanations of African and other non-European experiences. The Afrocentric paradigm is in conflict with key components of the positivist paradigm. According to Akbar (1994), Afrocentricity rejects three ideas central to positivism: (1) that research is value neutral, (2) that all valid knowledge is external, and (3) that human beings are fundamentally material. From an Afrocentric perspective, reality is fundamentally spiritual.

Finally, scholarship with Indigenous people speaks clearly to understanding subjective realities and truths. In her work with Indigenous communities in New Zeland, Linda Tuhiwai Smith (2012) uses a framework to engage subjective inquiry. She uses the metaphor of ocean tides to represent the movement, change, process, life, and inward and outward flow of ideas, reflections, and actions. The four directions identified—decolonization, healing, transformation, and mobilization (instead of north, south, east, and west)—represent processes. They are not goals or ends in themselves. They are processes that connect, inform, and clarify the tensions among the local, the regional, and the global. Each process is accompanied by questions related to its physical, economic, spiritual, and psychological antecedents.

The answers to these questions ultimately help identify and frame the culturally grounded practices and methodologies. Four major tides are represented as survival, recovery, development, and self-determination. These nonsequential conditions are states of being through which African communities move. Survival is subject to some basic prioritizing: survival of a people as physical beings; survival of languages, social and spiritual practices, personal relations; and survival of the arts. Recovery is a selective process, often responding to immediate crises rather than a planned approach. Recovery is related to the reality that African groups are not in control and are subject to a continuing set of external conditions. Development suggests stability, in that a group can engage in critical reflection and planned movement forward. Finally, at the core is self-determination—the ability of a people to name themselves, define themselves, and govern in their own best political, economic, and social interest.

The gap in public health research is simply that much of history and social scientific research is told from the perspective of people outside of the community being studied. As a result, what we "know" about other groups is based on an outsider's gaze of the "other" (Smith, 2012). Smith explains that researchers whose training is grounded in Western epistemology and methodology are trained to privilege their own beliefs over those being observed. As a result, their ability to truly understand marginalized groups is highly subject to flawed cultural analysis. Several examples of how this occurs include making comparisons between Blacks and other groups, assuming all Blacks are the same; respectability politics, assuming difference equates to deficiency; and the use of evidence-based best practices normed on predominantly White populations. Although all of these obstacles are important, I focus on one that I think is easiest to remedy, which is engaging research within the context of history and culture.

Oftentimes, researchers fail to consider the lived experiences of people in the inquiry process. In other words, researchers do not look at the context in which a phenomenon occurs. In connecting the present to the past, the researcher can develop a more nuanced approach to inquiry. For example, in my HIV-prevention education research with Black women, I study the treatment of the Black female body in history, literature, research, and popular culture. Research suggests that negative sexual stereotypes of Black women can affect their internalization of these images (Gordon, 2008; Townsend et al., 2010). By grounding my research in the history and culture of Black women's bodies, I have been better able to examine nuanced sites of harm and resilience in our sexual decision-making. It is the researchers' responsibility to understand not just what they see before them but the conditions under which it evolved.

What We Know about the Treatment of the Black Female Body

The Black female body has been contested space since our ancestors' abduction and forced exploitation on these shores. The very enslavement of Black bodies is predicated on the belief that Black bodies are inferior and therefore subhuman. For example, Menand (2001) points to the work of two anthropologists at Harvard University in the early 1800s who conducted research on the size of human skulls as a way to determine intelligence among various populations. The research of Samuel George Morton and Louis Agassiz promoted the inferiority of the Black race. In her book *Medical Apartheid: The Dark History of Medical Experimentation on Black Americans from Colonial Times to the Present* (2006), Harriet Washington details a comprehensive history of centuries of abuse and medical experimentation on African Americans, often without their knowledge or consent. Relevant to the topic of this chapter is Washington's discussion of the research conducted by J. Marion Sims. Sims is often referred to as the father of modern gynecology. He is best known for his pioneering surgical procedure correcting vesicovaginal fistula, which was a devastating complication of childbirth among nineteenth-century American women. The first consistently successful operation for this condition was developed by Sims, an Alabama surgeon who carried out a series of experimental operations on enslaved Black women between 1845 and 1849.

Sims conducted his research on these women without anesthesia because he didn't believe enslaved women felt pain as severely as White women. Numerous modern scholars and activists have attacked Sims's medical ethics, arguing that he manipulated the institution of slavery to perform ethically unacceptable human experiments on powerless, unconsenting women (Washington, 2006). The unscientific beliefs founded in the early days of medical experimentation evolved into stereotypes that permeated every aspect of American culture, thus becoming a faulty cornerstone of many institutional structures erected in American society.

I never fully considered the connection between culture, history, and Black women's bodies. Why? Because Black women rarely talk about our bodies in the context of sex or sexuality. Historically, these topics are generally considered taboo and heavily guarded by racially charged stereotypes like the Jezebel and mammy (Collins, 2004; Harris-Perry, 2011; Lomax, 2018; Thompson, 2012). Birthed during enslavement, these tropes depict Black women as lascivious and oversexed or as work horses who are sexually undesirable and only valuable in service to the slave owner. These ideas were so deeply embedded in the psyche of white supremacy and Southern culture that many Southern states established rape laws that stated the savage and highly sexual nature of the Black woman was so profound that it was not possible to rape her. In her book *At the Dark End of the Street*, the historian Danielle McGuire details the history of Black women, as the subtitle outlines, on the topics of "rape and resistance from the civil rights movement through the rise of Black Power." In the book, McGuire highlights the brutal rape of Recy Taylor in 1944. The married mother was abducted by several White men while walking home after church. She was raped and left on the side of the road, naked. McGuire (2010) says, "Growing up in the Jim Crow South, Taylor knew that black women were not even considered *ladies*. From slavery through most of the twentieth century, white Americans denied African-American women the most basic citizenship and human rights, especially the right to ownership and control of their own bodies" (p. 232). From the end of slavery until modern day, these stereotypes have effectively constructed a sexual purgatory from which Black women can't seem to escape and that, if they are not careful, passes down from one generation to the next.

The Effects of Stereotypes on the Sexual Health of Black Women

Matters of Black female sexuality are intertwined with complicated issues of race, class, slavery, and stereotypes. Many scholars have studied the effects of stereotypes and misinformation on Black women. The definition of *stereotypes* used here is from Hilton and von Hippel (1996), who state that "stereotypes are beliefs about the characteristics, attributes, and behaviors of members of certain groups" (p. 240); this includes those that affect Black women in the United States. Three pernicious stereotypes of Black women that date back to the period of American enslavement are the "mammy," "Sapphire," and "Jezebel" (West, 2008; Woodard & Mastin, 2005). The mammy stereotype is the image of an unattractive Black mother who is strong and content in her caregiving role for many children, in the service of White slave owners or White employers. The Sapphire (or "matriarch") stereotype is the image of an aggressive, dominating, angry, emasculating Black woman. The Jezebel (or "sexual siren") is the image of an immoral, sexually promiscuous, and sexually available Black woman (West, 2008; Woodard & Mastin, 2005).

Another, more recent stereotype of Black women is that of the "welfare queen," which is connected to images of Black women as "breeders" dating back to slavery (Collins, 2004). The welfare queen is an image of an uneducated, poor, single Black woman who does not want to work but has many children in order to take advantage of public assistance (Woodard & Mastin, 2005). An understanding of these stereotypes requires an intersectional analysis of the multiple stereotypical images of Black women that are distinct from those of Black men and White women and of the connection of these stereotypes to historical and contemporary structural oppression of Black women.

Research suggests that Black women are most certainly aware of these stereotypes and have experiences in which they believe that they have been treated differently because of these stereotypes. Specifically related to sexuality, Black women continue to be stereotyped as promiscuous, hypersexual, sexually available, and as having "animalistic" sexuality, all of which have a long history connected to the sexualized exploitation of Black women during enslavement and are consistent with the Jezebel archetype (Collins, 2004; A. Y. Davis, 1981; hooks, 1990; Thomas et al., 2008). In a recent experimental study of 435 predominantly White and Asian undergraduates, Rosenthal and Lobel (2016) found that a Black female was perceived as having had sex with more people in the past month; less likely to use birth control regularly during sex; more likely to have children and to have been pregnant at some time in the past; and more likely to receive some form of public assistance, to have a lower education, and to earn less income per year than a White female. These findings support the research hypotheses that there are negative stereotypes about Black women related to sexuality, motherhood, and socioeconomic status that are consistent with the historical images of the Jezebel and welfare queen stereotypes.

The effect of these stereotypes has profound implications for how Black women are treated generally in society, but more specifically in regards to their sexual and reproductive health. More importantly, how have these widely held stereotypes affected Black women's perceptions of their own bodies? In the following section, I explore the relationship between Black politics of respectability and sexual stereotypes.

Respectability Politics and Stereotypes

The term *politics of respectability* was first used in the context of Black women's efforts to separate themselves from derogatory stereotypical images imposed on them by larger society. The term was coined by Evelyn Higginbotham in her book *Righteous Discontent: The Women's Movement in the Black Baptist Church* (1994). Higginbotham documents the work of Black women leaders such as schoolteachers, nurses, church mothers, civic leaders, and others to exhibit strict public displays of sexual respectability to counter the dominate narrative of hypersexuality. To resist these stereotypes, Black women buried normal, innocuous expressions of sexuality in favor of being an image of either pristine asexuality or narrowly defined respectable married identity (Harris-Perry, 2011). The politics of respectability was widely practiced from the period of Reconstruction through the 1980s.

The problem with the politics of respectability is that it creates very narrow ways of being and demands unrealistic public performances of Black women. Some have argued that this practice of "disemblace" forced Black women to wear masks pertaining to matters concerning their bodies and sexuality (Higginbotham, 1994). In her work "Toward a Genealogy of Black Female Sexuality: The Problematic of Silence," Evelynn Hammonds argues that Black women reformers and scholars have been relatively silent about sexuality, especially in context of HIV/AIDS. She attributes this silence to the notion that the virus is associated with uncontrolled sexuality in mainstream culture, thus serving as the proverbial kryptonite in battle against HIV in the Black community.

The unique sexual history and cultural experience of Black women demands that any attempts to engage in meaningful sexual health education and HIV prevention include contextualization. Black women scholars are uniquely qualified to engage in this kind of work and offer the transparency of their experiences. To this point I offer a few of my own personal and professional experiences with stereotypes and respectability politics.

My parents officially divorced when I was in elementary school, although my father later returned because he regretted not being present in the lives of his two older children, born in his late adolescence. My parents were blue-collar workers. My father was a janitor at Grand Central Market in downtown Los Angeles. My mother, who earned an associate degree in nursing, never talked to me about sex. Never! Well, that's not totally true. When I got my period in the sixth grade, she told me, "Don't go behind buildings with boys." Early in her career my mother worked at General Hospital, the large public hospital in Los Angeles. Ultimately, she retired from the American Red Cross. My parents demanded that I work hard in school. They wanted me to go to college. They gave me everything I needed, and almost everything I wanted. The only thing they never gave me was "the sex talk."

My first husband and I never used condoms. When I didn't get pregnant, I just assumed the issue was his and not mine because of my previous pregnancies. Since I wasn't interested in having children, it was a moot point. I soon realized my first husband had a very violent temper, and the veneer of our marriage was cracking. It would be years later that I could admit I felt threatened in the marriage and was making an exit plan. The last straw that ended the marriage for me was when he was caught breaking and entering in the department that was fully funding my doctoral education. In one fell swoop, he tainted my standing in my program and colored me with the broad brush of "high-risk" inner-city youth. Would the faculty think I was in collusion with him? Would the program take away my fellowship? A few weeks later, I packed my things and left him living in the apartment that I was still paying for and driving the car my mother bought me.

In 1996, I had met and married the man of my dreams—my second husband. Initially, he didn't want children, but after a few years the topic of children came up. I had never been interested in having children. My mother encouraged me to focus on my education. But, I was willing to consider the possibility with him. I scheduled an appointment with my ob-gyn to explore my options. After a series of X-rays, I learned that my past had in fact caught up with me. My uterus had significant scar tissue from two abortions I had in college. The doctor also said that my uterus was compromised, so it would be unlikely that I could carry a child to term. My inability to have children resulted in the demise of my marriage. This was one of the lowest moments of my life, after the loss of my mother in 1994.

I regretted not knowing about birth control and how that lack of knowledge significantly altered my life. For most of my childbearing life, I didn't use birth control. I knew a few girls in college who took birth control pills or used a diaphragm, but I was too embarrassed to ask them about sexual protection. When I got pregnant, I told my boyfriend at the time, and he agreed to support whatever decision I made. I eventually told my mother, who encouraged me to have an abortion for the sake of my future. I had already made my decision to abort the pregnancy before telling my mother. I had dreams and aspirations of going to law school at the time, and a child was never something I wanted. When I got pregnant a second time, I was ashamed to tell anyone. How could I have been so stupid? So, my boyfriend and I went to the clinic alone. I wasn't totally irresponsible between my pregnancies. I did use birth control pills for a short period, but the dosage was too strong, and it made me sick to my stomach. I did not know that the dosage could be adjusted. There was so much that I did not know, but I was too ashamed to ask out of fear of being perceived as promiscuous.

Like many of the women I studied, I experienced early-onset sexual activity, multiple pregnancies, emotional domestic abuse, and single-parent upbringing (for a while). The stereotypical images of Black women were rarely critiqued in my master of social work program at UCLA. The scholarship we were given to study promoted pathologically driven narratives about the Black community, especially Black women—like the Moynihan Report (Moynihan, 1965). Fortunately, I had mentors who were grassroots community activists who helped me unpack the role of history and culture in the lives of Black folks—a practice I found instrumental later in my own research.

Late in life, I learned about the oppressive sexual history of Black women. This information helped me to better understand that my mother's silence on sex may have been a function of growing up in the era of the politics of respectability. While my mother certainly experienced a degree of economic freedom due to her education and career as a nurse in Los Angeles, she was still functioning under the complicated gender and racial norms fashioned in her segregated Southern upbringing. Recognizing this link helped me as a scholar to make important connections in own my research, which I explore below.

My Research

The young woman was hauntingly calm when she revealed that her uncle, her aunt's husband, raped her. She was seventeen years old at the time. While she had dated young men and engaged in heavy petting, she had never had sex before. Two years later, she had become a single Black mother raising her son alone. She sat awkwardly in the office chair with her shoulders slouching slightly forward. She appeared tired. She reminded me of the painting of the tired Black woman sitting on the edge of her bed looking like she was already weary from days' work not yet begun.

I immediately put down my interview guide, stunned by her confession. She was one of the earliest interviews in my research project, which examined the effects of living in low-income communities on

Black women's sexual decision-making and substance use. Her revelation shocked me. I was not expecting this kind of response. What she shared next shifted my entire research agenda because, sadly, I would later learn that her story was all too common.

This young woman said she was initially going to keep the rape to herself, but she felt so uncomfortable being around her uncle at subsequent family gatherings that she could no longer endure the stress. She told her aunt what happened, but, to her chagrin, her aunt became extremely angry at her. The aunt rebuked her niece's story and called her a liar. The aunt immediately told her sister, the young woman's mother. The mother also didn't believe her story, and both women began berating her. They told her if she repeated this "lie" it could break their family apart, as the Department of Family and Children's Services would surely get involved. The young woman acquiesced to the demands of her mother and aunt, at a cost often seen but rarely understood.

In an effort to reclaim her power, the young woman confided in me, she started engaging in casual sex. She said that she felt twice victimized: first by the rape, and second by her family's denial of her truth. She said that by sleeping around with other men she was choosing to be not a victim but rather an active agent in her sexual choices. While her choice of casual sex was troubling, I totally understood the sense of power she was attempting to reclaim and the often-complicated sexual history of Black women in America that influenced her current situation. This insight loosed the stereotypical chains from her narrative, allowing me to engage in a more nuanced analysis that considered her context, culture, and history.

There I was, another Black woman raised in a blue-collar community in South-Central Los Angeles who might have easily ended up a young Black single parent. Instead, I was an Ivy League–educated social scientist conducting federally funded research on the effects of social determinants of health on the HIV risk of Black women. In this particular study, I was trying to understand how living in low-income communities affects the sexual decision-making and substance use of Black female residents. Leaning into my childhood experiences of Black community support, formed in large part by the Great Migration stories of my parents, who relocated from the South to California, I embraced the supposition that low-income Black communities were not always negative places to live. My beliefs were informed by the stories my mother and father shared with me about growing up in their respective segregated neighborhoods in Austin, Texas, and Shreveport, Louisiana. While most Black families in their communities did not have a lot of money, neighbors were supportive of one another and looked out for each other, much like the stories detailed in Isabella Wilkerson's 2010 book, *The Warmth of Other Suns*. I grew up understanding that in spite of unequal access to educational, social, and economic opportunities, Black communities were also sites of resilience and communal uplift. These findings of communal resistance and resilience were often missing from the pathologically framed research studies I read in my graduate programs. I understood that Black women were always sexually vulnerable due to the history of enslavement in the United States. I also understood that young Black girls were often quietly guided away from potential sexual predators by mothers and aunties with words like "don't sit on uncle so and so's lap." So, this cultural reality influenced me to explore how some of the most economically disadvantaged and socially vulnerable Black women navigated these sexual land mines in contemporary settings.

Theoretically, the women in my study should have been very motivated to understand sex and their sexuality. Many of these women were economically disadvantaged, had not gone beyond a high school education, received some type of government subsidy (e.g., welfare, food stamps, public housing), and were single parents, raising multiple children as the head of their household. Consequently, the risks of unprotected sex significantly diminished the individual life opportunities of these women. I thought it particularly important to examine the sexual decisions and substance use of one of the most vulnerable groups from a historical and cultural lens to contextualize the findings.

However, after twenty-six of the fifty women in my study reported incidents of childhood sexual abuse, I realized that their sexual decision-making and substance use may be influenced by something far more insidious. Very few, if any, of the childhood sexual abuse victims reported their assault, let alone received counseling. The assaults these women experienced affected how they moved in the world. When asked about how the violation affected them, they reported classic victimization behavior (e.g., anger, withdrawal, distrust, overprotection of children; S. K. Davis & Tucker-Brown, 2013). The myth of the promiscuity of Black women caused a majority of the women to "small up" and attempt to become invisible in both their lifestyle and physical appearance. Even though most of the women had several children, their behavior was far from promiscuous. They were often involved in monogamous relationships with men who were at high risk of incarceration due to failure to pay child support, driving infractions, drug possession, or simply being Black in the wrong place.

When I surveyed the empirical literature on Black women, child-hood sexual abuse, and HIV, I discovered that the context in which Black women live was rarely discussed. While women only represent 19 percent of new HIV diagnoses in the United States, African American women constitute 61 percent of all women affected (Centers for Disease Control and Prevention [CDC], 2016). As such, the intersection of HIV-prevention research, Black female sexuality, culture, and history provides the perfect contextual storm for this conversation. The primary reason I am writing this chapter is to explore how research on the sexual and reproductive health of Black women has been fueled in large part by oppressive ste-reotypes, patriarchy, misinformation, and internalization of controlling images. These factors have contributed to underfunded HIV-prevention education programs and anemic public policies, further compromising the sexual health of Black women and girls.

HIV and the Black female body has rarely been examined in the context of slave history, Jim/Jane Crow oppression, and cultural norms. The absence of history and culture is a glaring omission in the approach to HIV-prevention education among Black women in public health.

Some Black feminist scholars have argued that Black women have never owned their bodies; rather, our bodies have been enslaved by the immoral propensities of slave owners, Jane Crow terrorists, patriarchal Black men, and conservative White politicians (Harris-Perry, 2011; McGuire, 2010). It is with this understanding that I began to question the relevance of existing HIV-prevention education strategies targeting heterosexual Black women. How can effective interventions be designed if they do not consider the history, culture, and sexual context in which Black women live?

These childhood and historical traumas had long-lasting effects on the lives of the women in my study. Several generations of women partic-ipated in my research (i.e., grandmother, mother, and granddaughter), so I was able to I observe intergenerational patterns. Childhood sexual abuse, lack of therapy, early onset of sexual activity, domestic violence, and single parenting—this pattern made me question the existing HIV-prevention efforts and their ability to address the complex personal, cultural, and historical issues affecting Black women.

I remember when HIV/AIDS came on the scene in the United States in the early 1980s. Stories of predominantly gay White men dying from the virus dominated the headlines and nightly news. The uninformed and religious conservatives often characterized the epidemic as God's wrath on the homosexual lifestyle. But out from the flames of devastating numbers of deaths arose a movement of those affected and infected. They were linked arm in arm with liberal and unflinching allies, especially in the Hollywood community. Gay men who were out, open, and unstigmatized by their lifestyle positioned themselves on the front lines of their own personal war. They became their own advocates, demanding that the government provide funding for drug research and myriad support services. As a recently minted social worker with my master's degree, I was excited by the social movement I was bearing witness to. The movement was a social worker's dream experience, grounded in the experiences of the people infected and affected by HIV/AIDS. It was community led and and refused to be silenced or shamed. After Magic Johnson made his historic announcement about his HIV status in 1991 (Diamond, 2016), I became excited. I thought, finally, the Black community can emerge from the shadows of its fears about sexuality, homophobia, and strangling religious dogma. But nothing could be further from the truth. Black men who have sex with men (MSM) and heterosexual African Americans have the highest HIV rates in the country.

After White and Black MSM, Black women are more profoundly affected by HIV/AIDS than any other group of women. In 2016, Black women were diagnosed with HIV at three times the rate of our White counterparts (CDC, 2016). In my own research and that of many of my colleagues, our risk is less influenced by promiscuous behavior and more by geographic, political, and cultural practices, such as slavery, rape laws, patriarchy, cultural norms, stereotypes, and anemic public policies. The history of sexual trauma among Black women has been discussed by many people, including historians, bench and social scientists, celebrities, and motivational speakers. While each documentation touches a part of the elephant, none have been able to paint a complete portrait of the elephant in the room of Black women's experience.

The intention of this chapter is to draw upon sociological, historical, political, and economic empirical data told through my personal and professional journey to frame the risk and resilience of Black women in the context of sexual health and HIV. My objective is to bridge the divide between the personal and the professional scholar.

Why Should the Personal Story and Professional Journey Be Told?

The best doctor, best medicine, best antidote for what ails us is the mirror reflection of ourselves: our friendships, our bonds, the comfort we seek and the support we receive from each other.

—Opal Palmer Adisa (1994)

The inspiration for this chapter owes its conceptual genesis to the 2017 conference titled "A Paradigm Shift: The Impact of HIV/AIDS on African American Women and Families," co-organized by Gail Wyatt and Cynthia Davis in Atlanta, Georgia, at Morehouse School of Medicine. It was here that I first witnessed the power of Black female scholars using their subjective knowledge to heal each other and themselves.

The conference attendees included a diverse group of HIV advocates, including researchers, clergy, physicians, national and local HIV service providers, policy makers, journalists, transgender women, cisgender women, professors, community organizers, and those who were HIV infected/affected. According to the conference program, the goal of the conference was to shine an urgent national spotlight on the plight of Black women and their families, as well as of trans women, as it pertained to HIV/AIDS and other issues surrounding reproductive health and social justice. The central theme of the conference was to "rise above" politics and greed to take control of our lives and our communities to end HIV/AIDS in our lifetime.

While some men were present at the conference, a majority of the attendees identified as Black women. These women shared their research, personal and professional experiences, tragedies, and hallelujah triumphs. The trans women shared some hard truths, sharp criticism, and disappointments about their interactions with cisgender women. Clergy shared strategies for moving past the stigma of HIV in the Black church. And political advocates shared their battle scars and tastes of victory in regard to increasing awareness and securing HIV funding on behalf of Black women. There were tears, cheers, hurt feelings, and revelations. In that moment, I had two revelations.

My first revelation was that everyone in that room had a compelling, nuanced, and complicated story about their relationship to their sexual history. As we shared our experiences, we were bearing witness to our wounds, but, more importantly, we were healing. Our stories shared many of the same types of characters (i.e., protagonists, antagonists, sidekicks, love interests, confidants, etc.). These characters were molded by our collective history and cultural reality. Like the creepy uncle that wanted you to sit on his lap, but your mother would quietly pull you away without making a scene. Or the little girl who wanted to be liked by the popular boy in her junior high school but felt pretty average and didn't think that her chocolate skin and kinky hair were attractive enough to capture his attention, so she snuck revealing clothing in her book bag and changed in the girls' bathroom during break. Or the mother who was inexplicably overprotective of her daughter—to the point of social isolation. Or the young girl who always knew she liked other girls but was afraid of speaking her truth for fear of alienating her family.

My second revelation was that for the first time in my research career I recognized that I was a part of a community of accomplished Black female scholars and activists who, like me, were touching different parts of the HIV elephant in the room. It was intense, personal, and profoundly moving. I realized that the value of my story does not lie solely in writing about the virtues of culturally grounded research and evaluation; there is also great value in sharing my experience as a Black woman and scholar who continues to unpack the socio/geo/political influences on the sexual health of Black women. Telling my story alongside my research increases authenticity, relatability, and the likelihood that culturally relevant practice, policy, and evaluative outcomes can be achieved. This point is made sharply by Evelynn Hammonds (1999) in "Toward a Genealogy of Black Female Sexuality: The Problematic of Silence," in which she suggests that contemporary Black feminist theorists must go through the work of "reclaiming the body as well as subjectivity." Hammonds says, "Black feminist theorists are themselves engaged in a process of fighting to reclaim the body—the maimed, immoral, black female body—which can be and is still being used by others to discredit them as producers of knowledge and as speaking subjects" (p. 99).

It is my hope that after reading this text you will not look at the intersection of Black women and public health research from the perspective of the one-size-fits-all model that currently dominates the public health discourse. Instead, I hope that you find another way of leading and learning that privileges your individual experience and our collective intersecting history and culture in the research context. So, I end this chapter where I began. It is of paramount importance that we embrace all our selves in order that we might save ourselves. It will be by *our* stripes that we are healed.

References

Akbar, N. (1994). *Light from ancient Africa.* Mind Productions.

Asante, M. K. (1987). *The Afrocentric idea.* Temple University Press.

Asante, M. K. (1990). *Kemet, Afrocentricity and knowledge.* Africa World Press.

Belgrave, F. Z., Townsend, T. G., Cherry, V. R., & Cunningham, D. M. (1997). The influence of an Afrocentric worldview and demographic variables on drug knowledge, attitudes, and use among African American youth. *Journal of Community Psychology, 25,* 421–433.

Belgrave, F. Z., Van Oss Marin, B., & Chambers, D. B. (2000). Cultural, contextual, and interpersonal predictors of risky sexual attitudes among urban African American girls in early adolescence. *Cultural Diversity and Ethnic Minority Psychology, 6,* 309–322.

Centers for Disease Control and Prevention. (2016). *Take charge. Get an HIV test.* Retrieved March 4, 2019, from https://gettested.cdc.gov/takecharge/about/index.aspx

Collins, P. H. (2004). *Black sexual politics: African Americans, gender, and the new racism.* Routledge.

Davis, A. Y. (1981). *Women, race, and class.* Random House.

Davis, D.-A., & Craven, C. (2011). Revisiting feminist ethnography: Methods and activism at the intersection of neoliberal policy. *Feminist Formations, 23*(2), 190–208.

Davis, S. K., & Tucker-Brown, A. (2013). The effects of social determinants on Black women's HIV risk: HIV is bigger than biology. *Journal of Black Studies, 44*(3), 273–289.

Davis, S. K., Williams, A. D., & Akinyela, M. (2010). An Afrocentric approach to building cultural relevance in social work research. *Journal of Black Studies, 41*(2), 338–350.

Denzin, N. K., & Lincoln, Y. S. (2011). Introduction: The discipline and practice of qualitative research. In N. K. Denzin & Y. S. Lincoln (Eds.), *The Sage handbook of qualitative research* (4th ed., pp. 1–19). Sage.

Diamond, J. (2016, November 7). Flashback: Magic Johnson makes earth-shattering HIV announcement. *Rolling Stone.* https://www.rollingstone.com/culture/culture-sports/flashback-magic-johnson-makes-earth-shattering-hiv-announcement-107302/

Few, A. L., Stephens, D. P., & Rouse-Arnett, M. (2003). Sister-to-sister talk: Transcending boundaries and challenges in qualitative research with Black women. *Family Relations, 52*(3), 205–215.

Gordon, M. K. (2008). Media contributions to African American girls' focus on beauty and appearance: Exploring the consequences of sexual objectification. *Psychology of Women Quarterly, 32*(3), 245–256.

Gould, S. J. (1981). *The mismeasure of man.* Norton.

Griffiths, K. (2018, February 27). "Black Panther" star Danai Gurira didn't let the world tell her what black women could be. She showed them. *Bustle.* https://www.bustle.com/p/Black-panther-star-danai-gurira-didnt-let-the-world-tell-her-what-Black-women-could-be-she-showed-them-8250971

Guest, G., & Namey, E. E. (Eds.) (2015). *Public health research methods.* Sage Publications.

Hammonds, E. M. (1999). Toward a genealogy of black female sexuality: The problematic of silence. In J. Price & M. Shildrick (Eds.), *Feminist theory and the body: A reader* (pp. 93–104). Routledge.

Harrison, F. V. (1991). *Decolonizing anthropology: Moving further toward an anthropology for liberation.* Association of Black Anthropologists / American Anthropological Association.

Harrison, F. V. (1995). Auto-ethnographic reflections on hierarchies in anthropology. *Practicing Anthropology, 17*(1/2), 48–50.

Harris-Perry, M. (2011). *Sister citizen: Shame, stereotypes, and Black women in America.* Yale University Press.

Higginbotham, E. B. (1994). *Righteous discontent: The women's movement in the black Baptist church, 1880–1920.* Harvard University Press.

Hilton, J. L., & von Hippel, W. (1996). Stereotypes. *Annual Review of Psychology, 47*(1), 237–271.

hooks, b. (1990). *Yearning: Race, gender, and cultural politics.* South End Press.

Hurston, Z. N. (2018). *Barracoon: The story of the last "Black Cargo".* Amistad Press.

Kershaw, T. (2004). *Developing the field of Africana studies: The importance of research methods* [Unpublished manuscript].

Lomax, T. (2018). *Jezebel unhinged: Loosing the black female body in religion and culture.* Duke University Press.

Madison, A.-M. (Ed.) (1992). *Minority issues in program evaluation.* New Directions for Program Evaluation, 53. Jossey-Bass.

McClaurin, I. (2001) *Black feminist anthropology: Theory, politics, praxis, and poetics.* Rutgers University Press.

McGuire, D. L. (2010). *At the dark end of the street: Black women, rape, and resistance—A new history of the civil rights movement from Rosa Parks to the rise of Black Power.* Vintage Books.

Menand, L. (2001). Morton, Agassiz, and the origins of scientific racism in the United States. *The Journal of Blacks in Higher Education, 34,* 110–113.

Mertens, D. M. (1999). Inclusive research: Implications of transformative theory for research. *American Journal of Research, 20*(1), 1–14.

Moynihan, D. P. (1965, March). *The Negro family: The case for national action.* Office of Policy Planning and Research, United States Department of

Labor. BlackPast.org (posted January 21, 2007). https://www.blackpast.org/african-american-history/moynihan-report-1965/

Ogbu, J. U. (1978). *Minority education and caste: TheAmerican system in cross-cultural perspective.* Academic Press.

Oliffe, J. L., & Greaves, L. (Eds.) (2012). *Designing and conducting gender, sex, and health research.* Sage Publications.

Palmer Adisa, O. (1994). Rocking in the sun light: Stress and black women. In E. C. White (Ed.), *The black women's health book: Speaking for ourselves.* Seal Press.

Prather, C., Fuller, T. R., Winifred, K., Brown, M., Moering, M., Little, S., & Phillips, S. (2006). Diffusing an HIV prevention intervention for African American women: Integrating Afrocentric components into the SISTA diffusion strategy. *AIDS Education and Prevention, 18*(Suppl. A), 149–160.

Prather, C., Fuller, T. R., Jeffries, W. L., Marshall, K. J., Howell, A. V., Belyue-Umole, A., & King, W. (2018). Racism, African American women, and their sexual and reproductive health: A review of historical and contemporary evidence and implications for health equity. *Health Equity, 2*(1), 249–59. https://doi.org/10.1089/heq.2017.0045

Reviere, R. (2001). Toward an Afrocentric research methodology. *Journal of Black Studies, 31*(6), 709–728.

Rosenthal, L., & Lobel, M. (2016). Stereotypes of Black American women related to sexuality and motherhood. *Psychology of Women Quarterly, 40*(3), 414–427.

Smith, L. T. (2012). *Decolonizing methodologies: Research and indigenous peoples* (2nd ed.). Zed Books.

Thomas, A. J., Witherspoon, K. M., & Speight, S. L. (2008). Gendered racism, psychological distress, and coping styles of African American women. *Cultural Diversity and Ethnic Minority Psychology, 14*(4), 307–314.

Thompson, L. B. (2012). *Beyond the black lady: Sexuality and the new African American middle class.* University of Illinois Press.

Tillman, L. C. (2002). Culturally sensitive research approaches: An African-American perspective. *Educational Researcher, 31*(3), 3–12.

Townsend, T. G., Neilands, T. B., Thomas, A. J., & Jackson, T. R. (2010). I'm no Jezebel; I am young, gifted, and Black: Identity, sexuality, and Black girls. *Psychology of Women Quarterly, 34*(3), 273–285.

Vogt, W. P. (1999). *Dictionary of statistics and methodology: A non-technical guide for the social sciences* (2nd ed.). Sage Publications.

Washington, H. A. (2006). *Medical apartheid: The dark history of medical experimentation on Black Americans from colonial times to the present.* Harlem Moon.

West, C. M. (2008). Mammy, Jezebel, Sapphire, and their homegirls: Developing an "oppositional gaze" toward the images of Black women. In J. Chrisler, C. Golden, & P. Rozee (Eds.), *Lectures on the psychology of women* (4th ed., pp. 286–299). McGraw Hill.

Wilkerson, I. (2010). *The warmth of other suns: The epic story of America's Great Migration*. Vintage Press.

Wingood, G. M., & DiClemente, R. J. (2000). Application of the theory of gender and power to examine HIV–related exposures, risk factors and effective interventions for women. *Health Education and Behavior, 27*(5), 539–565.

Wingood, G. M., DiClemente, R. J., Mikhail, I., Lang, D. L., McCree, D. H., Davies, Hardin, J. W., Hook, E. W., III, & Saag, M. (2004). A randomized controlled trial to reduce HIV transmission risk behaviors and sexually transmitted diseases among women living with HIV: The WiLLOW program. *Journal of Acquired Immune Deficiency Syndromes, 37*(Suppl. 2), 58–67.

Woodard, J. B., & Mastin, T. (2005). Black womanhood: *Essence* and its treatment of stereotypical images of Black women. *Journal of Black Studies, 36*(2), 264–281.

Wyatt, G. E. (1997). *Stolen women: Reclaiming our sexuality, taking back our lives.* John Wiley & Sons.

Wyatt, G. E., Longshore, D., Chin, D., Carmona, J. V., Loeb, T. B., Myers, H. F., Warda, U., Liu, H., & Rivkin, I. (2004). The efficacy of an integrated risk reduction intervention for HIV-positive women with child sexual abuse histories. *AIDS and Behavior, 8*(4), 453–462.

Afterword

"This is public health."

JASMINE WARD

"This is public health . . ."

I use this sequence of words daily! They sit on the edge of my tongue and roll off in convenience as either an affirmation or an unfortunate grievance. The statement happens to be a branding campaign of the Association of Schools and Programs of Public Health, but for me it typically signals work that must be done. However, there are times when the utterance of these words indicates a defining moment; it's when all of the public health education, experiences, sacrifices, and perseverance make sense!

Such a time is now.

Black women and public health—this is public health!

This text represents a lineage of professional and creative projects developed and led by several important voices that make up an interdisciplinary chorus: Dr. Stephanie Y. Evans, professor of Black women's studies and director of the Institute for Women's, Gender, and Sexuality Studies at Georgia State University; Dr. Sarita K. Davis, associate professor in the Department of Africana Studies and affiliate faculty in the Institute of Public Health at Georgia State University; Dr. Leslie R. Hinkson, chief officer for racial justice and equity at the League of Conservation Voters, formerly of Georgetown University and University of Michigan; and Dr. Deanna J. Wathington, executive board member of the American

Public Health Association, former executive dean of the Petrock College of Health Sciences, and former dean of the School of Graduate Studies at Bethune-Cookman University. These editors sought to create a space dedicated to scholarship and focus on Black women and public health. Much like the makeup of the editorial team and the interdisciplinary nature of public health, efforts to produce this text reached across many fields to engage researchers, practitioners, educators, and advocates.

Public health protects and improves the health of people and the health conditions of the communities in which people live, work, and play. For many within the field, the boundaries of public health are well defined and emphasized by title and degree. However, for those outside the borders of public health employment or academic training, the field can be a bit of an enigma. This explains, in part, the increasing need to name and in some regard explain public health!

Through inquiry, analysis, and action, public health addresses individual, institutional, and structural provisions and barriers to health. Public health is imperfect; it's hidden when it works, obvious when it doesn't, and often inadequate for those forced into the margins of society. A close examination of public health history reveals a certain fluidity of the profession; it defies all attempts to limit its reach. Over time, public health preparation, priorities, and practice have continued to usher in evolving pressures to address the ebbs and flow of disease and health.

More and more, public health students and professionals praise its applicability to everything! Lessons about the evolution of the field reveal great significance in the numerous professional wins, such as the reduction of infectious diseases and infant mortality. At the same time, students of public health go about the business of naming significant people, pioneers in the field, including Edward Jenner, John Snow, and Edwin Chadwick. This exercise is done in hopes of preserving the legacies of these "founding fathers," who all happen to represent White men in public health.

These advancements and historical accolades come at a cost. The cost is usually shared among communities enduring discrimination, highly burdened by disease, and the most divergent from hegemonic identities. As a result, generations of marginalized communities are haunted by the collective trauma of public health. To these groups of people and their communities, public health means unethical maltreatment and discrimination—such as racism, sexism, heterosexism, ableism, classism, and intentional efforts to erase their very existence. Presently, this discrimination is recreated and reinforced by social determinations of health.

Leading from the Black

For many Black people and other people of color, public health practice can be an act of cognitive dissonance. The concept of aligning oneself with public health evokes discomfort to varying degrees. The emotional labor required of Black public health professionals can be best described by enduring the constant reminders of membership in a population often disproportionately affected by disease and death while also recognizing the limitations and instability of funding and priority given the overwhelming reliance on political temperament and systemic discrimination. This is public health, so choosing it as a career requires a strong desire to effect change despite these realities.

In 2002, the *American Journal of Public Health* published "Who Does the Work of Public Health?" by Byllye Avery. A reproductive health researcher and activist, Avery penned the manuscript to chronicle her journey within the field of public health. She described how the death of a loved one increased her knowledge about her own health issues. After taking a job in public health, Avery admits she removed "public" from her conception of the field and solely focused on the health of Black women. Avery's journey was published over fifteen years ago, and, although dated, this article mimics the journey many Black women in the field of public health take to reduce health disparities that often represent them.

Reflective of Avery's lived experience, Black women bear the burden of negative health outcomes for most diseases compared to their counterparts of different genders and races. As highlighted throughout the chapters of this book, Black women experience higher morbidity rates for several heath issues. We cannot underestimate how occurrences in our personal lives impact our political and professional choices. The personal experience of identifying as a Black woman drives Black women into the field of public health. Subsequently, these stories are often overlooked, and little documentation has been published to support these narratives.

The honor of having an inside view to the development of this text has been one that I will always cherish. In essence, my involvement came as a result of my leadership role in an organization that attempts to secure and support space for Black women via social networks, much like the provisions in this text. In 2016, I started a small network for Black women within the public health profession, Black Ladies in Public Health (BLiPH). The invitation read, "OK Ladies, let's get in formation." This ode was to Black women needing support and collective strength after a couple of years exposed to several police killings of unarmed Black men; little mention of Black women dying in similar ways; the water crisis in Flint, Michigan; a political shift that seemed to predict more uncertainty for public health and social justice progress; and Beyoncé's 2016 song that became the edgy anthem known for the love shown to the Black aesthetic, sexual agency, confidence in feminine prosperity, and hot sauce (bat), which made complete sense given the video was set against the backdrop of Hurricane Katrina and early-twentieth-century-Creole-influenced New Orleans.

This group completely transformed the value I found in intentionally connecting with fellow public health professionals who not only shared my race and gender but also my insecurities about the true impact that the public health workforce had on making lives of Black people, women, and Black women better in 2016. We bonded; we shared experiences that did not require full explanation to be understood. One BLiPH member very poignantly stated, "we go home to disparity." We recognized that in some way our presence and attendance were affirmations of progress, now and to come. We began by supporting one another in day-to-day efforts, not just the major accomplishments. The peer mentoring, crowdsourcing, and networking came organically and reflected the most immediate needs of the women in the group.

Healing Doesn't Have to Come through Validation from Those Who Hurt You

BLiPH is now an organization of over 8,000 members. Our major focus has been to build and promote positive narratives about Black women in the field. We accept non-public-health-trained sisters in just about any field, as a way to help them consider the health implications of their work. We aim to shift the despair narratives to represent our resilient community with intersectional vantage points from a place of educational and experiential privilege. We hope to reintroduce public health to our communities by sharing who we are, what we do, and why we do it, while also sharing with the greater public health field what we need. Reconciliation of secondary trauma, moral injury, and emotional labor is required for full participation in a workforce plagued with historical abuse of Black people, women, and Black women.

The current work uses social solutions to catalyze the network of pupils, professionals, partners, and program participants committed to advancing public health. We are curating ecosystems that transform collective trauma narratives into narratives of healing and building communities that engage, enhance, and leverage the education, tenacity, and unique experiences of the Black community in an effort to dismantle barriers to equity in public health outcomes and career opportunities.

For members of a community vulnerable to discrimination, the decision to pursue public health requires an unwavering commitment to the interrogation of our—the public health profession's—response and inaction to threats in our communities. For Black women who are constantly called to pick a minority/priority, gender and race become extraordinarily meaningful to our service in the interest of the public's health. The intersections of identities privilege a worldview that is unique and valuable to our understanding of the injustice and opportunities around us.

This quick explanation of public health, along with considerations of Black women within the context of service to public health, is extremely relevant to the discussion of this body of work. As I read through this text, I found myself considering the inspirations and contributions of Black women to the field. I evaluated the importance of the layout and construction of the full text. The three thematic segments that provide connectivity include history, practice, and planning. As we move through these categories, Black women transform. The display of diversity supports the reality of our communities as patients and providers, mentors and mothers, the traumatized and the healed, women in the US and abroad all find their way into the pages of this book. Most importantly, these arrangements happen within the general public health space, but here, we've centered Black women's wellness!

Dr. Evans, along with the team of coeditors, made all this possible. Building on her priorities in prior work, it stands to reason that this book, specifically dedicated to Black women and public health, provides a great cross section of public health issues for and by Black women. I considered the methodical process of convening this group of editors and authors. Dr. Stephanie Evans's effort to fortify Black women researchers, authors, practitioners, and students in the space of this text provided the autonomy to produce works that represent the diversity of Black women and amplified public health priorities of Black women. Together, the chapters in this book harness overtones of strength and value, irrespective of the health burden or societal ill.

Dr. Evans's previous work reflects the centrality of Black women. As an innovative historian, Evans tells the stories of Black women across generations and mediums. Her work depicts the uniqueness of Black women, their nuanced life experiences, and the legacies of legendary people, including survivors, tenacious women facing immeasurable opposition, and architects of cultural and personal solutions to their own health and wellness. Evans anchors her public health perspective with a Black feminist, womanist consciousness that allows her to interrogate public health priorities and practices from a position of strength.

This text provided me the opportunity to take a critical look at the public health priorities happening around me, not simply as a recipient of social media news with passive attention. I paid attention to health messaging, whether intentional or unintentional; attended webinars and conferences; and conducted content reviews of my social media channels fairly frequently. Maternal mortality, global health, PrEP for HIV prevention, mentoring, community policing, health policy, self-care and mental health, and creativity for health equity are major topics of conversation and organizing. These priorities are driven by political and social interest that cuts across communication channels (social media, pop culture, and news broadcasts).

In consideration for projects that expand on this text, I'd like to offer comments that may manifest into ideas for future work. The limitations of the book are perhaps more of a universal dilemma for all readings that seeks to help communities where vulnerability and marginalization are major factors of life. The question is of how to disseminate this information so that it moves to action. Who's responsible for the task? The accountability for disseminating findings to the communities that need them has been a major shortcoming of academia. Professional advocacy efforts like #CiteBlackWomen and the Black Women's Studies (BWST) Booklist (bwstbooklist.net) hold professionals accountable for sharing ideas from Black women thought leaders. The BWST Booklist, in particular, is an open-access online resource that contains over 1,400 entries. This list, also curated by Dr. Stephanie Y. Evans, includes a diverse group of individuals and disciplines, much like this text. Will you take up this charge?

We also recognize the vast number of omitted health issues that could have found their way into this text. There are likely more pressing issues that are ushered into public health conversations and action daily. To be clear, the topics included reflect the submissions that met all scientific and publication standards.

Black women are not a monolith; this is supported and affirmed by this text. While we can see the diversity chapter to chapter, the unfavorable, unattractive, and uncomfortable truths are limited in most publications because they are also omitted from funding considerations or the efforts of many researchers. Examples of this could include a more in-depth look into protecting women engaged in sex work, name change and gender markers as determinants of health for people of trans experience (e.g., employment, housing, education), environmental racism and gentrification as concerns for community outreach, or the culpability of major anchor health organizations and funding sources in reinforcing the devaluation of Black women's public health issues and Black women professionals. Lastly, perhaps a very real bias that we must confront is the idea that Black women are exempt from mistreating and misrepresenting Black women or experiencing the consequences of mistrust bestowed upon the field of public health—we are public health. How we engage research, community involvement, and advocacy with people of color, including Black women, should reflect the highest standard of care, because we know public health requires active rebranding within many communities, and it's the right thing to do.

This book, *Black Women and Public Health*, is a commitment to ushering in the voices of current and new Black women researchers and activists. It serves as evidence of Black women knowing how and when to step up and take space and when to step back to give space. When I inquired about Dr. Evans's motivation for prioritizing the health issues of greatest concern to Black women and for creating this book, what she said echoed through the pages as I consumed the work of the various authors. I imagine this is something someone from the many target audiences represented in this text would say. It's simple and profound, something that is the hope of all Black women in public health. She summed up the ultimate goal and motivation for this book with absolute resolve: "Black women saved my life."

Contributors

Editors

Sarita K. Davis, PhD, is associate professor in the Department of Africana Studies (AS) and affiliate faculty in the Institute of Public Health at Georgia State University. Since 2009, she has served as director of the graduate program for AS. She is knowledgeable about culturally relevant research in HIV-prevention education targeting African American women. She has conducted research involving African American women at risk for HIV living in high-burden communities, with emphasis on the intersectional effects of race, class, and gender on health. Her research interests are sexual decision-making, HIV/AIDS-prevention education, and culturally relevant praxis.

Stephanie Y. Evans, PhD, is professor of Black women's studies and former director of the Institute for Women's, Gender, and Sexuality Studies at Georgia State University. She is the former chair of the Department of African American Studies, Africana Women's Studies, and History (AWH) at Clark Atlanta University and of African American Studies at the University of Florida. She researches Black women's intellectual history and examines Africana memoirs to study legacies of Black women's health and wellness. Her research on historical wellness offers context to contemporary self-care movements and lays a foundation for institutionalizing wellness—particularly in higher education, where stress is too often normalized. She is author of numerous articles and book chapters, as well as three books, *Black Women's Yoga History: Memoirs of Inner Peace* (SUNY 2021), *Black Passports: Travel Memoirs as Tools for Youth Empowerment* (SUNY Press, 2014), and *Black Women in the Ivory Tower, 1850–1954: An Intellectual*

History (2007). She is also lead coeditor of *Black Women and Social Justice Education: Legacies and Lessons* (SUNY Press, 2019), *Black Women's Mental Health: Balancing Strength and Vulnerability* (SUNY Press, 2017), and *African Americans and Community Engagement* (SUNY Press, 2010). Her portfolio is available online at professorevans.net.

Leslie R. Hinkson, PhD, MSc, is a sociologist whose research and consulting work focuses on processes of organizational change, stratification, and inequality within and across organizations as well as the role and meaning of race across institutional contexts and its effect on education, employment, and health outcomes. She is currently chief officer for racial justice and equity for the League of Conservation Voters. Before joining LCV, she was assistant professor of sociology at Georgetown University, with a courtesy appointment in African American studies (of which she was a founding member). A graduate of the sociology doctoral program at Princeton University, she completed a postdoctoral fellowship with the Robert Wood Johnson Health Policy Research Fellows at the University of Michigan. Her health- and medicine-related work focuses on race-based decision-making by physicians and the role that race-based medicine plays in our broader system of health-care delivery. Her edited volume *Subprime Health: Debt and Race in U.S. Medicine* explores the relationship between race-based medical interventions and debt as a means of revealing the unintended negative health and social consequences of race and racial profiling in medicine.

Deanna J. Wathington, MD, MPH, FAAFP, is a public health practitioner and family physician. She is the immediate past chair of the executive board of the American Public Health Association. Wathington is the chief medical officer for Commonsense Childbirth, Inc.; medical director of a Volunteers in Medicine clinic for the uninsured; and affiliate professor at the University of South Florida College of Public Health and College of Arts and Science. She formerly served as dean of the Petrock College of Health Sciences and dean of the School of Graduate Studies at Bethune-Cookman University. She has served as director of minority health for the Florida Department of Health. Wathington earned her doctor of medicine degree from the University of Medicine and Dentistry of New Jersey–New Jersey Medical School (now known as Rutgers University–New Jersey Medical School), master of public health from Temple University, and baccalaureate in zoology from Rutgers University. She completed residency training in family medicine at JFK Medical Center in New Jersey and Bayfront Medical Center in Florida. She is a Fellow of the American Academy of Family Physicians. Wathington served on the US Department of Health and Human Services National Partnership for Action to End Health Disparities Region IV Southeastern Health Equity Council and is a member of the founding editorial board of the *Journal of Healthcare Transformation*. Her work has centered on expanding diversity within the health professions, clinical–community linkages, equitable development and community health initiatives, women's health, and infant mortality disparities.

Afterword

Jasmine Ward, MPH, PhD, is a proud graduate of Tuskegee University, the University of Alabama at Birmingham, and the University of Alabama (Tuscaloosa). She's an experienced public health professional dedicated to creating a culture of health through servant leadership, community organizing, restorative service, education, and social action. Ward created the Black Ladies in Public Health (BLiPH) community as an initial effort to provide a platform to cultivate and support relationships between Black women in the field of public health. Her personal and professional interest in equity in the workforce and community health helped to shape the mission and vision of Black Ladies in Public Health. While BLiPH is an outgrowth of online social communities, Ward has a greater vision of creating a world where all Black ladies in public health are engaged, valued, and empowered in all aspects of their lives. BLiPH.org is a part of the goal to provide multiplatform social solutions that connect and engage Black women in public health with one another, the community, and their allies.

Authors

Ndidiamaka N. Amutah-Onukagha, PhD, MPH, CHES, is an associate professor in the Department of Public Health and Community Medicine at Tufts University School of Medicine. Her current research interests include health disparities, reproductive health, maternal and infant mortality, and HIV/AIDS in Black women. Amutah-Onukagha is a member of the American Public Health Association (APHA) and is currently the cochair of the Perinatal and Women's Health Committee in the Maternal and Child Health (MCH) Section. Amutah-Onukagha is the principal investigator of two multiyear studies on maternal mortality and morbidity, with an R01 funded by the National Institutes of Health and an interdisciplinary grant funded by the Robert Wood Johnson Foundation. Also, she is a member of the Massachusetts COVID-19 Maternal Equity Coalition and was honored with the APHA MCH Section's Young Professional of the Year Award in 2019. She is also in the 2020 class of the top 40 under 40 Leaders in Minority Health, an annual award given by the National Minority Quality Forum. Finally, Amutah-Onukagha is the founder and director of the Maternal Outcomes for Translational Health Equity Research Lab (MOTHER), which comprises thirty-five students from undergraduates to postdoctoral fellows with an interest in reducing maternal health disparities experienced by Black women.

Andrea Anderson, MD, FAAFP, is a bilingual family physician and associate chief of the Division of Family Medicine at the George Washington School of Medicine and Health Sciences. She codirects the Health Policy Scholarly Concentration and is the director for the Transition to Residency fourth-year required internship-readiness capstone course. In 2019, she was appointed to the National Board of Directors of the American Board of Family Medicine; she is the first African American woman to be appointed to this role in the organization's fifty-year history. Anderson is a Fellow of the American Academy of Family Physicians and a graduate of the Master Teacher Leadership Development Program. She is the chair of the DC Board of Medicine and has been active in DC health policy and medical regulation. In 2020, she was appointed to the DC Health Scientific Advisory Committee for the Development and Implementation of a Safe, Effective, and Equitable COVID-19 Vaccine Distribution Program. She serves in national leadership roles for the United States Medical Licensing Examination, the National Board of Medical Examiners, the Ethics and Professionalism Committee of the Federation of State Medical Boards, the national Academic Family Medicine Advocacy Committee, and the Society of Teachers of Family Medicine National Underrepresented Minority Faculty Development and Retention Task Force. Previously, Anderson spent fifteen years in practice. She is an alumna of Brown University and Brown School of Medicine. Anderson completed her family medicine residency at Harbor–UCLA Medical Center, where she served as chief resident and an academic medicine fellow.

Traci N. Bethea, PhD, MPA, is assistant professor of oncology in the Office of Minority Health and Health Disparities at the Georgetown Lombardi Comprehensive Cancer Center. Since 2011, she has worked extensively with the Black Women's Health Study (BWHS), a prospective cohort of 59,000 Black women, and with the African American Breast Cancer Epidemiology and Risk Consortium. Her research focuses on racially and socioeconomically patterned health disparities, with particular attention to estrogen receptor–negative breast cancer and to neighborhood socioeconomic status. Her more recent work involves breast cancer survivorship in the BWHS; insomnia symptoms in the BWHS; exposure to endocrine-disrupting chemicals in the Study of Environment, Lifestyle and Fibroids; and ovarian cancer in the Ovarian Cancer in Women of African Ancestry Consortium. Bethea's research program aims to bridge the gap between the biologic, individual, and macroenvironmental levels while working with multidisciplinary teams, which entails evaluating the complexity of social determinants of health and identifying modifiable risk factors at multiple levels. She seeks to identify aspects of both vulnerable and resilient individuals and communities in order to provide data that is actionable—either for future studies, policy development, or targeted interventions—to reduce health disparities.

Leslie Bronner, MPH, DrPH, MD, is an assistant professor in the Department of Psychiatry and Behavioral Sciences at Duke University Medical Center. Bronner received her bachelor of science in chemistry and mathematics from Duke University, her master of public health from Boston University, and her doctor of public health in epidemiology from Harvard University. She then returned to Duke for medical school, where she also completed her residency in psychiatry. She conducted research at Duke in cognitive behavioral therapy and worked at Southlight, a substance-abuse treatment center, where she soon became medical director. She was also chair and medical director at the Duke Regional Hospital psychiatry department. However, it was through her clinical work at Southlight, working with pregnant women and women with children, that she realized the effects of the intergenerational cycle of stressors such as abuse, neglect, and poor parenting on the social and emotional development of children, as well as the development of mental illness. She now dedicates her career to understanding this cycle and making a positive impact through her clinical work. She is also rededicating herself to public health research with a focus on stress and the social determinants of disease.

Yvonne Bronner, ScD, is a professor and founding director of the Public Health Program at Morgan State University and the Consortium of African American Public Health Programs. She specializes in nutrition and maternal and child health and has focused on stress and the social determinants of health in the Black family across the life cycle. Her research has involved complementary and alternative medicine, obesity reduction in schoolchildren, and promoting breastfeeding through a project that first highlighted the role of Black men. She was a member of the Institute of Medicine's Food and Nutrition Board, the Department of Health and Human Services (HHS) Secretary's Advisory Committee on Infant Mortality, the American Dietetic Association's editorial board, and the 2005 USDA/HHS Dietary Guidelines Advisory Committee.

Joedrecka S. Brown Speights, MD, FAAFP, is professor and chair of family medicine and rural health at the Florida State University College of Medicine, a Fellow of the American Academy of Family Physicians, and fellowship-trained in maternal and child health. She is the 2018 recipient of the Dr. Martin Luther King, Jr., Distinguished Service Award from Florida State University. Her experience includes serving as medical director of the National Community Center of Excellence in Women's Health at Turley Family Health Center (University of South Florida–Morton Plant Mease Family Medicine Residency), where she practiced the full scope family medicine including operative obstetrics and global health. She is an alumna of the Florida Agriculture and Mechanical University and completed medical training at Emory University School of Medicine before completing the St. Vincent's Family Medicine Residency in Florida. She is an inaugural fellow of the George Washington University Leaders for Health Equity International Fellowship, now Atlantic Fellows for Health Equity. Her interests include promotion of health equity through community-engaged research, clinical care, advocacy, and education. She is also focused on faculty vitality, mentoring, wellness promotion, and empowerment of women and girls. Her favorite times are with her husband, Gregory, family and friends, and traveling pre-COVID-19. She and her husband copastor University Ministries International.

Brittney Butler, MPH, is a Dual Postdoctoral Fellow at the FXB Center for Health and Human Rights and Center for Population and Development Studies at Harvard University. Her research focuses on how structural racism and interpersonal experiences of discrimination impact pregnancy complications in Black women. Butler is a Robert Wood Johnson Foundation Health Policy Research Scholar, where she receives supplemental training to translate scientific research to inform policy to build a culture of health. She is also president of the Society of the Analysis of African American Public Health Issues. Brittney graduated from the University of Miami in 2010 with a degree in biology and obtained her master of public health from Washington University in St. Louis in 2013.

Santiba Campbell, PhD, RYT-200, is an associate professor of psychology at Bennett College. Campbell received her BA in psychology from Winston-Salem State University and earned her MA and PhD in the field of social psychology from the University of Delaware in Newark. Her basic research question addresses what factors determine whether, in the face of perpetual threats posed by racism and racial discrimination, African Americans maintain positive psychological well-being and physical health, achieve success, and reach personal goals or adopt negative self-images and other destructive behaviors. Campbell studies this through the lenses of racial identity development, intersectionality, and contemplative practices with an interest in college-student success and satisfaction.

Jayme Canty, PhD, is a native of North Carolina. She graduated summa cum laude in 2006 from North Carolina Agricultural &Technical State University in Greensboro, where she received her bachelor of arts degree in political science. After working as a paralegal in North Carolina for two years, she returned to school to complete her master's degree in Africana women's studies at Clark Atlanta University in Atlanta, Georgia. For her master's thesis, she conducted a case study of Black women who participated in the Atlanta University Student Movement Protest in 1960 to determine how Black maternal figures passed down notions of activism. After completing her master's degree in 2011, she attended Clark Atlanta University to obtain a doctorate in humanities, with concentrations in Africana women's studies and political science. During her graduate studies, she taught several courses including Love and Sex, African Diaspora and the World, Black Feminism/The Black Woman, and Modern Period Humanities. She obtained her doctorate in fall 2017 with the dissertation entitled " 'The Swelling Wave of Oppression': The Intersectional Study of the Health Challenges of Black Heterosexual Women and Black Queer Women in the American South." Her research focuses on the health challenges of Black women in the South, the experiences of Black queer women in the South, and the significance of maternal figures among Black women in the South. She now works as a visiting assistant professor of African American studies at the University of Nevada at Las Vegas.

Sheila Carrette, MPH, is a public health specialist with a background in psychology, behavioral health, educational programming, and international health. As the founder and CEO of Overcomer, Inc., Carrette uses her diverse background and expertise to develop effective public health programming that focuses on the social determinants of health, including education, housing, and employment. In her position as a health consultant for the World Bank Group, Carrette focuses much of her time on improving health and nutrition outcomes for individuals in countries facing fragility, conflict, and violence. Through multistakeholder engagement, needs-assessment missions, and system analyses, she works with governments to address key operational and systemic challenges in vulnerable health systems. Prior to her current positions, Carrette founded and directed the Hope Center, a food bank and resource center dedicated to assisting low-income families in Prince George's County, Maryland, and Washington, DC. Carrette holds a bachelor of science from the University of Maryland and a master of public health from Liberty University; she is currently a doctor of public health candidate at Morgan State University.

Yvette C. Cozier, DSc, MPH, is associate professor of epidemiology and associate dean of diversity, equity, inclusion, and justice at Boston University School of Public Health and epidemiologist at Slone Epidemiology Center. Cozier is an investigator on the Black Women's Health Study (BWHS), a prospective follow-up of over 59,000 African American women begun in 1995. Cozier's overall research focus is on the influence of psychosocial factors in the development of sarcoidosis, obesity, cardiovascular disease, and cancer. She has published several analyses of perceived racism in relation to hypertension, breast cancer incidence, weight gain, and mortality in the BWHS. In addition, she has published analyses of the relationship between neighborhood socioeconomic status, including median household income and segregation, and the risks of hypertension, diabetes, and obesity. For the past several years, Cozier has been studying selected risk factors for sarcoidosis in the BWHS, including reproductive factors and genetic polymorphisms. She has also assessed the role of attitudes about spirituality and religiosity in health-promotion and disease-prevention efforts among Boston-area residents and clergy. New research areas in the BWHS include psychosocial factors and oral health, risk factors for lupus, and health conditions associated with aging.

Rebekah Israel Cross, MA, is a PhD candidate at the UCLA Fielding School of Public Health in the Department of Community Health Sciences and a Robert Wood Johnson Foundation Health Policy Research Scholar. Her research involves measuring racism-related social determinants of health. Broadly, she aims to unpack the relationships between racism, neighborhoods, and health. Specifically, she's interested in understanding how housing and community development policies influence health in Black communities. In 2011, she graduated from the University of North Carolina at Chapel Hill with degrees in sociology and political science. In May 2013, Cross earned a master's in sociology from American University.

Jenny Douglas, PhD, MSc, MA, completed her women's studies doctoral thesis on cigarette smoking and identity among African Caribbean young women in contemporary British society. Douglas is passionate about the health and well-being of Black women. Her research is both varied and wide ranging, spanning thirty years, on issues of race, health, gender, and ethnicity. The key theme unifying her research and activism is intersectionality—exploring how race, class, and gender affect particular aspects of African Caribbean women's health. Douglas's interdisciplinary research approach brings together sociology, public health, and women's studies, and she has published widely on public health, health promotion, and Black women's health. Douglas established and chairs the Black Women's Health and Wellbeing Research Network (www.open.ac.uk/Black-womens-health-and-wellbeing), and her ambition is to establish an international research institute on the health and well-being of Black women. Douglas is a senior lecturer in health promotion in the Faculty of Wellbeing, Education, and Language Studies at the Open University. She has a PhD in women's studies from the University of York, an MA in sociological research in health care from the University of Warwick, an MSc in environmental pollution control from the University of Leeds, and a BSc with honors in microbiology and virology from the University of Warwick. She is an honorary member of the Faculty of Public Health and a director of the UK Public Health Register. Douglas is a research affiliate of the Institute for Intersectionality Research and Policy, Simon Fraser University, Vancouver, Canada, and a Plumer visiting research fellow at St. Anne's College, University of Oxford. She is a member of the International Union of Health Promotion and Education.

Charlene A. Flash, MD, MPH, is the president and CEO of Avenue 360 Health and Wellness, a multisite health system in Houston, Texas, that includes six clinics, a dental center, an AIDS hospice, an adult day-activities program for people living with HIV, and a health equity program that provides supportive housing. Flash is a thought leader in health-care disparities and an expert on the implementation of HIV pre-exposure prophylaxis (PrEP), having developed one of the first comprehensive HIV-prevention programs in the United States to prescribe HIV PrEP to high-risk heterosexual people and men who have sex with men in a real-world setting outside the context of a demonstration project or clinical trial. Flash holds a voluntary faculty position as an assistant professor of medicine in the Division of Infectious Disease at Baylor College of Medicine and at the University of Houston. She served as the assistant medical director of HIV prevention services for Harris Health System in Houston. An infectious disease physician, Flash provides primary care to patients living with HIV and PrEP to at-risk individuals. Flash received her undergraduate degree in chemistry from Yale University, an MD from Robert Wood Johnson Medical School, and an MPH in quantitative health-care assessment from the University of Medicine and Dentistry of New Jersey School of Public Health. Flash completed a combined residency in internal medicine and pediatrics at Brown University and a fellowship in adult infectious disease at Harvard University. Flash is board certified in internal medicine and adult infectious diseases.

Mandy Hill, DrPH, MPH, is a dedicated and resilient public health practitioner whose core mission is to improve health by empowering the decision-making capacity of vulnerable populations and racial/ethnic minorities. Through this central theme, she establishes behavioral interventions to empower communities. By establishing relationships and sharing knowledge while developing and implementing programs, Hill touches a broad cross section of the population to restore their power and sense of self. Hill is the creator of an intervention (increasing pre-exposure prophylaxis, i.e., iPrEP) that motivates women to prevent an HIV diagnosis through PrEP uptake. Hill serves as the director of population health in the Department of Emergency Medicine and associate professor at UTHealth McGovern Medical School. A leader in this field for over a decade, Hill is working to move the needle on this critical initiative in the community. Making history as the first full-time public health research faculty member in the Department of Emergency Medicine, Hill leads development and implementation of public health–based prevention interventions to patients seeking care in the emergency department and community members at large. She is not only leading funded randomized studies in local emergency departments but also collaborating on county health department efforts and statewide programs in the University of Texas system.

Christy M. Gamble, JD, DrPH, MPH, is an experienced policy strategist and advocate with expertise in the law, policy, and research. Gamble currently works at the intersection of health, innovation, and social justice. Her work seeks to improve the public's health and well-being and achieve health equity through innovations that embrace the power of technology and improve access to quality, affordable, whole-person-centered care, especially for populations who have been historically marginalized and left out of the health-care system, while protecting patient data and privacy. Gamble has testified before Congress and state legislatures, published several opinion pieces in nationally recognized publications, and provided political and legal analysis and commentary for various radio and television stations on issues impacting the health and well-being of marginalized populations. Gamble received her JD from Duquesne University School of Law. She also holds a DrPH in epidemiology from the University of Pittsburgh Graduate School of Public Health and an MPH in epidemiology and biostatistics from Eastern Virginia Medical School.

Portia A. Jackson Preston, DrPH, MPH, is an assistant professor in the Department of Public Health at California State University, Fullerton. Her research focuses on multilevel approaches to self-care and stress as a driver of health inequity. She has published previously on professional quality of life, well-being, and self-care practices among university staff members serving high-need student populations and the role of organizations in mitigating workforce burnout. Her recent projects examine stress and coping practices among university staff and undergraduate students. She speaks widely on individual and organization-level strategies to promote well-being and sustainable performance. She received her bachelor's degree from Stanford University; her master's degree in public health from the University of Michigan, Ann Arbor; and her doctor of public health degree from the University of California, Los Angeles.

Tamara Y. Jeffries, MFA, is a former associate professor of journalism and media studies at Bennett College in North Carolina and is now a senior editor at *Yoga Journal.* She came to the academy after more than two decades as a writer and editor for national publications, including *Essence,* where she was executive editor from 2000 to 2004. She was also editor-in-chief of *HealthQuest: The Publication of Black Wellness* and a contributing editor for *Health* magazine. Her writing has appeared in national, local, and special-topics publications, and she has also coauthored and edited several health-related books. Jeffries teaches yoga at Bennett, where she has developed a model for yoga instruction called Whole Yoga, which helps intentionally infuse asana practice with philosophy, history, and culture to address issues related to race, gender, body image, religion, identity, and other diversities that impact students' experience of yoga and their ability to benefit from it. Jeffries and Campbell have presented their research on yoga and diversity at the Yoga Service Conference at Omega Institute, the University of Michigan Depression on College Campuses Conference, and other events. Their work is informed by a commitment to the academic study of yogic text and history, acknowledgment of the complex evolution of yoga in the West, and inclusivity in yoga-teaching practice. Both are members of the Yoga Service Council and registered with Yoga Alliance, where they also serve as members of the ethics committee.

Joylene John-Sowah, MD, MPH, received her BA from the State University of New York at Stony Brook in 1989 and her MD from Cornell University Medical College in 1994. She completed residencies in family practice at the University of Maryland and in general preventive medicine at the Johns Hopkins University Bloomberg School of Public Health, during which she received her MPH. John-Sowah served as a medical officer at the National Heart, Lung, and Blood Institute (NHLBI) Center for Translational Research and Implementation Science, where she was the Institute lead for Healthy People 2020 and also led the project that resulted in the landmark guidelines document *Evidence-Based Management of Sickle Cell Disease: Expert Panel Report, 2014.* John-Sowah has substantial experience in grant writing, scientific document editing, and conducting evidence-based reviews as a result of her positions at the NHLBI and her years at the American Medical Association (AMA). While with the AMA, she directed the development of the "Expert Committee Recommendations on the Assessment, Prevention, and Management of Child and Adolescent Overweight and Obesity," supported the AMA National Advisory Council on Violence and Abuse, and served as the AMA representative to the U.S. Preventive Services Task Force. Currently, John-Sowah is exploring new directions. She has launched Nansi Knows, an undertaking dedicated to supporting high school students as they aspire toward college, and hopes to develop work that will leave a positive and lasting impact on the souls of the people with whom she interacts.

Kelli Joiner, BS, has completed two years in the MPH program at the Chamberlain University School of Health Professions. She graduated from Sam Houston State University in 2016 with a bachelor of science in public health. She was a program coordinating intern at the Public Health Consulting Group, where she lead the group's social marketing campaign and coordinated onboarding of new clients and assignment of consultant teams to projects. Joiner transitioned from an interest in clinical practice as an aspiring nurse to a career plan in public health practice. As a student, she engaged as an author on peer-reviewed publications.

Dakota King-White, PhD, joined Cleveland State University (CSU) in fall 2016 in the Department of Counseling, Administration, Supervision, and Adult Learning. Within the department she is a core faculty member and coordinator of school counseling in the CACREP-accredited counseling program. Prior to coming to CSU, she received her PhD in 2012 in counselor education and supervision from the University of Toledo. She has an extensive background in working in K–12 education, where she has served as a school counselor, mental health therapist, and administrator. King-White studies the psychological, emotional, and behavioral effects of parental incarceration and strategies for developing mental health models in K–12 schools. Through her research she has designed a group-counseling curriculum for children of incarcerated parents, which has been implemented within K–12 education. Her most recent tool for children of incarcerated parents is a children's book, *Oh No! When a Parent Goes Away*. She has also created a mental health model that is used in K–12 education to help address the mental health needs of students within the academic setting. The model is an interdisciplinary approach to addressing mental health needs within schools. King-White is passionate about children succeeding and believes that all students can succeed if given the right tools and opportunities.

Kelly Yu-Hsin Liao, PhD, joined Cleveland State University (CSU) as an assistant professor in fall 2016 in the Department of Counseling, Administration, Supervision, and Adult Learning. She is part of the core faculty in the American Psychological Association–accredited counseling psychology specialization of the urban education PhD program. She received her PhD in counseling psychology in 2011 from Iowa State University after completing an internship at the University of Missouri-Columbia Student Counseling Center. Prior to joining CSU, she was a research scientist at the Culture and Health Research Center at the University of Houston. Liao studies coping with minority-related stress (e.g., acculturative stress, discrimination, stigma) among ethnic and LGBTQ individuals, positive psychology (e.g., self-compassion), and health psychology in ethnic minorities (e.g., psychosocial intervention for Chinese breast cancer survivors). Her current projects include developing a self-compassion writing intervention to cope with racism among African American students, exploring the Strong Black Woman stereotype and coping responses, examining the psychological benefits of gratitude among Chinese international students, and investigating the role of perceived burden in the health outcomes of Chinese cancer survivors.

Yasmeen J. Long, MA, is a public health and research professional with combined experience and expertise in academia, health policy, patient-centered research, stakeholder and community engagement, and global health. Her career in public health has primarily focused on improving health outcomes, eliminating disparities, promoting health equity, social determinants of health, and improving the quality of life for underrepresented and vulnerable communities particularly for women. She earned an MA in sociology and women's health from Suffolk University in Boston, Massachusetts, and a BSc in health sciences from Howard University in Washington, DC. She serves on advisory committees and leadership councils focused on addressing health inequities and disparities as well as health and wellness and advocates for policies that affect women's health and well-being throughout the life course.

Bisola Ojikutu, MD, MPH, is an infectious disease specialist and health equity researcher who has dedicated her career to overcoming racial and ethnic disparities and mitigating the impact of structural racism on infectious disease transmission and prevention, particularly HIV. Ojikutu is an associate physician within the Division of Global Health Equity at Brigham and Women's Hospital and the Department of Global and Social Medicine at Harvard Medical School. She is also a faculty member within the Infectious Disease Divisions at Brigham and Women's and Massachusetts General Hospitals. Her research explores medical and research mistrust and barriers to accessing HIV prevention and care, particularly among women of color and immigrant populations. She is a member of the Executive Leadership Committee for the Harvard University Center for AIDS Research and serves as the director of the Community Engaged Research Program and associate director of the Bio-Behavioral and Community Science Core. Ojikutu is coeditor of the comprehensive textbook *HIV in US Communities of Color* (first and second editions 2009 and 2020). She is cochair of the Comprehensive Care Committee within the Getting to Zero MA statewide coalition and a leader within the Suffolk County Ending the HIV Epidemic Steering Committee. She is the principal investigator of a Patient-Centered Outcomes Research Institute (PCORI) comparative effectiveness trial focused on PrEP uptake among Black women. In addition, Ojikutu maintains an active clinical practice focused on HIV and women's health, is board certified in internal medicine and infectious diseases, and is a fellow in the Infectious Disease Society of America.

Folake Olayinka, MPH, is a recent master of public health graduate in epidemiology and biostatistics as well as maternal and child health from Boston University School of Public Health. Currently, she works as an epidemiologist at the Texas Department of State Health Services. During her undergraduate studies, Olayinka conducted an independent research study for the honors track on the health care for and diagnosis of African Americans with schizophrenia, which opened her eyes to the health disparities often fueled by socioeconomic status. Her public health interest is a deep commitment to decreasing infant and maternal mortality in disadvantaged communities by promoting justice and health equity. In 2018, she was awarded the Mass NOW Feminist in Action Grant for founding the Feminist Guide organization and "round the table" podcast, which aims to educate women on the importance of feminism and ultimately create the next wave of African feminists. As the CEO of the

Feminist Guide, she spends her time writing various articles on topics including the importance of feminism, racial discrimination and sexism, and reproductive and other health discrepancies according to race. She also serves as the administrative executive of the New England Medical Association (NEMA), implementing changes to NEMA's structure and connecting with Black physicians in the New England area. Lastly, as an advocate for global childhood vaccination, she is part of the United Nations Shot at Life organization, which advocates for immunization of children in vulnerable countries by campaigning to members of Congress on Capitol Hill.

Esther Piervil, PhD, MPH, is a Certified Health Education Specialist (CHES) and public health consultant with over ten years of experience designing and conducting behavioral science and community health research. She currently serves as a research and evaluation specialist providing population health services to governmental and commercial agencies in the areas of chronic disease prevention and management among high-risk, vulnerable, and hard-to-reach populations. Her work aims to streamline wellness programs and health initiatives using evidenced-based theories to drive the application of culturally tailored, community-based implementation strategies. She is also an affiliate of Spelman College and Baylor University.

Mya L. Roberson, MSPH, is Assistant Professor of Health Policy, Vanderbilt University School of Medicine. As a graduate student, Roberson was a Robert Wood Johnson Foundation Health Policy Research Scholar; her dissertation examined differences in the surgical treatment of breast cancer for Black women residing in urban and rural areas of North Carolina. Broadly, she is interested in achieving health equity in cancer care delivery for Black people in the US South. She is the recipient of the American Association for Cancer Research Thomas J. Bardos Science Education Award and is a Truman Scholar.

Elice E. Rogers, EdD, is a tenured associate professor in adult learning and development at Cleveland State University. She serves as program coordinator of graduate programs in adult learning and development and is a member of the graduate faculty. Rogers is a Cyril O. Houle Scholar in the field of adult education and is recognized as a Kellogg Foundation scholar. Her publications include *Adult Education in an Urban Context: Problems, Practices, and Programming for Inner-City Communities: New Directions for Adult and Continuing Education* and "Afritics from Margin to Center: Theorizing the Politics of African American Women as Political Leaders" in the *Journal of Black Studies*.

Jovonni R. Spinner, MPH, CHES, is a results-driven, award-winning visionary public health strategist committed to improving health equity across the life span. She creates culturally competent health education and training programs and leads equity-driven conversations advocating for minority health. She builds multisector partnerships and oversees long-term strategic plans, guided by scientific evidence and regulatory policy to implement balanced decisions. While at the Food and Drug Administration, she uses a people-centric leadership style to inspire and boost team performance, build organizational culture, facilitate change management, and nurture talent, all while shifting mindsets of colleagues and advising senior leadership to use an equity lens to address health disparities, policies, and systematic change. She leads state and national health programs like the FDA's Diversity in Clinical Trials Initiative, NIH's Community Health Worker Health Disparities Initiative, and Virginia's Vaccines for Children Program, reaching millions of consumers to help each make better-informed health decisions, obtain health services, and advocate for healthier communities. She is an alumna of Virginia Commonwealth, Emory, and Morgan State Universities and remains active in her community serving on nonprofit boards, writing women's health articles, mentoring early-career professionals, and serving as a public health adjunct professor.

Tiffany D. Thomas, MCD, is the program coordinator and assistant professor of community development in the School of Architecture. While at Prairie View, she has led engaged research efforts in partnership with community-based organizations, rural and urban governments, and peer institutions focused in historically Black neighborhoods. Her work is featured in the *Journal of Community Development, Local Development and Society*, and *Contemporary Issues in Social Justice*. Thomas is an authority in community engagement and leverages divested neighborhoods as learning environments for social change. She is also affiliated with the Community Innovation Lab at the University of Kentucky, coteaching "Innovations in

Community Engagement," a project funded by Purdue University. Thomas was recently elected to Houston's City Council, the first Black woman to represent District F.

Alisa Valentin, PhD, is a technology policy advocate based in Washington, DC. She is the former Communications Justice Fellow at Public Knowledge, where she initially drafted "Rural Black Maternal Health in the Age of Digital Deserts." Valentin currently serves as the special advisor to FCC commissioner Geoffrey Starks, where she advises the commissioner on broadband access and adoption, the future of work, and prison phone justice policies. Valentin has taught communications and women's studies courses at several colleges and universities in the DC metropolitan area including Howard University, Trinity Washington University, Montgomery College, and Northern Virginia Community College. Valentin received her PhD in communications from Howard University. She also holds an MS in journalism from the Medill School of Journalism at Northwestern University and a BS in telecommunications from the University of Florida.

Judy Washington, MD, FAAFP, is an associate director and the women's health coordinator for Overlook Family Medicine. Washington has been involved in undergraduate medical and graduate medical education since 1996, when she joined the faculty of the East Tennessee State James Quillen School of Medicine as an assistant professor and residency program faculty member at the Chattanooga Family Medicine Residency Program. She was an assistant professor at the University of Medicine and Dentistry of New Jersey–New Jersey Medical School (now Rutgers School of Health Science) Family Medicine Department, assistant director of medical student education, and the family medicine clerkship director. Washington received her BS degree from the University of Montevallo in Montevallo, Alabama, and her medical degree from Meharry Medical College in Nashville, Tennessee. She completed her residency in family medicine at Mountainside Family Medicine in Verona, New Jersey. She is committed to physician wellness and completed yoga-teacher training and certification. Through her work as a trustee and officer of the Society of Teachers of Family Medicine Foundation, she is committed to increasing the number of underrepresented-in-medicine family medicine residents and faculty members and mentoring the next generation of family medicine educators.

Artist Statement

"Loving Comfort (Byllye Avery)"

COVER ART BY MADCOLLAGE

https://www.madcollage.com/

Allow me to explain, albeit briefly, how this image came about.

I envisioned Ms. Avery in a central position, commanding the image. She's looking at the horizon, which is a reference to hope, and she is standing tall with a strong posture. The background, in my opinion, needed to be simple so as not to detract from her.

I combined the muted purple and the rusty red of the flower petals with some traditional colors from handmade, block-printed African textiles that I found during my research. I feel they enhance each other quite well. The *duafe* symbol you introduced me to is enclosed in both red and purple circles as well as some print, which for me symbolizes Byllye Avery's ability to communicate and teach others through words. The lighter background offsets the symbol in a way that improves its visibility.

I then placed it over her heart. Its perimeter is punctuated with more rusty red petals from the passionflower. I chose this flower because it symbolizes not only suffering but also determination and sacrifice. To create a middle ground and to further make her face the main focal point of the image, I used a complementary ocher circle also bordered by passionflower petals. There is also a smaller circle made out of a semitransparent map that, in my interpretation, shows her reach being not just local but global.

Finally, in reading about the different adinkra symbols and their meanings, I learned that the *adinkrahene* (concentric circles) is considered the seminal and most powerful of these symbols. I use it in the very first and deepest layer of the collage, repetitively, not only due to its visual impact but because I think Byllye Avery embodies many of its characteristics: charisma and leadership within her field of expertise.

The image is an ephemeral mixed-media collage, which means that there's no final product other than the image itself. The elements are placed together, some glued, some painted, and they are later disassembled.

Biography

Born in Madrid, Spain, **Madcollage** started to make collage at a very early age, even before fully understanding the meaning of the word itself. After attending college in Spain and the United States, she settled in the Northeast, where she now lives and works. She splits her time between semirural Vermont and the city of Montreal, where she can recreate the urban experiences she had growing up in Europe. She enjoys museums, cafés, botanic gardens, and the solitude of her studio, where she reads, listens to music, and creates her artwork one tiny piece of paper at a time. She describes her work as "the confluence of two rivers: memory and imagination. They blend into each other to create something new. I love this process and I try to nurture it daily." She also adds, "I live with chronic pain. I also suffer from anxiety and depression, and I have been at the receiving end of the stigma surrounding mental illness many times. You will see glimpses of me and my personal struggle in every image I make, and that is as it should be. It is my objective to take one small brick off the ugly wall of silence surrounding invisible illnesses with honesty and perseverance, while pushing back on my own fears and feelings of inadequacy."

Index

Printed in the USA
CPSIA information can be obtained
at www.ICGtesting.com
LVHW091603071123
763288LV00001B/52